Modeling Economic Growth in Contemporary Slovakia

ENTREPRENEURSHIP AND GLOBAL ECONOMIC GROWTH

Series editor: Bruno S. Sergi, Harvard University, USA

Entrepreneurship and Global Economic Growth is Emerald's cutting-edge Global Economic Growth book series, presenting modern examinations of economic growth at national, regional, and global levels. Each book in this series discusses different dimensions of the changing economic and industrial contexts and examines in detail their impact on the nature of growth and development. For academics and senior practitioners, this series puts forward significant new research in the global economic growth field, opening discussions regarding new topics and updating existing literature.

Published Titles in This Series

Modeling Economic Growth in Contemporary Russia, edited by Bruno S. Sergi

Modeling Economic Growth in Contemporary Belarus, edited by Bruno S. Sergi

Modeling Economic Growth in Contemporary Malaysia, edited by Bruno S. Sergi and Abdul Rahman Jaaffar

Modeling Economic Growth in Contemporary Greece, edited by Vasileiois Vlachos, Aristidis Bitzenis and Bruno S. Sergi

Modeling Economic Growth in Contemporary Indonesia, edited by Bruno S. Sergi and Dedhy Sulistiawan

Modeling Economic Growth in Contemporary Hong Kong, edited by Michael K. Fung and Bruno S. Sergi

Modeling Economic Growth in Contemporary Poland, edited by Elżbieta Bukalska, Tomasz Kijek and Bruno S. Sergi

Modeling Economic Growth in Contemporary Czechia, edited by Daniel Stavárek and Michal Tvrdoň

Modeling Economic Growth in Contemporary India, edited by Bruno S. Sergi, Aviral Kumar Tiwari and Samia Nasreen

Modeling Economic Growth in Contemporary Slovakia

EDITED BY

MICHAEL AUGUSTÍN

University of Economics in Bratislava, Slovakia and Slovak Academy of Sciences, Slovakia

PETER JANČOVIČ

University of Economics in Bratislava, Slovakia

AND

BRUNO S. SERGI

Harvard University, USA and University of Messina, Italy

emerald PUBLISHING

United Kingdom – North America – Japan – India – Malaysia – China

Emerald Publishing Limited
Emerald Publishing, Floor 5, Northspring, 21-23 Wellington Street, Leeds LS1 4DL

First edition 2025

British Library Cataloguing in Publication Data
A catalogue record for this book is available from the British Library

ISBN: 978-1-83549-455-4 (Print)
ISBN: 978-1-83549-454-7 (Online)
ISBN: 978-1-83549-456-1 (Epub)

Printed and bound by CPI Group (UK) Ltd, Croydon, CR0 4YY

INVESTOR IN PEOPLE

Contents

II: Policies, Institutions, and Markets

III: Characteristics and Performance of Selected Industries

List of Figures and Tables

Figures

Tables

About the Editors

Michael Augustín is an Associate Professor at the Faculty of International Relations at the University of Economics in Bratislava, Slovak Republic. He also works as a Senior Researcher at the Institute of Political Science of the Slovak Academy of Sciences in Bratislava. His expertise spans political science and international relations. It covers various areas, including political theory, recent economic, social, and political development in Slovakia, France, Armenian-Azerbaijani relations, the Helsinki Process, and the OSCE. He is the author or coauthor of over 70 academic journal articles, conference papers, book chapters, textbooks, magazine, and newspaper columns.

Peter Jančovič holds a PhD in Economics. He is an Assistant Professor at the Department of International Economic Relations and Economic Diplomacy, Faculty of International Relations, University of Economics in Bratislava, Slovak Republic. He teaches the courses International Economic Relations and World Economy. His research area covers international economics and international economic relations, particularly focusing on international capital flows, personal remittances, and international development assistance. From a regional perspective, he specializes in the Latin American and Caribbean region, its economic development and position in the global economy.

Bruno S. Sergi teaches courses at Harvard, specifically focusing on development economics and the economics of emerging markets. His current research interests span the political economy of emerging markets and encompass sustainable development, technology, and global development practices. At Harvard, he is a Faculty Associate at the Harvard Center for International Development and an Associate at the Davis Center for Russian and Eurasian Studies. He also teaches International Political Economy at the University of Messina, Italy. He serves on multiple academic advisory boards in Europe and Asia. Furthermore, he is the Series Editor of Cambridge Elements in the Economics of Emerging Markets and the co-director of the Lab for Entrepreneurship and Development (LEAD), a research lab based in Cambridge that aims to generate and share knowledge about entrepreneurship, development, and sustainability.

About the Contributors

Kristína Baculáková, University of Economics in Bratislava, Slovakia, graduated in 2012 from the Faculty of International Relations, University of Economics in Bratislava, Slovakia. In 2016, she obtained a PhD degree in International Economic Relations at the same Faculty. She is currently working as an Associate Professor and Vice-Dean for Development at the Faculty of International Relations, University of Economics in Bratislava. She collaborated in several public projects to support culture and creative industry in Slovakia. She is an author of more than 70 publications. Her research interests include cultural and creative industries and smart city solutions. She leads the Model UN at the Faculty of International Relations.

Ingrid Brocková has been the Ambassador of Slovakia to the Czech Republic since September 2023. Prior to that, she was the State Secretary of the Ministry of Foreign and European Affairs (MFEA SR) of the Slovak Republic (2020–2023), the Ambassador and Permanent Representative of the Slovak Republic to the OECD (2011–2015, 2018–2020), the Director General for Economic Cooperation at the MFEA SR (2015–2018), and the Country Manager of the World Bank in Slovakia (2001–2008). She joined the MFEA SR in 1993; her expertise is mainly in economic diplomacy and development assistance agenda. Mrs Brocková was born in 1963. She holds a Doctorate in Economics (PhD) from the Slovak Technical University, Bratislava (1991). In 1999, she obtained a Master's in International Public Policy (MIPP) from the Paul H.Nitze School of Advanced International Studies at the Johns Hopkins University in Washington, DC, USA.

Jakub Csabay currently teaches at the Institute of European Studies and International Relations, Faculty of Social and Economic Sciences, Comenius University. He completed his PhD research on Institutional Dynamics of State-Minority Relations in Slovakia and Azerbaijan at the Center of Development Studies, University of Cambridge. He is a research affiliate of the Cambridge Central Asia Forum, and he co-founded the Cambridge Central European Conference. He has worked as a consultant to both private and public sector clients, and he had also previously supervised students at the Department of Politics and International Studies and Judge Business School in Cambridge. In Slovakia, he co-founded two civic associations, EDUSOC and RESDI, focused on educational and sustainable development projects for minorities, in particular Roma communities. Together with Anton Marcinčin, he co-edits the Yearbook of Regional Development in Slovakia, and he is also a collaborator of the Friends of the Earth-CEPA, working on energy poverty and engagement with academic institutions and municipalities.

Peter Daubner is a Political Scientist, Political Philosopher, and Political Economist. He works as a State Advisor in the Chancellery of the National Council of the Slovak Republic and as a researcher at the Institute of Philosophy of the Slovak Academy of Sciences. He specializes in neo- and post-Marxist political and social philosophy, environmental philosophy, European affairs, international relations, and political economy of capitalism.

Tomáš Dudáš is a Professor at the Faculty of Economics and Entrepreneurship of the Pan-European University. His research mainly focuses on international economic relations, with a specialization in the field of foreign direct investment and national competitiveness. Lately, he has been working on developing the national competitiveness of Central European countries, as well as studying the impact of FDI on the Slovak economy. He is a well-known Slovak expert on the global economy and is often featured in Slovak media. Additionally, he has authored several monographs and university textbooks, as well as more than a dozen articles in journals indexed in the Web of Science and Scopus databases.

Eva Horvátová is a Professor of Finance at the University of Economics in Bratislava and at the Masaryk University in Brno. She lectures on Banking and works with PhD students. She has written monographs and scientific articles on banking, financial regulation, and financial markets. She attended lectures and study stays in Luxembourg, Portugal, Germany, and Switzerland. Eva is also engaged in practical appraisal activities in the area of finance, controlling, and valuation of banks and financial institutions. In the period 2007–2020, she was the Head of the Department of Banking and International Finance at the Faculty of National Economy, University of Economics in Bratislava.

Ladislav Kabát is a Professor at the Bratislava University of Economics and Management (BUEM). He got his MS degree from the Economic University in Bratislava. The PhD program completed at the Plekhanov Institute of National Economy in Moscow in Operation Research and consequently continued as a University Teacher in Slovakia. As a Visiting Lecturer, he spent one semester at the University of Ghana in Legon (Accra). He established academic cooperation with US universities, namely Cornell University, Texas AM University, West Virginia University, and the University of Delaware (as a visiting professor). In 1996, he was appointed to the position of Director of the (UN) FAO Statistical Division in Rome, where participated in building statistical systems in developing countries until 2001. After completing this mission, he continues his academic career in Bratislava. His research is oriented on the quality of economic data and econometric models' applications.

Lubor Lacina is a Professor of Economics at Mendel University in Brno, Czech Republic. He is Jean Monnet Chair in Economic Studies and the Director of Jean Monet Center of Excellence. He is the author or editor of several monographs on European economic and political integration like Palgrave Macmillan (2008): Economic Performance of European Union. He is the editor of policy paper series providing suggestion for further process of deepening economic and political integration in EU.

Katarína Lukáčová is a Researcher who is involved in projects dealing with changing work and employment in the context of digital and green fair transformation, with expertise on transforming sectors (automotive, coal mining, energy, steel, metal, etc.). She specializes in economic/labor sociology, with a focus on social dialogue, work organization, and social dialogue/collective bargaining. She is currently finalizing PhD dissertation in Transnational Governance at the SNS/SSSA in Florence, Italy. As a junior human capital development expert in the ETF, she cooperates with various political and social partner organizations across European neighborhood on the projects related to governance of social partnership and skill development.

Anton Marcinčin is an economist, a former government plenipotentiary for underdeveloped regions, advisor to the Minister of Finance, member of parliament, and country economist at the World Bank in Bratislava. He published dozens of articles, lectured at several universities, and participated in many international research activities. Since 2021, he has co-edited and contributed to the Yearbook of Regional Development; in 2009, he coauthored Cost of Roma Non-inclusion; in 2000, the Economic Policy in Slovakia 1990–1999. Since 2007, he has regularly published columns in a daily Hospodárske noviny, and since 2015 in a daily Pravda. Marcinčin graduated from the Czech Technical University in Prague and CERGE-EI Prague and defended his PhD in Economics at Charles University in Prague. He has received scholarships and fellowships at the Tinbergen Institute Amsterdam and LSE London.

Monika Martišková, PhD, is a Researcher at Central European Labor Studies Institute (CELSI) Bratislava, Slovakia, and at the department of Social Geography and Regional Development at Charles University in Prague, Czechia. She is interested in industrial relations and collective bargaining in CEE countries focusing on automotive industry. In her most recent research, she focuses on effects of decarbonization on the labor market and working conditions in industrial sectors. She has been involved in several research projects supported by European Commission that concentrated on the responses of social partners on challenges on the labor market in Czechia and Slovakia in the private and public sectors. In 2022, she defended her PhD thesis at Charles University on the topic of labor in global production networks studied on the example of trade unions in the automotive industry in Czechia and Slovakia.

Renáta Pitoňáková is a Professor at the University of Economics in Bratislava, Faculty of International Relations, Department of International Economic Relations and Economic Diplomacy. She graduated from the University of Economics in Bratislava (Faculty of Commerce) and Comenius University in Bratislava (Faculty of Arts). Professor Pitoňáková teaches courses on international economic relations and world economy, finances, banking, and monetary policy. Her scientific and research areas cover international trade, finance, and monetary policy. She was the Principal Investigator of the International Project granted by the International Visegrad Fund and the leader of several domestic scientific projects of the VEGA framework granted by the Ministry of Education,

Research, Development and Youth of the Slovak Republic and APVV project financed by the Slovak Research and Development Agency.

Professor **Juraj Sipko** is a member of the European Academy of Science and Art, and he is a member of the European Economic and Social Committee. In this Committee, he is the President of the International Trade Follow-up Committee and the President of Economic and Fiscal Governance of the Euro Area. He is also a Lecturer at the Pan-European University in Bratislava and the Tomas Bata University in Zlin. The last 8 years, he was the Director of the Institute of Economic Research of the Slovak Academy of Sciences (SAS). He has worked as an advisor to governors of the National Bank of Slovakia. For six years, he advised the executive directors of the Belgium constituency in both the International Monetary Fund and the World Bank. Furthermore, he also served more than 6 years as a Director of International Relations of the Ministry of Finance of the Slovak Republic and as a negotiator with the European Union and the OECD. He spent one year as a Visiting Scholar at the Massachusetts Institute of Technology and participated in the executive programs at Harvard Business School (Harvard University) and the Wharton Business School (University of Pennsylvania). He also participated in research studies in St. Thomas University Cameron School of Business (Houston), Cass Business School (London), Lomonosovova University (Moscow). Mr. Sipko has published numerous research papers, articles, and books, and he has also participated in many foreign and domestic international conferences and workshops.

Dunja Spasojević is a master student at Mendel University in Brno, Czech Republic. Her research interest is in the area of economic impacts of EU enlargement from the point of view of candidate countries and the EU budget. She focuses empirically on economic development of new member countries of EU and candidate countries.

Jakub Szabó is a Postdoctoral Researcher at the Institute of European Studies and International Relations, Faculty of Social and Economic Sciences, at Comenius University in Bratislava. With teaching commitments and interests in quantitative social science, his research concentration includes comparative and international political economy with a focus on the European Union, Eurozone, and post-communist EU countries, EU economic governance, and differentiation in European integration.

Jaroslav Vokoun is a Researcher at the Slovak Academy of Sciences, Institute of Economic Research. His research focuses on competitiveness and the knowledge society. He has contributed to projects like "Vision and Strategy of the Slovak Society Development" (2008–2010) and "National Priorities for the Implementation of the Agenda 2030 Strategy" (2018). He is the co-author of publications: Attractiveness of the Territory and Mobility of Talents: Big Cities Attract Talents (2020), Creating and Evaluating the Knowledge Society Potential (2017), Motivation of Actors in the Direction to the Knowledge Society (2014), Cooperation of Actors in Technological and Innovative Development (2011), and Technological and Innovative Development in the Slovak Republic (2005).

Natália Zagoršeková is an Assistant Professor at the Faculty of International Relations, University of Economics in Bratislava, Slovakia. In her research, she focuses on the individual economies of the European Union and also on Africa. She currently teaches courses on the economies of the European Union and Africa in international relations. She recently wrote a textbook on the economies of the European Union.

Preface

Ingrid Brocková
Ministry of Foreign and European Affairs of the Slovak Republic

Slovakia is a successful story of the economic transition and integration into the transatlantic security and economic structures. The year 2024 is the year of commemoration of the 31st anniversary of establishing an independent state, 20 years of membership in the European Union (EU) and NATO, and 15 years in the Eurozone. The integration process was the anchor and accelerator of the economy's transition. It meant a long-term effort and required a whole-of-government approach. Membership in the European Union and Eurozone has become a key policy framework for Slovakia's economic policy; encoring Slovakia in the system of other international organizations has become a tool for the prevention of populism.

After an ambitious reform agenda (1999–2006), Slovakia deservedly earned a reputation as the leading reformer in Central Europe, as the Slovak economy became the fastest growing in the European Union. Comprehensive and significant changes in public policy enabled the country to achieve a qualitative turnaround in its international status: it gained membership in the OECD, NATO, and European Union, acquired one of the top credit ratings among transition economies, and attracted an increasing share of foreign investments. In January 2009, this success was emphasized when Slovakia joined the Eurozone.

The Slovak authorities established a solid track record of economic adjustment and broad-based reforms. As a matter of priority, Slovakia had to address fundamental systemic problems, particularly related to the transparency and effectiveness of financial flows in almost all sectors and to the building of institutional capacity. The robust driver of the economic changes was the accession to the OECD and European Union, complemented by the World Bank programs such as improving the stability and efficiency of the banking and enterprise sector, social benefits administration, provision of social services, public finance management, and the performance of the health care system. In the context of accession, this involved mainly advisory activities that played a vital role. In 2002, for example, the World Bank conducted a comprehensive economic review focusing on Slovakia's readiness for EU accession (Development Policy Review) as well as a key document on agriculture (Food and Agriculture in the Slovak Republic: the Challenge of EU Accession, published in 2003). Both documents recommended how to proceed in the accession process to maximize the benefits and minimize the costs related to the EU accession. The World Bank portfolio in the Slovak Republic had never been large in terms of the number of loans. However, in a few years, it succeeded in becoming quite diverse and substantive when it comes to the advisory role of the government.

The EU became the key policy framework for Slovakia's economic policy. Membership in the EU means the privilege and responsibility: the privilege to participate in many of the EU policymaking institutions, policymaking process, and to take full advantage of the resources that became available from the EU itself and to use those resources well to address the development challenges (especially well-equipped administrative structures and skills). Membership means responsibility for implementing EU legislation. Slovakia, being already a member of the EU, needed to build capacities that would allow Slovakia to fully benefit from the EU membership. That meant capacities to facilitate knowledge and expertise sharing, conducting analytical work, and evidence-based decision-making processes. At that time, Slovakia was facing three broad development challenges: (i) to continue the prudent management of the economy; (ii) to converge to European income levels and be competitive on the European and world markets; (iii) to reduce poverty and unemployment, and to address the problems of marginalized groups of the population, especially Roma community.

What was important after accession to the EU was maintaining the reform dynamism. In Slovakia, the spirit of reform and a new way of looking at economic and social challenges prevailed. During the initial process of acceding to the OECD and the EU, the requirements for successful accession heavily influenced the reform agenda in Slovakia. The reform process has been so well internalized and successful that Slovakia addressed problems in some areas by applying the best practices from the OECD and non-EU countries. Slovakia has introduced far-reaching economic systemic changes, often beyond the EU requirements: social security networks and pension systems were overhauled, the share of agriculture in GDP dramatically decreased, the business climate improved, the labor market was not overregulated, and the tax burden was relatively low. Managing economic policies meant converging to the EU and OECD levels as quickly as possible. The essential prerequisites for success were political leadership, commitment, and government ownership of the reform agenda. That was the so-called "Tatra Tiger" period.

Slovakia has made commendable progress, aiming to meet the Maastricht criteria to join the Eurozone in January 2009. The priority of the government then was to focus (i) on the quality and sustainability of growth (increasing employment and competitiveness), (ii) on protecting social cohesion and reducing poverty, and (iii) on strengthening public administration and capacities for the efficient utilization of the EU funds. Many challenges, such as investment in infrastructure, health care, and education, persist still today. The priority of the medium-term horizon is to ensure labor productivity growth to foster an efficient and competitive business environment to sustain the economic growth necessary to accelerate convergence. That means keeping the reform dynamics in the country.

Slovakia needs a new economic model. Slovakia's dynamic growth has depended mainly on export-oriented manufacturing and foreign direct investments; located largely in western Slovakia, the central and eastern parts of the country are lagging. Slovakia benefits from strong links with the world economy, especially the EU members. However, international trade tensions and volatility pose risks to Slovakia's open, export-oriented economy. To a greater extent, the Slovak economy's vulnerability is higher than most other OECD countries. Slovak production focuses mainly on low-value-added downstream activities. Strong productivity growth has arisen from joining global value chains, mainly in labor-intensive segments such as car assembly. Large foreign investment inflows have helped develop a competitive export-led manufacturing industry, with a strong specialization in the automotive and electronics sectors, fostering robust growth and productivity performance. To sustain economic progress, Slovakia will have to move beyond this approach. Low research and development expenditures limit productivity growth going forward. Sustaining past productivity improvements, primarily based on integration into global value chains, will require strengthening Slovakia's capacity to innovate and adopt new technologies. The quality of the academic research system must be improved, and collaboration with companies' R&D must be expanded.

The local value-added content of exports is relatively low, and skills shortages may deter future investment. Foreign investors have already asked for additional immigration to ease the supply of skilled workers. Success has been based on a narrow range of industries. Smaller or domestically owned firms, especially in services, have not benefited from spillovers, needing access to financial sources to innovate and develop, thus falling further behind in international productivity comparisons. Slovakia must invest in skills and adaptability to labor market developments, as the risk of automation is more acute than elsewhere. It also needs to develop its capacity to innovate and adopt new technologies.

The transition to a greener economy, supported by international environmental commitments and national policies, will entail structural changes in consumption patterns and industry structures and offer new drivers for potential growth. Slovakia will need to build a practical framework for green growth to maximize the exploitation of cleaner sources of growth and seize the opportunities to develop new green industries, jobs, and technologies. This requires addressing environmental externalities by extending environmental taxation and removing subsidies, together with improving the economy's adaptive capacities through eco-innovation.

The main priorities are to restore public finances while fostering domestic growth drivers and ensuring the funding of items to promote growth, such as education and active labor market policies. Educational outcomes have declined throughout the years in Slovakia, and the education system does not do a good enough job of preparing students for the labor market. At the same time, many young, talented Slovaks are studying and working abroad. Improving educational outcomes and investing in skills should be a priority. The decline in educational performance must be reversed, and more must be done to improve the chances of children from poorer backgrounds. Early childhood education and better trained and paid teachers are necessary for this transformation. Good vocational education is essential for improving the skills needed in the labor market.

Population aging in Slovakia, projected to be one of the sharpest in the OECD, will pose a long-term challenge for fiscal policy and higher living standards. As the old-age dependency ratio rises steeply in the longer term, fiscal pressure intensifies. In this respect, the parameters of the pension system would be essential. Reinforcing spending reviews and better integrating the results into medium-term budget planning could help increase efficiency and release funds for priorities such as education and social inclusion.

Slovakia has traditionally been a country with significant regional disparities. Regional inequality is among the highest in the OECD; not everyone has benefited equally from growth. Long-term unemployment remains prevalent in the east and some central regions. The socioeconomic situation of the Roma calls for urgent policy action. Skills shortages in the Bratislava region persist alongside skills mismatches and uneven availability of technological and human resources in the central and eastern regions. Inadequate transport infrastructure raises costs for those who might establish firms in the lagging regions. The mobility of low-skilled unemployed is hampered by the lack of affordable housing where the jobs are and the lack of prioritization of active labor market policies. At the same time, regional job creation is often hindered by the weak response of local labor costs to local labor market outcomes. The school-to-work transition is weak, and vocational education does not provide adequate skills, one of the main barriers to regional development. Unequal educational opportunities, particularly for the Roma population, also hold back inclusive growth. Most of the Roma (who make up around 8%–10% of the population) live in poverty and face social exclusion in most aspects of everyday life. Most suffer from long spells of unemployment and low life expectancy. The Roma needs better access to education, health, employment, and other public services. More live in isolated or segregated communities and have low educational levels and high school dropout rates. Although public services are available in principle, language barriers, a lack of awareness of available programs, and discrimination hamper access.

Slovakia is generally underperforming in terms of public sector efficiency, which reduces the room for maneuvering for fiscal consolidation and financing growth-friendly measures. The public sector lags on the application of e-government and e-procurement. Practiced human resource management has resulted in a high staff turnover. The regulatory framework and judicial system remain insufficiently supportive of business activity, and perceived corruption impedes growth. The efficiency of public spending and the absorption of EU funds suffer from a lack of systematic evaluation and coordination between ministries, cumbersome procedures, and weak administrative capacity. Public–private partnerships had to be canceled because of nontransparent procedures and high financing costs. Strong centralization has weakened the incentives for efficiency at the subnational level, and many municipalities are too small to provide public services efficiently.

Deploying reliable digital infrastructure and enhancing digital government services is critical to enabling digital transformation across the economy and society. Further improving the business environment can foster business dynamism. Despite progress in reducing administrative burdens, regulations in several areas, especially for start-up firms, remain more restrictive than in other EU countries. Continuing judiciary reforms are needed to fight corruption and foster efficiency and trust. Given the deterioration of public finances, there is little scope for higher spending without reprioritization. In such a situation, raising public sector efficiency can free up resources and help to stimulate productivity and, thus, potential growth.

Each government sets up an ambitious reform program, emphasizing reforms and investment in education, health care, and a greener economy and innovation. Further efforts are needed to raise Slovakia's chronically low absorption rate of EU funds by streamlining public procurement and enhancing public investment governance.

Historically, based mainly on integration into global value chains, sustaining productivity gains has been essential to revive economic convergence and boost living standards in Slovakia's aging society. It requires strengthening Slovakia's capacity to innovate and adopt new technologies also implementing necessary systemic measures such as:

- Building national capacity for strategic foresight to identify megatrends and their impact on vulnerability to external and internal shocks, thus building the resilience of the Slovak society.
- Slovakia needs a new economic model to ensure prosperity and competitiveness by addressing connectivity, education quality, the economy's structure (with the dominance of small- and medium-sized companies), and innovation capacity.
- Public administration needs to improve analytical capacity, evidence-based policymaking, and the ability to learn and be inspired by the good practices of other countries, especially in allocating available EU funds. That calls for a more efficient institutional structure, governance, and integrity of the public sector.
- Vision, political commitment, and stability. Slovakia is a country without continuity; what has been evident is sectors where changes require a more extended period than one election cycle. The country's vision is the fundamental prerequisite to spending wisely on EU funds to accelerate Slovakia's development challenges. Inclusive, sustainable, and green growth will not be achieved without the engagement and partnership of the private, public sector, and academic communities. Slovakia needs a whole-of-society approach.

I am convinced that the presented publication and its authors accurately reflect the state of play of the Slovak economy and outline recommendations on how to address the current challenges and create a new economic model for ensuring better prosperity in Slovakia.

Introduction

Michael Augustín[a], *Peter Jančovič*[a] *and Bruno S. Sergi*[b,c]

[a]University of Economics in Bratislava, Slovakia
[b]University of Messina, Italy
[c]Harvard University, USA

The story of Slovakia's economic journey over the past three decades is about how the country has undergone a remarkable transformation in its economic landscape. Emerging from the shadows of state socialism and the centrally planned economy, Slovakia embarked on a path of economic transition and reforms. The dissolution of Czechoslovakia marked the beginning of a new era for Slovakia, characterized by the need to establish its own economic policy, institutions, and legal frameworks. In the tumultuous years of the 1990s, the country faced numerous obstacles on its path to economic stability and growth. Through perseverance and strategic reforms, Slovakia emerged as a dynamic market economy with a strong export orientation and has been walking this path for over 30 years. However, the current economic model of Slovakia raises several concerns, particularly in light of global challenges, trends, and the necessity for transformation in order to increase economy's competitiveness and ensure its future economic growth.

The book *Modeling Economic Growth in Contemporary Slovakia* delves deep into the intricacies of Slovakia's economic trajectory, offering invaluable insights for policymakers, academics, and practitioners alike. Through a comprehensive analysis, the authors unravel the multifaceted factors that have shaped Slovakia's economic path, ranging from economic policies and institutional structures to trade dynamics, innovations, and external influences. The chapters of this book also identify some policy implications that might be useful in predicting the future trajectories of Slovakia's economic growth and development.

Chapter 1 discusses the economic challenges faced by Czechoslovakia after 1989 during its transition from a centrally planned system to a market economy. It focuses on the liberalization of prices and foreign trade, as well as small and large-scale privatization initiatives. Despite initial setbacks, the chapter highlights the successful transformation before the peaceful division of Czechoslovakia into the Czech Republic and Slovak Republic in 1993. The author explores the institutional and legal frameworks established by Slovak authorities and the economic pressures faced.

Modeling Economic Growth in Contemporary Slovakia, 1–4

doi:10.1108/978-1-83549-454-720241001

Chapter 2 examines Slovakia's economic transition since 1993. It analyzes pivotal reforms, political choices, and contextual elements impacting the country's economic path. The authors state that, despite growth, Slovakia faces challenges from oligarchic influence, socioeconomic disparities, over-reliance on the automotive sector, and insufficient investment in innovation and infrastructure. The chapter stresses the need for visionary leadership and a national discourse on Slovakia's future trajectory.

Chapter 3 discusses Slovakia's economic convergence within the global and European contexts. It analyzes Slovakia's progress against peers within the Visegrad Group and other new EU Member States using various metrics, such as Global Competitiveness Index, Ease of Doing Business, and GDP per capita. The chapter explores the factors driving these shifts and offers insights into the evolution of the Slovak economy.

Chapter 4 examines economic growth as the primary policy framework in Slovakia and explores alternative approaches that prioritize human welfare and environmental considerations. It analyzes indicators such as the Human Development Index (HDI) and the Planetary Pressures-adjusted Human Development Index (PHDI) to assess quality of life and environmental sustainability. The chapter questions the viability of growth-centric policies amid climate change challenges and the EU Green Deal, emphasizing the need for greater integration of sustainability principles in Slovakian policymaking. It concludes by identifying specific areas where insights from critical perspectives can inform policy decisions in Slovakia.

Chapter 5 discusses Slovakia's labor market dynamics from 2000 to 2020, which played a crucial role in accommodating the significant social and economic transformations during this period. The chapter provides insights into the status of the labor market, including unemployment rates and workforce composition. It examines the determinants of labor market changes and their interactions with the external environment.

Chapter 6 analyzes the real estate market in Slovakia, focusing on developments since 1990. It assesses factors influencing this market, including social, economic, and financial determinants. The chapter explores the impact of owner-occupied housing on housing issues and investigates ownership trends, particularly in Bratislava. It also examines the influence of financial indicators such as interest rates, housing loan availability, and banking sector regulations on residential real estate prices, determinants, and market risks in Slovakia.

Chapter 7 focuses on the Slovak Republic's external economic relations, namely its performance in foreign trade and foreign direct investment (FDI) flows, as well as the country's foreign economic policy and institutional framework in the field of export and investment promotion. The chapter points out that Slovakia is highly integrated into global value chains, but it mostly focuses on economic activities with a low domestic added value. Given that Slovakia is strongly dependent on exports and FDI inflows, the country should improve the effectiveness of its foreign economic policy, diversify the territorial and commodity structure of exports, support outward FDI flows, as well as attract FDI with higher added value and to less developed regions in order to increase international competitiveness and ensure future economic development of the Slovak economy.

Chapter 8 delves into the issue of regional inequalities in Slovakia. It explores the topic through a historical lens and draws comparisons between selected indicators and those of other areas within the European Union. The chapter highlights the negative impact that centralized governance structures in Slovakia have had on a regional welfare, resulting in weaker economic performance and labor market outcomes. Additionally, the text analyzes the effectiveness of financial transfers that have been put in place to address regional disparities. The chapter concludes with a set of public policy recommendations.

Chapter 9 discusses Slovakia's unique growth model and aims to explain the apparent differences through the politics of growth model approach. In the early 2000s, Slovakia implemented avant-garde neoliberal policies to outbid regional competitors in attracting FDI. Its growth model's strength lies in the interaction between a cross-class domestic growth coalition, meeting the needs of transnational manufacturing capital, and external constraints, like membership in the EMU.

Chapter 10 delves into Slovakia's automotive industry, which heavily relies on foreign capital. The industry faces an uncertain future due to digitalization and car electrification. The Slovak government seeks new foreign investments in battery production and a fifth car manufacturer. However, this strategy may affect long-term progress and innovation.

Chapter 11 focuses on innovation in Slovakia and its role in driving sustainable development and competitiveness. The chapter highlights the need for investment in research, development, and innovation from both private and public sectors. It also emphasizes the importance of digitalization and collaboration among stakeholders to foster a knowledge society. Lastly, it discusses the imperative of digital transformation for Slovakia to successfully adapt to ongoing changes.

Chapter 13 discusses Business Service Centers (BSCs) in the Slovak economy. These centers employ around 40,000 skilled workers and drive service export growth. The BSCs are expanding beyond Bratislava to cities like Košice, particularly in IT outsourcing. Government support is needed to secure a skilled workforce as the industry prepares for process automation.

Chapter 13 highlights the significance of tourism and culture industries in the Slovak economy and it also points out that Slovakia has an unexploited potential in this field that may be used for future economic development. The contribution of the cultural and creative industries to GDP has grown over the last 20 years, not only in the European Union but also in Slovakia. Therefore, culture and tourism play an increasingly vital role in the development of Slovakia's regions.

Chapter 14 compares the Czech and Slovak economies before and after joining the EU, focusing on the effects of EU membership and Slovakia's adoption of the euro on their economic trajectories. The aim of the chapter is to identify whether the two economies closely resemble each other or represent unique economic evolution cases. The authors investigate the behavior of the two economies throughout the transformation period.

The book paints a comprehensive picture of Slovakia's economic evolution through chapters delving into economic reforms, labor market dynamics, regional inequalities, innovation, external economic relations, and industry-specific analyses. It underscores the successes, challenges, and areas for improvement, particularly in the face of global trends and sustainability imperatives. *Modeling Economic Growth in Contemporary Slovakia* is a unique attempt to reflect the specific case of the Slovak economy. We believe this book represents a valuable addition to the existing book series Entrepreneurship and Global Economic Growth, focusing on another economy from the Central and Eastern European region.

I

Dynamics of the Slovak Economy

Chapter 1

Historical Development of the Czechoslovak and Slovak Economies in the Transition Period

Juraj Sipko

Slovak Academy of Sciences, Slovakia
Faculty of Economics and Entrepreneurship, Pan-European University in Bratislava, Slovakia
Faculty of Management and Economics, Tomas Bata University in Zlin, Czechia

Abstract

After 1989, the Czechoslovak economy faced very many challenges related to the transition process from centrally planned system to the market economy. The main goal of the transformation was the liberalization of prices and foreign trade. After the price and trade liberalization has been introduced a critical part of transformation, including the small and large scale of privatization. The price and foreign trade liberalization, including the small and large privatization, had very negative impact on the economic activities. After relatively successful transformation, the authorities from both the Czech and the Slovak Republic decided on a peaceful division on separate of two republics, the Czech and Slovak republics since January 1st, 1993. Historically, the main institutions during the Czechoslovak republic were located in the Czech Republic, in particular, central banks and other federal institutions. In addition, the structure of the Slovak economy was relatively less developed in comparison with the Czech economy. The Slovak authorities were able to build the institutional and legal frameworks for the Slovak economy. During 1993, the Slovak economy was under many pressures due to the relatively low level of the foreign exchange assets, deep external imbalances, and high level in inflation. Furthermore, it was needed the restructuring of the enterprises, dealing with bad debt in the banking sector etc. Despite all obstacles related to the overall transformation process, including the creation of new

Modeling Economic Growth in Contemporary Slovakia, 7–24

doi:10.1108/978-1-83549-454-720241002

institutions for a new country, the Slovak economy started to adjust to new market economic conditions relatively well.

Keywords: Transformation process; centrally planned system; market economy; liberalization of trade; deregulation of prices; privatization

1. Introduction

The goal of this chapter is to evaluate the historical development of the Czechoslovak and, subsequently, Slovak economy during the period from 1989 to 1993. After November 1989, the transformation process from a centrally planned system to a market economy began in the joint state of Czechs and Slovaks. A characteristic feature of this period was that the transformation process proceeded relatively quickly, primarily focusing on macroeconomic stability, price, and foreign trade liberalization. As the next stage in this transition process to a market economy, an extensive privatization of state property ensued.

From a macroeconomic perspective, creating conditions to ensure stability was necessary. Extensive changes were made in the fiscal area, both in the structure of public finances and in the introduction of transparency in public finances. In the monetary policy and exchange rate area, a series of measures were adopted to ensure the stability of price development and the exchange rate. Due to the extensive process of price deregulation, a relatively high level of uncertainty was observed during this period. The process of price liberalization led to a significant increase in the inflation rate.

The transformation process led to a gradual shift in foreign trade orientation from former member states of the Council for Mutual Economic Assistance (CMEA) to other European countries, especially industrially developed states and neighboring countries.

The change in orientation in foreign trade relationships and a decline in foreign exchange reserves prompted the former government to request additional financial resources from international monetary and financial institutions to ensure macroeconomic stability and an unprecedented adaptation to the newly emerging conditions.

Due to the radical transformation process, there was a noticeable lack of capital investments during this period. An analysis of the relationships in former Czechoslovakia is necessary to understand the developments in this period better.

Parts of this chapter have been published in the Slovak language in the section: Vývoj ekonomiky po roku 1989 [Development of the economy after 1989] (Sipko, 2021) of the monograph: Cesta Slovenska k vzniku samostatného štátu v roku 1993 [Slovakia's path to the creation of an independent state in 1993].

2. Economic Development in Former Czechoslovakia

During the interwar period, the Czechoslovak economy belonged to one of the leading developed economies in the global economic landscape. Industrial production with a relatively higher value added compared to some European states was predominant in the Czechoslovak economy (IMF, 1990). Therefore, the well-functioning economy enjoyed relatively high prosperity during this period.

Table 1.1. Development of Selected Indicators in Former Czechoslovakia (1987–1992).

	1987	1988	1989	1990	1991	1992
Inflation	0.1	0.2	1.4	10.8	59	13.1
Prices in the industry	0.1	0.1	−0.7	4.4	67.0	8.2
Trade balance	−0.3	0.4	0.1	−1.5	−2.3	−1.5
Current balance (PB)	0.4	1.1	−0.9	−1.3	−0.4	−0.6
Official foreign currencies	2.3	2.5	2.0	0.6	1.0	2.0
Foreign debt	6.7	7.3	7.9	8.2	9.1	10.6
Debt service (% share in exports)	24.0	24.8	24.4	19.5	16.8	12.4

Source: Own processing of data from the Czechoslovak Statistical Office and national statistical offices.

The Czechoslovak economy during socialism (1948–1989) was among the relatively most developed in terms of industrial production among the former states of the CMEA. Table 1.1 documents the development of selected macroeconomic indicators for the period 1987–1992 in former Czechoslovakia.

A characteristic feature of the macroeconomic policy in former Czechoslovakia was a very conservative approach. Therefore, thanks to this approach, the transition from a centrally planned system to a market economy was less vulnerable than other member states of the CMEA.

The table further indicates that relatively low inflation values were recorded until 1990 due to a prudent macroeconomic policy. Compared to other CMEA member states, former Czechoslovakia had relatively low foreign debt, USD 7.9 billion, at the end of 1989 (IMF, 1990, p. 10). In 1987, public debt was recorded at 6.7% of Gross Domestic Product (GDP), and in 1992, public debt remained at a relatively low level of only 10.6% of GDP.

A relatively high-quality and consistently improving comprehensive education system, among the best within the former CMEA states, also facilitated a high degree of industrialization. Despite these relatively favorable conditions and initial circumstances for transitioning from a centrally planned system to a market economy in former Czechoslovakia, there needed to be more experience with the transformation process compared to the Hungarian People's Republic and the Polish People's Republic.

After the elections in 1990, the government of Czechoslovakia prepared an extensive strategic plan for reforms. Based on a widely accepted consensus to initiate reforms, a legislative framework for the transition from a centrally planned system to a market economy was approved. The primary priority of the strategy was to expedite the transformation process, which was a precondition for membership in the EU (Fritsch & Hansen, 1997). In this context, the strategy for transitioning to a market economy involved the establishment of a financial sector, particularly banking and later the capital market, including the insurance sector (see Pavlík, 1997, pp. 89–96).

As a crucial measure during this period, efforts were made to stabilize the exchange rate to prevent speculative attacks on the Czechoslovak koruna. Until 1989, the State Bank of Czechoslovakia used a multirate exchange rate system. Exchange rates were divided into commercial and noncommercial rates. After adopting the reform plan for economic transformation, a very challenging period ensued with its implementation.

When assessing the development of the Slovak economy, it is necessary to reconsider the progress of specific comparable indicators within the common state of Czechs and Slovaks.

3. Development of the National Economies of Czechs and Slovaks From 1990 to 1992

In January 1990, the Czechoslovak government initiated a radical implementation of the transformation process. The principle of accelerating the transformation process, mainly through the strategy of the "big bang," was adopted and implemented, particularly in the areas of price liberalization and foreign trade.

A fixed exchange rate was introduced in external economic relations, which served as a nominal anchor for the Czechoslovak koruna. After abandoning the multirate exchange rate system, the official exchange rate for the Czechoslovak koruna was set at 18 Kčs (Czechoslovak koruna) for one West German mark and 28 Kčs for one USD (IMF, 1990, p. 25).

After adopting and implementing measures related to price deregulation and macroeconomic stabilization, the third area of transformation began – namely, the privatization process, which was divided into small and large privatization. The government introduced an import surcharge on consumer goods, initially set at 20% to stabilize the external macroeconomic balance, and it was reduced to 10% by January 1, 1992.

After the gradual achievement of relative stability in the macroeconomic area, further important measures were gradually adopted and implemented in the process aimed at a market-oriented economy. Prices increased by more than 50% in the second and third quarters of 1991. The processes of price and foreign trade liberalization, changes in foreign trade orientation, and macroeconomic stabilization were relatively successful. The transition to a market economy had relatively different developments in individual national economies.

4. The Development of Macroeconomic Indicators in Former Czechoslovakia

Despite Slovaks and Czechs living in the common state for decades, relatively divergent economic development was possible in both national economies. The macroeconomic development and its trajectory in the former Czechoslovakia stemmed from the principles of governance of the centrally planned system.

The performance in monetary and exchange rate policies was carried out by the State Bank of Czechoslovakia (see IMF, 1990, p. 29). The Czechoslovak Trade Bank represented the banking sector with a focus on foreign affairs, and also the Živnostenská Bank handled foreign exchange operations for selected individuals.

Price deregulation led to a significant price increase that led to high inflation. Therefore, the main objective of monetary policy, supported by a restrictive fiscal policy, was to eliminate shocks caused by the unfavorable development of the Terms of Trade index, thus reducing the potential impact on further inflation growth. The monetary program focused on using nonmonetary financial assets that arose due to small-scale privatization. Support for the business sector led to an increase in domestic loans.

Fiscal policy performance until 1990 was oriented toward and primarily fulfilled a redistributive function. Like the monetary policy during the period of the centrally planned system, fiscal policy also had a conservative approach. The preparation and implementation of the budget for 1990 also had a conservative but mainly restrictive character. One of the essential measures in the newly conceived budget was the abolition of the extra-budgetary funds for individual ministries and various forms of cross-subsidies between enterprises.

The main goal in fiscal policy management was to introduce measures against inflation growth. When designing the new federal budget, expenditures were considered within the federal government and national budgets. In addition, measures were adopted and implemented to increase transparency in public finances, especially in the area of subsidies for agriculture. One of the most important measures in macroeconomic policy was the adoption of systematic measures in exchange rate policy.

The exchange rate policy's basis during this period focused on price stabilization during its liberalization. The official exchange rate of the Czechoslovak koruna was determined using a currency basket. Because the exchange rate was directly linked to the currency basket, it performed as a nominal anchor during the price liberalization period.

The simplification of the exchange rate mechanism continued. "In a move toward a market-determined exchange rate system, a foreign exchange auction was introduced on an experimental basis in August 1989." (IMF, 1990, p. 26). On December 28, 1990, a unified exchange rate for the Czechoslovak koruna was introduced, expressing the mutual relationship between Kčs and USD.

The main basis for determining the value of the exchange rate of the Czechoslovak koruna was the currency basket, which consisted of five freely convertible currencies. The share of each currency in the basket was as follows: West German mark (40.93%), US dollar (32.88%), Austrian schilling (12.32%), Swiss franc (9.05%), and French franc (4.82%). After the introduction of the internal convertibility of Kčs on January 2, 1992, there was also a change in the composition of the currency basket. After this revision, the position of the US dollar strengthened: US dollar (49.07%), West German mark (36.15%), Austrian schilling (8.07%), Swiss franc (3.79%), and French franc (2.92%). Following the formation of two separate states, on March 5, 1993, the original basket of five currencies was reduced to a basket of two currencies with the following shares: West German mark (65%) and US dollar (35%). For more information about money and credit in the transition of the Czechoslovak economy, see Siebert (1992, pp. 307–326).

The challenging process of transformation led to devaluations in the exchange rate of the Czechoslovak koruna (Kčs) for tradable and nontradable payments. Given the devaluation of the Kčs exchange rate, which reached approximately 50% in 1990, the question arose of how to ensure the stability of the exchange rate with a relatively low volume of foreign exchange reserves. One option to increase the volume of foreign exchange reserves in the State Bank of Czechoslovakia was the possibility of obtaining additional financial resources to ensure macroeconomic stability from international monetary and financial institutions. Due to the decline in foreign exchange reserves, the former government of Czechoslovakia requested a stabilization loan from the International Monetary Fund (IMF) in 1991.

Given the different economic levels of the two national economies, it is necessary to compare their mutual development. One of the most crucial stages of the overall transformation process was the extensive privatization of state property.

5. The Privatization Process in Former Czechoslovakia

After the relatively successful liberalization of price, foreign trade, and payment systems, one of the most crucial and complex stages in the transition from a centrally planned system to a market economy emerged – the privatization process. The former Czechoslovak government decided to implement privatization, dividing it into small and large privatization (see Prust, 1993, pp. 61–64). Timing was crucial in the privatization process, and it was important to assess the state of the equity capital, fiscal aspects, and the actual implementation of privatization. One of the significant institutional shortcomings in the privatization process was the lack of a developed capital market.

In former Czechoslovakia, the entrepreneurial sector was relatively well-developed, with a substantial portion of the middle class involved. The restitution process played a crucial role in addressing historical injustices stemming from the nationalization of property belonging to individual citizens.

Many small businesses, including shops, underwent the restitution process within a relatively short timeframe. The total number of privatized small businesses and shops was estimated to be more than 100,000. The first stage of the privatization process was focused on small privatization.

6. Small-Scale Privatization

The process of small-scale privatization was incomparably more straightforward compared to large privatization. A characteristic feature of small privatization was that the selling price of small assets and the management of the entire process were much faster. The auction process of small privatization was relatively quickly implemented, and the achieved prices, in most cases, corresponded to the real value.

The privatization process was carried out through the national ministries of privatization in both national republics. National property funds in Slovakia and the Czech Republic played a significant role in the small privatization process. The National property funds created at the national level played an indispensable role in the privatization process. The main task of the established National property funds was to receive proceeds from the sale of state assets. In small privatization, leasing played a significant role and was utilized as an option. Only citizens of the former Czechoslovakia were allowed to participate in the first round of the auction process.

Even though most households did not have relatively high savings, a significant portion of state entities designated for small privatization was successfully realized through auctions. There was also an observed increase in loans to the private sector to support the small privatization process.

While small privatization was characterized by a relatively smooth process, large-scale privatization was associated with one of the most significant steps in the transition from a planned management system to a market economy.

7. Large-Scale Privatization

After a relatively quick and successful process of small privatization, a much more complex and challenging process of large privatization began. Given the complexity of the privatization process, various methods and approaches were employed. Negotiations, including the participation of foreign investors, auctions, and competitive bids, were used in selling state-owned enterprises. Additionally, the coupon privatization method was utilized, involving the sale through the National Property Fund, partial sales, or retaining a portion in the National Property Fund for potential sale to foreign investors. These privatization approaches were based on management proposals for selected state-owned enterprises, subject to review by specific ministries. After evaluating individual privatization projects, the relevant ministries provided feedback on the overall privatization project.

The direct sale to foreign investors began in 1991. One method within large privatization was coupon privatization, which took place from October 1991 to February 1992. In this form of privatization, every adult citizen of the former Czechoslovakia could register. Coupons could be used directly for investment or through newly created Investment Privatization Funds.

The sale of state-owned enterprises or parts of the assets within state-owned enterprises allocated through coupon privatization was carried out in five consecutive auction rounds. The initial round (also known as the zero round) occurred through auctions on February 17, 1992, and concluded only after the complete sale of state-owned enterprises or their parts. The first round of coupon privatization began in April 1992. If there was insufficient demand for individual state-owned enterprises or their parts, the residual value was transferred to the next round, sometimes with a reduction.

At the beginning of privatization, it was agreed that if a 97% stake in a state-owned enterprise was sold, the privatization wave would be considered complete. Revenue from the sale of state assets and their parts was used to create the Restitution Fund. It was established that 3% of the proceeds from the sale of state assets were earmarked for the Restitution Fund. Over 3.3 million citizens of the former Czechoslovakia participated in coupon privatization (see Marcinčin & Beblavý, 2000).

After the division of former Czechoslovakia into two separate states, the second major wave of coupon privatization continued in the newly formed independent states of Slovakia and the Czech Republic. At the national level, especially with foreign investors, there was an effort to gain additional capital, know-how, and access to foreign markets. During the joint state of Czechs and Slovaks, a common institutional and legislative framework was created for the transformation from a centrally planned system to a market economy. After creating two independent states, each proceeded according to its newly adopted national legislation. After the division of former Czechoslovakia into two separate states, it is important to compare the economic developments in each economy.

8. Comparison of GDP Development Between the Czech Republic and the Slovak Republic

The transformation process from a centrally planned system to a market economy had a very adverse impact on the economic development of both states. Until 1989, the GDP development, depicted in Fig. 1.1, was comparable between the two national economies in the common state.

The GDP growth in Slovakia reached in 1990 minus 5.3%, compared to minus 3.3% in the Czech Republic. The Czech economy historically achieved higher value-added, especially in industrial production, compared to the Slovak economy. A significant decline in GDP continued in both economies in 1991. That year, a substantial contraction of GDP was recorded at minus 17.6% in Slovakia and minus 13.6% in the Czech Republic. In 1992, the massive decline in Slovak GDP was reduced to minus 14%, while the Czech economic contraction reached minus 12.8%. The more favorable development of GDP in the Czech Republic resulted from the economic structure and foreign trade orientation. Industrial production played the highest role in generating GDP in both national economies.

9. Comparison of the Development of Gross Industrial Production Between Slovakia and the Czech Republic

One of the essential indicators in evaluating the economic growth in former Czechoslovakia was industrial production. Fig. 1.2 illustrates the period of the centrally

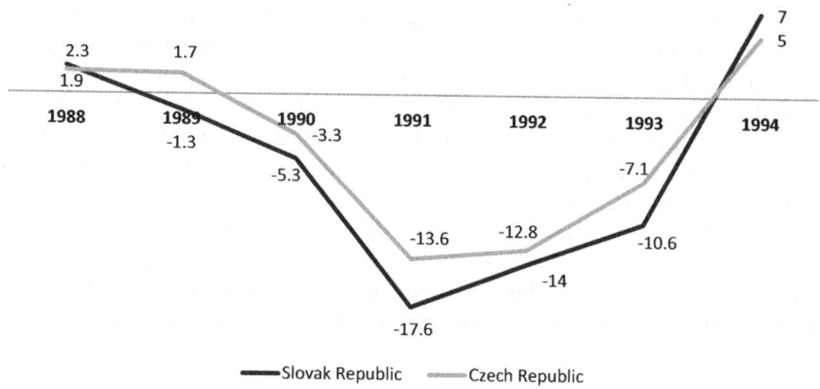

Fig. 1.1. Comparison of the Development of GDP Between Slovakia and the Czech Republic (1988–1994). *Source:* Own analysis based on data from the Slovak and Czech Statistical Offices and the Czechoslovak Statistical Bureau.

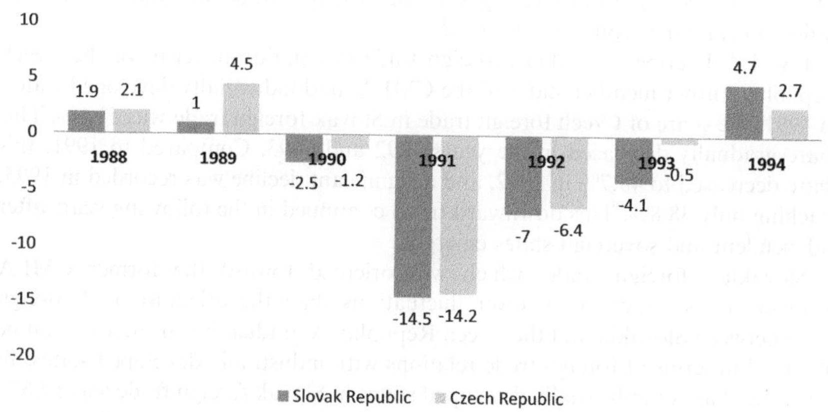

Fig. 1.2. Comparison of the Development of Gross Industrial Production Between Slovakia and the Czech Republic (1988–1994). *Source:* Own processing of data from the Slovak and Czech Statistical Offices and the ŠBČS.

planned management system compared to the unprecedented transformation process. In the conditions of the Slovak economy, industrial production declined already in 1990, reaching a value of minus 2.5%, compared to 1988, when the growth of industrial production was 1.9%.

With the ongoing transformation process, a significant decline in industrial production was recorded in the following years of transformation. In 1991, there was a decline of minus 14.5%. In the case of annual percentage changes in industrial production in the Czech Republic, relatively lower percentage changes in the decline of industrial production were recorded compared to Slovakia. In 1991, industrial production in the Czech Republic reached minus 14.2%. In the following years, that is, 1992–1993, a gradual linear increase in industrial production could be observed.

In 1994, there was a reversal in the development trend, where both already independent states achieved a very encouraging trend in industrial production and achieved positive values in this development. Foreign trade played a significant role in the structure of economic growth in both national economies.

10. Comparison of the Development of Slovak Foreign Trade

The former Czechoslovak economy was relatively more open than other CMEA member states. Its foreign trade policy was primarily oriented toward the former CMEA states, where trade with these countries accounted for 54% of total exports and 56% of total imports in 1989 (IMF, 1990, p. 30). With the onset of the radical reform process, significant changes in the foreign trade orientation of both national economies could be observed.

Fig. 1.3 describes Slovakia's foreign trade orientation in terms of the Czech Republic, former member states of the CMEA, and industrially developed states. In 1991, the share of Czech foreign trade in Slovak foreign trade was 51.6%. This share gradually decreased in the years 1992 and 1993. Compared to 1991, this share decreased to 48.7% in 1992, and a significant decline was recorded in 1993, reaching only 38.8%. This downward trend continued in the following years after independent and sovereign states emerged.

Slovakia's foreign trade, which was oriented toward the former CMEA member states, experienced lower fluctuations than the orientation of foreign trade between Slovakia and the Czech Republic. A gradual linear increase can be observed in terms of foreign trade relations with industrially developed states. In 1991, the share of industrially developed states in Slovak foreign trade was 19.6%; in 1992, this share reached 26.9%, and by 1993, it had increased to 32.5%.

This analysis shows that the most significant decrease in the share of Slovak foreign trade was recorded with the Czech Republic. Comparing changes in the development of Czech foreign trade is necessary to better understand the development of the two national economies.

11. Comparison of the Development of Czech Foreign Trade

The transformation process in the Czech economy led to more significant changes in its foreign trade orientation in the Czech Republic than in Slovakia. Foreign trade during the period of the common state of Czechs and Slovaks experienced significant changes (see Fig. 1.4).

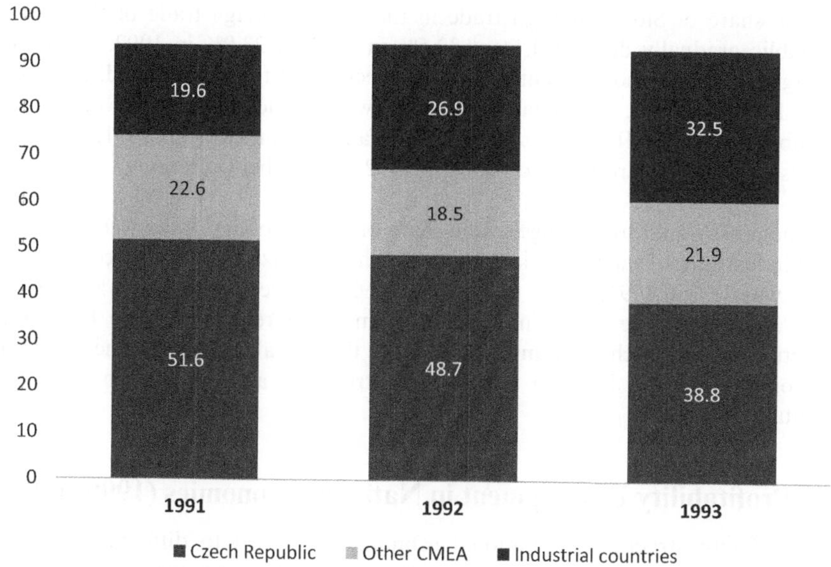

Fig. 1.3. Slovak Trade With Other Countries (1991–1993). *Source:* Own processing of data from the Slovak Statistical Office.

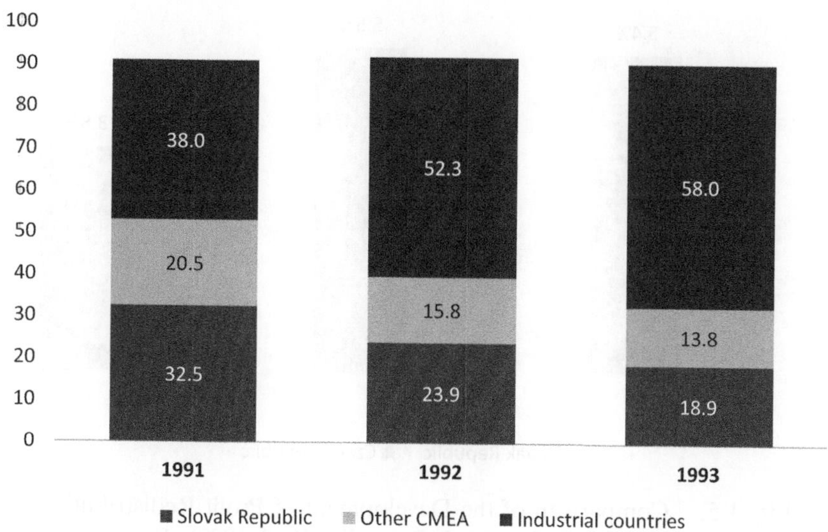

Fig. 1.4. Czech Trade With Other Countries (1991–1993). *Source:* Own processing of data from the Czech Statistical Office.

The share of Slovak foreign trade in the overall foreign trade of the Czech Republic gradually decreased from 32.5% in 1991 to 23.9% in 1992. After the emergence of two independent states, this decreasing trend continued, reaching only 18.9% in 1993. A similar linear downward trend in the share of former members of the CMEA on Czech foreign trade continued from 1991, where it represented 20.5%, dropping to 15.8% in 1992 and further decreasing to 13.8% in 1993.

The most significant change in the share of Czech foreign trade was observed with industrialized states. While the share of industrialized states in Czech foreign trade was 38% in 1991, it rose to 52.3% in 1992 and even further to 58% in 1993. This analysis of the share in Czech foreign trade reflects a more favorable structure of the Czech economy compared to the Slovak economy. The different economic structures between the two countries can also be seen in terms of profitability.

12. Profitability Development in National Economies (1990–1992)

The different structures of national economies also led to different levels of profitability for individual enterprises in the two national economies. In addition, Slovak companies had a relatively weaker financial position than Czech companies. Fig. 1.5 illustrates the differences in profit redistribution in the individual national economies between 1990 and 1992. In the observed period, relatively significant differences between companies in the individual states were recorded.

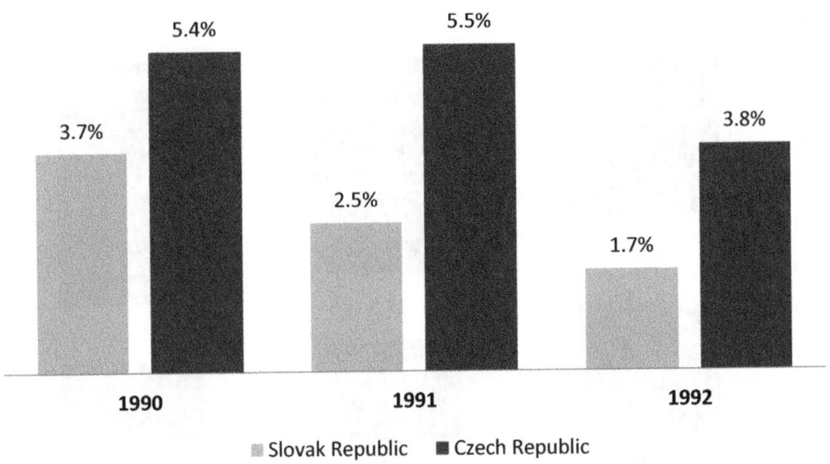

Fig. 1.5. Comparison of the Development of Profit Redistribution Between Slovakia and the Czech Republic (1990–1992). *Source:* Own processing of data from the International Monetary Fund and the OECD. Slovak and Czech Statistical Offices.

Gradually, with the ongoing transformation process, a linear decrease in profitability in Slovak companies could be observed. In 1990, the profitability was 3.7%; in 1991, a decrease of 2.5% was recorded; and in 1992, profitability reached only 1.7%. Czech companies achieved incomparably higher profits than Slovak companies. In 1991, the profitability of Czech companies reached 5.5%, which was 0.1% higher than in 1990. In the last year of the common state, the profitability of Czech companies decreased to 3.8%. From this analysis, it can be concluded that Czech companies entered the transformation with a relatively better financial position than Slovak companies. Considering the more sophisticated production in Czech companies, the higher added value was achieved compared to Slovak companies.

When evaluating the development of selected indicators in the real economy, it is important to compare the wage trends in individual states.

13. Development of Real Wages

A comparison of the development of real wages in Slovakia and the Czech Republic from 1991 to 1993 is essential when evaluating the progress of the two national economies. Fig. 1.6 illustrates a comparable linear decline in real wages in both countries during the transformation process. The implementation of a solid restrictive fiscal policy led to a significant decrease in real wages in 1991, reaching minus 29.8% in Slovakia and minus 26.6% in the Czech Republic. This highly unfavorable trend in reducing real wages resulted from the price liberalization process.

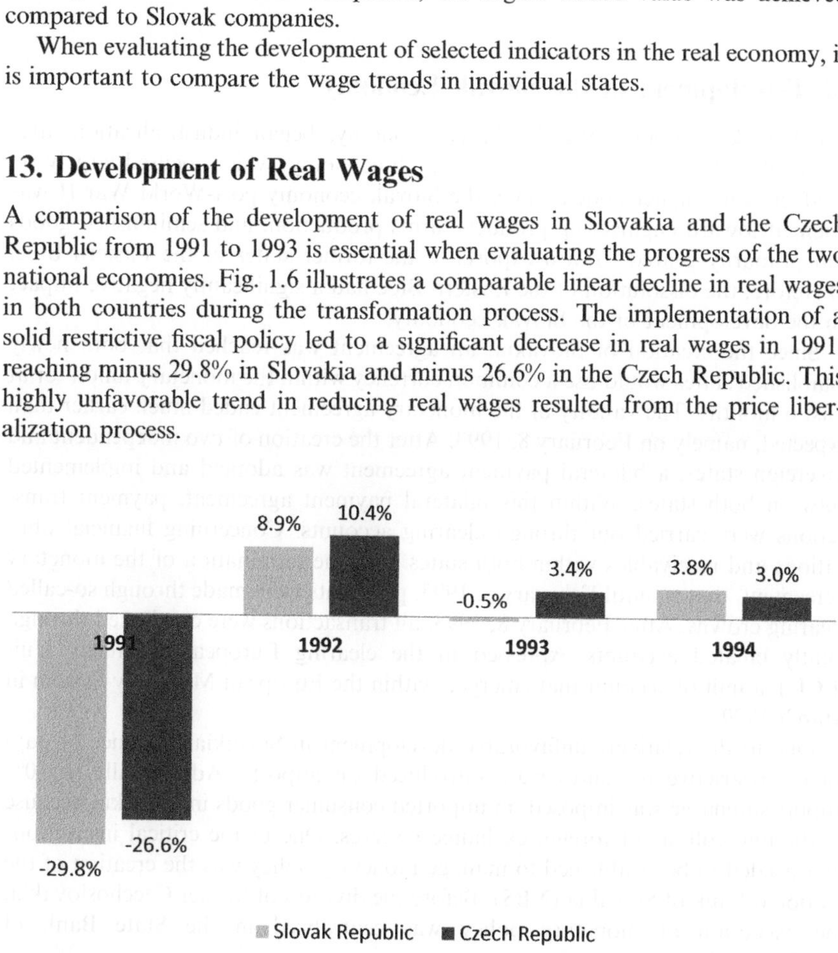

Fig. 1.6. Comparison of the Development of Real Wages in Slovakia and the Czech Republic (1991–1994). *Source:* Own analysis of data from the Slovak and Czech Statistical Offices.

In 1992, very favorable trends in real wage growth were observed, with real wages increasing by 8.9% in Slovakia and 10.4% in the Czech Republic. For 1993, it is noteworthy that there was a decline in the growth of real wages in Slovakia, reaching minus 0.5%. It was attributed to the reintroduction of a restrictive fiscal policy, mainly associated with establishing the independent Slovak state.

The further development of average real wages could be observed after the establishment of independent Slovakia and its separation from the Czech Republic. The trends from 1993 to 1994 might have been influenced by transformation processes and the new economic environment that emerged after the division.

14. Development of the Slovak Economy

The Slovak economy, like the Czech economy, began industrialization after World War II. In comparison to the Czech economy, which focused largely on products with higher added value, the Slovak economy post-World War II was oriented toward engineering products, arms production, and semifinished goods and primarily geared toward exports to the former states of the Eastern Bloc. Therefore, the dissolution of the Eastern Bloc had a significantly negative impact on the development of the Slovak economy.

Since the creation of Slovakia, an agreement was reached that both newly established states would use a common currency within the monetary union for at least 6 months. The validity of the monetary agreement ended much earlier than expected, namely on February 8, 1993. After the creation of two independent and sovereign states, a bilateral payment agreement was adopted and implemented between both states. Within this bilateral payment agreement, payment transactions were carried out through clearing accounts. Concerning financial obligations and receivables within both states until the termination of the monetary agreement, that is, until February 8, 1993, payments were made through so-called clearing crowns. After February 8, 1993, all transactions were conducted through jointly created accounts expressed in the clearing European Currency Unit (ECU), a unit of account that emerged within the European Monetary System in March 1979.

Due to the relatively unfavorable development in Slovakia's balance of payments, restrictive measures were introduced on imports. Additionally, a 10% import surcharge was imposed on imported consumer goods in Slovakia because of the low volume of foreign exchange reserves. One of the critical institutions that needed to be established to manage monetary policy was the creation of the National Bank of Slovakia (NBS). Before the division of former Czechoslovakia, the execution of monetary policy was centralized in the State Bank of Czechoslovakia.

In the early days of the independent state, the NBS faced the challenging task of managing monetary and exchange rate policy, including supervising the financial sector, especially the banking industry. The NBS began implementing monetary policy in Slovakia in early February 1993. In February 1993, the NBS introduced certain foreign exchange restrictions and limitations on access to foreign exchange reserves. Given the relatively favorable developments, these restrictions were lifted in mid-December 1993.

One of the most challenging tasks for the NBS after the creation of independent Slovakia was the creation of the national currency (see Marcinčin & Beblavý, 2000). The Slovak koruna (SKK) was established on February 8, 1993, following the conclusion of the monetary union between Slovakia and the Czech Republic.

The NBS started setting the official exchange rates of the Slovak crown against other freely convertible and national currencies based on a basket of five freely convertible currencies. For the determination of the official exchange rate of the Slovak koruna, a currency basket consisting of five currencies was used: Austrian schilling (ATS), French franc (FRF), German mark (DEM), Swiss franc (CHF), and U.S. dollar (USD). The individual weights of these currencies were regularly revised.

The high level of uncertainty was associated with future economic development and the sustainability of the monetary union within the two independent states. During this period, capital outflows from Slovakia were also observed. The NBS tightened credit conditions by introducing limits on loan applications for legal entities and households.

The high level of uncertainty manifested itself mainly in the unfavorable development of official foreign exchange reserves. As a result of the low level of foreign reserves, the Slovak crown was devalued by 10% on July 12, 1993. Moving from a centrally planned system to a market economy led to a significant reduction in the real economy in favor of the service sector.

15. Development of Selected Indicators of the Real Sector (1991–1993)

The transformation process had far-reaching consequences on the development of the structure of GDP. Fig. 1.7 illustrates the 3 years (1989–1994) of important selected sectors of the economy (agricultural and industrial production, construction, and services).

The presented Fig. 1.7 indicates a gradual and linear decline in the sectors of the real economy in favor of the service sector. The transformation process between 1990 and 1993 had long-term social and economic consequences. In 1989, agricultural production accounted for 9.4% of GDP, but by 1994, this share had decreased to 7.4%. The industrial production share of GDP, which was 49.3% in 1989, had dropped to 30.7% by 1994. Additionally, there was a decline in the construction sector from 9.1% in 1989 to 5% in 1994. However, the services sector increased from 32.2% in 1989 to 56.9% in 1994 (see Marcinčin & Beblavý, 2000).

Given the ongoing historical transformation process focusing on a green, digital, and socially equitable economy, there could be an emphasis on ensuring food self-sufficiency, similar to what has been achieved in Poland. Presently, a significant challenge for policymakers should be to create job opportunities and restore the quality of life in regions and rural areas to what it was before 1989.

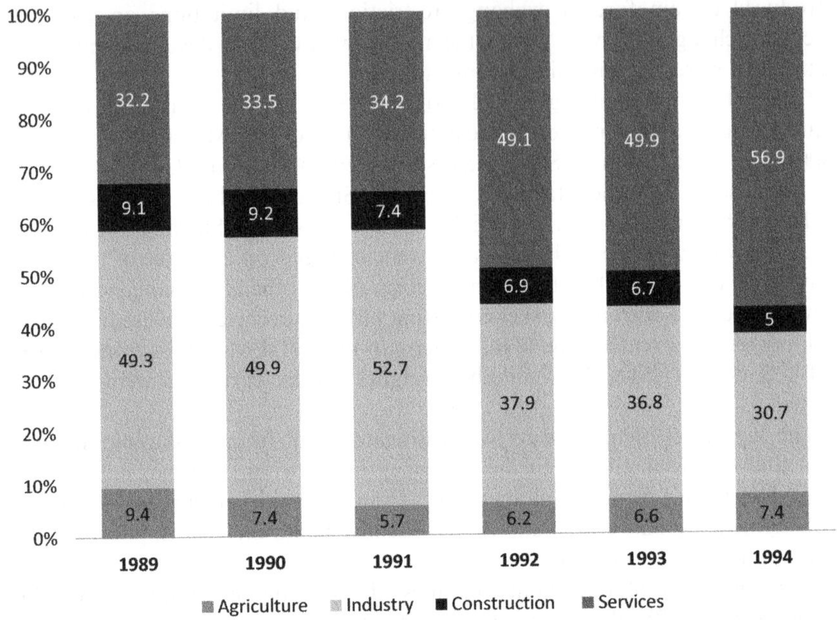

Fig. 1.7. Structure Development of GDP, by Selected Sectors of the Economy (1989–1994). *Source:* Own processing of data from the Slovak Statistical Office.

Since the establishment of independent Slovakia, insufficient attention has been devoted to education, medical care, and agricultural development. Food self-sufficiency and food security will be crucial in the ongoing process of further transformation. It can create favorable conditions for focusing on producing quality organic food, laying the groundwork for a healthy and high-quality life for all Slovaks.

16. Conclusion

The transformation from a centrally planned system to a market economy in the former Czechoslovakia after creating two separate states was marked by a high degree of uncertainty, macroeconomic instability, and the liberalization of prices, foreign trade, and payment systems. It was also associated with a challenging process of changing ownership relationships.

The transition to a market economy required the establishment of an institutional and legislative framework, both at the national and local levels of the former Czechoslovakia. Despite the complexity and unpredictability of developments during this period, the overall institutional and legislative change process was successfully implemented relatively quickly.

In the economic sphere, ensuring macroeconomic stability was crucial, both in terms of executing monetary policy and in the fiscal domain, with measures taken to secure stability in public finances. The process of price deregulation led to a significant increase in the inflation rate and a substantial decline in real wages in both states. The liberalization of foreign trade relations resulted in a shift in orientation toward individual territories and states.

The Czech economy's structure was better prepared for transformation compared to the Slovak economy, with historical differences playing a role. In particular, with a relatively higher added value of its products, it was more resilient and better able to withstand real shocks from the external environment.

Significant positive changes were made in the exchange rate mechanism. The State Bank of Czechoslovakia merged the long-standing multitiered exchange rate system into a unified official exchange rate for all types of payments. The introduction of a unified exchange rate for the Czechoslovak crown led to the gradual elimination of the black and parallel exchange rates with the Czechoslovak crown.

The transformation had an unprecedented negative impact on all real economic indicators. The process of changing ownership relationships was critical in the transformation. Small privatization was carried out relatively quickly. The process of large privatization continued even after the creation of the two separate states of the Czechs and the Slovaks.

The transformation process after the creation of the independent Slovak state was more challenging in Slovakia than in the Czech Republic. One crucial measure that needed to be addressed in Slovak conditions was the establishment of the NBS for the implementation of monetary and exchange rate policies, including supervising the financial sector. Additionally, the financial sector, especially the banking industry and the capital market, gradually began to take shape. The creation of the private sector also helped small and microentrepreneurs increase their business activities.

The overall process of transformation from a centrally planned system to a market economy was relatively short-lived. Despite the comprehensive transformation, it can be stated that both in the former Czechoslovakia and in Slovakia, the overall process was much faster compared to other transitioning economies.

After a relatively successful transformation from a centrally planned system to a market economy, Slovakia is currently facing a much more demanding social, economic, and overall transformation. The transition to a green, digital, and socially just society will require significant effort from all stakeholders, including the active involvement of civil society in the transformation process.

The current transformation will be unprecedented compared to the previous one in that, in many cases, due to climate change and environmental changes, it may involve existential threats to life on the planet. Therefore, now more than ever, it will be necessary to collaborate mutually to save lives on this beautiful planet and create a dignified and just life for future generations.

References

Fritsch, M., & Hansen, H. (1997). East-West integration and competition policy. In M. Fritsch & H. Hansen (Eds.), *Rules of competition and East-West integration*. Springer. https://doi.org/10.1007/978-1-4615-6087-6_2

IMF. (1990). *The Czech and Slovak federal republic. An economy in transition*. Occa Paper No. 72. International Monetary Fund. https://doi.org/10.5089/9781557751690.084

Marcinčin, A., & Beblavý, M. (Eds.). (2000). *Economic policy in Slovakia 1990–1999*. Centrum pre spoločenskú a mediálnu analýzu. https://www.academia.edu/6258072/Economic_policy_in_Slovakia_1990_1999

Pavlík, P. (1997). Economic transformation in central and Eastern Europe in the context of the process of European integration. *Perspectives*, *9*, 89–96. http://www.jstor.org/stable/23615993

Prust, J. (1993). The Czech and Slovak federal republic: Government finances in a period of transition. In *Transition to market*. International Monetary Fund. https://doi.org/10.5089/9781557752758.071

Siebert, H. (Ed.). (1992). *The transformation of socialist economies: Symposium 1991*. University of Kiel.

Sipko, J. (2021). Vývoj ekonomiky po roku 1989. In M. Pekník (Ed.), *Cesta Slovenska k vzniku samostatného štátu v roku 1993* (pp. 337–367). VEDA.

Chapter 2

Slovak Experience With Capitalism: The Myth of the Tatra Tiger

Michael Augustín[a] *and Peter Daubner*[b]

[a]University of Economics in Bratislava, Slovakia
[b]Slovak Academy of Sciences, Slovakia

Abstract

This chapter provides a detailed analysis of Slovakia's economic transformation since the end of the socialist era and its transition toward a market-based economy. The country had a slower start than Poland, Czechia, and Hungary in embracing capitalism, which earned it the nickname of the "Tatra Tiger" only after Dzurinda's administration. The chapter examines the crucial economic reforms, political decisions, and contextual factors that have shaped Slovakia's economic trajectory, particularly emphasizing the interplay between politics and economic policy. Additionally, it highlights the challenges posed by the legacy of previous governments, including oligarchic influence and socioeconomic disparities. Despite some periods of economic growth, Slovakia is currently facing a crisis of political and socioeconomic discontent, primarily due to overdependence on the automotive sector and a lack of investment in innovation and infrastructure. The chapter concludes by stating the need for more visionary leadership and a national dialog on Slovakia's future direction, indicating a concerning inertia in the face of pressing economic challenges.

Keywords: Slovak Republic; transformation process; privatization; neoliberalism; reforms; economic growth

1. Introduction

In the aftermath of the collapse of the Iron Curtain during the 1990s, several Central European countries experienced significant economic growth and modernization. The actors of the transformation's "success stories" of former

Modeling Economic Growth in Contemporary Slovakia, 25–48

doi:10.1108/978-1-83549-454-720241003

socialist economies in this region have often been called economic "Tigers." This term was inspired by the "Asian Tigers," such as South Korea, Taiwan, Singapore, and Hong Kong, which had also experienced impressive economic growth in the 20th century and a gradual transition from developing to developed economies. Among the Central European countries, Poland was one of the most successful in achieving rapid economic growth due to privatization, liberalization, and the opening up of its economy. Similarly, the Czech Republic, which underwent economic reforms after the division of Czechoslovakia, along with Hungary, achieved a relatively quick transition to a capitalist market economy. The informal label of these countries as "Tigers" was used extensively in journalistic jargon, as well as in academic literature. However, Slovakia was considered less successful than its neighboring countries in rapidly transitioning to capitalism. The nickname "Tatra Tiger" gained prominence much later concerning the liberal economic reforms implemented by the administrations of Mikuláš Dzurinda and Slovakia's economic performance during the first decade of the third millennium.[1]

Economists generally agreed upon four critical tasks necessary for a country's transition to a market economy. Fischer and Gelb (1991) perfectly summarized these tasks: (1) macroeconomic stabilization, (2) liberalization of prices and trade, (3) structural changes, (4) legal and institutional reforms. This transition can be generally described as the development that indicates the irreversible systemic change in the economy, political system, and political culture while heading toward political democracy, the rule of law, a functioning market economy, and an emerging civil society (Szomolányi, 2003). These milestones formed the bedrock of the economic transformation in Central and Eastern Europe. However, it is not easy to outline a unified direction of the transformation process in postsocialist Central Europe, as each country has its peculiarities. Nevertheless, academic literature does not contradict the claim that the transformation process in Central Europe was headed toward neoliberal capitalism. While in the Czech Republic, Hungary, and Poland, this process manifested itself as a necessary step toward economic modernization, in Slovakia, this development was hindered by the economic policy of Vladimír Mečiar's governments. During Mikuláš Dzurinda's tenure as the Prime Minister of Slovakia, the government successfully caught up with the country's rapid economic development, which led to Slovakia being nicknamed the "Tatra Tiger." However, the government led by Fico took a different approach, focusing on social welfare measures, increasing state intervention in the economy, and undoing some of the liberalization reforms implemented by the previous administrations.

In this chapter, we present a comprehensive analysis of the political events and decisions that have shaped the economic model of Slovakia since its establishment three decades ago. We focus on the sequence of governments, significant milestones, policies, reforms, and contextual factors that have accompanied Slovakia's

[1]The term "Tatra Tiger" pertains to the Tatra Mountains, situated in the northeastern region of Slovakia.

economic growth model. In examining Slovakia's economic trajectory, our primary aim is to dissect the intricate interplay between political dynamics and economic policy. Through a meticulous analysis of political events spanning three decades, we aim to elucidate the evolution of Slovakia's economic model. By scrutinizing successive governments, pivotal milestones, policy frameworks, and contextual influences, we seek to uncover the underlying drivers and implications of Slovakia's economic growth trajectory. Our investigation underscores the pivotal role of political decisions in shaping economic policies and steering the course of the nation's economic strategy. Through this comprehensive exploration, we endeavor to provide insights into the intricate relationship between politics and economics, offering a nuanced understanding of Slovakia's economic development journey and the primary factors contributing to the current depletion of this model.

2. Slovakia and the Vladimír Mečiar's Governments

Following the collapse of communism, the Czechoslovak Federal Republic decided to rapidly transform ownership relations. It was implemented through both small and large privatization, in addition to the restitution process. Small privatization was carried out through public auctions and embodied the privatization of retail stores, hotels, restaurants, and smaller factories. On the other hand, large privatization was divided into two waves, including one voucher privatization within each wave.

Vladimír Mečiar with his party Movement for a Democratic Slovakia (HZDS) led the Slovak government from the separation of Czechoslovakia until October 1998, with a break from March 1994 to November 1994, during which the interim government of Jozef Moravčík was tasked with organizing early parliamentary elections. The privatization model adopted by Mečiar quickly deviated from the federal model and became a symptomatic phenomenon of this era.

During his second term in office as Prime Minister from July 1992 to March 1994, Mečiar focused on gaining executive control over privatization. He took over the portfolio for privatization and managed the Ministry of Privatization directly after the departure of the Minister of Privatization in 1993. Mečiar ensured that party loyalists directed the state property portfolio at the National Property Fund (FNM). The FNM was an autonomous legal entity that primarily focused on executing privatization initiatives, finalizing purchase agreements and sales contracts, conducting public tenders and auctions, and temporarily overseeing the state's ownership stakes in transformed or partly privatized commercial enterprises. The policy favoring the domestic business class allowed for rewarding insiders and political allies, enabling them to purchase state-owned firms on advantageous terms (Gould, 2003).

The coalition of HZDS, The Union of the Workers of Slovakia (ZRS), and the Slovak National Party (SNS) came to power following the 1994 elections. Due to shady privatization deals, a disregard for the rights of ethnic minorities, and a lack of respect for the constitutional principles of democratic politics, the government that ruled from 1994 to 1998 tarnished Slovakia's reputation in the international community. As a result of these actions, both NATO and the EU rejected the country's attempts to forge closer ties with them (Haughton, 2004). Because of Mečiar's regime, Slovakia was not invited to negotiations on the enlargement of NATO or the EU (Laar, 2010). The economic policies of the third Mečiar Cabinet (1994–1998) witnessed a significant change in privatization strategy, with the second wave of voucher privatization being postponed and replaced by the sale of bonds through an amendment to the law on the transfer of state property to other entities. This move almost completely excluded employees and foreign parties from participating in privatization. The Mečiar government decided to distribute only 33 billion Slovak koruna among citizens through bonds. In contrast, the rest of the state property, valued at almost 170 billion koruna, was directly sold to privatizers. Unfortunately, most of what was sold off during Mečiar's term ended up in the hands of individuals closely associated with the Mečiar's party. The decision to put voucher privatization on the back burner adversely affected the development of emerging economic structures, specifically investment privatization funds that were established in the first wave of voucher privatization. Certain measures were introduced to limit the influence of investment funds, and some were even dissolved (in March 1995, the ministry revoked the activity permit of the First Slovak Investment Company). The abrupt alteration in the circumstances surrounding the privatization process had a significant impact on the investment funds, resulting in substantial financial losses.

In addition to the fact that nonvoucher methods became more pronounced during this period, different political decisions played a crucial role in shaping the privatization landscape. A significant change occurred at the initial meeting of the recently elected parliament on the night of November 3 to 4, 1994. The former members of the presidium and supervisory board of the FNM were dismissed by the parliamentary majority. New members, who were loyal to the parties of the parliamentary majority, were elected instead. Additionally, several decisions on direct sales made by Moravčík's government were instantly canceled. Finally, the parliamentary majority passed a bill that shifted the authority to make decisions regarding the direct sales of enterprises from the government to the FNM presidium. The FNM could make decisions with minimal public scrutiny as a quasi-private corporate entity. Consequently, the FNM presidium implemented a privatization program with little transparency and was quasi-legal, favoring insider interests (Gould, 2003). This decision weakened the control mechanism of privatization decisions. The control of the FNM did not fall within the powers of the Supreme Audit Office (NKÚ), which had an impact only on the government. The FNM could therefore only be controlled by parliament. In July 1995, the parliament passed a bill for privatizing state-owned enterprises in Slovakia. The Act on Securing the State's Interests in the Privatization of Strategically Important State Enterprises created two categories of enterprises. The first group included 27 companies that operated in critical fields such as gas, energy, post, telecommunications, pharmaceutical production, arms production, agriculture, water, and forest management. This group of enterprises should not have been subject to privatization. The second group represented 40 companies that were allowed to be privatized, but the state's majority share had to be maintained. However, in 1997, the Constitutional Court declared a law that transferred decision-making competencies to the Presidium of the FNM unconstitutional. As a result, the Ministry of Privatization regained authority. However, the Constitutional Court upheld the legitimacy of FNM's decisions based on the unconstitutional law, which remained in effect.

One of the most significant outcomes of privatization under the leadership of Vladimír Mečiar "as the father of the nation" (Haughton, 2004) was the creation of a concentration of property in the hands of a small group of loyalists of Mečiar's government. The privatization model, introduced by Mečiar's government, created spaces for clientelistic groups to gain a greater share of economic power, resulting in an imbalance in economic distribution. Concerning privatization processes and their impact on the inflow of innovation and foreign investors in Slovakia, Mečiar's efforts for a particular form of economic nationalism intended to create a "national capital-creating stratum" (Polák, 2004). It resulted in the accumulation of state capital in the hands of a regional oligarchy recruited from the ranks of successful managers of originally state-owned enterprises (Drahokoupil, 2007). However, this approach failed to create a proper market environment. It led to an insufficiently transparent and competitive climate that discouraged foreign investors and capital from bringing new ideas, technologies, and managerial expertise, except for a few exceptional cases. The more general experience of other postcommunist countries confirms that efforts to rapidly privatize on a large scale, focusing on insiders, have often failed to bring about the necessary restructuring for companies to thrive in competitive markets.

An excellent example is the company Calex, a prominent manufacturer of refrigerators and cooling equipment, which had a diversified export market that included the socialist bloc, North Africa, and Asian countries. The company employed over 5,000 people before 1989. However, the Velvet Revolution led to a significant change in the company's fortunes. Samsung-Calex, a new joint venture, was formed with the most profitable part of the factory, while the "old" Calex was left to deal with a massive loan burden. The Korean management was very protective of their business interests, for which they were draining the personal and production capacities of the "old" Calex and selling their products to a subsidiary company in Germany at a price that did not even correspond to the production costs. Even when the "old" Calex was designated as a strategic enterprise in 1995, it could not prevent its eventual collapse. Samsung withdrew from the joint venture project by selling its 46% stake back to the state in 1997, and parent company Calex went into receivership soon after. Despite the remerger of the two companies into "New Calex," it eventually went bankrupt in 2001. The privatization of Nafta Gbely and East Slovak Ironworks (VSŽ) are examples of state-owned assets being acquired by individuals with close ties to the ruling elites. In both cases, government loyalists gained access to significant state assets, allowing them to establish decision-making power over the companies.

During Mečiar's term, his policies significantly overlapped the state, political parties, and economic institutions. Deegan-Krause (2003) states that Meciar's governments, by linking economic interests with the power interests of political parties through the almost unlimited distribution of state assets, enormously increased the role of money in politics. Privatization was accompanied by legislation that did not improve the business environment but increased new owners' economic influence. Mečiar's strategy emphasized positive macroeconomic indicators to legitimize their policies, but in reality, it was only building the illusion of economic success. This development conveyed a time bomb for the next government, which took power during a complicated economic situation. The almost 7% economic growth was primarily possible thanks an increase in internal and external debt and was supported by demand-oriented economic policy instruments in 1995–1997 proved unsustainable. Instead, Mečiar's government switched to an expansionary policy. Investments and incentives flowed into infrastructure building and development impulses. Growth "on debt" itself would not be a problem, but projects that would increase the export potential of the given industries did not receive financing. Unfortunately, the growth that Slovakia achieved thanks to exports during this period relied excessively on semifinished goods. However, the structural weakness of exporting this type of product depends on the economic cycle of business partners. The latter was in the conjunctural phase, thanks to which an economic recovery could come to Slovakia. This expansionary fiscal policy was followed by the restrictive monetary policy of the central bank, which pushed out private loans through an increase in interest rates. Slovakia lacked adequate coordination with other segments of economic policy at the macroeconomic level, which would be followed by the necessary structural reforms (Marcinčin & Morvay, 2001). Since there was no restructuring and foreign investment, the unemployment rate reached almost 15% at the end of the Mečiar era. This time was wasted in terms of restructuring, modernization, and economic reform (Buček, 2010). We conclude that it was mainly the legacy of Mečiar's administrations and the controversial process of transformation of the economy in the 1990s that marked the economic development of Slovakia in the past three decades (Šikula, 2016). Moreover, Mečiar's legacy was a country "isolated in the heart of Europe" and at least temporarily excluded from the EU integration process (Miháliková, 2006) as a result of the "new Ostpolitik" implemented since the collapse of communism in Eastern Europe (Charillon, 2004). "It was the Slovak population who voted Mečiar out of office, knowing well the costs his government entailed in terms of possible exclusion from the EU accession process" (Le Gloannec & Rupnik, 2008, p. 55). Nevertheless, the process of democratization in Slovak society was much slower in the 1990s than in Hungary, Poland, and the Czech Republic (Haerpfer, 2006).

3. Slovakia Under Mikuláš Dzurinda's Political Leadership

Mečiar's third cabinet resulted in not only international political isolation and a weakened democratic institutional framework but also macroeconomic instability and socioeconomic problems (Gould, 2009; Miháliková, 2006). In fact, the unemployment rate increased dramatically. As a result, the challenging economic situation became the primary topic of discussion in sociopolitical debates, overshadowing the ongoing conflict between Mečiarism and anti-Mečiarism (Barański, 2020). After the elections in 1998, a broad anti-Mečiar coalition was formed. Ideologically diverse political groups were united by the goal of returning Slovakia to the path its neighbors were already following. The Slovak Democratic Coalition (SDK), the Party of the Democratic Left (SDĽ), the Party of the Hungarian Coalition (SMK), and the Party of Civic Understanding (SOP), which formed the government, represented an ideologically disparate coalition, but they were united by their antagonism toward Mečiar and their commitment to the idea of integrating the Slovak Republic into the European Union (see Gould, 2009).

In the wake of an economic crisis, the Slovak government, led by Dzurinda, adopted a series of measures to stabilize the macroeconomic situation and promote sustainable economic and political development. These measures included deep reforms in the economy, banking sector, public administration, and legal system. The government's first-year strategies were geared toward limiting the growth of domestic demand, completing the institutional framework, supporting microeconomic adaptation, and stimulating the supply side (Marcinčin & Morvay, 2001). To improve macroeconomic stability, the government adopted austerity measures aimed at reducing the current account deficit. While these measures initially led to a slowdown in GDP growth and a significant increase in the price level, they eventually brought about the expected result. Inflation gradually declined, and unemployment began to stagnate or decline slightly. By around 2000, it was clear that the economy was slowly recovering from the crisis and beginning to improve. And between 2000 and 2008, Slovakia had one of the highest GDP per capita growth rates in Europe, which was mainly caused by the growth of labor productivity (Biea, 2016). The increase in industrial production, mainly driven by expanding exports and foreign direct investments (FDIs), dropped rapidly after 2000 in Slovakia (Huffschmid, 2005).

Problem credits and poor asset quality hindered the efficient functioning of the banking sector (Šestáková & Ferenčíková, 2015). Banks often granted credits according to political criteria, while their business and financial returns were questionable. It led to the insolvency of the largest state banks. To address this issue, the Government of the Slovak Republic, in cooperation with the World Bank, implemented a program to restructure banks and the corporate sector to reduce internal indebtedness and stimulate economic growth. The program included the bank privatization process, preprivatization restructuring, work with receivables, and new legislation, including the Bankruptcy and Settlement Act. Restructuring the banking sector allowed the central bank, together with other steps taken by the government, especially in 1999–2000, to reduce interest rates fundamentally. Before privatization, the state banks had to undergo a recovery process primarily to retrieve politically motivated "bad credits" and replenish the required capital. Privatizing the banking sector aimed to attract strategic investors who could bring financial and managerial resources to modernize and stabilize the banking sector. The Slovak government organized tenders to sell majority shares in several state banks. Privatizing these banks contributed to modernizing and stabilizing the banking sector, improving its competitiveness, and enhancing its ability to offer credit and financial services in line with international standards. Among the first privatized banks in Slovakia in the years 1998–2001 were General Credit Bank (VÚB), Investment and Development Bank (IRB), and the largest of them – *Slovenská sporiteľňa* (SLSP).

Furthermore, the government created legislative conditions for privatizing strategic enterprises and natural monopolies. In September 1999, an amendment to the law on large-scale privatization was adopted, replacing the law of the third Mečiar Cabinet on privatizing strategic enterprises. The amendment identified 16 natural monopolies, which could be privatized after being approved by the government and legislators. Additionally, this amendment stipulated that the state had to retain a majority stake (at least 51%) in certain strategic enterprises. In the energy sector, the Slovak Gas Industry (SPP), Transpetrol, and energy distribution companies were privatized during the first Dzurinda. Privatization of SPP is still considered one of the most significant and most criticized privatization projects of the Dzurinda era. It was preceded by the reorganization of the company into a vertically integrated joint-stock company. The goal was to sell a 49% share of the shares, and the expected profits from the privatization were to reach 3 to 5 billion USD. In 2001, the state enterprise SPP was transformed into a joint stock company. A year later, the state sold 49% of the shares to Ruhrgas and Gaz de France for 2.7 billion USD. The remaining 51% of the shares remained in the hands of the National Property Fund. The most criticized moment of this privatization, in addition to the price itself, was the fact that the state gave up managerial control in the company. According to the privatization contract, only three members represented the Slovak Republic in the seven-member board of directors. Another typical example of controversial privatization is the case of the railway sector in Slovakia, specifically the Slovak Railway Company (ŽSR) (see Huffschmid, 2005).

After a change of government in 1998, there was a strong push toward adhering to the EU's political requirements. The first Dzurinda Cabinet was also eager to initiate accession negotiations as soon as possible. The impression made by the new administration's first decisions was so convincing that in December 1999, Slovakia was invited to begin accession negotiations at the Helsinki summit (Malová & Dolný, 2016). Slovakia was gradually integrated into other significant global institutional structures as part of the transformation process. In 2000, Slovakia was granted admission to the Organization for Economic Cooperation and Development (OECD). One year later, Slovakia became a new member state of the World Trade Organization (WTO).

In 2002, Slovakia held parliamentary elections that resulted in the formation of Mikuláš Dzurinda's second government, composed of four right-wing parties. This coalition enabled the implementation of significant economic reforms, thanks to a high level of program compatibility. This center-right government presented an opportunity for a network of liberal economic reformers to shape policy (Gould, 2009). Dzurinda's second coalition built on his previous government, with the added benefit of greater ideological coherence due to the absence of left-wing parties.

The main goal for the second Dzurinda Cabinet was to complete the integration process into the EU. During the negotiation process, Slovakia aimed to secure transition periods for many policy areas, which concerned the harmonization of rules so that Slovakia could become part of the single market and economic union. These transition periods were necessary to enhance the performance levels of the Slovak economy or to secure extensive capital investments.

These investments were part of a broader trend of increased FDI in Slovakia during the Dzurinda government. Cumulative FDI increased sevenfold to USD 18.45 billion by the end of 2006, with the largest portion the privatization of the state electricity producer to Italian Enel. The Italian company Enel definitively took control of a 66% package of shares in *Slovenské elektrárne* at the end of Dzurinda's government era. The Slovak Republic received 839 million euros for it. The automotive sector was a significant contributor to Slovakia's economic growth and industrial development during this period. During the government of Mikuláš Dzurinda, PSA, the manufacturer of Peugeot and Citroën cars, established its presence in Slovakia. The plant construction started in 2003 and the production of the first cars began in 2006. The Slovak government provided investment incentives amounting to 15% of the total investment value of 700 million euros, which is the maximum limit allowed by European Union competition laws. Kia Motors, another large investor, also decided to build a factory in Slovakia and was provided the same investment incentives by the Slovak government. These incentives included free land usage, cash contributions for job creation, tax credits, and resources for purchasing equipment. It is important to note that the determined limit by the European Commission only covers direct state support, whereas much higher funds were utilized for indirect, additional incentives such as the construction of a highway and modernization of the airport, housing for foreign company management, and other benefits. Slovakia has become a popular investment market in Europe due to several factors, including its low-cost skilled labor force, advantageous geographic location, and relatively liberal labor code. Several world newspapers and media described Slovakia as the "Detroit of Europe" (Landler, 2004) or "the world's next Hong Kong or Ireland" (see Stenning et al., 2011).

During the post-transition period, there was a noticeable push toward neoliberal restructuring in Central and Eastern Europe. Despite having to deal with various pressures, such as globalization, some postcommunist governments managed to navigate these challenges without resorting to neoliberal policies that would have weakened the strong welfare state that they inherited from the Communist era. As seen in Slovakia after 2002, a particular right-wing governmental configuration was a necessary precondition for neoliberal restructuring (Myant & Drahokoupil, 2010). In 2003 and 2004, the Dzurinda government implemented a comprehensive healthcare system reform as part of a broader neoliberal economic reform. The reform aimed to replace the social health insurance model with a market-oriented healthcare system based on user fees and managed competition. The government also introduced a public finance reform to reduce the budget deficit and improve fiscal discipline. It helped Slovakia achieve a budget deficit of less than 3% of GDP, a significant improvement from the previous periods. The two-tiered sales tax system was replaced with a universal value-added tax (VAT) of 19%. This change eliminated the lower tax rate for food, medicine, and other necessities. The previous income tax was also replaced by a flat personal income tax of 19%. Similarly, corporate taxes were reduced to a flat income tax of 19%. The government also canceled other taxes, including the dividend tax, real estate transfer tax, gift tax, and inheritance tax, to reduce the tax burden in Slovakia and attract foreign investments to reduce unemployment. The government also implemented a fiscal decentralization reform to distribute fiscal responsibilities to regional and local authorities, promoting economic development at the local level. However, as Sokol (2013) points out, within this neo-liberalization framework, regional development's responsibility gradually passed from the state to the regions, but without providing adequate resources. Furthermore, a second pillar of the pension system was created, with half of the contributions redirected toward the private pillar managed by pension management companies. The pension reform was introduced to improve its sustainability in the long term. Finally, the government implemented a reform to increase labor market flexibility, improve workforce employability, and reduce unemployment. Neoliberal policymakers at the Ministry of Education also tried to shift responsibility for higher education to individual students. However, there were conflicting opinions on whether to impose significant tuition fees or to maintain strict meritocracy regardless of income and background. The government failed to agree on an approach, leading to the failure of education reforms in the government's reform package (see Myant & Drahokoupil, 2010).

During the introduction of reforms in social welfare, especially in material need assistance, "Roma" riots broke out. These riots involved looting stores and were preceded by peaceful protests against the reforms. These protests included both Roma and non-Roma individuals. The Labor Minister at the time, Ľudovít Kaník, absolved himself of any responsibility for the riots and attributed the situation to a decade-long dependency on social benefits, which he deemed unacceptable. The media played a significant role in shifting the discourse from a social problem to an ethnic one, creating a narrative that portrayed the Roma as a security threat rather than a marginalized community in need of support (Dráľ, 2008). This approach led to the perpetuation of stereotypes about the Roma as being unwilling to work and undeserving of assistance. Unfortunately, the government and society as a whole have missed a crucial opportunity to address the underlying issue of social exclusion faced by the Roma minority.

The government's stance toward corporatism became unfriendly, leading unions to seek political support to advance their interests. In response to this growing tension between unions and the government, protests and rallies were organized. During these events, the unions' interests aligned with the priorities of the emerging opposition party Smer (Direction) which has merged smaller left-wing political parties and began to define itself as a social democracy. Following this, the Confederation of Trade Unions of the Slovak Republic began actively collaborating with Robert Fico and Smer starting from 2003 (Kahancová & Uhlerová, 2023).

During this period, financial investment groups such as Penta and J&T have emerged as the dominant players in the Slovak market. These groups were established during the privatization era of the 1990s and have since grown to become economic giants. Critics have raised concerns about the influence of oligarchs on political decision-making. Their close ties to politicians and government officials have raised questions about the transparency and fairness of Slovakia's political and economic process.

To understand why Slovakia underwent a shift toward neoliberalism (see Harvey, 2005), we can examine demographic and cultural factors or the influence of EU conditionality (see Sasse, 2007). While EU encouragement of the process of marketization and liberalization played a role, it did not mandate a strictly neoliberal approach. Fisher et al. (2007) suggest that we consider internal political factors as an explanation. The face and uncompromising advocate of the economic reforms of this period was Dzurinda's right-hand man – Minister of Finance Ivan Mikloš. However, Mikloš would not have been able to perform his role brilliantly without the support of young economists who were trained in the West. Although international financial institutions such as the World Bank provided support, the young economists were mainly inspired by the vast literature on market-based solutions in economics rather than the World Bank's wish to implement a neoliberal model. In fact, representatives from the World Bank raised concerns in 2003 that the government was implementing changes too quickly and too drastically (Fisher et al., 2007; see Myant & Drahokoupil, 2013). Indeed, a network of NGOs (MESA 10, F. A. Hayek Foundation, INEKO, IVO) and neoliberal thinkers gradually gained policy influence by establishing the center-right government in 2002 (Gould, 2009). Epistemic communities and members of the business community played critical roles in designing and implementing the reform process while serving as advisors to politicians. With enormous investments in the automotive and electronics sectors, Slovakia achieved remarkable economic performance, growing at over 8% in 2006.

The pressure to attract foreign investment was greater in Slovakia than in the Czech Republic or Hungary due to lower investment inflow during Mečiar's era in the 1990s than in other parts of Central Europe. The mantra of economic growth and GDP indicators helped to establish the neoliberal paradigm as a broadly recognized discourse supported by the mainstream media. Any signs of deviation from this path have been interpreted as a move toward the past, given Slovakia's negative experiences with Mečiarism in the 1990s (Fisher et al., 2007). However, there has been very limited space for a debate on whether a business environment built in a one-dimensional way can compete with the challenges of the future and if it represents a long-term sustainable economic model for Slovakia. Slovakia's competitiveness has been based on a workforce that is qualified, adaptable, but cheap (Šikula, 2016). Despite this fact, implemented policies enhanced Slovakia's global reputation as the "Tatra Tiger," a favorable location for investing in manufacturing facilities with moderate value addition, and resulted in increased international recognition (Malová & Dolný, 2016). In fact, it was the era of "growth without development" (see Becker & Lesay, 2019).

4. Fico Cabinets and Radičová "Intermezzo" Cabinet

The first government led by Robert Fico in Slovakia took office following the parliamentary elections held in June 2006. Fico's party, Smer-SD (Direction – Social Democracy), emerged as the winner of these elections due to the antisocial character of the right-wing government. This coalition with Slovak National Party (SNS) and Mečiar's ĽS–HZDS (People's Party – Movement for a Democratic Slovakia) represented a departure from the previous center-right governments in Slovakia, with Fico's Smer-SD advocating for more social welfare measures, a progressive tax system, and increased state involvement in the economy. We stress that during the period of 1999–2006, Fico was a strong adversary of social and economic liberalization reforms that were being implemented by the Dzurinda's governments (Gould, 2009; Nemčok & Spáč, 2020; Rybář, 2007). Despite his emphasis on his sociodemocratic background, Fico's rhetoric and actions have been ambiguous and inconsistent in terms of ideology throughout his career (Haughton, 2002).

Due to previously implemented reforms, Slovakia had one of the fastest-growing economies in the EU. Slovakia successfully reduced the economic disparity between it and the more developed Western European nations. Specifically, the GDP per capita of Slovakia increased from 43% of the EU-15 average in the year 2000 to 64% in 2008 (Biea, 2016). The significance of the automotive industry to the Slovakian economy should be highlighted within this context. In 2007, the Slovak Republic was the leading country in the world regarding car production. The exports of cars and their accessories accounted for over a quarter of the total exports. In 2008, the automotive industry employed approximately 80,000 individuals (Becker & Lesay, 2012). Although the economy has grown significantly, many believe this growth has not been evenly distributed among different regions and households, leading to increased income inequality. This perspective suggests that the western regions have primarily enjoyed the benefits of strong economic growth, while the majority of the eastern regions have been left behind (Banerjee & Jarmuzek, 2010).

Despite heavy criticism of Dzurinda's reforms, Fico's government managed to reverse only a few previous reforms, such as doctors' fees. In 2006, the government made only minor changes, primarily to restore a progressive element with differentiated VAT rates (Myant & Drahokoupil, 2010). The government implemented a series of measures to address the economic crisis right before it adopted the Euro on January 1, 2009. These measures aimed to boost consumer demand, introduce more stringent regulations, and raise income tax (Malová & Dolný, 2016). To stimulate domestic demand and consumption, the government implemented a program to stimulate the automotive industry and increase demand for new cars. The essence of this measure was to provide financial incentives (in the form of a financial contribution) to citizens who scrapped their old cars and purchased new, more environmentally friendly vehicles. This program was considered successful as it stimulated the domestic car market and helped reduce industrial decline during the global financial crisis. However, it also caused discussions regarding its long-term impact on the economy and the environment. While Fico also made some changes to the welfare system, they were not comprehensive and were mostly limited to one-time payments such as Christmas bonuses for pensioners (Gould, 2009). Fico preferred expensive state investments in the Keynesian style, which resulted in an 8% government budget deficit in 2009 (compared to previous years' deficits). However, the growth of the public finance deficit was a common phenomenon across the Eurozone and the EU during the recession (Euractiv, 2010). The biggest problem of the Slovak economic model during the financial crisis was the extreme sensitivity to the collapse of the German export sector and the narrow specialization in the automotive industry (Becker & Lesay, 2012).

The main achievement of this government was preparing the country's economy for the euro. The favorable economic development of the economy in the integration process led to Slovakia being the first country from the V4 to successfully meet the Maastricht criteria for joining the European Monetary Union (Myant et al., 2013; Šikula, 2016). The government successfully ensured the country met all the requirements and criteria to adopt the euro as its national currency in 2009 without any significant issues or debates (Buček, 2010). Slovakia completed its political and economic integration process by joining the EU in 2004, joining the Schengen area in 2007, and adopting the euro in 2009. However, at the same time, politicians and society lost the goal they had been striving to achieve for years. The country was left with no further vision of achieving further progress despite significant shortcomings in regional development, healthcare, and education. In the period after joining the EU, the following were specific for Slovakia: relatively low social expenditures, GDP per capita far below the EU average, relative poverty and income inequality (Keune, 2006).

In the 2010 elections, Fico received the highest number of votes. However, the opposition parties could still form a government without him. The government led by Iveta Radičová, which began its term in July 2010, pursued a consolidation policy. As a result, the deficit in the government budget decreased from 7.7% in 2010 to 4.8% in 2011 (Valentovič, 2013). Once again, Minister of Finance Ivan Mikloš took the lead in consolidating public finances and implementing austerity measures. The coalition also included the new political party Freedom and Solidarity (SaS), a center-right liberal political party in Slovakia founded by economist Richard Sulík, who designed Slovakia's flat tax system. It generally holds neoliberal economic positions. One of the most significant controversies during Radičová's tenure was the issue of Slovakia's participation in the European Financial Stability Facility (EFSF), a bailout fund established by the EU to assist the Eurozone in financial distress. Despite initial support from the government, the coalition faced internal opposition to the bailout, particularly from the SaS party. In October 2011, the Radičová government lost a vote of confidence in parliament over its decision to support the expansion of the EFSF. The SaS party withdrew its support, leading to the government's collapse and the calling of early elections.

In 2012, a major scandal known as the "Gorilla" case shook the Slovakian political sphere. At the heart of the scandal were leaked transcripts of wiretapped conversations between high-ranking members of the Penta group and influential figures in politics and business recorded during Dzurinda's era. The transcripts revealed that Penta had allegedly engaged in corrupt practices to sway political decisions, gain unfair advantages in business dealings, and manipulate the media landscape. These disclosures sparked widespread public protests aimed at exposing the connections between oligarchic groups and political elites and their impact on the political process.

After early elections in 2012, Smer-SD returned with an unprecedentedly strong mandate from the citizens. One single-party government focused on maintaining economic stability amid the ongoing Eurozone crisis and global economic uncertainty. Efforts were made to reduce budget deficits and public debt while promoting economic growth through targeted policies. It implied raising taxes and duties and limiting public spending. The flat tax system, which had been in place since 2004, was replaced by a system with two different tax rates (19% on income up to 37,981.94 euros and 25% above 37,981.94 euros). These policies were made more manageable since Slovakia's export markets were recovering, and moderate growth was returning after 2010. After the improved macroeconomic performance, Fico pragmatically aimed to promote Slovakia's status to that of a core EU member state (Malová & Dolný, 2016). Between 2012 and 2016, if we look at the differences between money received (especially structural funds) and money paid out, we find that the countries of the Visegrad Group, including Slovakia, received net transfers of 2%–4% of GDP (Piketty, 2020). In addition, freedom of travel, European funds and membership in the eurozone were clearly advantageous for the majority of Slovak citizens (Henderson, 2017). However, critics argued that the government pursued populist policies focusing more on short-term gains and political interests rather than addressing long-term structural issues. Government representatives justified redistribution policies through various "social packages": "When the economy is doing well, the citizens must feel it too." Even though the government had a comfortable majority in the parliament and the country was experiencing a period of economic prosperity, they did not initiate significant structural reforms in healthcare, education, or the labor market sector.

During this term, Jaguar Land Rover's arrival in Slovakia was a significant moment for the country's automotive industry. In December 2015, Jaguar Land Rover announced its plans to build a new manufacturing plant in Nitra, Slovakia, marking its first investment in Eastern Europe. The decision was influenced by various factors, including Slovakia's strategic location, skilled labor force, and favorable business environment. The "investment of the decade" reached a value of 1.4 billion euros. The investment incentives that the car manufacturer received from the government amounted to 130 million euros, which is approximately 9% of the total investment.

After the 2016 parliamentary election in Slovakia, the government formed was led by Prime Minister Robert Fico. This government was the third consecutive administration headed by SMER-SD with ideologically relatively disparate political parties SNS and the interethnic political party Most-Híd. Despite uninterrupted economic growth, low unemployment, and high public revenues, the government faced criticism for handling social issues, including healthcare, education, and welfare reform. There were concerns about the lack of transparency in decision-making processes, particularly regarding public procurement and government contracts. The government faced allegations of corruption and cronyism, with concerns about the misuse of public funds and unethical practices within various state institutions. During this period, the practices of the "agro mafia" in the east of Slovakia came to light. Organized crime groups exploit farmers through various fraudulent schemes, including embezzlement and theft, impacting the agricultural community negatively. The agro mafia's activities often lead to protests by farmers who have been victims of these criminal practices. Furthermore, the agro mafia in Slovakia is interconnected with political figures and parties, creating a complex web of corruption and criminal influence within the agricultural industry.

The fall of Fico's third government was triggered by the murder of journalist Ján Kuciak and his fiancee Martina Kušnírová. In the last article, Kuciak wrote about the connection of the Italian mafia 'Ndrangheta to state officials and representatives of Smer-SD. The opposition, activists, and citizens demanded the end of this government in large-scale protests. Robert Fico eventually resigned, and President Andrej Kiska entrusted the formation of a new government to Petr Pellegrini. While there were some positive economic indicators during the third Fico Cabinet, challenges related to corruption, economic crimes, and structural issues persisted and required further attention and reform efforts. Fico's government missed opportunities to implement more significant economic reforms to stimulate economic development and competitiveness.

In 2018 and early 2019, several signs of "overheating" of the economy could be observed, which indicated a likely slowdown. Growth of real estate prices and the lack of labor force have appeared, an unprecedented phenomenon in the Slovak labor market. Economists stated that the exhaustion of the price and cost factors of Slovakia's competitiveness is no longer a future threat but a current tendency. During this period, the number of seniors (65+) exceeded the number of children for the first time (Morvay et al., 2019). It represents a significant problem for the social security system and public finances' sustainability. However, the political elites have been unable to solve this issue satisfactorily. The absence of a vision or ideas about where Slovak society should go has led Slovakia to almost stop converging and approaching the most advanced states of the EU in recent years. The fragile Tatra Tiger got stuck.

5. From Matovič Through Ódor's Technocratic Government Back to Fico

The 2020 elections in Slovakia saw Smer-SD lose due to accusations of corruption, suspicions of its links to the oligarchy and connections to the mafia. None of their coalition partners were able to reach the 5% threshold. The coalition government formed after the elections was led by the populist OĽaNO party (Ordinary People and Independent Personalities), whose Prime Minister was Igor Matovič. Matovič campaigned on an anticorruption platform, promising to end

Fico's "Mafia State." The coalition government included various center-right parties, such as Sme rodina (We Are Family), SaS, and Za ľudí party (For the People). With a 3/5 majority in the parliament, the public had high expectations for significant reforms and a new governance culture.

The government faced considerable challenges in meeting the public's expectations due to pervasive internal disagreements and conflicts among coalition partners. Such political instability frequently resulted in tensions within the government. The government's response to the COVID-19 pandemic was criticized, primarily due to issues in the procurement of medical supplies, vaccination rollout, and communication of public health measures. The government's reaction saw concerns regarding transparency, efficiency, and coordination. Implementing lockdown measures to contain the spread of the virus had significant adverse effects on the economy, resulting in disruptions in business operations, loss of income for individuals, and economic uncertainty.

Eduard Heger became the Prime Minister of Slovakia following a political reshuffle within the coalition government in April 2021. The change in leadership was prompted by mounting criticism of the government's handling of the Covid-19 pandemic. Under Heger's administration, Slovakia has become one of the largest contributors to humanitarian aid for Ukraine, offering medical supplies, tents, sleeping bags, hygiene supplies, food, clothing, and even military aid such as air defense systems, fighter jets, helicopters, artillery, infantry fighting vehicles, engineering vehicles, demining systems, ammunition, and other material. Until the fall of 2023, Slovakia sent military aid to Ukraine with a total value of 671 million euros. Slovakia was also among Ukraine's largest donors of material and humanitarian aid per capita (RTVS, 2023).

During this period, Slovakia experienced a challenging economic climate characterized by record inflation rates. The country recorded the highest annual inflation rates in the Eurozone for several months, with food prices experiencing the sharpest increase. The costs of transportation and housing, particularly fuel and energy, were also among the highest. At the turn of 2022–2023, Slovakia's year-on-year inflation rates were approximately from 15.1% to 15.4% (ŠÚSR, 2023). Even in the fall of 2023, Slovakia still had the highest inflation rate in the Eurozone. According to Eurostat (2023), the highest annual inflation rates among EU Member States in 2023 were recorded in Hungary (17.0%), Czechia (12.0%), and Slovakia (11.0%). At the end of 2022 and the beginning of 2023, the Slovak government approved various decrees that guarantee the household electricity prices for 2023 will not increase from 2022 levels. Additionally, the maximum increase in final gas prices for households in 2023 will not surpass 15% (IEA, 2023).

The government led by Heger implemented education reforms aimed at enhancing the quality of education, modernizing curricula, and improving teacher training. In the healthcare sector, the government proposed measures to make the system more efficient and accessible, reducing bureaucracy, improving patient care, and addressing issues such as waiting times and hospital management. Following the expensive management of the pandemic, which was exacerbated by Matovič's wasteful policies, he continued his irresponsible fiscal approach even after transitioning from the role of Prime Minister to Minister of Finance. Consequently, public debt per capita in Slovakia increased by 41% (3,492 euros) to 12,039 euros in 2023 (Toma, 2023).

Heger Cabinet launched the implementation of the long-awaited plan of reforms, for which it is expected to receive 7.5 million euros from the Next Generation EU recovery fund. The goal is to help the country escape the middle-income trap and achieve 92% of the EU 27 average GDP per capita by 2030. In other words, to restart the convergence process and align it toward the most prosperous nations and the EU average. The Recovery and Resilience Plan is a one-of-a-kind opportunity to mitigate the pandemic's effects and transform the Slovak economy, creating opportunities and jobs. The plan includes investment and reform measures divided into 18 thematic components. It is worth 6.3 billion euros in grants. The Slovak recovery plan prioritizes neglected areas of health and education, efficient public administration, green transition, and digitalization (The Slovak Spectator, 2020). However, the plan mandates implementing key reforms for critical state functions such as healthcare, education, and justice to receive payments. Furthermore, it requires the effective functioning of state administration, digitalization progress, and climate change preparation (The Slovak Spectator, 2022).

After the no-confidence vote in the parliament, President Zuzana Čaputová named Slovak National Bank Deputy Governor Ľudovít Ódor to lead a technocratic government. Ódor's government worked toward maintaining continuity in the functioning of the state until the snap elections in September 2023. The caretaker government of economist Ľudovít Ódor has unveiled a package of consolidation measures worth almost 10 billion euros, which the future government could follow to reduce Slovakia's debt and general government deficit. The package features nearly 100 various measures, including an increase in the basic VAT by two percentage points, a proposed reduction in social spending, and a more effective tax-and-levy system (The Slovak Spectator, 2023).

The collapse of the previous ruling coalition, the citizens' disappointment, and the rising cost of living made possible the comeback of the Smer-SD party to power. Robert Fico won the 2023 Slovakian elections with sovereigntist rhetoric, which resonated with a significant portion of the electorate. His campaign was characterized by aggressive rhetoric against mainstream media and nongovernmental organizations. He stressed national interests and the necessity to conduct a sovereign foreign policy, which attracted voters who felt Slovakia's support for Ukraine was not in their best interests. The fourth Fico government was formed in October 2023. As one of its earliest actions, the new government fulfilled its promise to cease all military aid from the Slovak Republic to Ukraine, except for commercial military contracts. This decision was based on the argument presented by representatives of the governmental parties that supplying weapons only prolongs military conflicts.

Objectively, we state that the new government, which emerged from early parliamentary elections, took over public finances after two crises in a complicated state, which means that without government measures, the deficit would range from 2024 to 2027 at the level of 6% of GDP. Slovakia's debt would gradually increase to almost 70% of GDP. Public finances are in the zone of high risk of long-term sustainability. According to the Council for Budget Responsibility estimates, the current poor state of public finances was mainly impacted by the security and economic crisis and the pandemic, the initial high structural deficit at the end of good economic times, and the measures taken in 2023. The Council notes that the 2024 budget worsened long-term sustainability and was not created following spending limits. It thus lacks permanent measures that would reduce the deficit from the expected 5.7% of GDP to 5.2% of GDP this year (RRZ, 2024). The government has not yet decided to go down the path of fundamental cuts and consolidation of public finances.

Moreover, in February 2024, the European Commission put the evaluation of Slovakia's fourth recovery plan payment on hold, which amounts to 900 million euros. This decision was made due to several concerns the Commission has regarding Slovakia's adherence to the rule of law, spending limits, and pension measures. The European Commission has raised objections to the approval process and content of a controversial amendment to the Penal Code. Additionally, the Slovak government has violated the Budget Rules Act regarding spending limits. The government's economic and fiscal policies have also led to several credit rating agencies downgrading Slovakia's rating or lowering its outlook to negative. The European Commission also had a problem with the amendment of the Competence Act, which made it easier to dismiss the heads of independent offices in Slovakia. The European Commission has sent a letter to the Slovak government regarding multiple violations of the rule of law. In the letter from the end of March 2024, the Commission threatened Slovakia directly to stop the allocation of funds from the Recovery and Resilience Plan, which amounts to over 6 billion euros.

6. Conclusion

Slovakia is relatively often cited as a successful story of capitalist transformation strategically based on export manufacturing industries and FDIs (Becker & Lesay, 2019). Although the development of the last 30 years can be characterized rather as a success story, in general, the Slovak Republic is currently not in good shape. In 2024, two decades after joining the European Union and 15 years after joining the Economic and Monetary Union of the European Union, the Slovak Republic is in a permanent political and socioeconomic crisis. Slovak society is deeply polarized, frustrated, and dissatisfied with political and economic developments. The era of rapid economic growth and convergence, commonly referred to as the "Tatra tiger," has come to an end. The neoliberal growth model has suffered significant damage and exhaustion, yet no new coherent alternative has emerged in its place, particularly in the form of a Social Democratic model (Gál & Malová, 2021). As Kahancová and Uhlerová (2023) correctly pointed out, to reach the electorate, Smer-SD has recently flirted with conservative and nationalist issues, which conflict with social democracy.

Vladimír Mečiar's policies and the legacy of his government have had significant implications for Slovakia's economic development. The rough political lines drawn during his tenure created a challenging environment for subsequent governments to navigate. While many sought to distance themselves from the perceived failures and controversies of the Mečiar era, they also found themselves grappling with its lasting effects. The privatization processes initiated under Mečiar's government resulted in the emergence of powerful business entities known as "business clans" or oligarchs. These entities often had close ties to political elites, leading to concerns about cronyism, corruption, and the misuse of public funds. The concentration of economic power in the hands of a few influential individuals or groups hindered competition and innovation, stifling the growth of a more dynamic and diversified economy. According to Le Gloannec and Rupnik (2008), Slovakia had an "illiberal democracy" with delayed democratic consolidation and half-hearted economic reform in the 1990s.

The consolidation and completion of the transformation process, which included the integration of the Slovak Republic into key international organizations, the arrival of foreign investments, and the implementation of certain reforms, were crucial for the country. However, the transformation of the economic model from "real existing socialism" before 1989 to market capitalism, especially after the neoliberal turn in 2002–2006 (Fisher et al., 2007; Gould, 2009), was socially painful for a significant part of Slovak society. This adopted economic model failed to address the social inclusion of the marginalized Roma community or change the situation of the economically backward and depopulated islands of concentrated poverty represented by some southern and eastern regions of the Slovak Republic. This economic model mainly benefited multinational corporations, which need a free market, a minimum of state regulations, a disciplined and highly productive workforce, low labor costs, and, last but not least, state incentives. Additionally, neoliberal policies, once implemented, proved difficult to reverse, and even governments opposing Dzurinda's reforms struggled to offer alternatives to this widely accepted paradigm in Slovak politics. Besides that, as Mikloš (2008) acknowledges, the opinion of the majority in Slovakia is that the reforms were socially unbearable. In addition, according to the majority of the population, they represented enormous ballast for the people and negatively influenced mainly lower income groups. Despite Fico's promise to undo Slovakia's neoliberal order, Fico Cabinet did not tinker significantly with the Dzurinda government's basic capital-friendly measures (Gould & Malová, 2020).

Between 2012 and 2017, the Slovak economy's growth rate lost its previously held lead over the other Visegrad Group and Slovenia economies. This marks a significant shift from 2003 to 2008, when the Slovak economy was the growth leader of the group. After the recent recession, the Slovak economy managed to regain its status as a growth leader between 2010 and 2012 but has since lost its position (Morvay et al., 2019; Šikula, 2016). Overall, the Slovak economy's dynamics of GDP growth have declined in recent years. The limitations of the previous growth model of the Slovak economy are becoming increasingly evident. The growth pattern that relied on FDI inflows and low wages and cost levels (Myant & Drahokoupil, 2010) is losing its foundation. These issues have been highlighted in various documents, but they were considered as future warnings (Buček, 2010). Despite the positive fact of the Slovak economy's relative openness, these issues are now being recognized as immediate problems. In addition, poverty and social inequalities remain problems in Slovakia today (Gerbery, 2021) as well as regional disparities persist (see Banerjee & Jarmuzek, 2010).

Over the past two decades, Slovakia's political landscape has failed to introduce innovative measures and tools that could effectively reduce the vulnerability of its economy to potential economic and financial crises. Slovakia's economy became overly dependent on the automotive sector, making it too sensitive to fluctuations in the global automotive market. Moreover, governments squandered years of economic stability and missed several opportunities to push through costly reforms in health care and education. Slovakia's National Recovery and Resilience Plan can represent a game-changer only on the condition that the government will competently approach the implementation of milestone reforms and will simplify the administrative burden for drawing European funds.

The country's investment in science, research, and development, as well as innovation, has been negligible compared to its neighboring countries. Additionally, public investments in Slovak infrastructure have been low. As highlighted by Drahokoupil (2018), the primary political challenge for Central and Eastern European countries was establishing a framework that enables them to achieve competitiveness through innovation rather than merely relying on low labor costs. Despite the significant wage gap, there is still room for wage hikes without compromising a country's competitiveness. However, it is crucial to promote the modernization of the welfare state (see Häusermann, 2010), which goes beyond being a solution only for the poorest and is perceived as a burden on the economy (Šikula, 2016). Welfare regimes are labeled according to their defining power relations and key actors: social-democratic, liberal, and corporatist (Esping-Andersen, 1990). Slovakia has shifted from a predominantly continental social economic model to a liberal, Anglo-Saxon economic model (Mikloš, 2008) by providing only subsidiary poverty relief. Hence, people need to rely almost exclusively on their own earning capacity in the market. In our opinion, this "residual" model of the welfare state also belongs to one of the most significant factors contributing to the low sustainability of the Slovak economic model.

However, the current fourth Robert Fico's government has no vision regarding the economic development of Slovakia. In summary, the present landscape in Slovakia appears devoid of any meaningful dialog regarding the nation's future trajectory and desired identity, with scant enthusiasm from key stakeholders for engaging in such a comprehensive societal conversation. Instead of embarking on a journey of profound structural transformation, Slovakia seems to be languishing in a state of inertia, tending to the status quo rather than embracing the winds of change.

References

Banerjee, B., & Jarmuzek, M. (2010). Economic growth and regional disparities in the Slovak Republic. *Comparative Economic Studies*, *52*, 379–403. https://doi.org/10.1057/ces.2010.13

Barański, M. (2020). The political party system in Slovakia in the era of Mečiarism: The experiences of the young democracies of central European countries. *Eastern Review, 9*, 33–48. https://doi.org/10.18778/1427-9657.09.03

Becker, J., & Lesay, I. (2012). *Život na úver: Všetko, čo ste chceli vedieť o kríze.* Inaque.sk.

Becker, J., & Lesay, I. (2019). Slovakia's development model: Contours, vulnerabilities and strategic alternatives. *Journal of Contemporary Central and Eastern Europe, 27*(2–3), 139–154. https://doi.org/10.1080/25739638.2019.1692521

Biea, N. (2016). *Economic growth in Slovakia: Past successes and future challenges.* Publications Office of the European Union. https://doi.org/10.2765/01942

Buček, J. (2010). The financial and economic crisis in Slovakia – Its spatial aspects and policy responses. In G. Gorzelak & Ch. Goh (Eds.), *Financial crisis in Central and Eastern Europe: From similarity to diversity* (pp. 190–208). Scholar.

Charillon, F. (2004). Sovereignty and intervention: EU's interventionism in its 'near abroad'. In W. Carlsnaes, H. Sjursen, & B. White (Eds.), *Contemporary European foreign policy* (pp. 252–264). SAGE Publishers.

Deegan-Krause, K. (2003). Slovakia's second transition. *Journal of Democracy, 14*(2), 65–79.

Drahokoupil, J. (2007). *Political support of the competition state in the Visegrád four: The comprador service sector and its allies.* GARNET Working Paper No. 22/07. https://warwick.ac.uk/fac/soc/pais/research/csgr/garnet/workingpapers/2207.pdf

Drahokoupil, J. (2018). Zvyšovanie životnej úrovne prostredníctvom rastu založeného na inováciách. In P. Daubner (Ed.), *Budúcnosť Európy: Cesta k post-kapitalizmu?* (pp. 48–55). POLE.

Drál, P. (2008). Symbolic processes of social exclusion of Roma in Slovak public policy discourse. *Ethnicity Studies, 1–2*(3), 85–116.

Esping-Andersen, G. (1990). *The three worlds of welfare capitalism.* Princeton University Press.

Euractiv. (2010). Rozpočtový deficit i vládny dlh EÚ sa v roku 2009 výrazne zvýšili. *Euractiv.* https://euractiv.sk/section/all/news/eurostat-rozpoctovy-deficit-i-vladny-dlh-eu-sa-v-roku-2009-vyrazne-zvysili/

Eurostat. (2023). HICP – Inflation rate [prc_hicp_aind]. *Eurostat.* https://doi.org/10.2908/TEC00118

Fischer, S., & Gelb, A. (1991). The process of socialist economic transformation. *The Journal of Economic Perspectives, 5*(4), 91–105. https://doi.org/10.1257/jep.5.4.91

Fisher, S., Gould, J., & Haughton, T. (2007). Slovakia's neoliberal turn. *Europe-Asia Studies, 59*(6), 977–998. https://doi.org/10.1080/09668130701489170

Gál, Z., & Malová, D. (2021). Slovakia in the Eurozone: Tatra tiger or mafia state inside the elite club? In K. Arató, B. Koller, & A. Pelle (Eds.), *The political economy of the Eurozone in Central and Eastern Europe: Why in, why out?* (pp. 165–183). Routledge.

Gerbery, D. (2021). O čom hovoríme, keď hovoríme o chudobe detí a medzigeneračnej reprodukcii chudoby? In J. Košč & J. Ruman (Eds.), *K problematike chudoby a sociálnej neistoty na Slovensku v 21. storočí* (pp. 27–50). Pracujúca chudoba.

Gould, J. (2003). Out of the blue? Democracy and privatization in postcommunist Europe. *Comparative European Politics, 1*, 277–311. https://doi.org/10.1057/palgrave.cep.6110019

Gould, J. (2009). *Slovakia's neoliberal churn: The political economy of the Fico government 2006-8.* IESIR Working Papers no. 01/2009. Comenius University.

Gould, J., & Malová, D. (2020). Toxic ordoliberalism on the EU's periphery. In J. Bátora & J. E. Fossum (Eds.), *Towards a segmented European political order: The European Union's post-crises conundrum* (pp. 112–131). Routledge.
Haerpfer, C. W. (2006). Hungary: Structure and dynamics of democratic consolidation. In H.-D. Klingemann, D. Fuchs, & J. Zielonka (Eds.), *Democracy and political culture in Eastern Europe* (pp. 148–171). Routledge.
Harvey, D. (2005). *A brief history of neoliberalism*. Oxford University Press.
Haughton, T. (2002). Slovakia's Robert Fico: A man to be trusted or feared? Radio free Europe/radio liberty. *East European Perspectives*, *4*(11). https://www.rferl.org/a/1342505.html
Haughton, T. (2004). Explaining the limited success of the communist-successor left in Slovakia: The case of the party of the democratic left (SDĽ). *Party Politics*, *10*(2), 177–191. https://doi.org/10.1177/1354068804040499
Häusermann, S. (2010). *The politics of welfare state reform in continental Europe: Modernization in hard times*. Cambridge University Press.
Henderson, K. (2017). Euroscepticism and the 'missing left': The Slovak case study. *Politologický časopis-Czech Journal of Political Science*, *24*(3), 229–248. https://doi.org/10.5817/PC2017-3-229
Huffschmid, J. (2005). *Economic policy for a social Europe: A critique of neo-liberalism and proposals for alternatives*. Palgrave Macmillan.
IEA. (2023). *Electricity and gas price caps for households*. International Energency Agency. https://www.iea.org/policies/17135-electricity-and-gas-price-caps-for-households#
Kahancová, M., & Uhlerová, M. (2023). Trade unions in Slovakia: From politics to bread-and-butter unionism. In J. Waddington, T. Müller, & K. Vandaele (Eds.), *Trade unions in the European Union* (pp. 945–977). Peter Lang.
Keune, M. (2006). The European social model and enlargement. In M. Jepsen & A. S. Pascual (Eds.), *Unwrapping the European social model* (pp. 163–180). Policy Press. 167–188.
Laar, M. (2010). *The power of freedom: Central and Eastern Europe after 1945*. Unitas Foundation.
Landler, M. (2004, April 13). A 'Detroit' for Europe takes shape in Slovakia. *The New York Times*. https://www.nytimes.com/2004/04/13/IHT-a-detroit-for-europe-takes-shape-in-slovakia.html
Le Gloannec, A., & Rupnik, J. (2008). Democratization by extension: Seeking reinsurance. In Z. Laïdi (Ed.), *EU foreign policy in a globalized world: Normative power and social preferences* (pp. 51–67). Routledge.
Malová, D., & Dolný, B. (2016). Economy and democracy in Slovakia during the crisis: From a laggard to the EU core. *Problems of Post-Communism*, *63*(5–6), 300–312. https://doi.org/10.1080/10758216.2016.1200952
Marcinčin, A., & Morvay, K. (2001). Makroekonomická ilúzia a mikroekonomická realita – príklad Slovenska. *Finance a úvěr*, *51*(3), 130–146.
Miháliková, S. (2006). Slovakia: Pathways to a democratic community. In H.-D. Klingemann, D. Fuchs, & J. Zielonka (Eds.), *Democracy and political culture in Eastern Europe* (pp. 172–202). Routledge.
Mikloš, I. (2008). Slovakia: A story of reforms. In W. Bieńkowski, J. C. Brada, & M. Radło (Eds.), *Growth versus security* (pp. 54–88). Palgrave Macmillan.

Morvay, K., Dujava, D., Frank, K., Hudcovský, M., Jeck, T., & Lábaj, M. (2019). *Hospodársky vývoj Slovenska v roku 2018 a výhľad do roku 2020: Zaostrené na: prerušenie konvergencie*. VEDA, vydavateľstvo Slovenskej akadémie vied.

Myant, M., & Drahokoupil, J. (2010). *Transition economies: Political economy in Russia, Eastern Europe, and Central Asia*. John Wiley & Sons.

Myant, M., & Drahokoupil, J. (2013). Transition economies after the crisis of 2008: Actors and policies. *Europe-Asia Studies*, *65*(3), 373–382. https://doi.org/10.1080/09668136.2013.779459

Myant, M., Drahokoupil, J., & Lesay, I. (2013). The political economy of crisis management in East–Central European countries. *Europe-Asia Studies*, *65*(3), 383–410. https://doi.org/10.1080/09668136.2013.779460

Nemčok, M., & Spáč, P. (2020). The rise and sustainability of party leaders in Slovakia: Robert Fico and Mikuláš Dzurinda. In S. Gherghina (Ed.), *Party leaders in Eastern Europe: Personality, behavior and consequences* (pp. 241–264). Palgrave Macmillan.

Piketty, T. (2020). *Capital and ideology*. The Belknap Press of Harvard University Press.

Polák, M. (2004). Slovakia: From "National Capitalism" to EU liberalism (and beyond?). *Kurswechsel*, *1*, 70–78. http://www.beigewum.at/wordpress/wp-content/uploads/070_michal_polak.pdf

RRZ. (2024). *Hodnotenie rozpočtu verejnej správy na roky 2024 až 2026*. Council for Budget Responsibility. https://www.rrz.sk/hodnotenie-rozpoctu-verejnej-spravy-na-roky-2024-az-2026/

RTVS. (2023). *Slovenská pomoc Ukrajine v číslach: Patríme medzi svetových lídrov*. Radio and Television of Slovakia. https://spravy.rtvs.sk/2023/02/slovenska-pomoc-ukrajine-v-cislach-patrime-medzi-svetovych-lidrov/

Rybář, M. (2007). The parliamentary election in Slovakia, June 2006. *Electoral Studies*, *26*(3), 699–703. https://doi.org/10.1016/j.electstud.2007.04.007

Sasse, G. (2007). 'Conditionality-lite': The European neighbourhood policy and the EU's eastern neighbours. In N. Casarini & C. Musu (Eds.), *European foreign policy in an evolving international system: The road towards convergence* (pp. 163–180). Palgrave Macmillan.

Šestáková, M., & Ferenčíková, S. (2015). Restructuring of the banking sector in Slovakia over the last two decades. *Ekonomické rozhľady*, *44*(2), 168–187. https://euba.sk/www_write/files/SK/ekonomicke-rozhlady/er2_2015_sestakova_ferencikova_fulltext-20247.pdf

Šikula, M. (2016). Ekonomický vývoj samostatného Slovenska. In M. Pekník (Ed.), *Pohľady na slovenskú politiku po roku 1989. II. časť* (pp. 325–363). Ústav politických vied SAV & VEDA, vydavateľstvo SAV.

Sokol, M. (2013). Silicon Valley in Eastern Slovakia? Neoliberalism, post-socialism and the knowledge economy. *Europe-Asia Studies*, *65*(7), 1324–1343. https://doi.org/10.1080/09668136.2013.822714

Stenning, A., Smith, A., Rochovská, A., & Świątek, D. (2011). *Domesticating neo-liberalism spaces of economic practice and social reproduction in post-socialist cities*. Wiley.

ŠÚSR. (2023). *Indices of consumer prices – Detailed data – Monthly*. Database of the Statistical Office of the SR/DATAcube. [sp0029ms]. Statistical Office of the Slovak

Republic. https://datacube.statistics.sk/#!/view/en/VBD_INTERN/sp0029ms/v_sp0029ms_00_00_00_en

Szomolányi, S. (2003). Slovakia: From a difficult case of transition to a consolidated Central European democracy. In T. Hayashi (Ed.), *Democracy and market economics in Central and Eastern Europe: Are new institutions being consolidated?* (pp. 149–188). Slavic Research Center, Hokkaido University.

The Slovak Spectator. (2020, October 5). The finance ministry publishes its much-awaited reform plan. *The Slovak Spectator*. https://spectator.sme.sk/c/22502978/the-finance-ministry-introduced-a-reform-plan-for-slovakia.html

The Slovak Spectator. (2022, December 19). The recovery plan: An opportunity to bring Slovakia closer to a green future. *The Slovak Spectator*. https://spectator.sme.sk/c/23097910/the-recovery-plan-an-opportunity-to-bring-slovakia-closer-to-a-green-future.html

The Slovak Spectator. (2023, October 5). PM Odor reveals fiscal consolidation plan with Lego. *The Slovak Spectator*. https://spectator.sme.sk/c/23227547/pm-odor-reveals-fiscal-consolidation-plan-with-lego.html

Toma, B. (2023, June 27). Vlády vedené OĽaNO zavesili každému Slovákovi na krk nový dlh vo výške skoro 3 500 eur. *Trend*. https://www.trend.sk/ekonomika/vlady-vedene-olano-zavesili-kazdemu-slovakovi-krk-novy-dlh-vyske-skoro-3-500-eur

Valentovič, M. (2013). Slovakia: A struggle for reform. In V. Novotný (Ed.), *From reform to growth: Managing the economic crisis in Europe* (pp. 383–406). Eburon Academic Publishers.

Chapter 3

Slovakia's Changing Position Among Economies of the European Union and the World

Natália Zagoršeková

University of Economics in Bratislava, Slovakia

Abstract

During the short history of Slovakia as an independent state, economic convergence has been at the center of the attention of policymakers and public figures. Even after becoming a member of many important international organizations (e.g. European Union, OECD, NATO), Slovak discourse still focuses on comparison with the Visegrad Group countries or with so-called new EU Member States. In this chapter, based on several rankings covering relevant economic indicators, we describe the development of Slovak's position globally (Global Competitiveness Index, Ease of Doing Business, GDP p. c.) or specifically among the EU Member States (convergence to EU average in selected indicators). We also explain these changes in connection to the specific development of the Slovak economy.

Keywords: Slovakia; European Union; Central Europe; competitiveness; economic development; economic convergence

1. Introduction

Since 1993 when the Slovak Republic came into existence as a newly independent country, its economy and society went through many turbulent periods caused by internal and external factors. The country went through an economic transformation while building its statehood and finding its place in the wider European and global market. The process of political and economic integration was halted by political representation during the first years of independence, but Slovakia

Modeling Economic Growth in Contemporary Slovakia, 49–70

Published under exclusive licence by Emerald Publishing Limited
doi:10.1108/978-1-83549-454-720241004

successfully joined all relevant international organizations, including economically the most important, the European Union (EU).

After the change of political representation and many reforms, Slovakia recorded impressive economic growth and became popular among foreign investors. During this period Slovak economy was converging to the level of other European Union Member States and became the leader within the Visegrad Group based on several indicators.

Since the economic crisis, however, it became apparent that the trend of Slovak convergence to the EU average was reversed and that the Slovak Republic started to lag behind other economies of central and eastern Europe that were also members of the European Union. In recent years, Slovakia no longer competes with Czechia or Poland but is closer to the economic level of Bulgaria or Romania.

In this chapter, we document the trajectory of Slovak economic development based on several demographic and economic indicators. We compare Slovakia and its performance globally, on the European Union level, and regionally with other Visegrad Group Member States.

2. People

2.1 Demography

The 30 years of the independent Slovak Republic have been the age of strong global population growth. In 1993, the population of the world was 5.53 billion people and grew to 8.05 billion in 2023 (UN, 2022). While the global population grew every year, this trend was less clear in the European Union and Slovakia. Nevertheless, both the population of Slovakia and the European Union grew during this period. The population of Slovakia grew from 5.314 million in 1993 to 5.429 million in 2023 (Eurostat, 2023h).

The relative share of the Slovak population in the world is very small and declined during these 30 years from 0.096% to 0.067%. Similarly, the share of the Slovak population is growing slower than that of the European Union. Slovak population share in the European Union is currently 1.21%, which means Slovakia is the 18th most populous state in the EU (Eurostat, 2023h).

Demographic predictions for the European Union (Boussemart & Godet, 2018) and Slovakia similarly predict population decline after 2030, low fertility rates below replacement levels, aging population, and natural population decline. Unlike natural change, migration patterns are more difficult to forecast, but current data suggest that immigration pressures will be more dramatic in the European Union as a whole, than in Slovakia. Ďurček et al. (2019) predict that net migration will be lower than negative natural change in Slovakia and Slovakia remains one of the Member States with lowest levels of migration. Although population predictions indicate a population decline for both the European Union and Slovakia, the population of the EU should decline by 7.07% by 2100, and in Slovakia, the population is predicted to decline by 16.24% by 2100 (Eurostat, 2024k).

However, in 2022 (latest data), the Slovak population is younger than the EU average and has a lower old-age dependency ratio. The median age in the EU is 44.4 years, while in Slovakia, the median age is 41.8 years. The data on average median age in the EU are only available since 2001 and since then Slovak population has been aging faster than the European Union as a whole. The old-age dependency ratio (population 65 years or over to population 20–64 years) in Slovakia (28.2) is still lower than that of the EU average (36.0). Still, in both cases, the proportion is growing steadily since 2005 (Eurostat, 2024l).

Fertility rates in Slovakia reached their lowest level in 2002 with only 1.19; however, the negative trend has been reversed and in 2021 total fertility rate in Slovakia reached 1.63, which is still below replacement fertility, but higher than the EU average of 1.53. Slovak total fertility rate first surpassed the European Union average fertility rate in 2018 and is currently in ninth place in the EU (Eurostat, 2023b).

Within the EU Slovakia belongs to the countries with a very small immigrant population and in 2022 only 60 thousand inhabitants of Slovakia had other than Slovak citizenship, which is the fourth lowest value in the EU (higher only to Romania, Croatia, and Lithuania). The data reflect the situation on January 1, 2022 (Eurostat, 2024j) and since then the situation in Slovakia has changed significantly as a result of the Russian invasion of Ukraine and Ukrainian citizens' migration to EU Member States, including Slovakia. Until the end of June 2023, more than 4 million people from Ukraine were under temporary protection in the EU, but Slovakia as a neighboring country only housed 2.56% of these people. With 103,960 temporary protection beneficiaries, Slovakia falls behind countries that are further away from Ukraine like Spain, Italy, or the Netherlands. If we compare this number to population, Slovakia has 19 temporary protection beneficiaries from Ukraine to 1,000 inhabitants, which is the seventh highest value in the EU and far behind the Czech Republic (33 beneficiaries to 1,000 inhabitants) which is not even bordering Ukraine (Eurostat, 2024a). Based on the study by the Social Policy Institute (Veselková & Hábel, 2023), temporary protection beneficiaries from Ukraine were less successful in entering the Slovak labor market (34.2%) than in some other EU Member States, where more than 40% of temporary protection beneficiaries from Ukraine are now employed (Estonia, the Netherlands, Lithuania).

2.2 Education

An educated population is increasingly crucial for the future development of the Slovak economy in European and global competition. The level of education and its potential impact can be measured by various indicators. To cover different aspects of education and its connection to the labor market, we describe three different areas connected to it: tertiary education attainment, young people neither in employment nor in education and training, and results of the Program for International Student Assessment (PISA).

Tertiary education attainment in the EU in the age group 25–34 years old should reach 45% by 2030. Higher education is a necessary prerequisite for success in digital, innovative, and research-based economies like the European Union. Higher education also improves employment prospects (Council Resolution, 2021). In Slovakia, the unemployment level among people with primary education in 2022 is 40.2% (the highest in the EU), while it is only 2.4% among people with tertiary education (Eurostat, 2023i).

Tertiary education attainment in the age group 25–34 years (Eurostat, 2023g) increased significantly since 2000 (oldest available data) when it was only 11.1%, fourth lowest among EU countries with available data (data for Austria and Croatia were not available). While tertiary education attainment in 2022 did not yet reach the EU target of 45%, it grew to 39.1%. Although this share is lower than the EU average of 42%, it is higher than tertiary education attainment in Czechia, Hungary, and even in Germany.

While people with higher education have better employment prospects, youth unemployment continues to pose a problem for many developed economies including Slovakia. Youth unemployment can be solved through education and training where young people can acquire the skills demanded by the labor market. However, if young people remain unemployed and not in education or training, they risk disconnect from the labor market and social exclusion. The statistics on young people neither in employment nor in education and training (NEET) in Slovakia have been available since 2002 when the rate was 27.1%, the second highest among EU-27 countries after Bulgaria (Eurostat, 2023j). With continuous improvement, Slovak rates came close to the EU average since 2008 and in 2022 NEET in Slovakia was 9.6%, the same as the European Union average.

While most indicators related to education measure quantity, we decided to include the results of PISA as one of the measures of quality of educational outcome. PISA is the OECD's Programme for International Student Assessment. PISA measures 15-year-olds' ability to use their reading, mathematics, and science knowledge and skills to meet real-life challenges (OECD, 2023b). Slovakia has participated in PISA testing since 2003 (OECD, 2023a).

In reading, Slovak scores have been below the OECD average in all rounds of testing. Between 2003 and 2022, the average scores in reading in Slovakia dropped from 469 to 447. This downward trend was however not unique to Slovakia but followed the OECD average. While in 2003 Slovakia had the lowest score from participating EU-27 countries, in 2022 Slovakia surpassed Greece for the second worst place.

The results are very similar in mathematics performance. Slovak scores dropped between 2003 and 2022 from 498 to 464 and so did OECD average score. Slovak score surpassed the OECD average in 2006 and 2009 but in 2022 is again below the OECD average of 472. While the Slovak 2003 mathematics score was higher than many EU-27 countries participating in PISA testing (Greece, Italy, Portugal, Latvia, Spain, Hungary, Poland, Luxembourg), in 2022 Slovakia surpassed only the score of Greece.

The scores for science have only been available since 2006 and similarly to reading scores, Slovakia never performed above the OECD average. The score for science declined in Slovakia from 488 in 2006 to 462 in 2022, as well as the OECD average. While in 2006 Slovakia was similar to or better than Spain, Lithuania, Luxembourg, Italy, Portugal, and Greece in science scores among participating EU-27 countries, in 2022 only Greece had a lower score in science.

In addition to the decline in scores in all three measured subjects, the socio-economic status of students predicts their scores to a greater extent than on average in OECD countries. A higher proportion of students scored below baseline proficiency level than in 2012 in both mathematics and reading, while this proportion did not change significantly in science (Miklovičová & Galádová, 2023).

2.3 Labor Market

The labor market of Slovakia, specifically high levels of unemployment, has been a specific problem of the Slovak economy since independence in 1993 and fell below 10% only in 2016, more than 10 years after Slovakia joined the European Union. The data on unemployment in Slovakia come from different sources and are therefore difficult to compare. Eurostat data on the unemployment rate are only available since 2009 for Slovakia and other Visegrad Group countries. We will therefore use data from the Statistical Office of the Slovak Republic for the period between 1993 and 2008. These data are based on the number of registered unemployed persons and in Slovakia the unemployment rate based on this calculation is usually lower than Eurostat measured unemployment rate (TASR, 2007).

The unemployment rate in Slovakia in 1993 was almost 15% as Slovak industries were negatively affected by changes in global economic relations (with a particularly negative impact on the arms industry). Transformation in Slovakia continued slowly for several years and unemployment continued to grow to its peak in 2001 at almost 20% (Dudáš, 2013). European integration, economic reforms, and the growing attractiveness of Slovakia to foreign investors contributed to lowering the unemployment rate after 2002. Other contributing factors include high economic growth, emigration, and active labor market measures. However, there are factors still negatively influencing the unemployment rate in Slovakia including differences between demand and supply in the labor market, long-term unemployment, or low regional mobility (Rievajová, 2009).

Based on Eurostat (2023i) data, that have been available since 2009, even after almost 5 years in the European Union, the unemployment rate in Slovakia remained over 10% and over the EU average. The unemployment rate only decreased below 10% in 2016 (9.6%) and decreased below the EU average in 2017 (8.1% in Slovakia, and 8.3% in the EU). Since then, unemployment rates in Slovakia are steadily lower than the average of the EU-27, but within the Visegrad Group countries, unemployment rates in Slovakia remain high. While in 2022 Czechia, Poland, and Hungary are among the six EU Member States with the lowest unemployment rates, Slovakia is close to the EU average. If we compare the data on youth unemployment (15–24 years), unemployment rates in Slovakia remain higher than the EU average and significantly higher than in other Visegrad Group countries, which are below the EU average. In 2022, youth unemployment rate in Slovakia was 19.9%.

In addition to the relatively high unemployment rate, the biggest problem of the Slovak labor market is long-term unemployment. More than 66% of unemployed persons are unemployed for longer than 1 year and long-term unemployment is the highest in the European Union. In Eastern Slovakia region, the proportion of long-term unemployment is over 70%, which is the fifth highest rate of all NUTS 2 regions (Eurostat, 2023f).

Despite these problems, the employment rate in Slovakia in 2022 is above the EU average with 76.7% and has risen by more than eight percentage points since 2009. Similarly to the unemployment rate, other Visegrad Group countries have higher employment rates than Slovakia (Eurostat, 2023a).

2.4 Human Development Index

Slovakia is a developed country by any standard (OECD membership, EU membership, structure of economy) and ranks in the highest category among countries by the Human Development Index (HDI) as well. HDI is a composite measure that includes three dimensions of development: health, knowledge, and standard of living on a scale between 0 and 1. It groups countries based on their HDI into four categories: very high human development (0.8–1), high human development (0.7–0.8), medium human development (0.55–0.7), and low human development (0–0.55). According to the latest Human Development Report 2021/2022 (Conceição, 2022), Slovakia ranks 45th among 191 countries included in this report. The HDI of Slovakia in 2021 was 0.848. The value of HDI of Slovakia has grown steadily since 1993, when the value was 0.7, except for years 2020 and 2021, when it decreased for 2 years in a row. This decrease was primarily caused by a significant decrease in life expectancy during the COVID-19 pandemic and mirrored global trends.

Despite the decrease in global average HDI, the relative position of Slovakia worsened compared to the previous year. While in 2020, Slovakia was in 40th place, in 2021, it dropped to 45th place. Only three European Union Member States recorded lower values of HDI than Slovakia, Hungary, Romania, and Bulgaria. The best relative position of Slovakia is in mean years of schooling where Slovakia ranks in 17th place globally and 8th place within the European Union. However, in expected years of schooling, Slovakia is in 73rd place globally and 24th in the EU. In each of the indicators included in the HDI, Slovak values are higher than the world average.

The first Human Development Report in which Slovakia was included as an independent country was the Human Development Report 1995. The indicators included in HDI changed in 2010, but we can still regard the HDI ranking as continuous and comparable between 1995 and 2021, although the change in methodology favored Slovakia which improved its position from 42nd to 31st between Human Development Reports of 2009 and 2010. In 1995 (data from 1992), Slovakia ranked in 40th place by HDI, same as in 2020. The highest ranking of Slovakia was 31st place in 2010 after the change of methodology. The worst position for Slovakia is the 45th place in the latest Human Development Report.

3. Economy

3.1 GDP and GDP p. c.

Gross domestic product (GDP) and per capita gross domestic product (GDP p.c.) are two of the most commonly used measures to compare the economic power of the country and its economic level. Globally it is also useful to compare countries based on per capita gross national income (GNI p.c.), the indicator the World Bank uses to divide countries into four groups. Based on this indicator, Slovakia is among the high-income economies with GNI p.c. 22,070 USD (World Bank Group, 2024b). For comparison among European Union Member States, however, GDP-based indicators are used, and this chapter will therefore focus on these. GNI p.c. indicator is relevant in the context of the EU as it is a criterion used for Member State's eligibility for Cohesion Fund (Schwarz, 2023).

The first indicator showing the size and performance of the economy is total GDP. The Slovak economy belongs to the smaller economies globally and within the EU. It is also the smallest economy in the Visegrad Group with a total GDP of 109,645.2 mil. EUR in 2022, which is a 0.7% contribution to the European Union GDP.

Data about Slovak GDP and its comparison to other current Member States of the European Union are available at Eurostat beginning in 1995 (Eurostat, 2024c). Based on this we can not only describe the growth of the Slovak economy measured by GDP over the years (with just 3 years of decline) but also the strengthening position of the Slovak economy in comparison to the rest of today's European Union.

After the shock of 1989 when the whole economic system of Czechoslovakia collapsed together with its international economic relations system, Slovak GDP dropped and remained under its 1989 levels for several years. According to Neal (2007, p. 378), the Slovak economy reached a 1989 level of GDP in 1997, the same as Hungary. Meanwhile, Poland reached its 1989 GDP level in 1995, and the Czech Republic only in 2003.

The total GDP of Slovakia in 1995 was 15,322.9 mil. EUR and until Slovakia became a member of the EU in 2004, it more than doubled. Slovak GDP grew year by year with the exceptions of 1999, 2009, and 2020. In 1999, the slight decline was caused predominantly by a decline in domestic demand, while in 2009, the global financial crisis caused the decline in Slovak GDP (Haluška & Dolinič, 2018). The decline in 2020 was caused by the global COVID-19 pandemic and restrictions connected to it.

Slovak GDP in 1995 was only 0.2% of GDP of all 27 current members of the European Union. This proportion grew over time and reached its peak in 2015 at

0.7%. Slovak GDP has remained at this level compared to the rest of the European Union until these days. Slovak GDP is the 18th highest in the European Union, between Hungary and Bulgaria.

Slovak economy has grown almost every year since 1995 with three already mentioned exceptions (Eurostat, 2024b). GDP change rates in Slovakia during this period varied from a record 10.8% growth in 2007 to a decline of 5.5% during the global financial crisis in 2009. For most of the years during this period, the Slovak economy grew faster than the whole European Union economy. As Slovakia is in the process of catching up, higher growth rates are necessary for economic convergence. Slovakia lagged only in 1999 and 2000 when the economy underwent major economic reforms and in 2016 when the European Union economy grew 0.1 p.p. faster than the Slovak economy. However, in 2022, the European Union's average economic growth significantly outpaced the growth of the Slovak economy. While the GDP of the EU grew by 3.4% in 2022, the Slovak economy grew only by 1.8%. Slovak economy was the fourth slowest growing economy in the EU and its growth was outpaced by all other Visegrad Group economies.

The indicator used for measuring the convergence between European Union economies is the GDP p.c.. First, we can describe the undeniable improvement of this measure in Slovakia since 1995 if we look at GDP p.c. in EUR (current prices) (Eurostat, 2024i). While the GDP p.c. in Slovakia in 1995 was 2,860 EUR, the average GDP p.c. of the 1995 European Union Member States (then 15, including the United Kingdom) was 18,940 EUR. The average of all current 27 members of the EU in 1995 was 14,900 EUR. Among current EU members, Slovakia was in the 21st place based on GDP p.c. with GDP p.c. higher than Poland but below Hungary and Czechia. By 2004, the year when Slovakia and nine other countries joined the EU, Slovak GDP p.c. grew to 6,460 EUR. However, it fell to the 22nd place among current EU-27 members. Slovak GDP p.c. was still below those of Czechia and Hungary and above that of Poland. In the period between 1995 and 2004, Slovakia was outpaced by Estonia. Between 2009 and 2012 Slovak GDP p.c. was in the 19th place among current EU-27 Member States, which was the best position to date. In 2022, Slovak GDP p.c. is again in the 21st place with a value of 19,980 EUR.

As the cost of living varies within the European Union, it is useful to adjust GDP p.c. to reflect price level differences using the purchasing power standard (PPS). Based on this measure, the relative living standards of individual EU Member States can be expressed in relation to the EU average (set to equal 100) (Eurostat, 2023d). As the average GDP p.c. of EU-27 Member States is set to equal 100, we can compare the convergence of Slovakia to the current European Union since 1995 when GDP p.c. in PPS in Slovakia was below half of EU-27 average at 48.9, and by 2004, the year when Slovakia joined the EU, it grew to 58.6. The conversion of Slovak GDP p.c. in PPS continued until 2015 when it reached the highest value of 78.6. Between 2012 and 2015, Slovakia was the EU economy with the 17th highest GDP p.c. in PPS, its best position yet. Since 2016, however, the convergence trend has reversed and the position of Slovakia in this particular ranking worsened. Not only is Slovak GDP p.c. in PPS in 2022 only

71.1% of that of the EU, Slovakia is also the third poorest EU country surpassing only Bulgaria and Greece.

In the policy brief of the Institute for Financial Policy, this declining position is explained to be caused by two main reasons: calculation of countries' price levels and measuring convergence based on GDP at purchasing power parity (Dujava & Žúdel, 2023). The main problem (or methodological shortcoming) of Eurostat calculation is the overstating of housing prices in Slovakia. The authors argue that the above-described reversal of Slovak convergence is due to a change of methodology in the calculation of PPP and that there was no significant change in Slovak convergence or development of prices in Slovakia. However, the authors admit that living standards in Slovakia are negatively affected by the terms of trade loss and that an increase in the openness of the Slovak economy would strengthen the negative effect on living standards in Slovakia.

Other similar economies in the EU in terms of openness and development level, namely Czechia and Hungary, also experienced volatility in terms of convergence to the EU level of GDP p.c. in PPS, both are currently closer to the EU average than Slovakia. The only Visegrad Group country continuously converging to the EU average level in recent years is Poland. Its GDP p.c. in PPS in 2022 was 79.5% of the EU average.

3.2 Prices

The process of economic transformation to a market-based economy after 1989 and independence in 1993 brought about high levels of inflation in Slovakia, especially in 1991 when annual inflation reached 61.2%. Slovakia was not an exception, as inflation in Czechia reached 56.6%, in Hungary 35%, and in Poland 70.2%. Slovakia and the Czech Republic chose the strategy of rapid reduction of inflation, while the process was more gradual in Hungary and Poland (Bruchácová, 2000).

After the period of lower inflation, in 1999 and 2000, inflation rate in Slovakia rose again to a double-digit level, similar to the development in other countries applying for EU membership (Poland, Hungary, Romania, and Bulgaria). In Slovakia, the increase was mainly caused by the liberalization (and therefore rise) of regulated prices. However, this surge in inflation was only short-term and halted by a combination of policies like freezing wages in the administrative sector and restrictive monetary policy (Národná banka Slovenska, 2000a).

Between 2014 and 2016, Slovak economy experienced deflation for the first time in its short economic history. In 2014, the HIPC fell by 0.1%, in 2015 by 0.3%, and in 2016 by 0.5%. This development was not unusual within the EU and several other Member States experienced deflation during this period. This situation was caused mostly by external European-wide or global factors including low prices of oil and gas, sanctions against the Russian Federation and retaliatory measures by Russia, and the inability of European Central Bank policy to reverse the trend of very low inflation. Specific causes in Slovakia contributing to deflation were decreases in regulated prices and prices of transport (due to low oil prices and increased competition in the Slovak market) (Morvay et al., 2019).

After several years of a stable level of inflation around the ECB target of 2%, inflation in Slovakia reached double-digit levels again in 2022 and 2023. The increase in prices in Slovakia and many other economies was caused by two main factors: rebound after the COVID-19 crisis and war in Ukraine. During the 2020 and 2021 global pandemic, supply chains were disrupted, which led to bottlenecks resulting in inflation. The war in Ukraine strengthened the pressure mainly by the increase of prices of fuels globally. Different economies were hit by these shocks to varying degrees and especially the impact of war in Ukraine was hardest in the eastern part of the EU. These countries, including Slovakia, depended to a great extent on Russian imports of energy resources, and disruption in trade relations with Russia and discussions about alternatives on the EU level added to inflation pressures in the region (Plutzer et al., 2022). In 2023, Slovak inflation was the third highest in the EU after Hungary and Czechia, and followed closely by Poland (Eurostat, 2023d).

Not only was inflation in the EU lower than in Slovakia, but the structure of price increases in Slovakia and the EU in 2022 and 2023 was also different. While the highest price increase in both the EU and Slovakia was recorded in the category of food and non-alcoholic beverages, the increase was much higher in Slovakia. Meanwhile, the prices of nonessential goods and services like clothing and footwear or recreation and culture increased similarly in the EU and Slovakia (Eurostat, 2024e).

The price increase of food and nonalcoholic beverages in households in Slovakia partially reflects the household budget structure differences (Eurostat, 2024f) among EU Member States, as the weights of different categories of goods and services are adjusted for individual Member States (European Central Bank, 2023). While the average household in the EU in 2023 spent 17.25% of its budget on food and nonalcoholic beverages, the average Slovak household spent 26.35% on it. This is the second-highest value in the EU after Romania. The average Slovak household also spends a higher proportion of its budget than the average EU household on housing, water, electricity, gas, and other fuels, while lower proportions are spent on restaurants and hotels or recreation and culture.

3.3 Competitiveness

While the concept of a country's competitiveness is sometimes viewed as flawed and problematic, as this term stems from firm-level competition (Krugman, 1996), there are several international competitiveness rankings. The three most widely cited such rankings are the World Competitiveness Ranking (IMD, 2023a) by the International Institute for Management Development (IMD), the Global Competitiveness Index (GCI) by the World Economic Forum, and Doing Business by the World Bank Group.

The only one of these that has been continuously reported in recent years is the World Competitiveness Ranking. This ranking is based on 336 criteria grouped into four areas: Economic Performance, Government Efficiency, Business Efficiency, and Infrastructure (IMD, 2023a). Detailed data on the ranking are available from 2019 to 2023. In 2023, the ranking evaluates 64 economies, including Slovakia and almost all EU Member States except Malta. In 2023, Denmark was the most competitive economy for the second time in a row, while Slovakia ranked in 53rd place. The only EU Member State lower than Slovakia was Bulgaria in 57th place. Compared to the previous year's ranking, Slovakia was surpassed by Poland and Romania. Slovakia's 49th place in 2022 was its best position in the last 5 years. If we compare the 53rd place in 2023 with other Visegrad Group countries, Slovakia is closest to Hungary in 46th place, while Poland is in 43rd place and Czech Republic is far ahead in 18th place.

If we look at ranking in four areas evaluated by the IMD, we see that Slovakia ranks highest in Infrastructure (44th) and that its position in this area remains the same as it was in 2019. Meanwhile, Slovakia dropped from 42nd to 56th place in Economic Performance since 2019 and its strongest area became its weakest, while the ranking in Government Efficiency and Business Efficiency improved. These four areas are further divided into five segments each and ranked. The worst evaluated segment for Slovakia was International Investment where Slovakia outranked only Botswana for 63rd place.

The International Institute for Management Development also evaluates the same list of countries in the World Digital Competitiveness Ranking and World Talent Ranking. In the World Digital Competitiveness Ranking (IMD, 2023b), Slovakia reached 46th place in the world and 22nd place in the EU (without Malta). In this ranking, Slovakia ranked higher than Bulgaria, Greece, Cyprus, Romania, and Hungary within the EU. However, the Czech Republic was in the 24th place. This ranking rates three aspects of digital competitiveness: Knowledge, Technology, and Future readiness.

In World Talent Ranking Slovakia ranked 51st in the world and outperformed only Bulgaria and Romania among EU Member States. This ranking also evaluates three dimensions: Investment & Development (of home-grown talent), Appeal (for foreign talent), and Readiness (skills and competencies in the talent pool). The Czech Republic is 21st in this ranking, which is especially interesting for Slovakia, as many Slovak students and professionals choose Czechia as their destination country due to common history, mutual language comprehension, and cultural and geographical proximity. The flow of workforce between the two countries is disproportional. In 2022, there were 33 times more Slovaks working in Czechia (214,907) than Czechs working in Slovakia (6,480) (Dedinský, 2022). Slovaks leave for Czechia even before they enter the labor market, as almost 21 thousand Slovak students study at Czech universities. The main reasons they cite for choosing Czechia over Slovakia are better quality and reputation (Beňušová, 2023).

Another widely cited competitiveness ranking was based on the GCI reported until 2019. In 2020, Global Competitiveness Report did not include GCI ranking due to disruptions in the global economy caused by the COVID-19 pandemic and after 2020 the Global Competitiveness Report was also discontinued. The GCI evaluated countries based on more than 100 indicators (methodology changed several times during the period described in this chapter) sorted into 12 pillars. The development of the ranking of Slovakia and other Visegrad Group Member States is illustrated in Fig. 3.1.

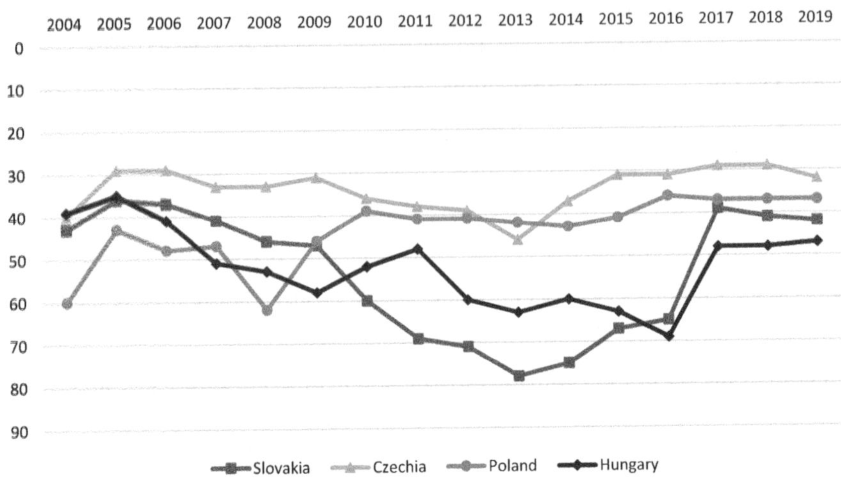

Fig. 3.1. Global Competitiveness Index Ranking. *Source:* Author's own elaboration based on World Bank Group (2017) and World Bank Group (2019).

Between the 2016 and 2017 rankings, the methodology of the GCI changed and became more based on hard data than soft data (Olczyk et al., 2022). This change improved the ranking of all Visegrad Group countries, most significantly Slovakia and Hungary.

Slovak competitiveness diverged from the development in other Visegrad Group countries since 2009 when the steep decline began. In 2013, Slovakia fell to 78th position globally, historically its worst ranking. In 2013, the most problematic aspects of Slovak competitiveness were indicators from first pillar – Institutions. Out of 146 countries included in the ranking, Slovakia ranked 144th in Favoritism in decisions of government officials, 143rd in Efficiency of the legal framework in settling disputes, and 139th in Public trust in politicians (Schwab & Sala-i-Martín, 2016). Business Alliance of Slovakia states that the main reasons behind this ranking in Slovakia are inefficient public institutions, low enforceability of law, bureaucracy, clientelism, unattractive tax system, low transparency and efficiency of public spending, growing state indebtedness, rigid labor code, and the low quality of the education system (Podnikateľská aliancia Slovenska, 2013). Since then, there have been improvements in almost all pillars in Slovakia and also in the overall position of Slovakia in GCI ranking from 78th to 65th position. The most problematic areas of Slovak competitiveness were still institutions and the labor market, where Slovakia ranked 102nd and 93rd, respectively (Knošková & Donovalová, 2017).

In the last ranking from 2019, Slovakia was the 42nd most competitive economy in the world with 67 points out of 100. The best pillar for Slovakia was

Macroeconomic stability, where it achieved first place with 32 other countries. The worst pillar for Slovakia was the Product market where Slovakia was 89th. Upon detailed analysis, we can see that there are five indicators where Slovakia is among the 10 worst performing countries in the world: Efficiency of the legal framework in challenging regulations (132nd), Ease of hiring foreign labor (133rd), Burden of government regulation (135th), Distortive effect of taxes and subsidies on competition (137th), and Labor tax rate (138th). On the other hand, there are some indicators where Slovakia is in the first (shared) position: Credit gap in the financial system, Workers' rights, Inflation, and Debt dynamics (Schwab, 2019).

The third indicator used to compare countries based on various competitiveness-related indicators was Doing Business, which the World Bank discontinued in 2021 (The World Bank, 2021) after the scandal where the staff of the World Bank claimed being pressured to boost the ranking of China (Shalal & Lawder, 2021). In 2021, the corrected ranking was published. Doing Business Report ranks countries based on 13 categories relevant to the business environment including labor market regulations, taxes, and administrative procedures for businesses. This ranking is more narrowly focused on benefits for businesses unlike World Competitiveness Ranking and GCI; therefore, the ranking might be quite different.

Based on available data (World Bank Group, 2024a) on rankings since 2010, we can see that the position of Slovakia in this ranking worsened almost every year (the only exception is 2016), although the overall score improved from 69.5 points in 2010 to 75.3 points in 2020. From the 33rd position in 2010, Slovakia fell to the 45th position. While in 2010 Slovakia was the best country for business in the Visegrad Group, in 2020, it fell to the third position behind the Czech Republic and Poland. Among current EU Member States, Slovakia fell from 14th place to 17th place.

The score of Slovakia worsened in some categories; however, this was caused by changes in methodology. It seems that while Slovakia improved its business environment, other countries improved it to a greater extent. The most problematic aspects of the Slovak business environment in 2020 were construction permits and starting a business (World Bank Group, 2020).

We can summarize that Slovak position in competitiveness rankings has been worsening in recent years globally and regionally. While Slovakia used to be a leader in some aspects within the Visegrad Group, currently it is last or second to last when it manages to surpass Hungary.

3.4 Sectors of Economy

The position of sectors of the economy in Slovakia is determined by Slovak economic history and current position as a developed economy and member of the European Union. In accordance with this, the service sector has the highest share in GDP and employment, followed by industry and agriculture. Slovakia also belongs among central European members of the EU for which a relatively higher share of industry is typical. Based on the latest data, the share of industry in total added value in Slovakia is 33.4%, which is the second highest share after Ireland (Zagoršeková, 2024). The industry also employs 31% of employees in Slovakia, the second highest share after the Czech Republic. Consequently, the share of services in added value and employment is relatively lower compared to other EU Member States of the EU average.

The importance of the agricultural sector in the Slovak economy, especially in employment, fell dramatically since 1989. Employment in the agricultural sector has fallen by 85% since then. However, since 1995 the share of agriculture in Slovak GDP has not changed significantly, as it was 2.6% in 1995 and 2.5% in 2022, which is slightly higher than the EU average (Eurostat, 2024d). Employees in this sector are also older than in other sectors, the average age is nearing 50 years. The aging of farmers is a problem in the EU as a whole, but the proportion of farmers over 50 years is higher in Slovakia than in the EU (Drapáková & Koreň, 2020). Based on Global Food Security Index by the Economist Intelligence Unit that evaluates the agricultural and food sector based on four categories (Affordability, Availability, Quality and Safety, and Sustainability and Adaptation), Slovakia is in 36th place out of 113 countries and only Romania has worse position than Slovakia among the EU Member States (The Economist Group, 2022).

The Slovak industrial sector was indispensable in the period of rapid growth of the Slovak economy and its convergence with the rest of the EU. The attractiveness of the Slovak industry for foreign investors contributed to the fact that the industry has the same share in GDP as it had in 1995, while in similarly industry-oriented economies like the Czech Republic or Germany, the share of industry declined during this period. Slovak industry was attractive for foreign investors mainly due to low costs and this alone cannot sustain the competitiveness and ensure continuous growth in the future. Most FDI in Slovakia was not directed to research, development, or high-tech production, which is necessary for the future and should be increasingly covered by Slovak investment capacities (Ministerstvo hospodárstva SR, 2018).

The most important sector of the Slovak industry is automotive, with its significant share in production, employment, investment, and international trade. Based on the data from The European Automobile Manufacturers' Association, 16% of manufacturing jobs in Slovakia are in direct automotive manufacturing, which is the highest share in the EU (ACEA, 2023). In Slovakia, this means 77.5 thousand jobs. In 2022, Slovakia produced almost 1 million vehicles and is the fourth biggest producer of cars in the EU surpassing even France. According to SARIO (2023a) data, the automotive industry accounts for 50% of total industrial production in Slovakia and 11% of Slovak GDP. It employs 261 thousand people directly and indirectly. Slovakia remains the global leader in car production per capita with four major car producers and the fifth producer, Volvo, planning to start the production in 2026. Slovakia is also the country in the EU most specialized in the manufacture of motor vehicles, trailers, and semitrailers, as this sector contributes 17.9% of industrial value added. In the EU, the average share of this sector is 7.7% (Eurostat, 2023e, p. 37).

The service sector in Slovakia retained its share in GDP since 1995, which is circa 65.5%. However, the shares of different subsectors changed during this period with declines in financial and insurance activities and real estate activities and increases in information and communication and professional, scientific, and technical activities. Slovakia is interesting for investors in business services. Business Services Centers employ more than 40,000 people in Slovakia and the sector continues to grow (SARIO, 2023c). Another important service sector in Slovakia is ICT, where employment has grown by 58% since 2008 (SARIO, 2023b).

3.5 Government Finance

Despite a succession of crises in the global and European economy, Slovakia is usually not among the countries cited as the worst examples of government finance. Slovakia received loans from IMF in 1993 and 1994, but these have been repaid by 2000 (Národná banka Slovenska, 2000b). Since then, Slovakia joined the European Monetary Union and had to adhere to convergence criteria regarding government deficit and debt. Since independence, Slovakia never achieved a budget surplus, and the lowest budget deficits of 1% GDP were achieved in 2017 and 2018. Excluding the first years of independence when Slovakia underwent many economic reforms, the worst years for government budget results were the crisis years right after Slovakia joined the Eurozone in 2009 and the years of the global COVID-19 pandemic (Eurostat, 2023c).

Unlike the budget deficit, government debt was very low in the first years after independence and grew until 2001 (51.1% GDP). After 2001, the debt declined during the years of rapid economic growth and fell to 28.6% GDP in 2008. After the crisis in 2009, the development of Slovak debt varied and in 2021 it surpassed the 60% GDP level required by the Stability and Growth Pact. Despite negative developments in recent years, Slovak government debt remains well below the EU average.

Government finance data for 2023 and 2024 differ in predictions by the Slovak Ministry of Finance and the European Commission. Both institutions agree that in 2023 and 2024, Slovak government budget deficit will be over 6% of GDP and that in both years the government debt will remain below 60% of GDP (Európska komisia, 2024).

3.6 International Trade

Slovakia is a small open economy heavily dependent on international trade, mainly within the European Single Market. Slovak external trade amounts to 204% of its GDP, and Slovakia is the fourth most open economy in the EU after other small economies like Luxembourg, Malta, and Ireland (Zagoršeková, 2024). The size of the Slovak economy is a precondition for high levels of openness and since independence openness fell below 100% only once, in 1999. Since then, it has grown rapidly due to economic reforms and the subsequent interest of foreign investors. A similar development can be seen in data on other Visegrad Group Member States, however, on lower levels of openness, especially in Poland due to the size of its economy (World Bank Group, 2024c).

For external trade in goods, Slovakia depends on the EU more with its exports than imports (Eurostat, 2024h). While in 2022, Slovakia imported 76.8% from other EU Member States, 80.1% of its exports went to the EU market. These shares are among the highest in the EU, only three countries import higher shares from the EU and two countries export higher shares to the EU. Although the importance of EU-27 in Slovak external trade in goods fluctuated, its share never fell below 70% in imports and 78% in exports.

Slovak external trade is dominated by European Union Member States in general, but particularly important trade partners are Germany and Czechia, followed by Hungary and Poland. Based on the latest data, these four countries receive 46.29% of Slovak exports and Slovakia imports 51.01% of its imports from these four countries (The Growth Lab, 2024). In 2021, the fifth biggest importer to Slovakia was the Russian Federation with a 5.9% share in total imports. According to the detailed statistics of the Statistical Office of the Slovak Republic, the share of Russia in Slovak imports in 2022 grew to 7.3% with 94.1% of these imports being mineral fuels (DATACube, 2024). Preliminary data from 2023 show that imports from Russia fell to about 55% of the previous year's values and are still dominated by mineral fuels. In the period between January and October 2023, the share of Russia in imports to Slovakia was 4.07%. The importance of Russia as a market for Slovak exports is minimal, its share in 2023 was only 0.3%.

Despite strict sanctions against Russia and the import of Russian oil, Slovakia negotiated some exemptions and continues to import oil from Russia via the Druzhba pipeline. Slovak refinery Slovnaft, owned by Hungarian MOL, needs more time to adjust its technology to the processing of non-Russian oil, which currently covers 30% of its production. A similar exemption for the Czech Republic expired on December 5, 2023. However, in the 12th package of sanctions by the EU, Slovakia managed to negotiate a 1-year extension allowing Slovnaft to export fuels produced from Russian oil to the Czech Republic until December 5, 2024 (Reuters, 2023).

The most important exported (and imported) category in Slovakia is SITC7 – machinery and transport equipment, which includes vehicles, and products of the most important industry in Slovakia – the automotive industry. In 2022, SITC7 category had a 57.6% share in Slovak exports of goods, which is the highest value in the European Union, before Czechia and Hungary with over 50% shares (Eurostat, 2024h). This shows the similarity in the importance of the automotive industry in the overall Central European region. On the other hand, Slovakia has the lowest share within the EU of chemicals in its exports, only 4.8%. The second most important exported category from Slovakia is other manufactured goods with 25.7%. The share of other export categories is below 10%. The same two categories are also the most important in Slovak imports of goods. In imports, another relatively important category is mineral fuels, lubricants, and related materials with an 11.8% share, followed by chemicals and related products with an 8.5% share.

The importance of the SITC7 category in Slovak exports grew significantly over the last 20 years. In 2002, its share was 39.6%, lower than the share of Other manufactured goods. Since then, it has grown steadily and reached its peak in 2020 with a 64% share in exports as its share grew at the expense of Other manufactured goods.

The trade balance of Slovakia in trade with goods since 2002 was very volatile and underwent significant changes in trends. After a long period of negative trade balance since independence, in 2009, Slovakia reached a positive trade balance for 1 year. Between 2012 and 2018, the positive trade balance seemed like a new normal for Slovak external trade, but it changed again to significant year-by-year fluctuations. In 2022, Slovak negative trade balance reached its 20-year maximum at 3849.5 million EUR. Despite the growth of exports, the negative balance was caused by the increase in prices of imported mineral fuels and the trade balance of almost all EU Member States worsened compared to 2021 (FinReport, 2023).

While external trade with goods shapes the Slovak economy, external trade with services lags (Eurostat, 2024g). Slovakia is the fifth smallest exporter of services in the European Union, the position far behind the importance of its overall economy. Slovak exports of services are growing and the trade balance in trade with services remains positive.

4. Conclusion

Based on the comprehensive examination of Slovakia's development since its independence, focusing on demographic challenges, economic transformation, and integration into the global economy, we drew several conclusions. Slovakia's journey postindependence illustrates the challenges and opportunities faced by transitional economies in integrating with the global and European markets, however, Slovak economic development is unique even within the region of Visegrad Group countries. With series of important reforms and political changes, Slovakia managed to start the process of convergence to the EU average economic level. However, after several successful years, the process was reversed, and Slovakia is again among the poorest countries of the European Union Member States despite spurred economic growth and improved living standards.

There are still challenges hindering further development that we identified in this chapter. While advancements in tertiary education and a decrease in youth unemployment align with EU goals, challenges in educational outcomes and long-term unemployment underscore the need for continued reform and investment in human capital. Slovakia's reliance on automotive industry and the need for diversification and innovation in the face of global economic shifts underscore the importance of evolving economic policies to ensure sustainable growth. Slovak development trajectory can therefore serve as an example of successful transformation and economic integration, but also as a reminder of the need for continuous adaptation in the rapidly changing global economy.

References

ACEA. (2023). *The automobile industry pocket guide 2023/2024.* https://www.acea.auto/files/ACEA-Pocket-Guide-2023-2024.pdf

Beňušová, L. (2023, July 26). *Prečo odchádzajú slovenskí študenti na vysoké školy do Česka?* Vysoké školy. https://www.vysokeskoly.sk/clanok/preco-odchadzaju-slovenski-studenti-na-vysoke-skoly-do-ceska

Boussemart, J.-M., & Godet, M. (2018). *Europe 2050: Demographic suicide (n. 462).* Fondation Robert Schuman. https://server.www.robert-schuman.eu/storage/en/doc/questions-d-europe/qe-462-en.pdf

Brucháčová, A. (2000). *Comparation of the economic and monetary development of Slovakia, the Czech Republic, Hungary, Poland and Slovenia.* Institute of Monetary and Financial Studies of the NBS. https://nbs.sk/_img/documents/publik/2000_comparation%20of%20the%20economic%20and%20monetary.pdf

Conceição, P. (2022). *Human development report 2021–22: Uncertain times, unsettled lives: Shaping our future in a transforming world.* https://hdr.undp.org/system/files/documents/global-report-document/hdr2021-22reportenglish_0.pdf

Council resolution on a strategic framework for European cooperation in education and training towards the European Education Area and beyond (2021–2030) 2021/C 66/01. (2021). *Official Journal of the European Union, C 66*, 1–21.

DATACube. (2024). *Zahraničný obchod s vybranými krajinami podľa tried nomenklatúry SITC Rev. 4.* [Data set]. Štatistický úrad SR. https://datacube.statistics.sk/#!/view/sk/VBD_INTERN/zo0018ms/v_zo0018ms_00_00_00_sk

Dedinský, M. (2022, December 30). 30 rokov po: V Česku pracuje rekordný počet Slovákov, Čechov to k nám za prácou neťahá. *Aktuality.* https://www.aktuality.sk/clanok/a8dTrAz/30-rokov-po-v-cesku-pracuje-rekordny-pocet-slovakov-cechov-to-k-nam-za-pracou-netaha/

Drapáková, D., & Koreň, M. (2020, July 13). Slovenské poľnohospodárstvo sa vyľudňuje rýchlejšie ako vo zvyšku EÚ. *Euractiv.* https://euractiv.sk/section/ekonomika-a-euro/infographic/slovenske-polnohospodarstvo-sa-vyludnuje-rychlejsie-ako-vo-zvysku-eu/

Dudáš, T. (2013). Vplyv prílevu priamych zahraničných investícií na nezamestnanosť na Slovensku. *Medzinárodné vzťahy, 11*(1), 22–32.

Dujava, D., & Žúdel, B. (2023). *On purchasing parity.* Inštitút finančnej politiky, MF SR. https://www.mfsr.sk/files/archiv/14/ppp_web_EN.pdf

Ďurček, P., Šprocha, B., & Bleha, B. (2019). Populačná dynamika. In D. Gurňák et al. (Eds.), *30 rokov transformácie Slovenska* (pp. 84–113). Vydavateľstvo.

European Central Bank. (2023). *HICP – Indices, breakdown by purpose of consumption: December 2023.* https://www.ecb.europa.eu/stats/ecb_statistics/escb/html/table.en.html?id=JDF_ICP_COICOP_INX

Európska komisia. (2024, January 16). *Stanovisko Komisie z 16. 1. 2024 k návrhu rozpočtového plánu Slovenska.* C(2024) 343 final. https://economy-finance.ec.europa.eu/document/download/92121c21-aed7-4183-943f-76dbe20122d1_sk?filename=C_2024_343_1_SK_ACT.pdf

Eurostat. (2023a). *Employment and activity by sex and age – Annual data.* https://ec.europa.eu/eurostat/databrowser/view/LFSI_EMP_A__custom_2883233/bookmark/table?lang=en&bookmarkId=ce403f20-69c2-4071-9c70-b0a22d9283d9

Eurostat. (2023b). *Fertility indicators.* https://ec.europa.eu/eurostat/databrowser/view/DEMO_FIND__custom_2453892/bookmark/table?lang=en&bookmarkId=213cadfc-3a95-483e-bd77-5de1c3a756ab

Eurostat. (2023c). *Government deficit/surplus, debt and associated data.* https://ec.europa.eu/eurostat/databrowser/view/GOV_10DD_EDPT1__custom_2523873/bookmark/table?lang=en&bookmarkId=1b8a9e10-03aa-4947-925d-b95e4026f0b5

Eurostat. (2023d). *Key figures on Europe: 2023 edition.* European Commission. https://ec.europa.eu/eurostat/documents/15216629/17706595/KS-EI-23-001-EN-N.pdf/5df7a393-8461-9270-7eaa-91a4b1c2acc6?version=3.0&t=1697616189434

Eurostat. (2023e). *Key figures on European business: 2023 edition.* European Commission. https://ec.europa.eu/eurostat/documents/15216629/16825859/KS-04-23-195-EN-N.pdf/3f72cb73-0ba3-bcfe-0a2f-7bbc03ea5361?version=2.0&t=1685428985626

Eurostat. (2023f). *Long-term unemployment (12 months and more) by sex, age, educational attainment level and NUTS 2 regions (%).* https://ec.europa.eu/eurostat/databrowser/view/lfst_r_lfu2ltu/default/table?lang=en

Eurostat. (2023g). *Population by educational attainment level, sex and age (%).* https://ec.europa.eu/eurostat/databrowser/view/edat_lfs_9903/default/table?lang=en

Eurostat. (2023h). *Population change – Demographic balance and crude rates at national level.* https://ec.europa.eu/eurostat/databrowser/view/DEMO_GIND__custom_3073107/bookmark/table?lang=en&bookmarkId=a996e8aa-0aea-49ae-a3c0-083a1369476b

Eurostat. (2023i). *Unemployment by sex, age and educational attainment – Annual data.* https://ec.europa.eu/eurostat/databrowser/view/une_educ_a/default/table?lang=en

Eurostat. (2023j). *Young people neither in employment nor in education and training by sex, age and labour status (NEET rates).* https://ec.europa.eu/eurostat/databrowser/view/EDAT_LFSE_20__custom_2454629/bookmark/table?lang=en&bookmarkId=a16b142a-938a-4528-8dd0-5e6e73520189

Eurostat. (2024a). *Beneficiaries of temporary protection at the end of the month by citizenship, age and sex – Monthly data.* https://ec.europa.eu/eurostat/databrowser/view/MIGR_ASYTPSM__custom_5996564/bookmark/table?lang=en&bookmarkId=c1c734bb-fa84-49d0-a163-7b5d911990d6

Eurostat. (2024b). *GDP and main aggregates – International data cooperation annual data.* https://ec.europa.eu/eurostat/databrowser/view/NAIDA_10_GDP__custom_2524606/bookmark/table?lang=en&bookmarkId=37ee036f-b035-4c99-adb8-05b26dc18569

Eurostat. (2024c). *GDP and main components (output, expenditure and income).* https://ec.europa.eu/eurostat/databrowser/view/NAMA_10_GDP__custom_2523828/bookmark/table?lang=en&bookmarkId=1a92af2f-d64d-402a-a623-d0b045d60397

Eurostat. (2024d). *Gross value added and income by A*10 industry breakdowns.* https://ec.europa.eu/eurostat/databrowser/view/NAMA_10_A10__custom_2523951/bookmark/table?lang=en&bookmarkId=28346bb0-c092-44ef-8427-b6d432ab7554

Eurostat. (2024e). *HICP – Annual data (average index and rate of change).* https://ec.europa.eu/eurostat/databrowser/view/PRC_HICP_AIND__custom_2523854/bookmark/table?lang=en&bookmarkId=61da8b4e-0479-4d94-a3be-bcabfda224aa

Eurostat. (2024f). *HICP – Item weights*. https://ec.europa.eu/eurostat/databrowser/view/PRC_HICP_INW__custom_2523858/bookmark/table?lang=en&bookmarkId=f30337fc-6fd2-41dc-86ef-18d3fdd54952
Eurostat. (2024g). *International trade in services (since 2010) (BPM6)*. https://ec.europa.eu/eurostat/databrowser/view/BOP_ITS6_DET__custom_2523930/bookmark/table?lang=en&bookmarkId=a4a28900-a7aa-4ed2-91d1-d0bbefceaa02
Eurostat. (2024h). *Intra and extra-EU trade by member state and by product group*. https://ec.europa.eu/eurostat/databrowser/view/EXT_LT_INTRATRD__custom_2523915/bookmark/table?lang=en&bookmarkId=78829166-885c-47b1-a0f6-94546adb03fe
Eurostat. (2024i). *Main GDP aggregates per capita*. https://ec.europa.eu/eurostat/databrowser/view/NAMA_10_PC__custom_2523843/bookmark/table?lang=en&bookmarkId=4a6b307b-10eb-4b37-82cd-9e5f402137ec
Eurostat. (2024j). *Population on 1 January by age group, sex and citizenship*. https://ec.europa.eu/eurostat/databrowser/view/MIGR_POP1CTZ__custom_2565787/bookmark/table?lang=en&bookmarkId=add9abbe-41fc-4d98-b5cf-fbd255eea3ca
Eurostat. (2024k). *Population projections*. https://ec.europa.eu/eurostat/web/population-demography/population-projections/database
Eurostat. (2024l). *Population structure indicators at national level*. https://ec.europa.eu/eurostat/databrowser/view/DEMO_PJANIND__custom_2453944/bookmark/table?lang=en&bookmarkId=2a8747cf-18e7-41b0-9e85-ef2e4aaa7cde
FinReport. (2023, February 8). Deficit zahraničného obchodu Slovenska dosiahol rekordných 4,3 miliardy eur. *FinReport*. https://www.finreport.sk/ekonomika/deficit-zahranicneho-obchodu-slovenska-v-roku-2022-dosiahol-rekordnych-4-3-miliardy-eur/
Haluška, J., & Dolinič, J. (2018). Makroekonomická výkonnosť slovenskej ekonomiky v rokoch 1995–2017. *Slovenská štatistika a demografia*, *28*(3), 57–76.
IMD. (2023a). *IMD world competitiveness booklet 2023*. https://imd.cld.bz/IMD-World-Competitiveness-Booklet-2023/2/
IMD. (2023b). *IMD world digital competitiveness ranking 2023*. https://www.imd.org/centers/wcc/world-competitiveness-center/rankings/world-digital-competitiveness-ranking/
Knošková, Ľ., & Donovalová, A. (2017). Hodnotenie vývoja konkurencieschopnosti Slovenskej republiky v rokoch 2014 až 2016. *Studia commercialia Bratislavensia*, *10*(37), 54–65.
Krugman, P. (1996). Making sense of the competitiveness debate. *Oxford Review of Economic Policy*, *12*(3), 17–25. https://doi.org/10.1093/oxrep/12.3.17
Miklovičová, J., & Galádová, A. (2023). *Správa o realizácii medzinárodnej štúdie PISA 2022 a prvé výsledky za SR*. Národný inštitút vzdelávania a mládeže. https://www2.nucem.sk/dl/5715/PISA_2022_Kratka_sprava_SVK.pdf
Ministerstvo hospodárstva SR. (2018). *Priemyselná výroba a jej postavenie v hospodárstve SR*. https://www.economy.gov.sk/uploads/files/ezNh8gXF.pdf
Morvay, K., Frank, K., Hudcovský, M., Hvozdíková, V., Jeck, T., & Šikulová, I. (2019). *Hospodársky vývoj Slovenska v roku 2015 a výhľad do roku 2017*. VEDA.
Národná banka Slovenska. (2000a). *Annual Report 1999*. https://nbs.sk/_img/documents/_publikacie/annualreport/arnbs99.pdf
Národná banka Slovenska. (2000b). *Splatenie pôžičky od MMF*. https://nbs.sk/historia/splatenie-pozicky-od-mmf/

Neal, L. (2007). *The economics of Europe and the European union*. Cambridge University Press.

OECD. (2023a). *OECD skills surveys*. https://pisadataexplorer.oecd.org/ide/idepisa/dataset.aspx

OECD. (2023b). *PISA 2022 results (Volume I): The state of learning and equity in education*. PISA, OECD Publishing. https://doi.org/10.1787/53f23881-en

Olczyk, M., Kuc-Czarnecka, M., & Saltelli, A. (2022). Changes in the global competitiveness Index 4.0 methodology: The improved approach of competitiveness benchmarking. *Journal of Competitiveness*, *14*(1), 118–135. https://doi.org/10.7441/joc.2022.01.07

Plutzer, V., Šilan, J., & Hojdan, D. (2022, June). *How did high inflation come about?* Inštitút finančnej politiky, MF SR. https://www.mfsr.sk/files/archiv/47/Policy_brief_Inflation_2022.pdf

Podnikateľská aliancia Slovenska. (2013). *SR v rebríčku konkurencieschopnosti padla na 78. miesto*. https://www.alianciapas.sk/sr-v-rebricku-konkurencieschopnosti-padla-na-78-miesto/

Reuters. (2023, December 19). Slovakia wins EU OK on Russian oil-based products sales to Czech Republic. *Reuters*. https://www.reuters.com/business/energy/slovakia-wins-eu-ok-russian-oil-based-products-sales-czech-republic-2023-12-19/

Rievajová, E. (2009). Trh práce a očakávané zmeny v kontexte procesu globalizácie. In V. Páleník (Ed.), *Ekonómia trhu práce a jej implikácie pre Slovensko: Zborník príspevkov z vedeckej konferencie* (pp. 77–88). Inštitút zamestnanosti.

SARIO. (2023a). *Automotive sector in Slovakia*. https://www.sario.sk/sites/default/files/2023-10/sario-automotive-sector-in-slovakia-2023-10-26.pdf

SARIO. (2023b). *Information & communications technology sector in Slovakia*. https://www.sario.sk/sites/default/files/sario-ict-sector-in-slovakia-2024-01-19.pdf

SARIO. (2023c). *Shared service & business process outsourcing centers in Slovakia*. https://www.sario.sk/sites/default/files/sario-ssc-2024-01-15.pdf

Schwab, K. (2019). *The global competitiveness repot 2019*. World Economic Forum.

Schwab, K., & Sala-i-Martín, X. (2016). *The global competitiveness report 2013–2014: Full data edition*. World Economic Forum.

Schwarz, K. (2023). *Cohesion fund*. European Parliament. https://www.europarl.europa.eu/factsheets/en/sheet/96/el-fondo-de-cohesion

Shalal, A., & Lawder, D. (2021, September 17). IMF chief called out over pressure to favor China while at World Bank. *Reuters*. https://www.reuters.com/business/sustainable-business/world-bank-kills-business-climate-report-after-ethics-probe-cites-undue-pressure-2021-09-16/

TASR. (2007, July 31). ÚPSVaR: Najvyššia miera nezamestnanosti SR v EÚ je kvôli inej metodike merania. *Sme Index*. https://index.sme.sk/c/3419182/upsvar-najvyssia-miera-nezamestnanosti-sr-v-eu-je-kvoli-inej-metodike-merania.html

The Economist Group. (2022). *Global food security index 2022*. https://impact.economist.com/sustainability/project/food-security-index/reports/Economist_Impact_GFSI_2022_Global_Report_Sep_2022.pdf

The Growth Lab. (2024). *Slovakia*. Harvard University. https://atlas.cid.harvard.edu/countries/206

The World Bank. (2021). *World Bank group to discontinue doing business report*. https://www.worldbank.org/en/news/statement/2021/09/16/world-bank-group-to-discontinue-doing-business-report

UN. (2022). *World population prospects: The 2022 revision*. https://population.un.org/dataportal/data/indicators/70/locations/900/start/1990/end/2023/table/pivotbyage?df=d5bf0f3e-1f4c-4aaf-aa59-78ca99c17018

Veselková, M., & Hábel, B. (2023). *Pracovným migrantom z Ukrajiny sa na Slovensku darí lepšie ako odídencom*. Inštitút sociálnej politiky, MPSVaR SR. https://institutsocialnejpolitiky.sk/wp-content/uploads/2023/09/Veselkova_Habel_2023_Pracovnym_migrantom_z_UA_sa_na_SK_dari_lepsie_ako_odidencom-1.pdf

World Bank Group. (2017). *Global competitiveness index*. https://govdata360.worldbank.org/indicators/h93b3b7a4?country=SVK&indicator=632&countries=CZE,POL,HUN&viz=line_chart&years=2007,2017

World Bank Group. (2019). *GCI 4.0: Global competitiveness Index 4.0*. https://govdata360.worldbank.org/indicators/ha03bec65?country=SVK&indicator=41472&countries=CZE,POL,HUN&viz=line_chart&years=2017,2019

World Bank Group. (2020). *Doing business 2020: Economy profile Slovak republic*. https://archive.doingbusiness.org/content/dam/doingBusiness/country/s/slovakia/SVK.pdf

World Bank Group. (2024a). *Doing business data*. Doing Business Archive. https://archive.doingbusiness.org/en/data

World Bank Group. (2024b). *GNI per capita, Atlas method (current US$)*. https://data.worldbank.org/indicator/NY.GNP.PCAP.CD?most_recent_value_desc=true

World Bank Group. (2024c). *Trade (% of GDP) – Slovak Republic, Czechia, Hungary, Poland*. https://data.worldbank.org/indicator/NE.TRD.GNFS.ZS?locations=SK-CZ-HU-PL&utm_source=twitter.com%2Fthewebvy

Zagoršeková, N. (2024). *Ekonomika štátov Európskej únie*. Vydavateľstvo EKONÓM.

Chapter 4

Critical Perspectives to Growth-Based Approach as Policy Goal and Dominant Measure of Policy Performance in Slovakia

Jakub Csabay

Comenius University, Slovak Republic and University of Cambridge, UK

Abstract

The aim of this chapter is to combine a number of critical approaches to economic growth as the dominant policy framework and measure of performance in Slovakia. The dominant policy discourse in Slovakia continues to perceive economic growth, GDP per capita as well as the other economic indicators as the primary measures not only of economic performance but also of public policy and standards of living. Recognizing that as important as they are, they remain measures and means rather than outcomes and goals, it will explore more human welfare-centered and environmentally considerate measures in the context of Slovakia, arguing that both scholars and policymakers need to go beyond the national level of analysis and traditional quantitative methodologies. From a human and welfare perspective, the chapter will look at the Human Development Index (HDI) in Slovakia as an example of an indicator to study the quality of life. It will also problematize more broadly whether focus on growth in the context of climate change-related challenges and the EU Green Deal is still a viable and the most appropriate measure to follow, and to what extent sustainability has been sufficiently integrated and used in Slovakia, in this regard. The chapter will also offer concrete areas where insights from the critical perspectives might be most relevant in the context of Slovakia.

Keywords: Slovakia; economic growth; critical approaches; sustainable development; human development; degrowth; postgrowth; green growth; doughnut economics; public policy

Modeling Economic Growth in Contemporary Slovakia, 71–83

doi:10.1108/978-1-83549-454-720241005

1. Introduction

"People in Slovakia consider the public finance deficit and economic inequalities to be the country's greatest challenges shortly before elections," said one of the news reports on public opinions before the national elections in September 2023 (Kern & Hrivňák, 2023). While the public finance deficit and economic inequalities scored 35% and 31%, respectively, climate change was, together with racism, considered a major problem only by 5% of respondents in this survey (Tomek, 2023). As true and unbelievable some of these outcomes may be, making one think who the responsible deficit considerate respondents are, the outcomes for climate change and economic inequalities are perhaps not the most surprising ones. However, the important message here is that framings and measurements show relative importance of different policy areas not only in public discourse, be it media or political, before the elections but also in the policy design and subsequent implementation itself.

In comparison with other contributions in this volume, this chapter will take a more critical and potentially dissenting perspective to the overall framing of the volume that is focused on economic growth and its modeling in Slovakia. Without undermining their value, this chapter will open a question of whether economic growth should be still perceived as the main policy goal and measurement of policy performance in Slovakia, and to what extent the policy debate has been or rather should be shifting to more human well-being and sustainability-centered domains, which had previously been and to some extent still are considered merely the factors of growth. Such a discussion is relevant not only in the context of the UN Sustainable Development Goals but more recently in relation to the European Green Deal and the Fit for 55 initiatives, which provide a framework for the European Union (EU)green transition (European Council, 2024), thus unavoidably having a policy impact on Slovakia.

The first part of the chapter will discuss and provide an overview of the different variations and perspectives that are critical to the growth dominated policy framing in international literature, including degrowth, postgrowth, green growth, and doughnut economics. The subsequent parts will contextualize the debate to Slovakia. It will use them as a framework to analyze the policy framings and measurements to see where Slovakia stands in these debates in the country's key strategic documents, notably the Program Slovakia 2021–2027, the Recovery and Resilience Plan, and the Program Statements of the Governments 2020–2023 and 2023–2027. The chapter will then present how Slovakia performs in terms of more human-centered and sustainability-focused indicators. It will also provide a brief reality check discussion, while highlighting some of the main challenges as well as opportunities for application of the critical approaches in policy framing and measurement in the context of Slovakia: (1) focus on impact rather than spending in the EU financial instruments; (2) subnational levels of analysis are vital for accurate picture and informed policy design; (3) special attention needs to be paid to the conditions of marginalized communities who often live in informal settings; (4) overcoming disciplinary boundaries in the expert community.

2. The Critiques to Growth as a Policy Goal

The critiques to growth-based policy models are not new to the academic or policy debates, but given the limited scope of this chapter, it will not dive into Malthusian or other historical debates of that sort. Instead, this chapter will look into more recent critical perspectives, drawing from categorization used in the European Environment Agency's (2023) briefing that groups them in the following way: degrowth, postgrowth, green growth, and doughnut economics. All critical of the current modus operandi of the economy, they each take slightly different perspectives in their respective focus, with their calls for a radical change stretching across a large spectrum.

First, highly critical of modern capitalism, the degrowth academic and policy approach originated in early 1970s, with two notable publications coming to the world, *The Club of Rome's The Limits to Growth* (Meadows et al., 1972) and Georgescu-Roegen's (1971) *the Entropy Law and the Economic Process*. While diverting, respectively, on the topic of zero growth versus declining growth policy recommendation among other matters, they both agreed on the fact that the system of economy based on continuously increasing production and consumption produces severely negative environmental impacts. At the same time, it does not necessarily lead to improvement of the quality of life of society, which should be the primary policy goal rather than the economic growth itself (Georgescu-Roegen, 1971; Meadows et al., 1972). Hickel's (2020) *Less is More* constitutes a more contemporary account of this critical approach.

Second, the postgrowth approach is coming from a slightly less critical standpoint and offers somehow less radical and more flexible policy implications in comparison with the degrowth perspective. Recognizing limited availability of natural resources as well as the impact of their extraction, it acknowledges benefits that economic growth can offer to improvement of the quality of life yet argues that these are limited at a certain point and alternative pathways need to be sought. A seminal publication, in this regard, is Jackson's (2009) report for the Sustainable Development Commission, *Prosperity without Growth?* which defined prosperity as the key goal and proposed steps toward a sustainable economy. The important difference with the degrowth critique is that the postgrowth approach does not have a single policy pathway, but instead provides guiding principles and argues that solutions need to be context specific (Jackson, 2009).

Thirdly, the green growth approach may be considered the least critical to the mainstream economic growth perspective. As such, it does not really question the underlying notion of the current mode of production and consumption, but rather suggests that the market should move to greener solutions (OECD, 2011). These should come about from increased investments in green technologies and innovations as the new market for growth, which should go hand in hand with more responsible use of natural resources and support for distributional policies and reduction of poverty (OECD, 2011). While remaining largely abstract in the macroperspective in the proposed policy pathways (OECD, 2011), it has been advocated for by a number of international organizations, including the

Organization for Economic Cooperation in Europe, the World Bank, and the United Nations Environmental Program (Green Growth Knowledge Platform, 2012).

Last but not least, doughnut economics has constituted the most recent critique of growth-based policies. Originating in Kate Raworth's Oxfam paper in 2012 (Raworth, 2012), the author has subsequently developed her ideas further and offers a way to rethink and restructure the system of the economy, which is visualized through a culinary approachable doughnut form. Placeable somewhere in between the degrowth and postgrowth notions and ignoring the growth as the main focus altogether, Raworth's doughnut economics concentrates on the balance between basic needs and environmental limitations (Raworth, 2012). While the center represents the proportion of people lacking basic conditions for quality of life, the outer line represents the environmental boundary in terms of available resources that cannot be overused (Raworth, 2012). According to this logic, a successful economy fulfills all the inner conditions without falling outside of the outer boundary (Raworth, 2012).

The above constitute, in their own right, idealistic critiques and proposed alternatives to the growth-based model of the economy, with none realistically constituting a single bullet solution. They all have their limitations and barriers to practical application as well as respective political barriers, which will be partly explored in the context of Slovakia in the latter part of this chapter; for the purposes herein, they offer a critical lens in the form of an alternative analytical and policy framework to understand the context of policy developments in Slovakia.

3. Strategic Documents and Policy Framings in Slovakia: Confusion Between Means and Goals?

This part will analyze Slovakia's policy framings and measurements in terms of growth versus its alternatives using the country's key strategic documents. It will focus on the documents that provide the overall policy framework and carry most recent relevance (as of February 2024), specifically the Program Slovakia 2021–2027, the Recovery and Resilience Plan, and the Program Statements of the Governments 2020–2023 and 2023–2027. While the former two constitute the largest sources of public investment in the country (financed from the European Union), the latter two represent outlines of policy goals as perceived by the two most recently elected national governments coming from different ends of the political spectrum. In other words, the previous opposition is the current government. The chapter will not dive into the details of political reshuffling in the government between 2022 and 2023 or the temporary caretaker government in 2023 as it does not deem it relevant for the overall picture. It will neither explore older policy frameworks given the fact that some of the critical approaches are relatively recent, and as unfortunate as it may sound, the notions of sustainable development and environmental and social dimensions were not considered a priority until relatively recently.

Both Program Slovakia 2021–2027 and the Recovery and Resilience Plan constitute documents which were negotiated between the EU and national institutions, and as such they incorporate EU level and national priorities. In terms of the above frameworks, they can be placed somewhere in between the traditional economic growth approach, combined particularly with the green growth and to a lesser degree postgrowth perspective. With its overall allocation of more than 6 billion Euros in Slovakia, the Recovery and Resilience Plan was designed to respond to pandemic and divided in between six components defining the relevant priority areas: (1) green economy; (2) quality education; (3) science, research, innovations; (4) better health; (5) effective public services and digitalization; (6) REPowerEU focused on energy transformation (Office of the Government of the Slovak Republic, 2023). While highlighting that 37% of the investment is directed toward green policies and innovations (Office of the Government of the Slovak Republic, 2021), which is very much the focus of the components 1 and 5, it also mentions considerations for the needs of the disadvantaged groups across the different components (Office of the Government of the Slovak Republic, 2021). Therefore, this approach largely corresponds with the green growth perspective as the overall narrative of the Plan and its different components, such as education, green economy investments and innovations, are aimed at restarting economic growth, although through a more climate sensitive and energy effective production and consumption. The economic growth, remaining at the very core of the document, should then lead to and not be achieved at the expense of other aspects of the quality of life and lead to achieving the EU goal of carbon neutrality by 2050 (Office of the Government of the Slovak Republic, 2021). This places the plan outside of the degrowth and doughnut economics framing.

Unlike the Recovery and Resilience Plan, which is as described above aimed at strengthening economic growth in its very essence, the Program Slovakia 2021–2027 with a total allocation of more than 12 billion is leaning closer to the post-growth approach yet still abiding to the green growth notion. While not denying the growth as such, the core priority targets carry stronger well-being and environmentally considerate focus as the primary expected outcomes: (1) smart and competitive Europe; (2) greener low-carbon Europe; (3) more connected Europe; (4) more socially inclusive Europe delivering the European pillar of social rights; (5) Europe closer to its citizens; (6) Just Transition Fund (MIRRI, 2022). Even though growth is mentioned and highlighted as one of the key priorities (MIRRI, 2022), it is nuanced within the framework of the climate neutral and circular economy based on smart specialization and innovations. The core aspects of the Program (priority target 4) focus on achieving concrete goals for improved socioeconomic conditions of quality of life even for the most disadvantaged groups, for instance, in terms of access to education and the labor market (MIRRI, 2022), as well as improving biodiversity and reducing environmental impacts (priority targets 2 and 6), even energy consumption (MIRRI, 2022). Overall, these assessments are coherent with primary purposes of these instruments. While the Recovery and Resilience Plan is meant to deliver postpandemic economic reawakening, the EU structural funds programs have historically served as more redistributive and mitigating mechanisms.

How about the Program Statements of the Governments in 2020–2023 and 2023–2027? One can argue that these equally reflect their authors and the context they were written in, but neither would effectively fit within any of the critical frameworks. Although they are both narrative-based political pamphlets that do not include specific targets in contrast to the previous documents, they remain heavily grounded in a growth-based policy approach. The former was authored at the start of the pandemic and hence one can identify strong overlaps with the documents discussed above. However, the economic growth, or rather supporting measures for this policy goal, possess a much more important position across different chapters of the Program (National Council of the Slovak Republic, 2021), yet with a considerable attention paid to climate mitigation measures and environmental considerations as well as improvement of socioeconomic conditions (National Council of the Slovak Republic, 2021). In the case of the more recent document, economic growth retains its core policy priority across the different thematic chapters (National Council of the Slovak Republic, 2023). At the same time, the Program emphasizes the priority of improving the social and economic conditions but contrary to other documents, it directly expresses a critical stance toward EU climate targets if they were to be harmful to economic performance and the quality of life (National Council of the Slovak Republic, 2023).

To sum up, the brief analysis of the key strategic documents has shown that economic growth remains an essential policy maxim in Slovakia with a very limited presence of the critical approaches, especially in the Program Statements of the Governments. The critical approaches can be observed to a certain extent in the EU negotiated financial instruments, the Recovery and Resilience Plan and the Program Slovakia 2021–2027, containing green growth and to a lesser degree postgrowth elements. However, even in their case the narrative is predominantly set in a way that economic growth is a policy goal rather than a mean to deliver the improvement of the quality of life and the environmental conditions. The academic and policy scholarship has by now reached a consensus that the desired policy framing and outcome should go beyond economic growth as such, but the other question is what indicators we should then use to measure the performance of the policies instead of the economic growth. The following part will critically engage with this question in the context of Slovakia.

4. Measures of Development and Policy Performance in Slovakia: How to Move Toward Human Welfare and Sustainability Indicators?

It would be unfair to say that Slovakia only uses economic growth as a measurement of policy performance as the different documents discussed above do include a number of partial measurable targets for specific components (reduction of CO_2 emissions, air quality, participation in the labor market, performance in school, and others). However, economic growth does continue to be an overall target as well as a measure in these documents. In other words, if the economy is growing, policies are expected to be well-implemented and improve people's well-being. Is this necessarily true? Fig. 4.1 shows a continuous growth in Slovakia's PPP adjusted GDP per capita over the years, with a decline displaying only in the case of the 2008 financial crisis and the first pandemic year in 2020. In both cases, there was a subsequent return to a growing trend in the following years. This section will discuss how Slovakia performs using more complex indicators that would more closely align with some of the critical approaches. It will use UNDP's Human Development Index (HDI), including its subnational measures, as an example of human or welfare centered indicator as well as Planetary pressures-adjusted Human Development Index (PHDI) in order to consider the sustainability dimension.

Does the trend stand also in terms of the improvement of human welfare in Slovakia in terms of its HDI? The country's score as of 2021 is 0.848, which ranks Slovakia 45 out 191 and a "very high" category, but also behind most of the other EU countries (UNDP, 2022). HDI constitutes a composite measure entailing indicators for health (life expectancy), education (mean years of schooling and expected years of schooling), and income which is included in the form of GNI per capita rather than GDP (UNDP, 2022). As such it provides a more complex picture of the quality of life over time while allowing for comparison and covers some of the social dimensions and/or basic necessities included in the critical approaches. Figs. 4.1 and 4.2 (showcasing Slovakia's GDP and HDI progress) show very similar trends, with the noteworthy moments when the trends differed. While Slovakia's HDI continued to grow in the case of the 2008 financial crisis as the indicators for health and education continued to grow, the reverse can be

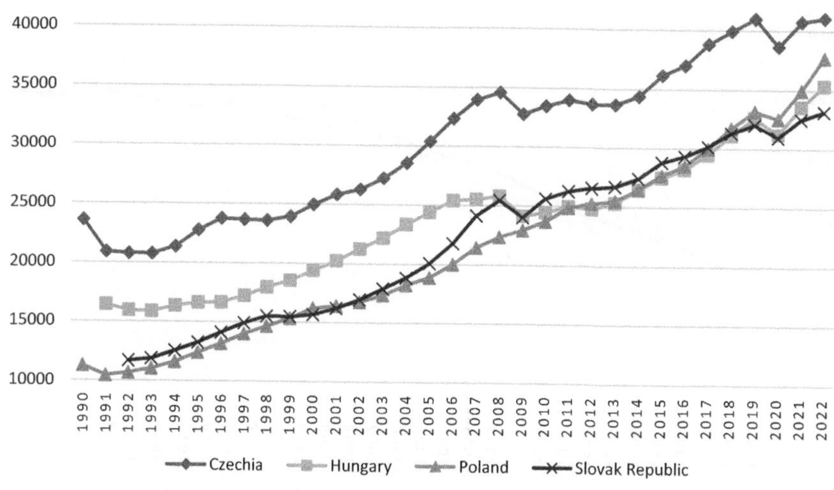

Fig. 4.1. PPP-Adjusted GDP per Capita of Slovakia and Other V4 Countries (Constant 2017 International $; 1990–2022). *Source:* World Bank (2022).

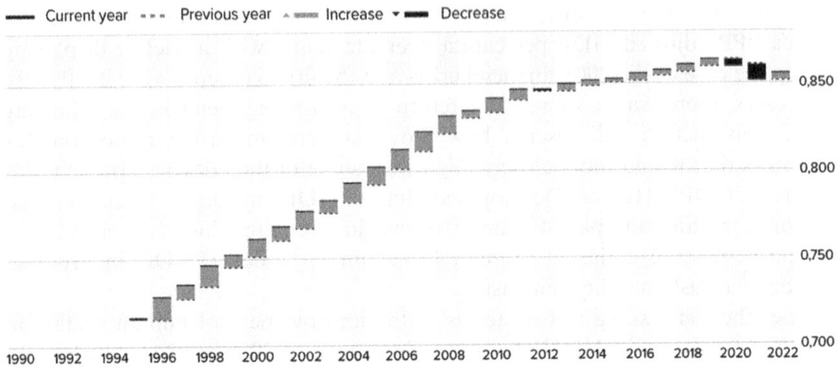

Fig. 4.2. Slovakia's HDI Trend (1990–2021). *Source:* UNDP (2022).

observed for the pandemic years of 2020 and 2021. Even though the economy was starting to grow again in 2021, the HDI continued to fall as a result of the falling life expectancy.

Even more unsurprising are the regional and subnational comparisons. Fig. 4.3 shows Slovakia's decline in its HDI toward Hungary's level. Although it still scores higher than its southern neighbor as of 2021 which is a contrasting trend to the GDP levels, Czech Republic and Poland are leading both HDI and GDP ranks. In terms of subnational levels, Table 4.1 demonstrates that HDI levels

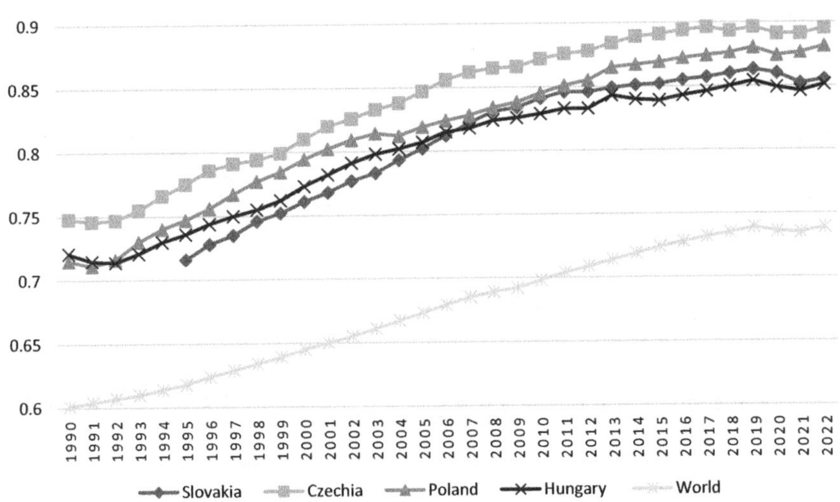

Fig. 4.3. HDI Trend of Slovakia and Other V4 Countries (1990–2021). *Source:* UNDP (2022).

Table 4.1. Slovakia's Subnational HDI per Region in 1990 and 2021.

Subnational HDI in Slovakia 1990; 2021		
Region/Year	**1990**	**2021**
Bratislava	0.818	0.944
Central Slovakia	0.710	0.827
Eastern Slovakia	0.694	0.811
Western Slovakia	0.720	0.839

Source: Global Data Lab (2022).

continued to grow for all regions in the last decades but considerable differences between Bratislava and other regions of the country remain, implying that on average people in the capital continue to live longer, earn more, and get better access to education, which is reflecting a long-lasting policy problem of regional disparities highlighted in all the documents described in the previous section. County, microregional or municipal levels might show even greater inequality, although such data is not currently available.

If the HDI is one of the ways how social dimension from the critical approaches can be measured, how shall sustainability be included in the formula in order to take into consideration the environmental dimension from the critical approaches? And how does Slovakia perform in this regard? This chapter uses the Planetary pressures-adjusted Human Development Index (PHDI). For the first time used in UNDP's Human Development Report 2020, it is a measure of "human development adjusted by carbon dioxide emissions per person (production-based) and material footprint per capita to account for the excessive human pressure on the planet" (UNDP, 2022). In other words, in a world where doughnut economics rationale is followed, HDI and PHDI would be equal. As Table 4.2 is showing, Slovakia scored 0.738 as of 2021 values, which places the country at the very end of the V4 behind Hungary. However, Slovakia is the only

Table 4.2. V4 Planetary Pressures-Adjusted Human Development Index in 2019 and 2021.

V4 Planetary Pressures-Adjusted HDI 2019; 2021		
Country/Year	**2019**	**2021**
Slovakia	0.720	0.738
Czech Republic	0.768	0.748
Hungary	0.781	0.755
Poland	0.752	0.753

Source: UNDP (2020) and UNDP (2022).

country showing notable improvement when compared with 2019 values (Table 4.2), while others either showed decline (Hungary and Czech Republic) or produced practically the same outcome (Poland). As this is a very recent indicator, there are no data available on pre-2019 PHDI; therefore, it is not possible to observe a longer trend similar to HDI.

Using the logic of the critical approaches, this brief analysis showed some diverting trends of how Slovakia performed beyond economic growth in terms of social well-being and sustainability as represented in the HDI and PHDI. The purpose was not to propose these two indicators as the ideal or ultimate measures but as available alternatives which could be easily integrated in Slovakia's relevant policy documents, yet so far remain absent. While there are many other composite or thematic indexes for quality of life and/or sustainability that may be even more elaborate, for example, OECD Better Life Index (OECD, 2020) or Environmental Performance Index (EPI, 2022), these are often collected on a periodical basis and the level of their elaboration and complexity might be at the expense of their applicability. Given the importance of applicability to the real world, critical approaches need not remain only in the theoretical realm as alternative policy frameworks or overlooked measures and indicators. The final part will reflect on some of these challenges in the context of Slovakia.

5. Conclusion and Final Remarks: Opportunities and Challenges for the Application of Critical Approaches to Growth in Slovakia

This chapter has applied the alternative approaches to growth as a critical lens to analyze Slovakia's policy framework. By analyzing its key strategic documents, it has shown that economic growth continues to dominate the policy vision, and remains a crucial measure of the country's policy performance, so far leaving a very limited space for the alternative approaches and more encompassing measurements. The concluding part will discuss some of the practical aspects and potential areas where the critical approaches could not only be of benefit but could also be positively received in terms of their practical application. It is probably unrealistic to see all of the European Union, or for that matter Slovakia, suddenly turning to the degrowth movement or the doughnut economy. However, these approaches, frameworks, and methods strongly align with some of the EU Green Deal notions and can thus pose an opportunity to deliver them more effectively on the national or local level in some concrete actionable areas.

Firstly, it was already mentioned that the EU funding, whether it is from the Recovery and Resilience Plan or the Program Slovakia 2021–2027, constitutes the main source of public investment in Slovakia. However, the expert and public debates are largely focused on the public finance deficit (as shown at the start of the chapter) or on more effective spending. The latter should be understood as a faster way to spend more money, if put very bluntly, as Slovakia is notoriously performing very poorly on this front. Certain recommendations were proposed by the caretaker government last year, which even led to some results (MIRRI, 2023; Office of the Government of the Slovak Republic, 2023). Nonetheless, the main issue is that the question is still posed as whether a country is spending too much or too little, rather than what the desired impact is, and how it should be evaluated, so that not only policy design and outputs can be measured, but also that people can easily observe the benefits, and ideally take part in the decisions. Some efforts on this front were conducted by the Value for Money Initiative, although it has been rather quiet for the past months (Denník N, 2023), while other efforts were aimed at, for instance, decentralization of the funds to the regions (MIRRI, 2023). Participatory sides of the postgrowth or doughnut economics approaches, with a special focus on combining social and environmental dimensions, could not only provide effective tools for policy design but also easy to understand rationale for the communities and actors at the local and regional levels. This can be, for instance, in underdeveloped areas such as the social economy, which provides a lot of beyond-growth opportunities.

Secondly, following up on the above, it is not only the design, decision-making, and implementation that need to take the bottom-up into account, it is also the data collection and measurements that need to dive into subnational levels of analysis in order to be able to have accurate picture of the living and environmental conditions and to facilitate informed policy design in line with the social and environmental needs of the particular regions or localities. The critical approaches provide a more comprehensive framework based on which local and environmental conditions can be captured in connection with each other. The data need to be collectable, adjustable, storable, and applicable from the local to national level, as well as pairable with other public sector databases. An example of such efforts is the currently commencing national project on Regional Centers for Sustainable Energy, which will support both data management and policy support functions to the regions and municipalities to address socioenvironmental challenges and needs from the perspective of energy across Slovakia (SIEA, 2023).

Thirdly, when it comes to data and the need for context tailored solutions, special attention needs to be paid to the living conditions of vulnerable and marginalized communities who often live in informal settings. In the context of Slovakia, it is particularly marginalized Roma communities, who constitute the most disadvantaged ethnic group in Europe and nearly half of the total of approximately 400,000 Roma living in Slovakia (Ravasz et al., 2020). These communities face significant socioeconomic inequality and hardship, including long-term unemployment, unequal access to healthcare or education, but also spatial marginalization, environmental injustice, and energy poverty (Ravasz et al., 2020). However, neither in academic literature nor in the relevant strategic policy documents, such as the Recovery and Resilience Plan, have their social and environmental challenges been sufficiently interlinked. Furthermore, many traditional indicators do not take into account the nature of the informal settlements and local semiformal ecosystems they are living in. Once again, these constitute the very questions the critical approaches described above provide a framework for addressing of – taking into consideration both – improvement of marginalized groups' living standards and decrease in environmental burden.

Finally, the disciplinary boundaries in the expert community need to be more inclusive and open for at least a conversation with alternative approaches, and vice-versa. Such conversations do not need to begin at high-level policies but may very well commence in teaching and research. "Sustainable development is a topic for ecologists," said one of my colleagues, who is an economist, some months ago at the times when some of the more radical critiques no longer consider the sustainable development approach sufficient in terms of the nature of change and its propositions. One can argue that there are historical reasons related to state socialism why in Slovakia economic thinking tends to lean in a more mainstream direction. However, almost 35 years after the Velvet Revolution, there is no reason why the expert academic and policy community should not be open to exploring the relevance of alternative approaches to critical contemporary challenges.

References

Denník N. (2023, November 10). Blog N: Value for money unit. *Denník N.* https://dennikn.sk/autor/uhp/

EPI. (2022). *Slovakia.* Environmental Performance Index. https://epi.yale.edu/epi-results/2022/country/svk

European Council. (2024). *European green deal.* Council of the European Union. https://www.consilium.europa.eu/en/policies/green-deal/

European Environment Agency. (2023). *Briefing: Growth without economic growth.* https://www.eea.europa.eu/publications/growth-without-economic-growth

Georgescu-Roegen, N. (1971). *The entropy law and the economic process.* Harvard University Press.

Global Data Lab. (2022). *Slovakia: Subnational HDI.* Global Data Lab. https://globaldatalab.org/shdi/table/shdi/SVK/?levels=1+4&interpolation=0&extrapolation=0

Green Growth Knowledge Platform. (2012). *Inaugural conference of the green growth knowledge platform: "Green growth: Addressing the knowledge gaps".* https://www.greenpolicyplatform.org/sites/default/files/GGKP_Conference_Summary.pdf

Hickel, J. (2020). *Less is more: How degrowth will save the world.* William Heinemann.

Jackson, T. (2009). *Prosperity without growth? Transition to a sustainable economy.* Sustainable Development Commission. https://www.sd-commission.org.uk/data/files/publications/prosperity_without_growth_report.pdf

Kern, M., & Hrivňák, T. (2023, September 24). SMER and extremist electorate consider migration as the biggest challenge, HLAS voters are less concerned. *Denník N.* https://e.dennikn.sk/minuta/3585205

Meadows, D. H., Meadows, D. L., Randers, J., & Behrens, W., III. (1972). *The limits to growth. The club of Rome.* Universe Books.

MIRRI. (2022). *Partnership agreement of the Slovak Republic 2021–2027.* https://www.eurofondy.gov.sk/wp-content/uploads/2022/07/220713_SK_Partnersk%C3%A1-dohoda-SR_21_27_do-SFC.pdf

MIRRI. (2023). *Spending of EU funds improved by more than one billion – The most successful is the IROP programme managed by the Ministry of Finance.* https://mirri.gov.sk/aktuality/cko/cerpanie-eurofondov-sa-zvysilo-o-viac-ako-miliardu-najlepsi-je-program-irop-ktory-riadi-ministerstvo-investici/

National Council of the Slovak Republic. (2021). *Program statements of the governments in 2021–2024*. https://www.nrsr.sk/web/Dynamic/DocumentPreview.aspx?DocID=494677

National Council of the Slovak Republic. (2023). *Program statement of the government 2023–2027: "Better, more peaceful and safer to live in"*. https://www.nrsr.sk/web/Dynamic/DocumentPreview.aspx?DocID=535376

OECD. (2011). *Towards green growth*. OECD Green Growth Studies. OECD Publishing. https://doi.org/10.1787/9789264111318-en

OECD. (2020). *Slovak Republic*. OECD Better Life Index. https://www.oecd betterlifeindex.org/countries/slovak-republic/

Office of the Government of the Slovak Republic. (2021). The recovery and resilience plan: Chapter 1. https://www.planobnovy.sk/site/assets/files/1069/01_kapitola_1_vseobecne-ciele-sudrznost-planu_1.pdf

Office of the Government of the Slovak Republic. (2023). *15 years of (un)used EU funds? The caretaker government offers solutions on how to make spending more effective*. https://www.vlada.gov.sk/15-rokov-nevyuzitych-eurofondov-vlada-odbornikov-prinasa-navod-ako-zefektivnit-ich-cerpanie/

Ravasz, Á., Kovács, Ľ., & Markovič, F. (2020). *Atlas of Roma communities 2019*. Publishing House of the Slovak Academy of Sciences.

Raworth, K. (2012). *A safe and just space for humanity: Can we live within the doughnut?* Oxfam Discussion Papers. https://www.oxfam.org/en/research/safe-and-just-space-humanity

SIEA. (2023). *Supporting the development of local and regional energy*. Slovak Innovation and Energy Agency. https://www.siea.sk/podporne-programy/podpora-rozvoja-regionalnej-a-lokalnej-energetiky/#rcue

Tomek, R. (2023, November 10). Economic newsfilter: People fear budgetary deficit much more than they fear migrants. *Denník N*. https://e.dennikn.sk/3585829/ekonomicky-newsfilter-ludia-sa-boja-rastuceho-rozpoctoveho-deficitu-omnoho-viac-ako-migrantov/

UNDP. (2020). *Human development report 2020. The next frontier: Human development and the Anthropocene*. United Nations Development Programme. https://hdr.undp.org/content/human-development-report-2020

UNDP. (2022). *Human development reports: Slovakia*. United Nations Development Programme. https://hdr.undp.org/data-center/specific-country-data#/countries/SVK

World Bank. (2022). GDP per capita, PPP (constant 2017 international $). https://data.worldbank.org/indicator/NY.GDP.PCAP.PP.KD

II

Policies, Institutions, and Markets

Chapter 5

Empirical Study of the Slovak Labor Market in the Breakthrough Development Period

Renáta Pitoňáková[a] *and Ladislav Kabát*[b]

[a]University of Economics in Bratislava, Slovakia
[b]Bratislava University of Economics and Management, Slovakia

Abstract

The globalized economic environment is a reality of our time, and the free market is an organic part of it. In the European Union, the free market is one of the key pillars of its functioning. The free movement of labor, capital, goods, and services contributes to long-term and stabilized economic and social development. When monitoring and analyzing the free market, the labor market deserves special attention. The information provided reflects Slovakia's labor market for 2000–2020, in which the country was undergoing significant social and economic changes. It was joining the European Union and the euro area. Many privatization projects continued, as well as modernization and building of new business capacities. However, their successful use required new sources of labor and a new labor market organization. Therefore, in this chapter, we provide information about the status of the labor market in the context of economic development. We also point out the level of unemployment in relation to the structure of the labor force. The chapter aims to provide principal information about changes in the labor market in Slovakia and its determinants from the external environment.

Keywords: Gross domestic product; population; labor market; employment; unemployment; labor productivity

Modeling Economic Growth in Contemporary Slovakia, 87–99

Published under exclusive licence by Emerald Publishing Limited
doi:10.1108/978-1-83549-454-720241006

1. Introduction

The labor market and its characteristics, such as volume, structure, rate of employment, and unemployment rate, are among the most sensitive tools for assessing the status of the economy. Therefore, economic theory and management practice examine economic growth, employment, and unemployment as the key components of the labor market. The strategic mistakes of the governments of Slovakia (after 1993) in regulating the privatization processes led to the rapid collapse of inefficiently managed businesses, resulting in higher levels of unemployment.

This chapter focuses on the Slovak labor market between 2000 and 2020. During this period, the country was undergoing significant political, economic, and social changes. The newly adopted legislative framework was essential for expanding cooperation with the industrially advanced EU countries and for the privatization processes. The outcome of the following transformations and privatization projects brought relatively high economic growth, however, simultaneously the high level of unemployment, with a negative impact on the labor market and social atmosphere.

The chapter is structured as follows. After the introductory part, there is an overview of the corresponding literature, followed by methodology and analysis of labor market indicators. The last part contains the core findings of the labor market analysis.

2. Literature Overview

The political, economic, and social changes that Slovakia underwent in the first decade of its existence attracted the attention of a wide range of professional public, both domestic and foreign. Of particular interest was the course and forms of privatization. According to Djankov and Pohl (1997), the process of privatization and restructuring, compared to other countries of the region, was successful. These results were achieved even without significant investment support from abroad. The more detailed information on schemes of economic restructuring and its bottlenecks during the discussed period is presented by Ježek (1997). When evaluating the results of the privatization and restructuring process, it is necessary to point to the situation on the labor market separately. According to Djankov and Pohl (1997), economically inefficient enterprises have ceased to exist, or their production programs have changed significantly. Consequently, the number of jobs on the labor market decreased by up to 50%, which was subsequently reflected in a growing level of unemployment. The detailed statistical analysis of the previous years is presented by Machlica et al. (2014).

The complicated period in the history of Slovakia's labor market is studied by Kubicova and Sergi (2005). They analyzed the performance and effectiveness of the Slovak labor market over the period 1994–2004. Authors applied practical tools such as Beveridge's curve and the Okun Law, as well as the advanced regression analysis to identify the responsiveness of unemployment in Slovakia under the policy restructuring of the economy rather than in economic cycles. The various aspects referring to the large movement of labor force also bring various conflict situations requiring deeper economic analysis and explanation. According to Pekarskiene et al. (2017), the globalization of national economies and markets has been a prominent tendency in recent decades, and the expansion of activities of multinational enterprises is one of the dominant features of the global economy. An interesting methodological contribution offer Ziolo and Sergi (2020), who provide new and original knowledge about Sustainable Finance and its role in the economy including ESG risk and propose the original research methodology in sustainable financing. Fang et al. (2021) empirically analyzed the effects of globalization on labor market regulations. They also point to globalization measures as potential determinants of de jure labor market conditions. The overview of the relevant articles on labor market issues is discussed by Fasani et al. (2020). Their paper presents the summarization of articles and contributions in the context of the main developments in this field. Under their methodology, the articles are split into broad thematic areas relevant to their contribution to the labor market. The first set of papers provides novel evidence on migrant selection. The second group of articles delves into the core literature identifying the impact of immigration on the labor market.

A detailed analysis of the labor market development over the last decades is offered by Dorn and Zweimüller (2021). They discuss the past, present, and potential future of the European labor market by documenting patterns of labor mobility across European countries. They also ask whether and to what extent the labor markets of these countries have become more integrated over time. A detailed examination of the impact of active and passive labor market policies is analyzed by Theodoropoulos and Voucharas (2023). Qerimi and Sergi (2017) identified the effects of the global economic downturn, its nature and impacts on the state of employment in the region of South East Europe.

Kureková and Žilinčíková (2023) analyzed the Slovak labor market from the perspective of intra-EU migration and return. Their study focused on the less skilled returnees. The findings suggest that returning migrants are more exposed to job instability than migrants and stayers. Klacso and Štulrajterová (2021) analyzed labor market flows between employed, unemployed, and inactive stages within 2005Q1–2020Q1 and separately for 2009–2010. Education, marital status, or the number of years in the current job are the main factors impacting the flows in the case of employment. Education level seems to impact holding or finding a job significantly. The effects of technology development on the future labor market of Slovakia were inspected by Novakova (2020). The outcomes suggest that automation could negatively affect the labor market and that existing artificial intelligence applications replace only human jobs with low value-added. Kiner and Štefančík (2022) identified the effects of the COVID-19 pandemic on unemployment growth in the Slovak Republic using a time series methodology from February 2020 to February 2021, considering several variable factors, such as gender, level of education, and employment sector. Female migrants seem more resilient to the negative impacts of the pandemic. Přívara (2021) analyzed labor market conditions and emigration trends in Slovakia and EU neighboring countries. The analysis of emigration trends showed that among EU neighboring countries, the Slovak migrant population tends to migrate mostly to the Czech

Republic. Karšay (2021) focused on the main structural and cyclical drivers of unemployment rate developments in 2014–2019. The findings reveal that active labor market policies, demography, workforce mobility, higher quality of human capital, and labor productivity drove the structural decline. Machlica et al. (2017) stressed the need to improve the education system to raise quality that would better align students' skills with new labor market needs. Gerbery and Miklosovic (2020) analyzed the transitions between employment and unemployment and identified a low labor market mobility in Slovakia.

The role of the further progressing restructuring and modernization of the country's industry is elaborated by Biea (2015). In his view, "while increasing employment and labor force participation could have a significant impact on Slovakia's GDP level, there are substantial gains to growth to be achieved by closing the still large labor productivity gap between Slovakia and more developed European economies." The role of education in achieving the needed technological changes goals in the transforming countries is discussed by Popescu et al. (2022).

3. Methodology

3.1 Data

This section introduces the data and methods used in elaborating the inspected topic. The data on an annual basis were derived from the publicly available database of the Statistical Office of the Slovak Republic (SO SR). The period of the observation starts in 2000 and finishes in 2020 (21 observations). The time series data are graphically presented. Table 5.1 deploys the list of indicators with short explanatory comments and sources.

3.2 Methods

An analytical method was primarily used for preparing this text and presenting the results. In addition, we applied comparative analysis to find out similarities and differences between observed indicators within the specified time of observation (2000–2020). Historical insight was utilized in order to delve into Slovakia's political and economic past.

4. Labor Market

The labor market in Slovakia in the first decades was significantly determined by the consequences of changes on the political scene and the impacts of transformation and privatization changes. Its fundamental changes were made by the Labor Code (Act no. 311/2001 Coll.). In line with this legislative frame, the important changes in the organization of the labor market took place. Namely the Trade Union lost its effective veto power over the organizational changes and firing of workers, and their power was generally weakened. Moreover, the compensation of their representatives for the time they spent on trade union

Table 5.1. List of Labor Market Indicators.

Indicator	Description	Source
Gross domestic product (GDP)	GDP in current prices	SO SR
Population	Total (women and men)	SO SR
Preproductive age population	People aged 0–14	SO SR
Productive age population	People aged 15–64	SO SR
Postproductive age population	People aged 65+	SO SR
Employment	Employees and entrepreneurs	SO SR
Employment (%)	Employees and entrepreneurs of the total population	Authors' own calculation
Unemployment	Unemployed persons aged 15 to 74	SO SR
Unemployment (%)	Unemployed persons aged 15 to 74 of total population	Authors' own calculation
Economically active population (labor force)	Employment + unemployment	SO SR
Unemployment rate (%)	Number of people unemployed as a percentage of the labor force	SO SR
Labor productivity per calendar day	GDP per 1 calendar day in current prices (million euro)	SO SR
Labor productivity per working day	GDP per 1 working day in current prices (million euro)	SO SR

Source: Authors' own elaboration.

duties was abolished. On the other hand, the power of works councils was strengthened. Collective bargaining, however, remained in the hands of trade unions only. The current situation in the labor market in Slovakia is coordinated between government bodies, trade union representatives, and representatives of business sector (Uhlerová & Králik, 2015).

The labor market is a socioeconomic area continuously monitored and analyzed as an organic part of a country's economic system. Its importance lies in the fact that labor market is a conditioning factor for the successful functioning of the standard markets of capital, goods, and services. An interesting finding on the structure, effectiveness, qualification aspects, and migrant situation is presented by Přívara (2021).

It is known that the labor market refers to the supply of and demand for labor. Employees offer their labor, employers demand. When analyzing the labor market, the size and structure of the population, its dynamics, and its qualification structure should be considered. *Age structure* allows us to identify and quantify the current situation in the labor market and estimate its development. This information is essential for profit-oriented businesses for their strategic planning and for governmental institutions for projecting and building social welfare programs and their inclusion in governmental expenditures. The knowledge of the *population qualification structure* is necessary for projecting educational and training programs (Lahti et al., 2024). An important aspect of the labor market is its *sectoral breakdown*. For strategic development programs, it is important to know which factors are essential for the success and competitiveness of individual sectors. Knowledge of the market environment and the ability to estimate its development reduces conflict between labor supply and demand.

Concerning the situation on the labor market over the period of the early 2000s, unemployment rates were relatively high but gradually declined as the economy grew and structural reforms were implemented. Over the mid-2000s, unemployment continued to decrease as the economy expanded, driven by strong growth in manufacturing and services sectors as well as foreign investment projects. The late 2000s brought the Global Financial Crisis with unemployment rising temporarily but remained relatively moderate compared to other European countries. During the 2010s, unemployment fluctuated but generally trended downward, confirming the gradual recovery of the economy. In the late 2010s, unemployment reached the precrisis levels and confirmed the recovered economy potential.

4.1 History of the Labor Market in Slovakia

Slovakia, as an independent country, has a brief history. It was a part of Czechoslovakia until 1992. A unified state political and economic policy determined economic and social development. Principles of state governance stem from the role of the central political and economic authorities. Due to this fact, the labor market was characterized by full employment. Unemployment was a nearly unknown category, according to the legislation, it was considered illegal. Since 1990, Slovakia changed its political orientation. The initial legislative steps resulted in creating a new market environment. In 1993, Czechoslovakia split into two separate states, the Czech Republic and Slovakia. In subsequent years, additional strategic political decisions and important economic reforming measures were adopted. New rules of the market economy were gradually implemented. Slovakia started a new economic history in 2004, joining the European Union. Its membership in the EU opened new challenges, for example, access to structural funds and foreign direct investment projects from Germany, France, and the Netherlands. The following significant step in the history of Slovakia was undertaken on January 1, 2009, when the country adopted a single euro currency. This step brought economic and financial stability and increased investors "confidence in trading with Slovak companies." The milestones in 2004 and 2009 offered new possibilities for domestic and EU countries in their labor markets.

Many Slovaks benefited from the possibility of a better-paying job in the EU labor market.

4.2 Analysis of Labor Market Indicators

4.2.1 Gross Domestic Product

Economic development in Slovakia experienced since 2000 relatively high GDP growth rates. The core factors were economic reforms, privatization, and increased foreign investment inflows following its transition from a centrally planned to a market-oriented economy. The GDP growth in the following decade continued. It was supported by strong exports, particularly in the automotive and electronics industries. Over the late 2000s, the Global Financial Crisis occurred. Like other countries, Slovakia faced a slowdown in GDP growth. Over the 2010s, the economy gradually recovered, with GDP growth rates at a slower pace compared to the precrisis years. During the late 2010s, the GDP growth remained steady, supported by domestic demand, foreign investment, and exports.

Gross Domestic Product (GDP) is a key economic indicator. It reflects an economy's overall health and performance and has significant implications for the labor market. As part of the GDP analysis, we present the fastest and slowest-growing industry clusters. Employment is the main category according to which these industries were categorized. Fig. 5.1 shows the dynamics of final consumption (*household final consumption and general government final consumption*), investment, export, import, and GDP over 2000–2020.

Special attention must be paid to developing the final consumption values within 2007–2009. During the global financial and debt crisis (2007–2009), higher values of the final consumption resulted from the rising governmental expenditures allocated to social protection schemes. Fig. 5.2 deploys the fastest (G-I) and slowest growing industry clusters (A).

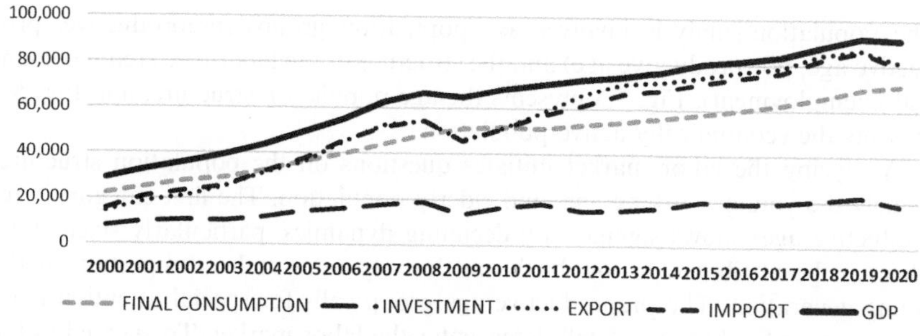

Fig. 5.1. GDP and GDP Components (in Million Euros). *Source:* Authors' own elaboration based on the Database of the Statistical Office of the Slovak Republic (2023).

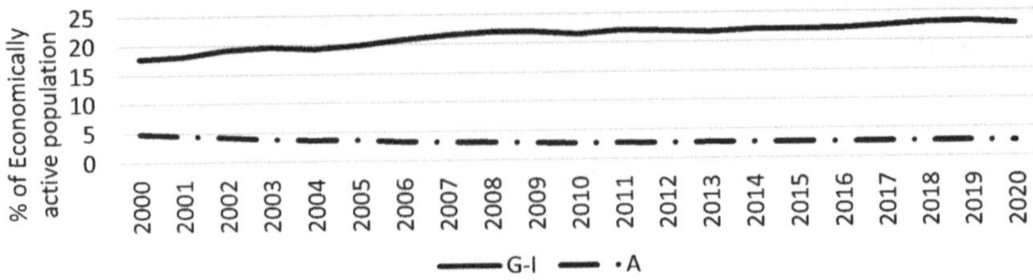

Fig. 5.2. Fastest/Slowest Growing Clusters of Industries of the Slovak Economy. *Source:* Authors' own elaboration based on Database of the Statistical Office of the Slovak Republic (2023) and Statistical classification NACE rev. 2 (Eurostat, 2023). *Note:* Industry clusters follow the categorization according to the Statistical Office of the Slovak Republic. A – Agriculture forestry and fishing, G – Wholesale and retail trade repair of motor vehicles and motorcycles, H – Transportation and storage, I –Accommodation and food service activities.

Group G-I represents the commercial sector, transport, and gastro, and accommodation services. About 17% of the economically active population was employed in this G-I industry at the beginning of the analyzed period. During the observation period, employment in this cluster achieved over 22%. This situation is consistent with the development of the final consumption category presented in Fig. 5.1. Cluster A involves the agriculture, forestry, and fishing industries. Over a long time, the agriculture industry has been facing a declining number of permanently employed labor forces. It is a result of continuing to replace the human factor with sophisticated machinery and a broad spectrum of various chemicals.

4.2.2 Population

The population analysis involves age population groups (preproductive, productive age, postproductive age) and the structure of the labor force (employment and unemployment). Fig. 5.3 presents the age population structure, and Fig. 5.4 presents the economically active population.

Analyzing the labor market initiates questions on the population structure, namely the young, working age, and elderly population. The first category (preproductive age) shows significantly declining dynamics, particularly since 2009. This can be attributed to low birth and fertility rates and outmigration of the young generation. The preproductive age group calls for special attention from governing bodies because it will, later, enter the labor market. To succeed in the labor market, it is necessary to enhance and improve their knowledge and professional skills.

The category of productive age consists of a population aged 14–64 and suggests a sharp decline. The possible factors could be attributed to the

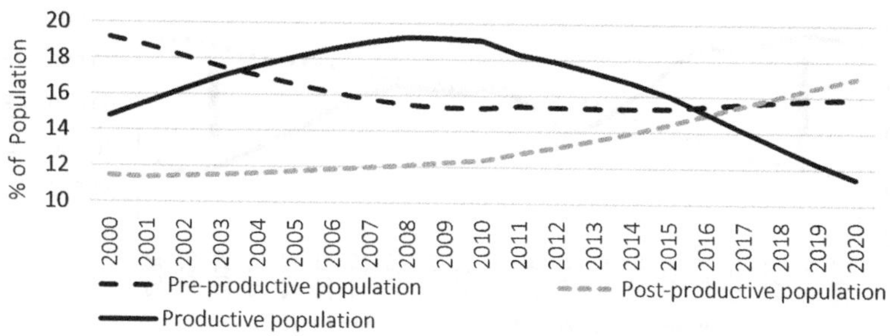

Fig. 5.3. Population Structure According to Age Groups. *Source:* Authors' own elaboration based on Database of the Statistical Office of the Slovak Republic (2023).

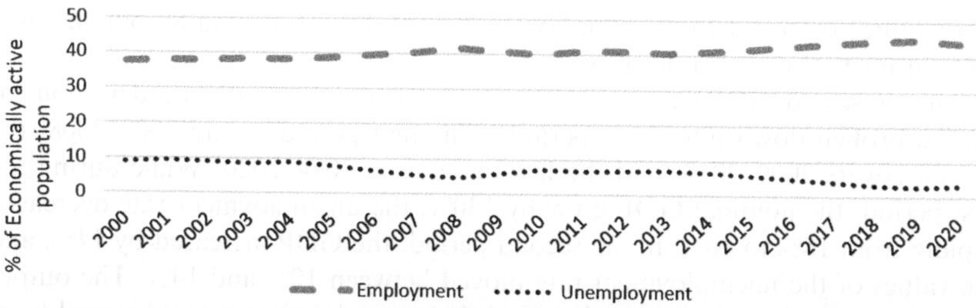

Fig. 5.4. Structure of Economically Active Population. *Source:* Authors' own elaboration based on Database of the Statistical Office of the Slovak Republic (2023).

deteriorating health status of the Slovak population. For example, the healthy life expectancy in Slovakia is significantly shorter than in developed Western countries.

The curve of the postproductive group confirms the aging of the Slovak population. Governmental bodies must pay more attention to social and health care programs for the elderly.

In line with our introductory formulation, we assume a positive impact of GDP on unemployment. This expectation complies with economic theory and was frequently discussed in economic literature. The following picture confronts the dynamics of GDP and the unemployment rate. The shape of both curves indicates an inverted relation, meaning that the increase in the output is reflected in the decreasing unemployment rate. Fig. 5.5 presents the dynamics of nominal GDP and unemployment. As an example, in the year 2001, at the volume of GDP (around 20 billion euros), the level of unemployment was close to 20% of the

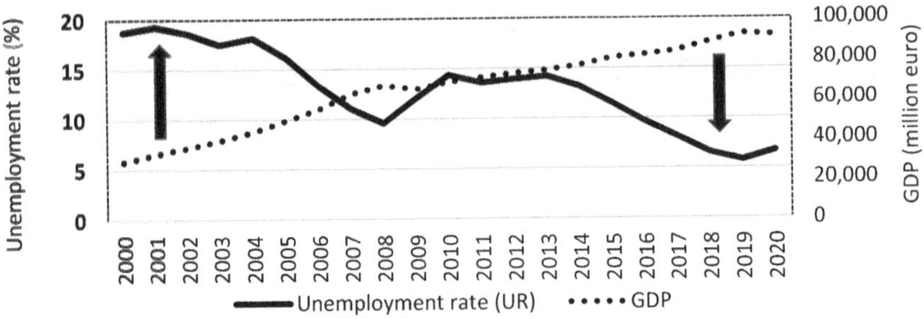

Fig. 5.5. GDP and Unemployment Rate. *Source:* Authors' own elaboration based on Database of the Statistical Office of the Slovak Republic (2023).

labor force compared to the situation in 2018 (GDP of around 80 billion euros with an unemployment rate of 6.5%).

The presented GDP in nominal terms and unemployment rate development can be broken down into three periods. The first period covers 2000–2008, the second covers 2009–2013, and the last one covers 2014–2020. While during the first period, the nominal GDP grew by 130%, the unemployment rate decreased rapidly from 18% to 10%; in the second period, the GDP increased by 14%, and the values of the unemployment rate moved between 12% and 14%. The output expanded by 19% in the last period, and the unemployment rate decreased from 13% to 6.7%.

4.2.3 Labor Productivity

Labor productivity is essential for monitoring the effectiveness of the labor market as to the output result per person in observed industries. In our case, the output is expressed by the nominal volume of GDP, while the unit of labor is represented by one working (WD) or calendar day (CD). According to the Eurostat (2024) data, development of labor productivity (amount of goods and services produced per day) seems to have a rising tendency apart from two periods of external shocks (global financial and debt crisis in 2009–2010 and COVID-19 in 2020–2022). In 2009, the labor productivity for calendar days decreased annually by almost 12 million euros and by 18 million euros for working days. In 2020, labor productivity for calendar days dropped by 3.4 million euros, and for working days, it dropped by 5.4 million euros. These declined values should be analyzed in relation to changes in the labor market, particularly with the unemployment rate between 2008–2009 and 2019–2020. The rate of unemployment in 2008 and 2009 achieved about 9.6% and 12.1%, respectively, while within 2019–2020, the rate was at 5.7% and 6.8%.

4.2.4 Trade Union Roles and Social Policies

Trade unions are one of the participants creating labor market rules. In the 2000s, trade unions played a key role in negotiating better working conditions in industries undergoing restructuring. As the Slovak working population is decreasing (see Fig. 5.3), unions' bargaining power is increasing and employers' flexibility in managing the labor market is decreasing. Similarly, trade union bodies have a rigid attitude to migration policy (hindering the competitiveness of the labor market). Employers fear the reduction in preproductive and productive population will require a new migration inflow, which could cause tension in the labor market.

5. Conclusion

The period 2000–2020 is a small part of independent Slovakia's history. However, significant sociopolitical and economic changes occurred in the country during this period. During the first years of the reported period, the country faced problems of high unemployment, which resulted from the economic collapse of many manufacturing enterprises due to a lack of competitiveness in foreign markets. However, the necessary changes in the legislative framework gradually created suitable conditions for foreign investors to enter Slovakia's business environment. As a result, job vacancies significantly increased, and unemployment decreased (from 20% in 2000 to 6.7% in 2020). The external effects of the global financial and debt crisis between 2008 and 2013 brought about some changes. A significant outcome was the structural shift in employment. Sectors with low competitiveness, unsuccessfully confronted with the business environment of developed EU countries, had reduced the labor market potential. The agricultural sector is a good example. About 4.8% of the total labor force was employed in this sector in 2000, dropping to 2.6% in 2020. The period of years 2000–2020 is a short part of Slovak's history as an independent country.

The monitored periods of the labor market cover the most important development stages of the Slovak economy as an independent unit. The presented results indicate that despite several problematic political decision-making, the country managed to integrate into the economic space of the European Union and created prerequisites for the successful continuation of this development.

References

Biea, N. D. (2015). *Economic growth in Slovakia: Past successes and future challenges.* Economic Brief 008, European Commission. https://economy-finance.ec.europa.eu/system/files/2017-01/eb008_en_2.pdf

Djankov, S., & Pohl, G. (1997). *Restructuring of large firms in Slovakia.* Working Paper Number 73. https://www.researchgate.net/publication/23724059_Restructuring_of_Large_Firms_in_Slovakia

Dorn, D., & Zweimüller, J. (2021). Migration and labor market integration in Europe. *The Journal of Economic Perspectives*, *35*(2), 49–76. https://www.aeaweb.org/articles?id=10.1257/jep.35.2.49

Eurostat. (2023). *NACE Rev. 2 – Statistical classification of economic activities*. https://ec.europa.eu/eurostat/web/products-manuals-and-guidelines/-/ks-ra-07-015

Eurostat. (2024). *National accounts based productivity indicators at total economy, industry and regional level (nama_10_prod)*. https://ec.europa.eu/eurostat/web/national-accounts/database?node_code=nama_10_prod

Fang, J., Gozgor, G., & Nolt, J. H. (2021). Globalisation, economic uncertainty and labour market regulations: Implications for the COVID-19 crisis. *The World Economy*, *45*(7), 2165–2187. https://doi.org/10.1111/twec.13230

Fasani, F., Llull, J., & Tealdi, C. (2020). The economics of migration: Labour market impacts and migration policies. *Labour Economics*, *67*, 101929. https://doi.org/10.1016/j.labeco.2020.101929

Gerbery, D., & Miklosovic, T. (2020). Labour market transitions and their determinants in Slovakia: Path from crisis to recovery. *Ekonomický časopis*, *68*(7), 651–676. https://doi.org/10.31577/ekoncas.2020.07.01

Ježek, T. (1997). The Czechoslovak experience with privatization. *Journal of International Affairs*, *50*(2), 477–488. https://www.jstor.org/stable/24357627

Karšay, A. (2021). *Structural and cyclical drivers of unemployment rate*. NBS Working Paper Nr. 1/2020. https://nbs.sk/_img/documents/publik/wp_01_2021_en_structural_and_cyclical_drivers_of_unemployment_rate.pdf

Kiner, A., & Štefančík, R. (2022). Immigrants on the Slovak labour market: Who is more resilient to the impacts of COVID-19? *Eastern Journal of European Studies*, *13*(1), 60–80. https://doi.org/10.47743/ejes-2022-0103

Klacso, J., & Štulrajterová, E. (2021). *Determinants of labour market flows in Slovakia*. NBS Working paper 5/2021. https://nbs.sk/_img/documents/publik/wp_5_2021_klacso_stulrajterova_determinants_of_labour_market_flows_in_slovakia.pdf

Kubicova, J., & Sergi, B. S. (2005). *Job matching and the Slovak labour market. Market economy, competition and competitiveness*. University of Szczecin, Microeconomics Department. https://ssrn.com/abstract=2165957

Kureková, L. M., & Žilinčíková, Z. (2023). Examining labour market hierarchies in Slovakia from the perspective of intra-EU migration and return. *Journal of Ethnic and Migration Studies*, *49*(16), 4140–4168. https://doi.org/10.1080/1369183X.2023.2207338

Lahti, J., Reinikainen, J., Kontto, J., Laaksonen, M., Partonen, T., Elonheimo, H., & Tolonen., H. (2024). Work ability trends 2000–2020 and birth-cohort projections until 2040 in Finland. *Scandinavian Journal of Public Health*, 1–9. https://doi.org/10.1177/14034948241228155

Machlica, G., Toman, J., Haluš, M., & Martinák, D. (2017). *Enhancing advanced skills to better meet labour market demand in the Slovak Republic*. OECD Economics Department Working Papers No. 1416. https://doi.org/10.1787/72c55c64-en

Machlica, G., Žúdel, B., & Hidas, S. (2014). *Unemployment in Slovakia*. Economic analysis – Policy paper, Inštitút finančnej politiky MH SR. https://www.mfsr.sk/files/archiv/priloha-stranky/19979/96/2014_30_Trh_prace.pdf

Novakova, L. (2020). The impact of technology development on the future of the labour market in the Slovak Republic. *Technology in Science*, *62*(C). https://doi.org/10.1016/j.techsoc.2020.101256

Pekarskiene, I., Laskiene, D., Saboniene, A., & Susniene, R. (2017). The impact of economic globalization on the labor market of an open small economy. In M. Bilgin, H. Danis, E. Demir, & U. Can (Eds.), *Financial environment and business development* (pp. 199–216). Springer.

Popescu, L. M., Dobre, F., Barladeanu, T. V., & Petrică, A. (2022). Aspects of education and employment in the European Union. In *BASIQ 2022 International Conference on New Trends in Sustainable Business and Consumption*. https://www.conference.ase.ro/wp-content/uploads/2022/06/22010_Final.pdf

Přívara, A. (2021). Labour market efficiency and emigration in Slovakia and EU neighbouring countries. *Economic Research-Ekonomska Istraživanja, 34*(1), 1850–1869. https://doi.org/10.1080/1331677X.2020.1858131

Qerimi, Q., & Sergi, B. S. (2017). The nature and the scope of the global economic crisis' impact on employment trends and policies in South East Europe. *Journal of International Studies, 10*(4), 143–153. https://ssrn.com/abstract=3091314

Statistical Office of the Slovak Republic. (2023). *Databases*. https://slovak.statistics.sk/wps/portal/ext/Databases

Theodoropoulos, N., & Voucharas, G. (2023). *Firm closures and labor market policies in Europe: Evidence from retrospective longitudinal data*. GLO Discussion Paper No. 1288. Global Labor Organization (GLO). https://www.econstor.eu/bitstream/10419/271668/1/GLO-DP-1288.pdf

Uhlerová, M., & Králik, J. (2015). *Social dialogue in local and regional government as a tool for effectiveness increase in public service sector (chosen problems)*. https://www.researchgate.net/publication/268430527_Social_Dialogue_in_Local_and_Regional_Government_as_a_Tool_for_Effectiveness_Increase_in_Public_Service_Sector_Chosen_Problems

Ziolo, M., & Sergi, B. S. (2020). *Financing sustainable development. Key challenges and prospects*. Palgrave Macmillan.

Chapter 6

The Residential Real Estate Market in the Slovak Republic

Eva Horvátová

University of Economics in Bratislava, Slovak Republic and Masaryk University in Brno, Czech Republic

Abstract

The residential real estate market represents the entire complex of economic and social relations at the macroeconomic and microeconomic levels. This publication aims to evaluate developments in the field of financing and the development of the residential real estate market in Slovakia, with a special focus on the determinants affecting the demand, supply, and prices of residential real estate in Slovakia and Bratislava. Owner-occupied housing is the dominant type of housing and has a significant impact on the development of housing issues. Research into the issue of multiple ownership of real estate provides answers to questions about the growth of real estate prices in the conditions of Bratislava. The influence of financial indicators, especially interest rates, the availability of housing loans, and the regulation of the banking sector explain the essential connections in the area of the development of residential real estate prices and factors of their development. The analysis points to the need for the development of rental housing in Slovakia.

Keywords: Residential real estate market; housing policy; owner occupied and rental housing; real estate prices; cyclicality of housing prices

1. Introduction

The real estate market is part of a complex economic and financial system that connects the macroeconomic environment, the financial market, investments, banking, social conditions, and territorial development. The real estate market and the stability of the economic environment are in mutual interaction.

Modeling Economic Growth in Contemporary Slovakia, 101–120

doi:10.1108/978-1-83549-454-720241008

According to Schwartz (2020), housing finance serves to understand how government policy affects financial markets, because mortgages are a central element of both banks and households balance sheets. Determinants affecting the prices of residential real estate are divided into supply and demand factors. As stated by Cár (2009), demand factors include credit availability, location, economic situation, demographic factors, political situation, housing policy, and savings rate. On the side of supply factors, the author mentions mainly the place of housing construction in the spatial plans of cities and municipalities, the availability of building plots as well as economic and technical factors such as the construction stage and the state of the housing stock. He considered the interest rate as a key factor in the real estate market.

Real estate market research focuses on various groups of approaches, such as regional, socioeconomic, investor, financial, banking, psychological, and others.

The regional approach looks for key factors of regional development and solutions to regional disparities, for example, Arundel and Hochstenbach (2020). Plešivčák and Buček (2017), using the example of the analyzed region, pointed out that the innovative capacity of the region and the support of the business environment are key development factors arising from the internal environment. From the external environment, the development of regions is mainly influenced by foreign direct investments and the social cohesion of the EU.

The authors Wu and Lux (2018) identified factors affecting real estate prices at the regional and national level, as well as potential price bubbles. They used Gordon's dividend discount model and treated house prices as the present value of future rental income. The analysis of regional trends showed that the growth of real estate prices in the regions was influenced by different factors in the short and long-term, so regional aspects are important.

The socioeconomic approach solves issues of housing policy, housing affordability, and thus has several aspects of research. For example, Lux and Sunega (2014) analyzed the conditions of eight European countries (Austria, Germany, Czech Republic, Hungary, Poland, Slovakia, Slovenia, and Italy) from the point of view of subsidies and housing options for seniors. They found that in countries with lower rates of home ownership and a higher share of rental housing, the range of housing subsidies for the elderly is wider and includes more innovative features. Szüdi and Kováčová (2016) applied a socioeconomic approach to housing issues for marginalized groups of Roma in Slovakia when they described the social housing project "Building hope" in the municipality of Rankovce in Eastern Slovakia.

2. Factors Influencing the Supply and Demand of Residential Real Estate

The analytical approach is related to the analysis of housing affordability. Housing affordability is an important social and economic indicator. It is evaluated from the financial aspect as housing affordability, and from the material point of view as housing accessibility. Questions of financial affordability of housing were addressed by Endel and Kuta (2018) and others. According to the authors Kuda and Lux (2010), the unaffordability of housing can be a cause of social exclusion. The concept of housing affordability has become the basis for assessing the housing situation.

Bohle (2018) analyzed the mortgage markets and found that factors such as the liberalization of financial flows and the privatization of the banking sectors directed predominantly international liquidity into mortgage financing.

Nemcová (2016) points to the importance of the concept of state housing policy in terms of strengthening purchasing power in the national economy. Kelly et al. (2018) evaluated that an increase in the availability of loans leads to an increase in the value of real estate. Their results indicate that market conditions such as LTV (Loan to Value) and PTI (Payment to Income) also had a significant impact on property prices.

Several economic, social, and demographic factors support owner-occupied housing. Kropáčková et al. (2022) state the advantages of owner-occupied housing through the advantages of mortgages compared to renting. Mikeszová et al. (2018) consider real estate ownership as an investment for old age. Property ownership can be motivated by own consumption, but it can also be an investment. Lennartz et al. (2019) stated that the motive for buying a second property is intergenerational support. Multiple property ownership affects housing affordability. Bieger et al. (2007) reported that retirees prefer secondary ownership due to living in nature. Lux (2009) stated that the taxation of financial income increases the price of rent. Therefore, people prefer to own property.

The influence of cultural and social factors was addressed by Acolin (2022), when he presents own housing as ontological certainties and the subjective feeling of creating one's own decisions. Hubert and Schmidt (2019) also found that cultural preferences influence homeownership decisions.

Palacin and Shelburne (2005), Winkler (2010), and Syrový (2009) found that homeowners move less compared to renters and therefore homeownership seems to be negatively correlated with labor mobility. Broulíková et al. (2018) analyzed the common assumption that home ownership promotes unemployment, because it is said that ownership limits the search for a job in the labor market. Empirical tests have produced mixed results, possibly due to the endogeneity of home ownership. The article documents that the privatization of apartments in Central and Eastern Europe after the fall of the Iron Curtain resulted in a quasiexperimental allocation of ownership of apartments to individual households. The authors found only weak evidence that homeowners are less willing to move and no evidence of a higher risk of unemployment compared to renters.

The authors Mnasri (2015) and Syrový (2009) connected the advantages of rental housing with the flexibility of the workforce. The authors De Boer and Bitetti (2014) found that the deregulation of social housing does not automatically mean the emergence of a stable private rental sector.

3. History of Housing Development and Real Estate Market in Slovakia

3.1 History of Housing Development in Slovakia

Housing policy and the residential real estate market in Slovakia have undergone major changes, especially in the period of economic transformation after 1989. In Slovakia, owner-occupied housing is currently the dominant form. We believe that it is largely an economic question, as well as a psychological and cultural one. As stated by Lux (2009), until 1989, housing consisted mainly of state, cooperative, and state enterprise apartments. To a lesser extent, there were privately owned houses. Until 1989, the area of housing was generally affected by central planning and administrative interventions. The construction of prefab houses before 1989 was typical for most socialist states and helped to overcome the housing need, according to Hegedüs et al. (2013). The development of the residential real estate market after 1989 was significantly contributed by the stabilization of the macroeconomic indicators of the Slovak economy, the reduction of interest rates, the growth of employment and economic performance, and last but not least, the adoption of the common euro currency in 2004. Policy changes in the area of housing after 1989 were dealt with by Szelény (2014), Špirková (2018), and Szolgayová et al. (2019).

According to Szolgayová et al. (2019), the first population census in 1991 showed that the rental sector made up 26.7% of the total housing stock and 22.1% were cooperative apartments. Szolgayová et al. (2019) found that the prevailing owner-occupied housing was caused by the privatization of apartments after 1989 in Slovakia. State apartments and apartments of state enterprises were transferred free of charge to the property of municipalities. The subsequent transformation of housing cooperatives after 1993 made it possible to privatize cooperative housing. The price of privatized apartments represented the unpaid part of investment loans, which was far below the market price. In this context, Špirková (2018) writes that as a result of privatization, up to 90% of apartments came into private ownership and there was a complete elimination of public and private rental apartments. Owned housing in Slovakia continues to grow continuously, when according to Eurostat (2024) in 2010, it represented 90%, in 2018, it was 91.3%, in 2020, it was 92.3%, and in 2022, up to 93% of the population had their own housing. This is broken down in Fig. 6.1 below:

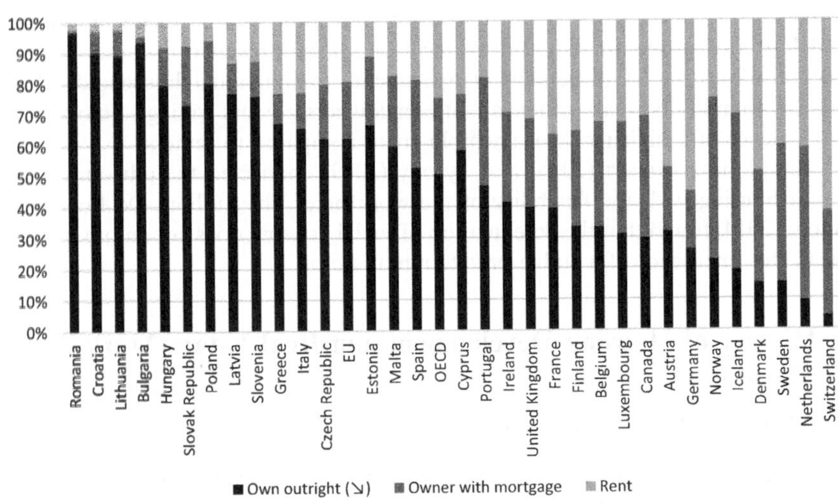

Fig. 6.1. Share of Owner-Occupied Housing in Selected Countries and Slovakia. *Source:* OECD (2022). *Note:* In each column, the first dark color indicates owner-occupied housing, followed by owner with mortgage, then rent private, rent subsidized and others.

3.2 The Situation on the Housing Market After Slovakia's Accession to the European Union

In 2004, the Slovak Republic joined the European Union. It was the beginning of a new phase of development for the Slovak residential real estate sector. As a result of positive macroeconomic developments, stable economic growth was recorded which was manifested in increasing foreign direct investments, increasing liquidity, decreasing inflation, and lowering interest rates. After joining the EU, Slovakia was perceived as a fast-growing economy, which joined the Eurozone in 2009. In the period after the global financial crisis after 2008, the Slovak banking sector maintained the growth of real estate loans. This phenomenon persisted until 2023. Real estate financing was the dominant element of lending, as loans were directed not only to the purchase of real estate but also to the financing of developers' development projects. Since 2015, Slovak households have been among the fastest-indebted households in the EU. The ratio of loans to GDP increased from 25% in 2015 to 36.7% in 2020.

The housing market includes owner-occupied, rental, and state-owned sectors. Mansfeldová and Tuček (2002) and Hegedüs et al. (2013) stated that the rental sector contains the state (often seen as social) and the private sector.

Rental housing in Slovakia lags behind after 1989. In practice, there exist basic forms of rental housing, namely market, regulated, and social rental housing. Social and regulated rental housing have a weak offer in Slovakia, where market rental housing prevails. Market rental housing is concentrated in the Bratislava region and in large regional cities such as Košice and Banská Bystrica. There are differences in the definition of social rental housing in EU countries. The authors De Boer and Bitetti (2014) and Cár (2009) pointed to the need to approach it according to specific national conditions. Hegedüs et al. (2017) addressed the issues of the private rental sector, and they predict its dynamic development in the future.

According to Eurostat (2024) data, the share of people living in rental housing in Slovakia is continuously maintained at a low level. In 2017, 9.9% of the population used rental housing, in 2018, it was 8.7%, and in 2022, it was only 7.8%. Statistical data also point to the threat of poverty from the point of view of rental housing. In Slovakia, in connection with the growth of rental prices, the threat of poverty in the area of rental housing has increased compared to owner-occupied housing. The risk of poverty increased during the period between 2005 and 2023 from 18% to 40% in rental housing, while the risk of poverty remained at 12% in owner-occupied housing.

In 2023, rental prices have increased significantly. The growth of interest rates, the decrease in the financial availability of housing, and the related reorientation of a part of the population to rental housing contributed to the growth of the rent.

The Average Monthly Rental Prices of Two-Room Apartments (EUR) are shown in below Table 6.1.

Developments in the housing market after 2015 were influenced by low interest rates and available housing loans. Several studies shown below in Fig. 6.2 that the increase in the availability of credit causes an increase in real estate prices. The

Table 6.1. Average Monthly Rental Prices of Two-Room Apartments (EUR).

	1Q 2010	4Q 2018	4Q 2020	4Q 2021	4Q 2022	3Q 2023*
Bratislava I	670	790	646	676	739	1,163
Bratislava II	530	570	561	537	665	838
Bratislava III	540	570	558	542	619	889
Bratislava IV	500	540	550	558	622	843
Bratislava V	531	600	561	509	605	794
Košice I	530	590	545	561	670	n.a
Košice II	380	560	532	548	656	n.a
Košice III	370	430	510	495	570	n.a
Košice IV	510	490	526	516	659	n.a
Banská Bystrica	410	440	514	531	604	n.a
Nitra	390	580	528	534	585	n.a
Prešov	370	410	456	482	560	n.a
Trenčín	360	400	520	549	596	n.a
Trnava	410	560	551	553	618	n.a
Žilina	380	550	539	505	623	n.a

Source: Author's own processing using data reality.sk, nehnuteľnosti.sk and bencont.sk.
Note: *Bruchánik (2023).

increase in the availability of loans was mainly caused by the drop in interest rates. Research in Slovakia confirmed that these factors, combined with the growth in demand, also influenced the growth in real estate prices. There was continuous growth in real estate prices until 2023. In 2023, real estate prices fell. The fall in real estate prices was caused by the rise in interest rates, the reduction in the availability of loans, and the limitation of loans by the regulator through LTV, DSTI (Debt Service to Income), and DTI (Debt to Income).

The stability of the real estate market is also influenced by the development of apartment construction. The number of completed apartments in this area is growing, but the demand for apartments in cities exceeds their supply. The following Fig. 6.3 shows the development of construction in the conditions of the Slovak Republic in parts of Western, Central, and Eastern Slovakia, as well as in individual regions of the Slovak Republic.

4. Real Estate Market Developments

4.1 Determinants of the Development of Real Estate Prices

The development of the real estate market is influenced by several determinants. According to the authors Schiller and Weiss (1999), real estate prices are essentially predictable. A drop in prices on the real estate market may not be news

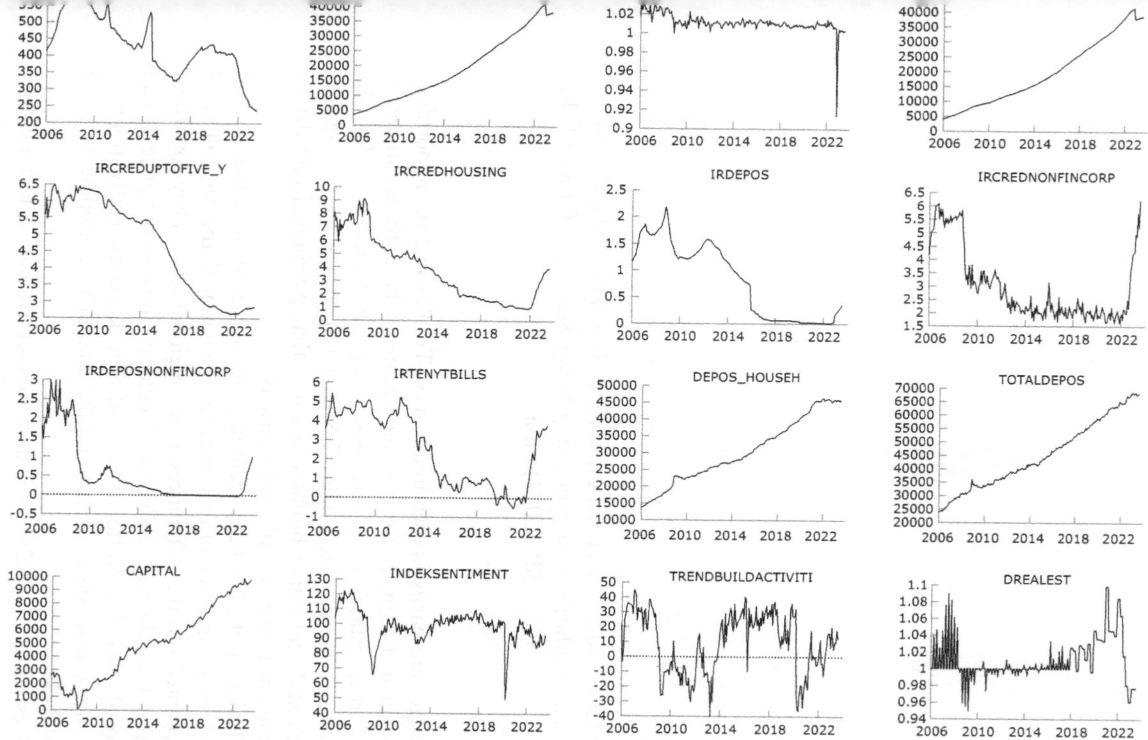

Fig. 6.2. Selected Indicators Influencing the Property Market. *Source:* Author's own processing using NBS (2024) data. *Note:* HOUSINGCREDONETOFIVE = housing loans with maturity 1–5 years; DHOUSINGCREDOVERFIVE = changes in housing loans with maturity over 5 years; TOTALHOUSINGCRED = total housing loans; IRCREDUPTOFIVE_Y = interest rate for loans up to 5 years; IRCREDHOUSING = interest rate on housing loans; IRDEPOS = interest rates on deposits; IRCREDNONFINCORP = interest rate on loans for non-financial corporations; INDEKSENTIMENT = economic sentiment index; DWAGES = wage changes; INFL = inflation; IRDEPOS = interest rate on deposits; DEPOS_HOUSEH = household deposits; TOTALDEPOS = total deposits; CAPITAL = capital of banks; DREALEST = changes in real estate prices in Slovakia.

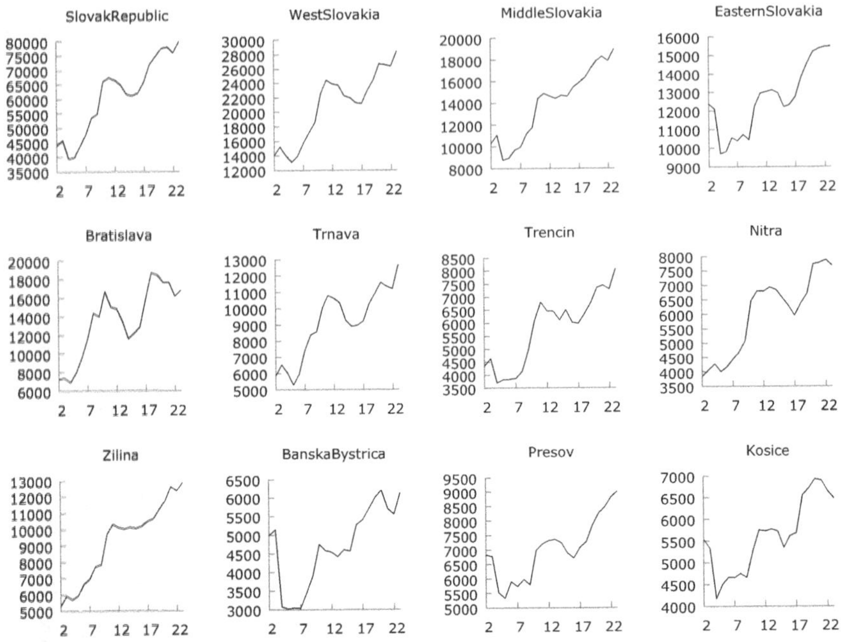

Fig. 6.3. Flats Under Construction Within Slovakia in the Period 2002–2022. *Source:* Author's own processing using Statistical Office of the SR (2024) data.

because price changes are partly known in advance. To illustrate the importance of real estate market inefficiencies for risk management, the authors estimate a simple model of real estate price forecasts using an indicator called the "Case-Shiller quarterly Home Price Index." Shiller (2016) has warned against both tech bubbles and real estate bubbles, arguing that psychologically driven volatility is an inherent feature of all asset markets.

The authors Tkacova et al. (2024) identified the influence of economic and sociological variables on the price of real estate at the national and regional level in Slovakia and pointed out the differences at the regional level. They confirmed the assumption about the different influence of determinants on the price of real estate at the regional level. The National Bank of Slovakia consistently monitors the development of the real estate market and the quarterly development of real estate prices in Slovakia.

The authors Cesnak et al. (2024) provide a market evaluation methodology through indices used for real estate market analysis, such as the housing affordability index or macroeconomic models estimating real estate price fundamentals.

The authors Vogel and Werner (2015) analyzed bubbles in real estate markets and found that extreme market events were basically caused by excessive expansion of bank credit and leveraged transactions.

Cronin and McQuinn (2016) found that the reduction in LTV ratios that may occur as a result of regulatory caps will lead to greater demand for rental housing, which will lead to higher rents at a given housing price level.

This result is suitable for explaining the housing market in Slovakia after 2022. Greenwald (2018) found that the PTI indicator is a more effective tool for dampening the growth of real estate prices compared to the LTV indicator.

Brauner and Plottová (2017) found that the rental price depends on the purchase price of the property, interest rates, developments on the financial market, and the rate of inflation. They confirmed that there is interdependence between property prices and rental prices. Dröes and Francke (2018) found a strong correlation between property prices and market turnover. GDP and interest rates could also explain the correlation between price and turnover indicators.

As Schwartz (2020) points out, large-scale mortgage markets only work where the government influences the banking system to eliminate maturity risks and limit excessive credit creation.

Using quarterly data covering house prices in different countries over four decades, Aizenman et al. (2019) find that house price appreciation is positively associated with economic growth, while the relationship between house price depreciation and economic growth is highly nonlinear depending on country-specific characteristics. Ehrenbergerová and Bajzík (2020) found that an increase in the interest rate by one percentage point causes a decrease in real estate prices by 0.7% after 1 year and by 0.9% after 2 years.

The authors Pittini et al. (2019) identified these problems when it comes to the Slovak real estate market: a high share of owner-occupied housing in Slovakia, high prices of private rental housing, and large price differences between Bratislava and other regions.

The article from Lennartz et al. (2019) addresses three key topics: how to produce more affordable housing units, how to better allocate scarce housing resources among residents and between regions; and how to reduce the speculative element in the current housing market.

Cunha and Lobão (2021) consider factors such as gross domestic product (GDP), interest rates, housing starts, and tourism to be the main cause of real estate price growth but not in all the geographical levels of analysis.

The development of interest rates on loans and the drop in interest rates on deposits stimulated households to buy residential real estate or to buy secondary and investment real estate. Limited investment returns on the capital market during the period of low interest rates stimulated to invest in real estate. The growing demand for loans and the increasing availability of loans in combination with a limited supply caused the growth of real estate prices on the Slovak market. These are displayed below in Fig. 6.4:

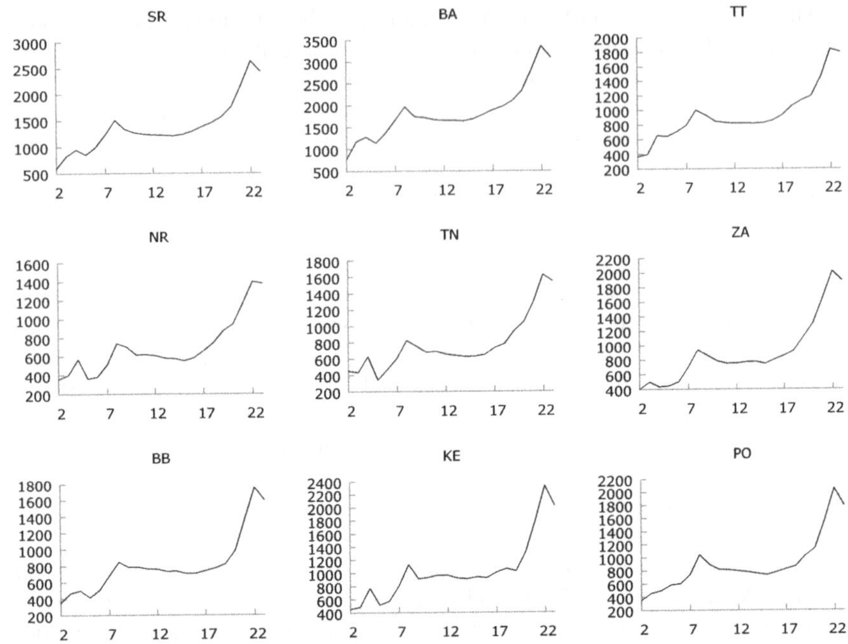

Fig. 6.4. Development of Real Estate Prices in Slovakia (EUR/m^2).
Source: Author's own processing using NBS (2024) data.

The author Cár (2009) states that the growth of interest in private rental housing is limited by the economic disadvantages of renting an apartment compared to purchasing it, while in addition the apartment becomes the property of the buyer.

4.2 Analysis of Housing Prices in Slovakia and Bratislava

The following models shown in Fig. 6.5 are compiled in such a way that it is possible to identify the main factors of the development of the real estate market in Slovakia.

The growing demand for loans and the increasing availability of loans have caused an increase in real estate prices on the Slovak market. The models show the strong influence on real estate prices in Slovakia when it comes to such factors as changes in housing loans over 5 years, interest rates on loans over 5 years, interest rates on housing loans, economic sentiment index, construction activity trends, and total housing loans. The development of real estate prices in Bratislava was influenced by the development of wages and savings, which we explain by the fact that investors prefer investing in real estate over alternative forms of

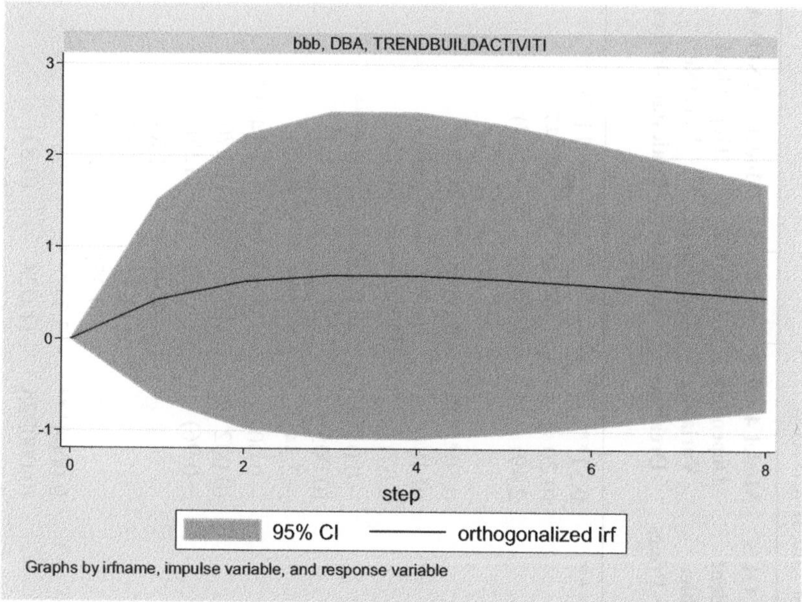

Fig. 6.5. Impulse-Response Function: Impulse – Real Estate Prices in Bratislava Changes; Response – Build Activity. *Source:* Author's own processing using NBS (2024) data.

investment and also by multiple ownership of real estate as investment real estate or for rental purposes.

The residential real estate market is influenced by macroeconomic factors and the development of the banking and financial market. When it comes to macroeconomic influences, it was mainly inflation that had a significant impact on the growth of real estate prices in both, Slovakia and Bratislava. The positive development of employment was reflected in the growth of real estate prices in Bratislava.

We analyzed the impact of individual variables on the prices in Bratislava and on the average prices of residential properties in Slovakia. The conclusions about the impact of the growth of deposits on the growth of real estate prices in Bratislava were confirmed. The conclusions about the impact of growth in construction activity on price changes in Bratislava were based on the theoretical assumptions that rising prices cause growth in construction activity. The growth of residential real estate prices in Bratislava was driven by demand from investors, as well as a reaction from construction contractors.

Models of Real Estate Price Factor Estimations in Slovakia and Bratislava are shown in the below Table 6.2.

Table 6.2. Models of Real Estate Price Factor Estimations in Slovakia and Bratislava.

	Model 1 WLS Dependent Variable: BA	**Model 2 OLS Dependent Variable: DBA**	**Model 3 OLS Dependent Variable: Realestate-Prices**	**Model 4 OLS Dependent Variable: Drealest**	**Model 5 ANOVA Dependent Variable BA**	**Model 6 ANOVA Dependent Variable Realestate-Prices**
Const	−3800.66 *** (1063.98 −3.57)	0.53*** (0.18 2.84)	−2909.67*** (866.87 −3.35)	0.51*** (0.20 2.49)	− 1504.45*** (260.89 −5.77)	−1311.58*** (212.47 −6.17)
DHOUSINGCREDOVERFIVE	1380.54 (962.96 1.43)	0.17** (2.56 0.01)	793.46 (785.12 1.01)	0.50*** (0.18 2.67)	0.06** (0. 02 2.74)	0.05** (0.01 3.02)
IRCREDUPTOFIVE_Y	263.23*** (31.88 8.25)	−0.01* (0.005 −1.96)	226.04*** (26.48 8.53)	−0.01** (0.005 −2.34)	243.44*** (28.32 8.59)	206.57*** (23.07 8.95)
IRCREDHOUSING	163.05*** (14.60 11.16)	−0.002 (0.002 −1.09)	141.31*** (12.33 11.46)	−0.002 (0.002 −0.96)	178.52*** (15.59 11.45)	151.14*** (12.70 11.90)
IRCREDNONFINCORP					−4.95 (14.17 −0.35)	−1.83 (11.54 −0.16)
INDEKSENTIMENT	3.74*** (1.05 3.53)	0.0009*** (0.0002 4.49)	2.28** (0.936 2.44)	0.0008*** (0.000225 3.39)	3.77*** (1.028 3.67)	1.93* (0.83 2.31)

DWAGES	343.410 *** (2.901 2.901)	−0.00378 (0.0219 −0.17)	215.58** (98.57 2.18)	−0.01 (0.02 −0.50)	261.28* (107.80 2.42)	163.12* (87.79 1.83)
INFL	82.62*** (16.71 4.94)	0.005* (0.003 1.70)	68.49*** (13.84 4.96)	0.006* (0.003 1.82)	68.23*** (13.84 1.70)	58.90*** (12.22 4.82)
IRDEPOS	61.68 (49.19 1.25)	0.02** (0.008 2.53)	48.82 (41.77 1.16)	0.02** (0.009 2.31)	80.94* (44.58 1.82)	75.64* (36.30 2.08)
DEPOS_HOUSEH	0.020** (0.009 2.122)	0.04 (0.0006 0.06)	0.01* (0.008 1.71)	−0.0002 (0.00007 −0.38)	0.09*** (0.01 7.34)	0.07*** (0.01 7.42)
TOTALDEPOS					−0.07*** (0.008 −8.41)	−0.06*** (0.007 −8.79)
IRTENYTBILLS	−9.78 (10.62 −0.92)	−0.016*** (0.001 −5.25)		−0.009 (0.002 −4.52)	−12.94 (9.36 −1.38)	−3.73 (7.26 −0.49)
UNEMPL	−22.71*** (5.80 −3.91)	−0.0007 (0.001 −0.71)		−0.0008 (0.001 −0.68)	−25.08*** (5.50 −4.56)	−20.76*** (4.48 −4.63)
TRENDBUILDACTIVITI	−2.83*** (0.55 −5.12)	−0.0006 (0.001 −6.14)	−2.42*** (0.46 −5.19)	−0.0006 *** (0.001 −5.25)	−1.63** (0.52 −3.12)	−1.27** (0.42 −2.99)
DGDP		−0.001 (0.007 −1.61)	−2.13 (3.22 −0.66)	−0.001 (0.0008 −1.42)	−1.91 (3.41 −0.56)	−0.57 (2.77 −0.21)

(Continued)

Table 6.2. *(Continued)*

	Model 1 WLS Dependent Variable: BA	**Model 2 OLS Dependent Variable: DBA**	**Model 3 OLS Dependent Variable: Realestate-Prices**	**Model 4 OLS Dependent Variable: Drealest**	**Model 5 ANOVA Dependent Variable BA**	**Model 6 ANOVA Dependent Variable Realestate-Prices**
TOTALHOUSINGCRED	0.08*** (0.008 9.92)		0.07*** (0.007 10.49)		0.04* (0.02 1.85)	0.03* (0.01 1.82)
	R-squared 0.967 S.E. of regression 97.72	*R*-squared 0.47 S.E. of regression 0.01	*R*-squared 0.96 S.E. of regression 80.17	*R*-squared 0.95 S.E. of regression 87.17614	*R*-squared = 0.97 Prob > *F* = 0.000	*R*-squared 0.97 Prob > *F* = 0.000

Source: Author's own processing using NBS (2024) data.

Note: Values in parentheses are std. error and *t*-value; *** denotes statistical significance at the 1% level, ** at the 5% level and * at the 10% level. Variables: DHOUSINGCREDOVERFIVE = changes in housing loans with maturity over 5 years; IRCREDUPTOFIVE_Y = interest rate for loans up to 5 years; IRCREDHOUSING = interest rate on housing loans; IRCREDNONFINCORP = interest rate on loans for non-financial corporations; INDEKSENTIMENT = economic sentiment index; DWAGES = wage changes; INFL = inflation rate; IRDEPOS = interest rate on deposits; DEPOS_HOUSEH = household deposits; TOTALDEPOS = total deposits; IRTENYTBILLS = interest rate on 10-year government bonds; UNEMPL = unemployment rate; TRENDBUILDACTIVITI = the trend of construction activity; DGDP = change in GDP growth; TOTALHOUSINGCRED = total housing loans.

The current development after the increase in interest rates confirms the validity of general results and connections between loan prices, their availability, real estate prices, and interest rates. Last but not least, in the real estate market, there is inertia and downward price inflexibility. How can this be explained? It is also necessary to start from the position of individual subjects on the market and their preferences. If we think about whose interest is the reduction of real estate prices, we come to the following conclusions: Banks and developers perceive a possible fall in real estate prices as a risk. Banks because they not only finance real estate but also, they have real estate as collateral for housing loans. A reduction in the value of collateral requires additional security of receivables or reporting them as more risky, which requires the holding of higher capital. Developers are interested in selling real estate at a profit, which also threatens the rise in input prices at the time of real estate construction. Real estate agents are also interested in maintaining high real estate prices, as their commissions depend on the value of transactions. In essence, it can be concluded that from a microeconomic point of view, there are only a few entities that are interested in reducing real estate prices. These include entities on the demand side, that is, households and also the state, which is interested in increasing the availability of housing.

Based on all the known contexts, the growing trend in the real estate market has broken and currently a drop in prices is already noticeable throughout the Slovak Republic. This can be explained mainly by the growth of interest rates and inflation. Despite the reduction in real estate prices, the affordability of residential real estate has decreased in Slovakia. In order to reduce risks, the National Bank of Slovakia limited the LTV, DSTI, and DTI indicators to housing loans.

As a result of rising interest rates, access to own housing became more difficult and therefore residents had to solve their needs through rental housing. The growth of rental housing in 2023 was largely caused by the inaccessibility of own housing, which the inhabitants of Slovakia prefer not only for economic but also for psychological reasons. The growth of rental housing in the last year is not the result of household preferences, but is a solution from the point of view of economic constraints.

The Hodrick–Prescott filter was used to estimate the cyclicality of the development of housing prices in Slovakia. As the graph in Fig. 6.6 shows, during the period 2022–2023, significantly increasing cyclical component appears which indicates an overvaluation of residential real estate prices.

This figure points to two significant periods of cyclical growth in real estate prices. The first period with significant cyclical component can be recognized during the global financial crisis in 2008 and the second period with significant growth in real estate prices was during the period 2021–2022. Cesnak and Klacso (2021) did not find the presence of a price bubble on the real estate market in the Slovak Republic, although they admitted the overvaluation of real estate in some regions of the Slovak Republic. Similar results are also reported by Tkacova et al. (2024).

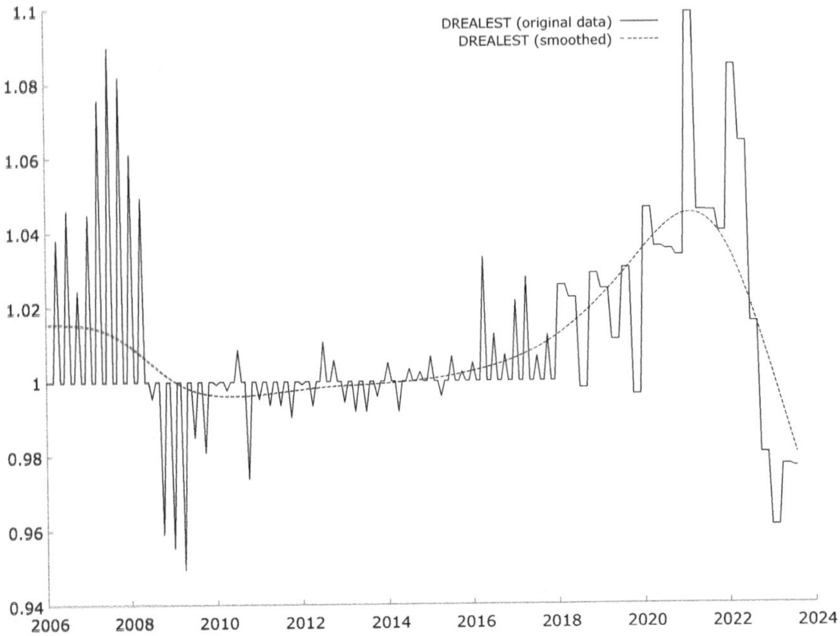

Fig. 6.6. Hodrick–Prescott Filter of the Time Series of Changes in the Prices of Residential Real Estate in Slovakia. *Source:* Author's own processing using NBS (2024) data.

5. Conclusion

The development of the residential real estate market in Slovakia shows certain general features that can be theoretically predicted, but it also has its own specifics, which are connected to historical, cultural, and other elements specific to Slovakia. The general factors that significantly influenced the development of the residential real estate market include mainly the effects of the macroeconomic environment. In Slovakia, it has been confirmed that the financing and development of the real estate market requires a stable economic environment. The stabilization of the macroeconomic indicators of the Slovak economy contributed significantly to the development of the real estate market and its financing, especially the reduction of interest rates, the growth of employment, the performance of the economy, and last but not least, the adoption of the common currency, the euro.

The reduction of interest rates caused an increase in the availability of housing loans, which on the other hand, along with the growth in demand, caused an increase in the prices of residential properties. In the period after 2015, Slovak households were evaluated as the fastest indebted households within the EU, which caused the need to limit the availability of loans. The decrease in the availability of loans was also caused by the increase in interest rates and the limits and restrictions on housing loans by the National Bank of Slovakia. Although rental housing began to increase after 2023, it was forced due to the unavailability of housing loans. Preference for owner-occupied housing still persists, due to the economic disadvantage of rental housing compared to housing loan repayments.

The analysis points out that individual factors affect real estate prices in Bratislava and Slovakia to a different extent. Real estate prices in Bratislava reacted more strongly to changes in interest rates and credit availability. In Bratislava, the influence of multiple ownership of properties held for rent, was also evident. We explain the connection with savings by the fact that the saved funds are invested in the secondary ownership of real estate, which is subsequently sold at a profit or used for renting. This is manifested to a greater extent in Bratislava. Of the macroeconomic influences, inflation had a significant impact on the growth of real estate prices in both groups, Slovakia and Bratislava. The positive development of employment was reflected in the growth of real estate prices in Bratislava.

The situation on the residential real estate market is undergoing major changes resulting from rising interest rates and inflation. At all levels of residential real estate market research, the need to develop affordable or rental housing, comes to the fore.

References

Acolin, A. (2022). Owning vs. renting: The benefits of residential stability? *Housing Studies*, *37*(4), 644–667. https://doi.org/10.1080/02673037.2020.1823332

Aizenman, J., Jinjarak, Y., & Zheng, H. (2019). Housing bubbles, economic growth, and institutions. *Open Economies Review*, *30*, 655–674. https://doi.org/10.1007/s11079-019-09535-9

Arundel, R., & Hochstenbach, C. (2020). Divided access and the spatial polarization of housing wealth. *Urban Geography*, *41*(4), 497–523. https://doi.org/10.1080/02723638.2019.1681722

Bieger, T., Beritelli, P., & Weinert, R. (2007). Understanding second home owners who do not rent – Insights on the proprietors of self-catered accommodation. *International Journal of Hospitality Management*, *26*(2), 263–276. https://doi.org/10.1016/j.ijhm.2006.10.011

Bohle, D. (2018). Mortgaging Europe's periphery. *Studies in Comparative International Development*, *53*(2), 196–217. https://doi.org/10.1007/s12116-018-9260-7

Brauner, R., & Plottová, S. (2017). Factors that affect the market prices of flat renting. In *Proceedings of the 14th international scientific conference European financial systems 2017*. Masaryk University. https://munishop.muni.cz/en/catalog/free-e-books/european-financial-systems-2017-munispace_948

Broulíková, H. M., Huber, P., Montag, J., & Sunega, P. (2018). *Homeownership, mobility, and unemployment: Evidence from housing privatization*. ISE Working Paper No. 7. https://papers.ssrn.com/sol3/papers.cfm?abstract_id=2896765

Bruchánik, R. (2023). *Staršie byty majú za sebou rok poklesu cien, nájomné stále rastie.* Kvartálna analýza realitného trhu, ročník 2023, 3. kvartál. https://www.bencont.sk/app/cmsSiteAttachment.php?ID=520&disposition=inline

Cár, M. (2009). Výber faktorov ovplyvňujúcich ceny nehnuteľností na bývanie na Slovensku. *BIATEC, 17*(3), 2–8. https://www.nbs.sk/_img/documents/_publik_nbs_fsr/biatec/rok2009/biatec0309.pdf

Cesnak, M., & Klacso, J. (2021). *Assessing real estate prices in Slovakia – A structural approach.* NBS Working paper 3/2021. National Bank of Slovakia. https://www.nbs.sk/_img/documents/publik/wp_3_2021_cesnak_klacso_assessing_real_estate_prices.pdf

Cesnak, M., Klacso, J., Kupkovič, P., Moravčík, A., Rychtárik, Š., & Vrbovský, R. (2024). *Assessing residential real estate prices in Slovakia: Possible approaches and indices.* NBS Occasional paper, No 1/2024. https://nbs.sk/dokument/b5de6821-fe5b-4cd9-9e1b-af4043d75e21/stiahnut/?force=false

Cronin, D., & McQuinn, K. (2016). Credit availability, macroprudential regulations and the house price-to-rent ratio. *Journal of Policy Modeling, 38*(5), 971–984. https://doi.org/10.1016/j.jpolmod.2016.06.002

Cunha, A. M., & Lobão, J. (2021). The determinants of real estate prices in a European context: A four-level analysis. *Journal of European Real Estate Research, 14*(3), 331–348. https://doi.org/10.1108/JERER-10-2020-0053

De Boer, R., & Bitetti, R. (2014). *A revival of the private rental sector of the housing market? Lessons from Germany, Finland, Czech Republic and The Netherlands.* OECD Economics Department Working Papers No. 1170. OECD Publishing. https://doi.org/10.1787/5jxv9f32j0zp-en

Dröes, M. I., & Francke, M. K. (2018). What causes the positive price-turnover correlation in European housing markets? *The Journal of Real Estate Finance and Economics, 57*(4), 618–646. https://doi-org.ezproxy.muni.cz/10.1007/s11146-017-9602-7

Ehrenbergerová, D., & Bajzík, J. (2020). *The effect of monetary policy on house prices – How strong is the transmission?* Working Papers Series 14/2020. Czech National Bank. https://www.cnb.cz/en/economic-research/research-publications/cnb-working-paper-series/The-Effect-of-Monetary-Policy-on-House-Prices-How-Strong-is-the-Transmission-00001/

Endel, S., & Kuta, V. (2018). *Bydlení v souvislostech.* Vysoká škola báňská – Technická univerzita Ostrava.

Eurostat. (2024). *Distribution of population by tenure status, type of household and income group – EU-SILC survey.* https://ec.europa.eu/eurostat/databrowser/view/ILC_LVHO02__custom_2618682/default/table?lang=en

Greenwald, D. (2018). *The mortgage credit channel of macroeconomic transmission.* MIT Sloan Research Paper No. 5184–16. http://dx.doi.org/10.2139/ssrn.2735491

Hegedüs, J., Lux, M., & Horváth, V. (2017). *Private rental housing in transition countries: An alternative to owner occupation?* Palgrave Macmillan.

Hegedüs, J., Lux, M., & Teller, N. (2013). *Social housing in transition countries.* Routledge.

Hubert, J. S., & Schmidt, T. (2019). *Cross-country differences in homeownership: A cultural phenomenon?* Deutsche Bundesbank No 40/2019. https://www.bundesbank.de/resource/blob/812762/f8a280904a736a138a8f7d2e09dcd2f2/mL/2019-11-01-dkp-40-data.pdf

Kelly, R., McCann, F., & O'Toole, C. (2018). Credit conditions, macroprudential policy and house prices. *Journal of Housing Economics, 41*, 153–167. https://doi.org/10.1016/j.jhe.2018.05.005

Kropáčková, S., Čudová, M., Šimeček, T., Podškubka, T., Laipold, M., Brodecká, V., & Hlúšková, R. (2022). *Bytové domy, zdroj příjmů i povinností.* Wolters Kluwer.

Kuda, F., & Lux, M. (2010). *Bydlení v regionech: Důsledky regionálních rozdílů v dostupnosti bydlení.* Professional Publishing.

Lennartz, C., Baarsma, B., & Vrieselaar, N. (2019). Exploding house prices in urban housing markets: Explanations and policy solutions for the Netherlands. In R. Nijskens, M. Lohuis, P. Hilbers, & W. Heeringa (Eds.), *Hot property: The housing market in major cities* (pp. 207–221). Springer.

Lux, M. (2009). *Housing policy and housing finance in the Czech Republic during transition: An example of the schism between the still-living past and the need of reform.* Delft University Press.

Lux, M., & Sunega, P. (2014). The impact of housing tenure in supporting ageing in place: Exploring the links between housing systems and housing options for the elderly. *International Journal of Housing Policy, 14*(1), 30–55.

Mansfeldová, Z., & Tuček, M. (2002). *Současná česká společnost: sociologické studie.* Sociologický ústav AV ČR.

Mikeszová, M., Sunega, P., Lux, M., & Aresta, V. (2018). *Vlastní bydlení jako finanční bonus k důchodu.* Sociologické nakladatelství SLON/Sociologický ústav AV ČR.

Mnasri, A. (2015). Renting vs. buying a home: A matter of wealth accumulation or of geographic stability? *Journal of Economic Dynamics and Control, 60*, 42–72. https://doi.org/10.1016/j.jedc.2015.08.008

NBS. (2024). *Štatistika.* https://nbs.sk/statisticke-udaje/

Nemcová, D. (2016). State housing policy in Slovak Republic as the mean of stimulating demand in the real estate market. In *Drive your knowledge be a scientist: Conference proceedings of the 12th annual international Bata conference for Ph.D. students and young researchers.* Zlín. https://digilib.k.utb.cz/handle/10563/45980

OECD. (2022). *HM1.3 housing tenures.* https://www.oecd.org/els/family/HM1-3-Housing-tenures.pdf

Palacin, J., & Shelburne, C. R. (2005). *The private housing market in eastern Europe and the CIS.* Discussion Paper Series No. 2005.5. United Nations. https://unece.org/fileadmin/DAM/oes/disc_papers/ECE_DP_2005-5.pdf

Pittini, A., Dijol, J., Turnbull, D., & Whelan, M. (2019). *The state of housing in the EU 2019.* Housing Europe, the European Federation of Public, Cooperative and Social Housing. https://www.housingeurope.eu/resource-1323/the-state-of-housing-in-the-eu-2019

Plešivčák, M., & Buček, J. (2017). In the centre, but still on the periphery: Is there any room for development of socio-economically deprived region in Slovakia? *International Journal of Social Economics, 44*(11), 1539–1558. https://doi.org/10.1108/IJSE-01-2016-0023

Schiller, R., & Weiss, A. (1999). Home equity insurance. *The Journal of Real Estate Finance and Economics, 19*(1), 21–47. https://link.springer.com/article/10.1023/A:1007779229387

Schwartz, H. M. (2020). Covering the private parts: The (re-)nationalisation of housing finance. *West European Politics, 43*(2), 485–508. https://doi.org/10.1080/01402382.2019.1582254

Shiller, R. (2016). *Irrational exuberance*. Princeton University Press.

Špirková, D. (2018). *Housing policy in the Slovak Republic*. IntechOpen.

Statistical Office of the SR. (2024). *Statistics*. https://slovak.statistics.sk/

Syrový, P. (2009). *Financování vlastního bydlení*. GRADA Publishing.

Szelényi, I. (2014). Pathways from and crises after communism: The case of central Eastern Europe. *Belvedere Meridionale*, *16*(4), 7–23. http://www.belvedere-meridionale.hu/?page_id=444

Szolgayová, E., Hlaváčová, V., Kaliňák, M., Kollár, E., Kurňavka, J., Pilát, E., & Reháková, V. (2019). *Podpora nájomného bývania*. https://www.zmos.sk/oznamy/podpora-najomneho-byvania.html

Szüdi, G., & Kováčová, J. (2016). "Building hope: From a shack to 3E house"—Innovative housing approach in the provision of affordable housing for Roma in Slovakia. *Journal of Housing and the Built Environment*, *31*(3), 423–438. https://www.jstor.org/stable/43907394

Tkacova, A., Gavura, S., Fulajtarova, M., & B.asistova, L. (2024). Determinants of real estate prices in Slovakia at the national and regional level. *AD ALTA Journal of Interdisciplinary Research*, *13*(2), 250–256. https://www.magnanimitas.cz/ADALTA/1302/PDF/1302.pdf

Vogel, H. L., & Werner, R. A. (2015). An analytical review of volatility metrics for bubbles and crashes. *International Review of Financial Analysis*, *38*, 15–28. https://doi.org/10.1016/j.irfa.2014.11.003

Winkler, H. (2010). *The effect of homeownership on geographic mobility and labour market outcomes*. University of California.

Wu, Y., & Lux, N. (2018). U.K. house prices: Bubbles or market efficiency? Evidence from regional analysis. *Journal of Risk and Financial Management*, *11*(3), 54. https://doi.org/10.3390/jrfm11030054

Chapter 7

External Economic Relations of the Slovak Republic: Trade, Investment, and Related Policies

Peter Jančovič

University of Economics in Bratislava, Slovakia

Abstract

Given the fact that Slovakia is a small, open, export-oriented economy strongly dependent on foreign trade and foreign direct investment (FDI) inflows, this chapter seeks to analyze the country's performance in international trade and investment flows as well as its foreign economic policy in the field of export and investment promotion. This chapter points out that Slovakia's foreign trade and inward FDI flows are highly interconnected due, inter alia, to the lion's share of foreign companies in Slovak exports. In addition, Slovakia's largest comparative advantages in exports are "acquired" through FDI inflows and include products of the automotive and electronics industries. However, the way in which Slovakia is involved in international trade and investment flows reflects its reliance on lower value-added economic activities, such as, in particular, the assembly of motor vehicles from imported intermediate products. In order to increase international competitiveness of the Slovak economy and ensure its future economic growth, it is important to improve the effectiveness of Slovakia's foreign economic policy and economic diplomacy, diversify the territorial and commodity structure of Slovak exports, support the expansion of Slovak companies abroad, as well as attract FDI with higher added value and to less developed regions.

Keywords: External economic relations; foreign economic policy; European Union; foreign trade; international specialization; foreign direct investment

Modeling Economic Growth in Contemporary Slovakia, 121–143

Published under exclusive licence by Emerald Publishing Limited
doi:10.1108/978-1-83549-454-720241010

1. Introduction

The Slovak Republic represents a small, open, export-oriented economy that is heavily dependent on foreign trade and foreign direct investment (FDI) inflows. With trade openness, measured as the ratio of total trade (exports plus imports) in goods and services to gross domestic product (GDP), higher than 204% in 2022, Slovakia belongs to the 10 most open economies in the world (World Bank, 2024a). From a historical perspective, Slovakia's trade openness shows an increasing trend, indicating the growing importance of trade flows in the economy. Slovakia's foreign trade is closely related to FDI. Multinational corporations operating in Slovakia make a significant contribution to the Slovak Republic's GDP, employment, and export volumes. Given the fact that Slovakia has a small domestic market, the inflows of FDI are predominantly export-oriented, which has a major impact on the export structure of the Slovak economy (Ministry of Economy, 2024a).

In this context, this chapter examines various aspects of Slovakia's external economic relations, specifically its performance in foreign trade and FDI flows, as well as the country's foreign economic policy in the field of export and investment promotion. The external economic relations of the national economy are defined as all its relations with other global economy's actors, which involve the movement of goods, services, capital, and people across borders, while these activities are affected by foreign economic policy (Ministry of Economy, 2024b). As an integral part of the overall economic policy, foreign economic policy can be seen as the government's deliberate action that influences the country's external economic relations through the determination of foreign economic rules, principles and objectives, as well as methods and tools necessary for their achievement. Given that Slovakia is part of the European Union's (EU's) common commercial policy, which falls within the exclusive responsibility of the EU, this chapter deals with export and investment promotion policies that continue to be managed by the Member States.

This chapter is structured as follows. The first section provides an overview of Slovakia's foreign economic policy in the field of foreign trade and investment, with a special focus on strategic documents and the institutional framework in this area. The second section identifies the main characteristics of the territorial and commodity structure of Slovakia's foreign trade in goods and analyzes international specialization of the Slovak economy. The third section describes Slovakia's position in foreign investment flows, especially the structure of inward and outward FDI as well as the importance of FDI for the Slovak economy. The final section of this chapter is devoted to concluding remarks along with some policy implications.

2. An Overview of Slovakia's Foreign Economic Policy in the Field of Trade and Investment

Foreign economic policy of the Slovak Republic is significantly influenced by its membership in the European Union and the Eurozone. With the accession to the EU in 2004, Slovakia adopted rules of the EU's common commercial policy and lost its autonomy in the field of external trade policy. The common commercial policy falls under the exclusive competence of the European Union, which means that the EU manages trade and investment relations with non-EU countries through its trade and investment policy. The EU's responsibilities in this area include trade in goods and services, the commercial aspects of intellectual property, public procurement, and FDI (European Commission, 2024). The EU makes laws on trade and investment matters, as well as negotiates and concludes international trade and investment agreements. In addition, Slovakia joined the euro area in 2009 implying that monetary policy, which can also be used to influence external economic relations, is conducted by the European Central Bank. It should also be noted that Slovakia is part of the EU single market with free movement of goods, services, capital, and persons, which limits the possibilities of determining its foreign economic policy.

The current strategic document that covers Slovakia's foreign economic policy in the field of foreign trade and investment is the *Concept of External Economic Relations and Economic Diplomacy of the Slovak Republic for the Period 2022–2030* (hereafter "Concept") developed by the Ministry of Economy of the Slovak Republic and the Ministry of Foreign and European Affairs of the Slovak Republic (MFEA). The Concept has replaced the previous two strategic documents such as the *Strategy of External Economic Relations of the Slovak Republic for the Period 2014–2020* (hereafter "Strategy") and the *Focus of Economic Diplomacy in the Field of Bilateral and Multilateral Relations until 2020*.

According to the Concept, Slovakia's foreign economic policy is primarily aimed at "supporting inclusive and sustainable economic growth, creating jobs with higher added value and increasing the competitiveness of the Slovak economy on an international scale" (Ministry of Economy, 2024a). To achieve the main goal in the field of external economic relations, the following partial objectives are set out: (i) diversification of the territorial structure of Slovak foreign trade, (ii) attracting FDI with higher added value, (iii) creating a favorable international environment to promote the economic interests of the Slovak Republic, (iv) improving the use of pro-export policy instruments, and (v) increasing the efficiency of economic diplomacy. The objectives of the Concept are broad, unspecified, and therefore difficult to measure. The Concept states that based on the above-mentioned partial objectives, the so-called action plans with specific tasks and measurable indicators will be developed for the effective implementation of the Concept (Ministry of Economy, 2024a). However, such an action plan has not yet been published.

The Strategy, as the previous strategic document in the field of Slovakia's external economic relations, contains significantly more objectives which are divided into four groups, such as commercial policy objectives, investment objectives, objectives in the field of research and innovation cooperation with other countries, and objectives in the field of unified presentation of the Slovak Republic (Ministry of Economy, 2024b). Commercial policy objectives consist of general and specific objectives. The general objectives are to increase export volumes, increase the number of exporters, and ensure stable supplies of strategic goods. The specific objectives are to (i) diversify the territorial structure of exports – increase the share of exports to non-EU markets, (ii) diversify the commodity structure of exports – increase the share of exports in commodity groups other than HS85 (electrical machinery and equipment) and HS87 (motor vehicles), (iii) increase the share of exports of small and medium-sized enterprises (SMEs), and (iv) increase the share of services exports, including tourism. Investment objectives of the Strategy include increasing FDI inflows particularly to higher added-value sectors and less developed regions, increasing export performance through investment, increasing investment in industrial R&D, and supporting established investors in expanding their activities in the Slovak economy. To sum up, the objectives of Slovakia's external economic relations defined in the strategic documents are primarily focused on export and investment promotion, emphasizing the need to diversify territorial and commodity structure of foreign trade and attract FDI with higher added value.

In light of the above-mentioned strategic documents and the fact that Slovakia is part of the EU's common commercial policy, the Slovak Republic's foreign economic policy focuses primarily on export and investment promotion, that is, pro-export policy and policy supporting FDI inflows. Pro-export policy is defined as all activities, objectives, and corresponding tools of the state aimed at enhancing the country's export performance (Ministry of Economy, 2024b). Pro-export policy instruments can be divided into financial, fiscal, and functional instruments (Ministry of Economy, 2024b). Financial instruments include banking and insurance products. Fiscal instruments consist of the so-called structural instruments, that is, instruments financed from EU sources, and instruments falling under development cooperation programs that may potentially enhance export performance. Functional instruments include a wide range of services provided to exporters by various stakeholders.

Economic diplomacy, as an integral part of Slovakia's foreign policy, represents the coordination of activities carried out by state and nonstate actors, which are aimed at supporting commercial and business activities of Slovak entrepreneurs when they enter foreign markets, as well as supporting flows of FDI into the Slovak economy (Government Office of the SR, 2016). Slovak economic diplomacy is primarily focused on promoting exports, FDI inflows, and interests of the Slovak Republic in international organizations (Ministry of Economy, 2024b). Economic diplomacy promotes exports and investments through the provision of assistance, advisory, consultancy, and information services. Economic diplomats identify investment and export opportunities for Slovak companies abroad and investment opportunities for foreign companies in the Slovak economy, look for opportunities to present Slovakia and organize such presentations, establish contacts with local entrepreneurs, monitor tenders and selection procedures, and perform many other functions.

Investment policy instruments can be divided into acquisition and marketing activities, consultancy and assistance activities, investment aid (investment incentives), and postinvestment assistance (Ministry of Economy, 2024a). Acquisition investment activity is carried out by various actors in Slovakia and abroad through the active promotion of Slovakia as an attractive investment destination. Marketing activity consists in the creation of promotional materials about the Slovak investment environment. Before starting a business in Slovakia, potential investors are usually provided with consultancy and assistance services in a variety of domains, such as, for instance, assistance with the selection of location and real estate, organization of meetings with local stakeholders, and consultancy on labor market situation, tax system, and investment incentives. Postinvestment assistance is intended to help established companies with expanding their production and operations, solving potential problems with the public administration bodies, and identifying local suppliers and service providers.

The main fiscal instrument for supporting FDI flows into the Slovak economy is investment aid regulated by European and Slovak legislation, which is divided into extraordinary investment aid and regional investment aid. Extraordinary investment aid can be granted to support investment projects related to industrial production in sectors strategic for the transition to a net-zero economy (Ministry of Economy, 2024d). These strategic sectors include, for instance, the production of batteries, solar panels, and wind turbines, as well as the production of critical raw materials necessary for their manufacture. The Ministry of Economy (2024d) defines regional investment aid as state aid "designed to foster competitiveness and reduce regional disparities." Regional investment aid may be granted for investment projects of new or established companies in the field of industrial production, technology centers, and shared services centers. In Slovakia, investment incentives are provided in the form of grants for tangible and intangible fixed assets, corporate income tax relief, contribution for newly created jobs, and rental or sale of publicly owned real estate at a discounted price (SARIO, 2024a).

The provision and amount of regional investment aid are influenced by various factors, such as the size of a company, minimum investment amount, number of newly created jobs, share of new technologies in a given investment, unemployment rate, and economic development of a district where the investment is made. Maximum aid intensity, which means the maximum amount of investment incentives calculated as a portion from the eligible costs, varies depending on particular regions and districts of Slovakia, while the Bratislava region's districts are completely excluded from the investment aid scheme. From August 2002 to February 2024, the Slovak government granted 267 investment incentives with a total value of almost 2.5 billion euros for investment projects that planned to create approximately 72 thousand new jobs (Ministry of Economy, 2024e). In that period, the most widely used forms of investment aid were grants for tangible and intangible fixed assets (46% of the total aid granted) and income tax relief (44% of the total aid granted). The main beneficiaries of regional investment aid were car manufacturers such as Volvo Car Slovakia, Kia Slovakia, PSA Slovakia, and Jaguar Land Rover Slovakia. From a territorial point of view, the highest number of investment incentives were granted to the companies from Germany, Slovakia, Austria, the Republic of Korea, the Netherlands, and the United States.

2.1 Institutional Framework of Slovakia's External Economic Relations

The institutional framework of Slovakia's external economic relations and economic diplomacy consists of the following actors:

- The Ministry of Economy of the Slovak Republic, including Slovak Investment and Trade Development Agency (SARIO), Slovak Innovation and Energy Agency (SIEA), and Slovak Business Agency (SBA);
- The Ministry of Foreign and European Affairs of the Slovak Republic (MFEA), including the Slovak Republic's diplomatic missions and Slovak Agency for International Development Cooperation (SAIDC);
- The Ministry of Finance of the Slovak Republic, including Export-Import Bank of the Slovak Republic (EXIMBANKA SR) and Slovak Guarantee and Development Bank (SZRB);
- Other ministries and specialized agencies such as the Ministry of Tourism and Sport of the Slovak Republic, including Slovakia Travel, the Ministry of Investments, Regional Development and Informatization of the Slovak Republic, and the Ministry of Agriculture and Rural Development of the Slovak Republic;
- Nonstate actors such as Slovak Chamber of Commerce and Industry (SOPK), Council of Slovak Exporters, Klub 500, National Union of Employers, Entrepreneurs Association of Slovakia, and many others.

The Competitiveness and Productivity Council of the Government of the Slovak Republic (hereafter "Council") is an advisory, coordinating and initiative body of the Slovak Government aimed at increasing the productivity and competitiveness of the Slovak economy and the better regulation policy (Ministry of Economy, 2022). In 2021, the Council replaced the more narrowly focused Export and Investment Promotion Council of the Government of the Slovak Republic, which was created in 2012 with the purpose of strengthening the support for international business and economic cooperation and presentation of the Slovak Republic abroad, while the priority objective was to promote exports and FDI inflows (Government Office of the SR, 2024). The Council's mission is to (i) support internal competitiveness and productivity, improve the business environment, promote investment and innovation in the economy, as well as (ii) improve international competitiveness, including the promotion of export, foreign investment, and international cooperation in the field of innovation. Its main function is to monitor, analyze, and evaluate the productivity and competitiveness of the Slovak economy. The Council brings together state and nonstate actors in the area of the Slovak Republic's external economic relations. It consists of 23 members, among whom are representatives of the state administration bodies, business and employer organizations, and self-governing associations (Ministry of Economy, 2022).

"Team Slovakia" is an informal interministerial platform seeking to enhance cooperation and mutual awareness of central state authorities in the field of export and investment promotion, supply chain development, science, research and innovation development, tourism promotion, and other areas (MFEA, 2022). It is made up of representatives at the level of directors-general of the Ministry of Economy, Ministry of Transport, Ministry of Agriculture and Rural Development, MFEA, Government Office, SBA, SARIO, and Slovakia Travel. The coordination group focuses on sharing information on projects, sectoral policies, and ongoing activities with foreign partners. It creates synergistic effects for selected activities and projects by involving human and financial capacities of the relevant members. In summary, the Council and "Team Slovakia" play an important role in coordinating the activities of various stakeholders in the area of external economic relations and economic diplomacy of the Slovak Republic.

The Ministry of Economy of the Slovak Republic and the Ministry of Foreign and European Affairs of the Slovak Republic are the main actors in Slovakia's external economic relations. In 2011, the MFEA took over the responsibility for economic diplomacy from the Ministry of Economy, but foreign trade remained under the competence of the Ministry of Economy. According to Csabay and Cséfalvayová (2022), the division of competencies in the field of external economic relations has naturally led to a rather forced, but necessary cooperation, as well as frictions between these two ministries. Parízek, a chairman of the Council of Slovak Exporters, argues that this division of competences causes unsystematic and ineffective foreign trade promotion (Oláhová, 2023). The Ministry of Economy is the central state administration body responsible, inter alia, for foreign trade and investment aid, including the formulation and implementation of foreign trade policy and investment policy (Ministry of Economy, 2024c). In close cooperation with the MFEA and other actors in the field of Slovak external economic relations, the Ministry of Economy proposes policies to promote exports, FDI, and innovation. The specialized agencies SARIO, SIEA, and SBA fall under the remit of the Ministry of Economy of the Slovak Republic.

SARIO was founded in 2001 as an implementation and facilitation state agency for export and investment promotion. Its main mission is "to accelerate the investment, export and innovation potential of the Slovak Republic with the intention of turning the country into a technology center attractive to foreign investors, experts and potential business partners" (SARIO, 2024b). It aims to attract FDI flows into the Slovak economy and support export performance of Slovak companies. In terms of investment promotion, SARIO focuses on consultancy, technical and assistance activities. It provides a wide range of services for potential and established investors related to the Slovak business environment, investment location, labor market, cooperation opportunities, investment incentives, local suppliers, and other areas. SARIO supports investors in three main phases such as location assessment phase, market entry phase, and postinvestment phase (i.e., continuous support). Furthermore, SARIO acts as an intermediary that facilitates communication between the companies and relevant state or public administration bodies. Regarding foreign trade support, SARIO provides information, assistance, consultancy, and educational services for Slovak companies with the aim of supporting their exports, as well as services for foreign companies interested in Slovak production and production cooperation (SARIO, 2024c). The agency supports Slovak companies and their international sales by organizing business missions and cooperation events, supporting the participation of Slovak companies in international fairs, searching for business partners abroad, training exporters, and other activities.

Between 2002 and 2022, SARIO concluded more than 630 investment projects amounting to a total of almost 15 billion euros. These investments created more than 140 thousand direct jobs (SARIO, 2024d). From a sectoral point of view, the majority of investment projects were related to automotive industry (30% of concluded investment projects between 2002 and 2022), electrical engineering industry (13%), and machinery industry (12%). Regarding territorial breakdown, SARIO supported the most investment projects of companies from Germany, the Republic of Korea, the United States, and Austria. During the same period, SARIO supported thousands of Slovak companies through more than 1,889 business missions, cooperation events, and participation in international fairs (SARIO, 2024e). Based on data from 2022, SARIO employs 88 people (SARIO, 2024e). Its budget for 2024 amounts to 4.7 million euros, representing an increase of 29% compared to the previous year (Ministry of Economy, 2024f). SARIO currently has three regional (domestic) offices in Bratislava, Banska Bystrica, and Kosice. It does not have any foreign offices, although the Strategy states that a network of SARIO foreign offices will be created to support exports. In the near future, SARIO plans to have its representation in the United States, Germany, and the Republic of Korea through seconded experts whose main task will be to present the Slovak business environment, as well as identify investment and trade opportunities directly in the selected territories (SARIO, 2024f).

However, Slovakia still lags behind some other countries in certain aspects of government support for trade and investment. Compared to the Czech Republic's trade and investment promotion agencies (there are two separate agencies, namely CzechInvest and CzechTrade), SARIO has almost three times fewer employees (CzechTrade and CzechInvest employed a total of 250 people in 2022) and approximately six times lower annual budget according to data from 2022. In addition, CzechTrade and CzechInvest together have 18 regional offices in the Czech Republic and more than 50 foreign offices (CzechInvest, 2024a; CzechTrade, 2024). Between 2002 and 2022, CzechInvest mediated 1,938 investment projects (CzechInvest, 2024b), which is three times more than SARIO mediated during the same period. According to the OECD (2018) report, which evaluates investment promotion agencies of its member countries, SARIO has a smaller number of staff and a higher number of mandates compared to the median of OECD countries, while its activity mix is focused on image building and targeting. In addition, Slovakia's investment promotion agency belongs to the group of agencies with a lower average budget and fewer domestic and foreign offices.

The SBA, founded in 1993, is a public–private institution that specializes in supporting SMEs during all phases of the business cycle, including strengthening their competitiveness within the EU single market and third country markets (SBA, 2024). It provides financial services (i.e., microcredits), as well as nonfinancial services (i.e., education, training, and consultancy) to SMEs. The SIEA, founded in 1999, is an implementation agency that promotes Slovak exports indirectly through comprehensive support for the development of innovative activities with the aim of increasing the efficiency of the domestic economy and its competitiveness (Ministry of Economy, 2024a).

The MFEA is responsible for the coordination and implementation of Slovakia's economic diplomacy. As part of the Slovak foreign policy, economic diplomacy focuses on promoting exports and FDI inflows, increasing the involvement of entrepreneurs in development cooperation, developing foreign cooperation in the field of science, research and innovation, and promoting Slovakia's economic interests in international organizations (MFEA, 2024a). The MFEA promotes foreign trade, investment, and international cooperation through the Business Center Department and the network of diplomatic missions. Economic diplomacy activities carried out by the MFEA include business missions, fairs and exhibitions, presentation events, Innovation Days, Company Days, "From Regions to the World," Export Forum, and other activities. With 91 diplomatic missions abroad, the Slovak Republic is represented in 64 countries (MFEA, 2024b). According to the latest available information, Slovakia has 70 economic diplomats in 62 countries (MFEA, 2024c). In recent years, the number of economic diplomats has increased significantly. However, it is important to note that economic diplomacy activities are carried out by all representative offices, regardless of the presence or absence of an economic diplomat. The heads of diplomatic missions (representative offices and consulates general) are responsible for the performance of economic diplomacy. Among the weaknesses of the Slovak Republic's economic diplomacy are insufficient human and financial resources allocated to economic diplomacy, performance of multiple functions at the same time by some economic diplomats, weak evaluation of the results achieved by economic diplomacy, low effectiveness of supporting SMEs in non-EU markets, and other aspects (e.g., MFEA, 2018; Oláhová, 2023; Ružeková et al., 2021).

The Slovak Republic started to provide bilateral development assistance in 2003. The SAIDC, founded in 2007, represents an implementation agency of Slovakia's official development assistance. An important role of SAIDC is, inter alia, to support the creation of new business partnerships of Slovak companies involved in development cooperation activities and to facilitate their penetration into the markets of developing countries (Ministry of Economy, 2024a). In this regard, the Private Sector Engagement Program was designed to support synergies between the Slovak Republic's development cooperation objectives and the business goals of Slovak companies, especially SMEs, in developing countries (SlovakAid, 2024). It engages the private sector in Slovakia's development cooperation activities and helps Slovak businesses to establish themselves or expand their activities in developing countries through cofinancing projects in the form of grants from the national budget.

In the field of external economic relations, the Ministry of Finance of the Slovak Republic is responsible for bilateral investment treaties (BITs) and double taxation conventions (Ministry of Economy, 2024a). The Export-Import Bank of the Slovak Republic and the Slovak Guarantee and Development Bank fall within the sphere of authority of the Ministry of Finance of the Slovak Republic. The SZRB is a specialized banking institution that may support Slovak exports indirectly through the financing of SMEs.

EXIMBANKA SR, founded in 1997, is a state export credit agency and the only direct instrument of the state for export financing (EXIMBANKA SR, 2024). Its main mission is to support Slovak exporters, regardless of their size, business sector, or destination country, through financial operations and expertise in the field of export, thereby increasing their competitiveness on foreign markets. Besides export promotion, EXIMBANKA SR also supports FDI of Slovak enterprises. EXIMBANKA SR plays a complementary role for commercial financial institutions, enabling Slovak companies to enter riskier projects, sectors, and territories. It provides a wide range of banking and insurance products, as well as other forms of export promotion, such as, for instance, consultancy on financial, commercial, and territorial export-related issues and the organization of various specialized events and workshops. Unlike other EU countries, the position of EXIMBANKA SR is specific, in that it provides comprehensive institutional support for exports, that is, banking and insurance activities, under one roof (Pavelka et al., 2021, p. 120). Banking products include financing, namely preexport credits, investment loans, foreign investment loans and buyer credits, as well as bank guarantees when exporting to foreign markets. Insurance products are intended for businesses or banks, allowing them to eliminate commercial, political, or combined risks. In addition, EXIMBANKA SR also supports Slovak companies that want to implement development projects and thus establish themselves in developing countries by providing preferential export credits, that is, concessional financing to a foreign buyer from the public sector in selected developing countries (SlovakAid, 2024). Under the so-called PSLO mandate, EXIMBANKA SR provides companies with information on the opportunities for participation in tenders of international financial institutions in developing countries, for which they may obtain financing from these institutions.

The Ministry of Tourism and Sport of the Slovak Republic is responsible for tourism promotion. Since its establishment in February 2024, the Ministry of Tourism and Sport has taken over competences in the field of tourism from the Ministry of Transport of the Slovak Republic (Ministry of Transport, 2024). Slovakia Travel, which falls under the remit of the Ministry of Tourism and Sport, represents a national marketing and promotion agency in the field of Slovak tourism. The Ministry of Investments, Regional Development, and Informatization of the Slovak Republic coordinates the agenda of Slovak innovation diplomacy. The Ministry of Agriculture and Rural Development of the Slovak Republic is responsible for export promotion of agricultural and food products.

3. Foreign Trade of the Slovak Republic

Slovakia as a small open economy is highly dependent on foreign trade, while applying an export-driven growth model (European Commission, 2023b). With the share of total trade in GDP exceeding 204% in 2022, Slovakia is the most open Visegrad Group country, the fourth most open EU Member State and one of the 10 most open economies in the world (World Bank, 2024a). Slovakia's trade openness reveals an increasing trend (the total trade accounted for 112% of GDP in 1993), which indicates the growing importance of foreign trade for the Slovak economy over time. Regarding the performance in goods exports, Slovakia ranked first among EU countries, as the share of exports of goods accounted for 88.6% of the Slovak GDP in 2022 (Eurostat, 2024b). However, a high degree of trade openness is closely linked to a high vulnerability to external economic shocks, which is also the case in Slovakia.

The territorial structure of Slovak foreign trade has changed considerably over the last few decades. Until 1989, the vast majority of Czechoslovakia's foreign trade was carried out with the Soviet Union and other Central and Eastern European countries, that is, members of the former economic organization Comecon. In the 1990s, during the period of transition to a market economy, the country's geographic pattern of foreign trade changed fundamentally, as the share of Slovakia's merchandise exports to Western Europe increased from 19% in 1989 to 71% in 1994 (WTO, 1995). In a subsequent period, the most important factor that affected Slovakia's trade patterns was the country's accession to the EU in 2004. The Czech Republic was Slovakia's largest trading partner from the dissolution of Czechoslovakia in 1993 until 1997, and since then Czechia has been the second most important trading partner due to geographical proximity as well as historical, linguistic, and cultural ties. Since 1998, Germany has been the largest trading partner of the Slovak Republic (UNCTADstat, 2024a).

Slovakia naturally has the closest commercial and economic ties with other EU Member States. Intra-EU (intraregional) trade accounted for 80.1% and 76.8% of Slovakia's exports and imports of goods, respectively, in 2022 (Eurostat, 2024c). Slovakia's most important export partners are Germany (21% of total merchandise exports in 2022), Czechia (12%), Hungary (9%), Poland (8%), and France (6%) (UNCTADstat, 2024a). On the other hand, when it comes to intra-EU trade, the majority of Slovakia's imports come from Germany (14% of total merchandise imports in 2022), Czechia (9%), Poland (5%), Hungary (5%), and France (3%) (UNCTADstat, 2024a). Extra-EU trade, that is, trade with non-EU countries, accounted for 19.9% and 23.2% of Slovakia's exports and imports of goods, respectively, in 2022 (Eurostat, 2024c). Outside the EU, important export partners are the United Kingdom (4% of total merchandise exports in 2022), the United States (3%), and China (3%). The largest non-EU import partners include China (8% of total merchandise imports in 2022), Russia (7%), and the Republic of Korea (6%) (UNCTADstat, 2024a). In summary, the territorial structure of Slovakia's foreign trade is relatively concentrated, as most of its trade is carried out with a few trading partners, mainly from the EU. However, some non-EU countries are important partners due to imports of oil, natural gas, and components for the Slovak manufacturing sector. It can also be observed that Slovakia does not have developed trade relations with developing countries.

Regarding the commodity structure of foreign trade, Slovak export is dominated by motor vehicles for the transport of persons (24.4% of total merchandise exports in 2022), parts and accessories of vehicles (5.1%), television receivers (4.4%), telecommunication equipment (3.8%), and refined petroleum products (2.5%) (UNCTADstat, 2024a). From a long-term perspective, the road vehicles, electric machinery and appliances, and machinery make up more than half of Slovakia's total exports in goods, indicating a low level of diversification of the Slovak export basket. This is confirmed by the UNCTAD's export product concentration index (i.e., Herfindahl-Hirschman index), according to which Slovakia has a moderately concentrated export structure, but with a growing concentration tendency (UNCTADstat, 2024c). Compared to the other Visegrad countries, Slovakia has the most concentrated commodity structure of exports. On the other side, Slovakia's most important import items include parts and accessories of vehicles (11% of total merchandise imports in 2022), telecommunication equipment (6.1%), natural gas (5.6%), electrical machinery (3.6%), and electric current (3%) (UNCTADstat, 2024a). Except for energy imports, the commodity structures of Slovakia's exports and imports are similar, suggesting the importance of intraindustry trade.

In Slovakia, the terms of trade, measured as the ratio between the index of export prices and the index of import prices, deteriorate over time (OECD, 2024a), which indicates an unfavorable position of the economy in international trade flows. This is caused by various factors, such as the increasing prices of imported inputs, including fossil fuels and other commodities, as well as the way of Slovakia's integration into global value chains, that is, assembling of imported intermediate products (European Commission, 2023a), resulting in a low domestic added value in Slovak exports (Fidrmuc et al., 2020). According to OECD (2024b) data, Slovakia has the fourth highest share of foreign value added in gross exports (47.7% in 2020) among OECD countries. In addition, Slovakia records the lowest share of high-technology exports, that is, products with high R&D and innovation intensity, in the total manufactured exports (8.4% in 2022) among the Visegrad countries and the fifth lowest within the EU (World Bank, 2024b). Other weaknesses of Slovakia's exports include a high concentration of exporters, weak involvement of SMEs in total exports, and insufficient export performance of Slovak companies. The 10 largest exporting companies, predominantly foreign owned, accounted for 33% of total Slovak exports in 2020 (Hrabina, 2021). Slovak exports are generated mostly by foreign companies, whereas domestic companies accounted only for 12% of total exports in 2021 (Steinhauser & Boros, 2022). SMEs, that is, companies with less than 250 employees, accounted for 29.5% of total Slovak exports in 2022 (SBA, 2023).

Table 7.1 reports five commodity groups with the highest degree of international specialization of the Slovak Republic in four selected years (1995, 2007, 2015, and 2022). It was calculated by using the Lafay index of international specialization. In 1995, Slovakia's greatest comparative advantages were in the

Table 7.1. The Highest Values of the Lafay Index of International Specialization of the Slovak Republic.

No.	1995	2007	2015	2022
1	Iron and steel products, not clad (4.94)	Passenger motor vehicles (7.17)	Passenger motor vehicles (7.79)	Passenger motor vehicles (10.71)
2	Petroleum products, refined (1.57)	Television receivers (4.62)	Television receivers (3.06)	Television receivers (1.55)
3	Textile yarn (1.32)	Petroleum products, refined (1.37)	Rubber tires (0.81)	Rubber tires (0.57)
4	Iron and steel products, clad (1.12)	Iron and steel products, not clad (1.09)	Petroleum products, refined (0.72)	Iron and steel products, not clad (0.46)
5	Wood, simply worked (0.87)	Sanitary, plumbing and heating fixtures (0.41)	Iron and steel products, not clad (0.42)	Petroleum products, refined (0.32)

Source: Author's own calculations, using UN Comtrade (2024) data.

Note: The values of the Lafay index of international specialization (LFI) are given in brackets.

The LFI is calculated using the following formula: $\mathrm{LFI}_j^i = 100\left(\frac{x_j^i - m_j^i}{x_j^i + m_j^i} - \frac{\sum_{j=1}^{N}(x_j^i - m_j^i)}{\sum_{j=1}^{N}(x_j^i + m_j^i)}\right)\frac{x_j^i + m_j^i}{\sum_{j=1}^{N}(x_j^i + m_j^i)}$,

where x_j^i and m_j^i are export and import of a commodity group j at the 3-digit level of SITC classification of a country i to and from the rest of the world, respectively, and N is the total number of commodity groups. A positive value of the LFI indicates the existence of comparative advantage in a given commodity group, whereas a negative value indicates comparative disadvantage. The higher the LFI value, the greater the comparative advantage. For more information, see Zaghini (2003).

export of lesser sophisticated and low-skill products, such as iron and steel products, textile yarn, and wood (Table 7.1). In 2022, Slovakia achieved the strongest comparative advantage in the export of passenger motor vehicles. The degree of Slovakia's international specialization in motor vehicles shows a growing trend from the mid-2000s when PSA Peugeot Citroën (currently Stellantis) and Kia started their operations in the Slovak economy. Slovakia also shows relatively high degree of specialization in exporting television receivers, rubber tires, iron and steel products, and refined petroleum products. As can be seen in Table 7.1, the patterns of Slovakia's international specialization are relatively constant in the 21st century. Broadly speaking, Slovakia shows "acquired" comparative advantages, in particular through FDI inflows, rather than "natural" comparative advantages that are based on factor endowments.

4. Foreign Direct Investment

The inflow of FDI plays a vital role in the Slovak economy. Foreign companies operating in Slovakia hold an important share of Slovak exports, employment, industrial production, as well as overall GDP. At the beginning of the 21st century, FDI inflows contributed to the modernization and restructuring of the Slovak economy. Foreign investments significantly contributed to labor productivity growth, primarily due to the import of efficient technologies, and thus also to Slovakia's economic convergence toward the EU average (Ministry of Economy, 2018). However, FDI flows into the Slovak economy were not adequately accompanied by investments into R&D, innovation, and high-tech industries, which resulted in the current stagnation of higher added-value sectors and international competitiveness of the Slovak economy (Ružeková et al., 2021). Although multinational corporations are more productive than Slovak companies, they mostly transfer lower added-value economic activities to the Slovak economy, rather than research activities that usually remain in their home countries. This led to the result that Slovakia represents a "top assembly plant" and not a leader in research and innovation (Habrman et al., 2022).

Fig. 7.1 depicts FDI inflows as a percentage of GDP to the Slovak Republic and other Visegrad Group countries from 1993 to 2022. Inward FDI flows to the Slovak economy can be divided into three periods. The first period, dated from Slovakia's independence in 1993 until 1998, is characterized by relatively low FDI inflows to the Slovak economy compared to other Visegrad countries, mostly due

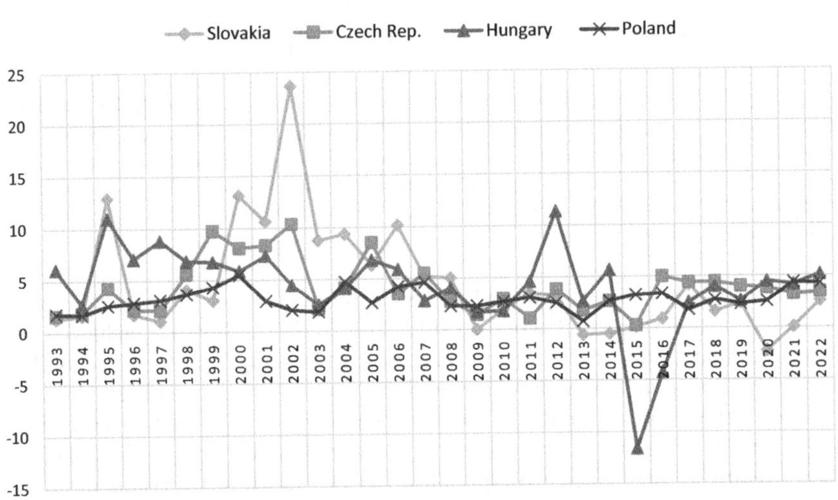

Fig. 7.1. FDI Inflows to the Visegrad Countries in the Period 1993–2022 (% of GDP). *Source:* Author's own elaboration based on UNCTADstat (2024b) data.

to political instability and unfavorable investment environment during the era of "Mečiarism" (1993–1998). In this period, FDI inflows to the Visegrad countries were mainly driven by the privatization process. The government of Vladimír Mečiar publicly prioritized domestic investments over foreign ones (Wemer, 2013), which also contributed to relatively low FDI flows into Slovakia. Between 1993 and 1998, FDI inflow to GDP ratio in Slovakia averaged 3.8% per year (UNCTADstat, 2024b). In the second period, dated from 1999 to 2008, the Slovak economy experienced a boom in FDI inflows, primarily thanks to economic reforms (tax, pension, labor market, and other reforms) implemented by the two governments of Mikuláš Dzurinda (1998–2006), investment aid that started to be provided by the Slovak government, Slovakia's accession to the EU in 2004, as well as continuation of the privatization process. Between 1999 and 2008, the share of FDI inflow in Slovakia's GDP was on average 9.5% per year (UNCTADstat, 2024b), while the highest inward FDI flows were recorded between 2000 and 2006, when Slovakia became a leader in FDI inflow to GDP ratio among the Visegrad countries (Fig. 7.1). The change was triggered by the Global Financial Crisis, as a result of which Slovakia experienced a negative FDI inflow in 2009. In the postcrisis period, FDI inward flows did not reach the level of the first decade of the 21st century. The third period, dated from 2009 onwards, is characterized by a relative slowdown in FDI inflows expressed in relation to GDP compared to the previous period as well as other Visegrad countries (Fig. 7.1). Between 2009 and 2022, FDI inflow to GDP ratio in Slovakia averaged 1.2% per year (UNCTADstat, 2024b). This slowdown may be caused, inter alia, by the loss of Slovakia's competitive advantage based on a relatively cheap, available, and skilled labor force.

Slovakia's position in foreign investment flows is highly inward-oriented, given that inward FDI stock was equivalent to 50.6% of Slovakia's GDP in 2022, while outward FDI stock represented only 4.8% of its GDP in a given year (UNCTADstat, 2024b). The share of inward FDI stock in Slovakia's GDP has increased more than tenfold since 1993, when the stock represented 4.7%. However, over the recent years, inward FDI stock to GDP ratio has shown a downward trend (e.g., inward FDI stock accounted for more than 62% in 2017) (UNCTADstat, 2024b). Compared to the Czech Republic and Hungary, as well as EU27 average, inward FDI stock to GDP ratio in Slovakia is significantly lower. The large imbalance between FDI inflows and outflows reflects the need of the Slovak economy to import foreign capital and not to export it abroad. The share of outward FDI stock in Slovakia's GDP has more than quadrupled between 1993 and 2022. However, Slovakia records the second and fourth lowest outward FDI stock to GDP ratio among OECD and EU countries, respectively (UNCTADstat, 2024b). This may indicate the low ability of Slovak companies to expand abroad due to a lack of capital and low competitiveness in foreign markets caused by insufficient innovation capacity (IHA, 2023), as well as an inadequate state support for FDI outflows.

Inward FDI stock in Slovakia accounted for 53.8 billion euros in 2022 (NBS, 2024). As shown in Fig. 7.2, the largest foreign investors in Slovakia are the

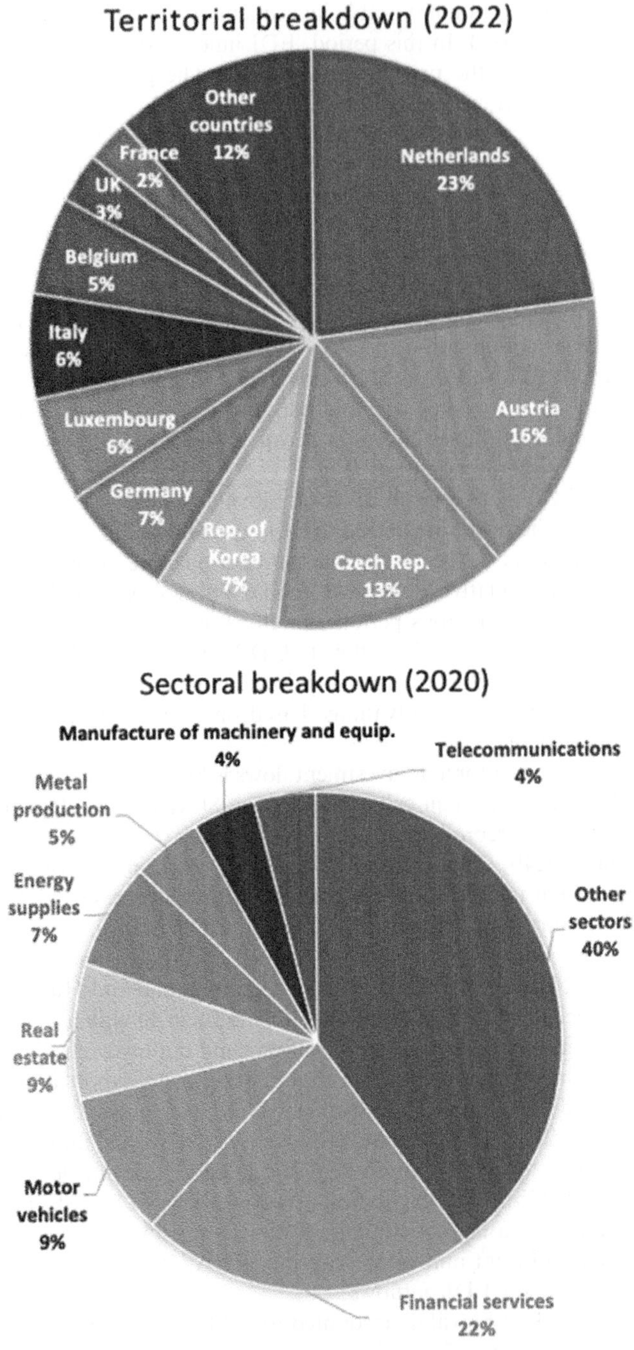

Fig. 7.2. Structure of Inward FDI Stock. *Source:* Author's own elaboration based on NBS (2024) data.

Netherlands (due to the fact that many non-Dutch multinational corporations are registered there because of tax advantages), Austria, and the Czech Republic. Despite the fact that Germany accounts for only 7% of inward FDI stock in Slovakia (Fig. 7.2), German companies belong to the most important foreign investors in the Slovak economy. Most FDI in Slovakia is carried out by EU-based multinational corporations. In 2022, EU countries accounted for 86.4% of inward FDI stock in the Slovak Republic, while the share of OECD countries represented 96.8% (NBS, 2024). Among non-EU countries, the largest investors include the Republic of Korea and the United Kingdom, followed by the United States and Norway.

In the Slovak economy, inward FDI stock is very unevenly distributed. From a territorial point of view, 81% of inward FDI stock is concentrated in Western Slovakia, including the Bratislava Region, 12% in Central Slovakia, and only 7% in Eastern Slovakia (NBS, 2024). Roughly two thirds of inward FDI stock is concentrated in the Bratislava region, with 63.6% located in Bratislava. Although state investment aid is aimed at reducing regional disparities, the regions of Presov and Banska Bystrica account for only 1.6% and 2.4% of Slovakia's inward FDI stock, respectively (NBS, 2024). Regarding the sectoral breakdown, 59.4% of inward FDI stock in the Slovak economy is concentrated in the service sector, particularly financial, real estate, and telecommunication services, and 31.6% in manufacturing sector, especially automotive, metallurgical, and mechanical engineering industries (Fig. 7.2). The automotive industry is the most important manufacturing sector for FDI inflows and, at the same time, the driving force of the Slovak economy. Slovakia's automotive industry produces more than one million vehicles per year, accounts for half of the total industrial production, directly employs (four established car manufacturers and their direct suppliers) about 176 thousand people, and contributes by 11% to Slovakia's GDP (SARIO, 2024f). The fifth global car manufacturer in Slovakia, Volvo, is expected to start its production in 2026 with a planned annual capacity of 250 thousand vehicles (SARIO, 2024f). It is important to note that inward FDI stock is largely concentrated in low value-added manufacturing, such as assembly activities in the car industry (IHA, 2023).

Determinants that positively influence FDI flows into the Slovak economy include favorable geographic location in the center of Europe, high degree of trade openness, membership in the EU and euro area, relatively skilled and educated labor force, positive attitude of the Slovak government toward inward FDI flows (e.g., investment incentives, SARIO activities, industrial parks), heavily industrialized economy (especially a highly developed automotive industry and a dense network of automotive suppliers), and other factors. Regarding the types of FDIs according to the main motivation of multinational corporations when investing abroad, efficiency-seeking FDI or, in other words, export-oriented FDI dominate from the Slovak economy's perspective (e.g.,

Habrman et al., 2022; Ministry of Economy, 2024a). In the early 21st century, FDI inflows were mostly driven by relatively cheap and qualified workforce, which is no longer the case due to increasing labor costs as well as a shortage of skilled labor (e.g., European Commission, 2023a). This suggests that Slovakia should build a new competitive advantage and improve its nonprice competitiveness in order to attract the necessary amount of FDI, especially to higher added-value sectors.

On the other hand, the factors that can adversely affect multinational corporations' decision to invest in Slovakia include small domestic market with 5.4 million inhabitants, mineral resources scarcity, inland location of the country, significant regional disparities, high vulnerability to external economic shocks due to Slovakia's dependence on industry, exports and high integration in global value chains, suboptimal quality and availability of transport infrastructure, relatively low R&D and innovation spending, poor availability of labor force and unfavorable demographic situation (e.g., shrinking working-age population and population aging), low labor productivity (measured as GDP per person employed and hour worked) compared to the EU average (Eurostat, 2024a), low efficiency of public administration, inefficient judiciary system, and uncertain macroeconomic environment (e.g., European Commission, 2023a, 2023b; U.S. Department of State, 2024).

Slovak companies have not made significant outward FDI, as the total cumulative value of direct investments from Slovakia abroad amounted to 5.1 billion euros in 2022 (NBS, 2024). As shown in Fig. 7.3, Slovakia records a high territorial concentration of outward FDI stock. Approximately 54% of Slovakia's outward FDI stock is concentrated in the Czech Republic (Fig. 7.2). It can also be observed that Slovak companies tend to expand to geographically close European countries, such as the Czech Republic, Poland, Austria, and Hungary, which together accounted for 72% of Slovakia's outward FDI stock in 2022 (Fig. 7.3). Most of these host countries have similar economic structures with comparable level of economic development, which, to a certain extent, limits the potential economic benefits that outward FDI can bring, such as the transfer of new technology and know-how from abroad (Fidrmuc et al., 2020). Therefore, state support for FDI outflow to Western European countries and non-EU countries might be beneficial for the Slovak economy. Among non-EU countries, the United Kingdom, Ukraine, and China have the largest share in outward FDI stock of the Slovak Republic (NBS, 2024). As illustrated in Fig. 7.3, Slovakia's outward FDI stock is predominantly concentrated in the service sector, namely wholesale, real estate, and management consultancy services.

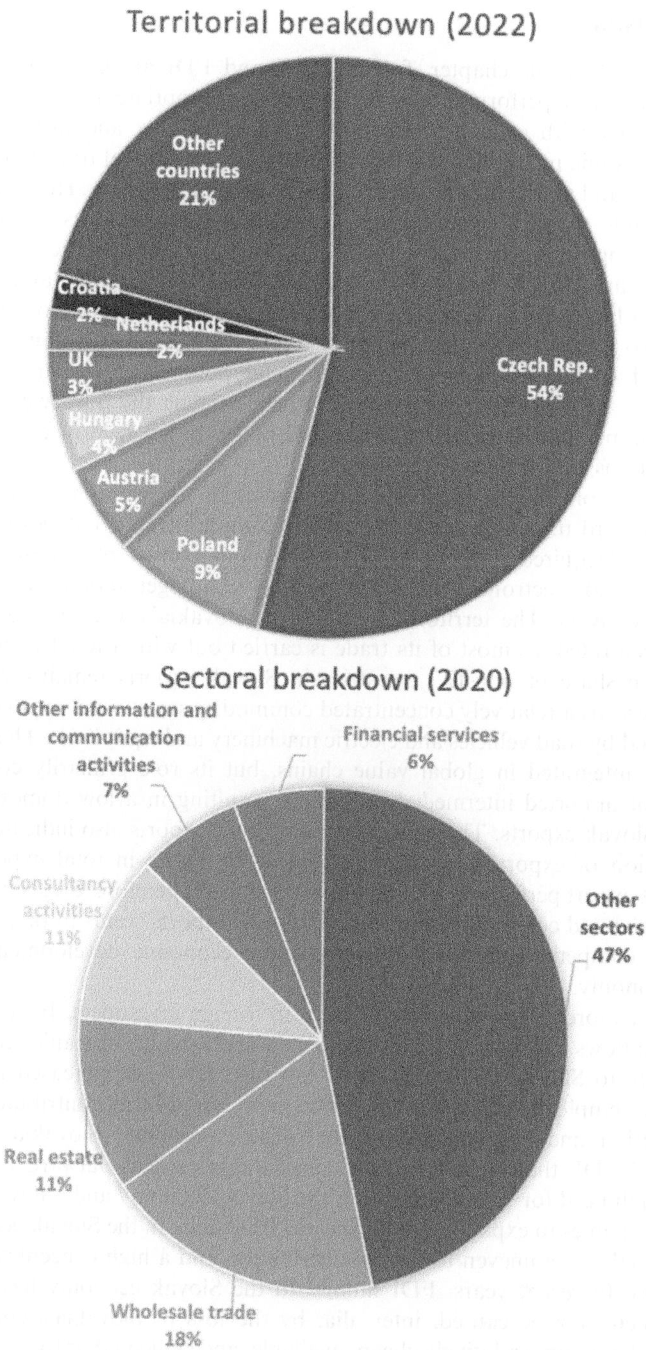

Fig. 7.3. Structure of Outward FDI Stock. *Source:* Author's own elaboration based on NBS (2024) data.

5. Conclusion

As emphasized in this chapter, foreign trade and FDI are key drivers of the Slovak economy's performance. Therefore, an appropriate foreign economic policy together with clearly defined strategies, objectives, and instruments of external economic relations, as well as an effective institutional framework in the field of trade and investment promotion are more than necessary. However, there is considerable scope for further improvements in various areas, such as, for instance, strengthening the efficiency of Slovak economic diplomacy, enhancing cooperation among different stakeholders, allocating more human and financial resources to the national system of export and investment promotion. It is also important to note that Slovakia's membership in the European Union, especially with regard to the EU's common commercial policy and investment policy measures, as well as being part of the Eurozone define the framework for the formulation and implementation of national policy in the field of external economic relations.

Slovakia is one of the most open economies in the world with a growing tendency toward trade openness. The largest comparative advantages in Slovak exports are "acquired" through FDI inflows and consist of the products of automotive and electronics industries, namely passenger motor vehicles and television receivers. The territorial structure of Slovakia's foreign trade is relatively concentrated, as most of its trade is carried out with a few EU countries, whereas the share of non-EU countries in Slovak exports remains very low. Slovakia records a relatively concentrated commodity structure of exports, which is dominated by road vehicles and electric machinery and equipment. The country is strongly integrated in global value chains, but its role primarily consists in assembly of imported intermediate products, resulting in a low domestic value added in Slovak exports. The analysis of Slovakia's exports also indicates a high concentration of exporters, weak involvement of SMEs in total exports, and insufficient export performance of Slovak companies. Therefore, diversification of the territorial and commodity structure of Slovak exports seems to be crucial for increasing competitiveness and ensuring future economic development of the Slovak economy.

Slovakia's foreign trade is closely linked to foreign investment due to the fact that FDI inflows are primarily export-oriented and foreign companies contribute significantly to Slovakia's total exports. Inward FDI flows increased industrial production, employment, and labor productivity, as well as contributed to the modernization and restructuring of the Slovak economy. Slovakia is a net importer of FDI, that is, inward FDI considerably exceeds outward FDI, indicating a high need for foreign capital in the Slovak economy and a low ability of Slovak companies to expand abroad. Inward FDI stock in the Slovak economy is characterized by an uneven territorial distribution and a high concentration in a few sectors. In recent years, FDI inflows to the Slovak economy have slowed down, which may be caused, inter alia, by the loss of Slovakia's competitive advantage based on a relatively cheap, available, and skilled labor force. Slovakia faces the challenge of ensuring FDI inflows of the necessary amount, attracting FDI with higher added value and to less developed regions, as well as supporting investments by Slovak companies abroad.

References

Csabay, M., & Cséfalvayová, K. (2022). Reconciling institutional actors of economic diplomacy: The case of Slovakia. *Czech Journal of International Relations*, *57*(2), 7–37. https://doi.org/10.32422/cjir.2

CzechInvest. (2024a). About CzechInvest. https://www.czechinvest.org

CzechInvest. (2024b). Business and Investment Development Agency. Investment project statistics. https://www.czechinvest.org/en/Uber-CzechInvest/Statistika-investicnich-projektu

CzechTrade. (2024). O CzechTrade. https://www.czechtrade.cz/czechtrade

European Commission. (2023a). *In-depth review 2023. Slovakia*. European Commission, Institutional Paper 223. https://economy-finance.ec.europa.eu/system/files/2023-05/ip223_en.pdf

European Commission. (2023b). *2023 country report – Slovakia*. European Commission, Commission Staff Working Document, SWD (2023) 625 final. https://economy-finance.ec.europa.eu/system/files/2023-05/SK_SWD_2023_625_en.pdf

European Commission. (2024). *Trade. Making trade policy*. https://policy.trade.ec.europa.eu/eu-trade-relationships-country-and-region/making-trade-policy_en

Eurostat. (2024a). *Labour productivity per person employed and hour worked (EU27_2020=100)*. https://ec.europa.eu/eurostat/databrowser/view/tesem160/default/table?lang=en

Eurostat. (2024b). *Exports of goods and services in % of GDP*. https://ec.europa.eu/eurostat/databrowser/view/tet00003/default/table?lang=en

Eurostat. (2024c). *Intra and extra-EU trade by member state and by product group*. https://ec.europa.eu/eurostat/databrowser/view/ext_lt_intratrd/default/table?lang=en

EXIMBANKA SR. (2024). *About Eximbanka*. https://eximbanka.sk/en/about-eximbanka/

Fidrmuc, J., Gardoňová, K., Hulényi, M., & Zavarská, Z. (2020). *Report on productivity and competitiveness of the Slovak Republic 2019*. National Productivity Board of the Slovak Republic. https://isa.gov.sk/narodna-rada-pre-produktivitu-nrp/

Government Office of the SR. (2016). *Návrh Zamerania ekonomickej diplomacie v oblasti bilaterálnych a multilaterálnych vzťahov do roku 2020*. https://rokovania.gov.sk/RVL/Material/21556/1

Government Office of the SR. (2024). *Rada vlády Slovenskej republiky na podporu exportu a investícií*. https://www.vlada.gov.sk/rada-vlady-slovenskej-republiky-na-podporu-exportu-a-investicii/

Habrman, M., Habodászová, Ľ., & Šrámková, L. (2022). *Reformný Kompas slovenskej ekonomiky*. Inštitút finančnej politiky. https://www.mfsr.sk/files/archiv/7/27257_material_hlasovanie.pdf

Hrabina, J. (2021, December 9). Najväčších exportérov na Slovensku trápia klesajúce príjmy z export. *Trend*. https://www.trend.sk/nazory-a-komentare/najvacsich-exporterov-slovensku-trapia-klesajuce-prijmy-exportu

IHA. (2023). *Správa o produktivite a konkurencieschopnosti za rok 2022*. Inštitút hospodárskych analýz. Inštitút hospodárskych analýz, Ministerstvo hospodárstva Slovenskej republiky. https://www.mhsr.sk/uploads/files/5GnvPQ8A.pdf?csrt=7448239595103812314

MFEA. (2018). *Informácia o stave siete zastupiteľských úradov SR v zahraničí v roku 2018*. https://www.economy.gov.sk/uploads/files/LzpzKORk.pdf
MFEA. (2022). *Tím Slovensko*. https://www.mzv.sk/diplomacia/ekonomicka-diplomacia/spolupraca-so-statnymi-instituciami/tim-slovensko
MFEA. (2024a). *Ekonomická diplomacia*. https://www.mzv.sk/diplomacia/ekonomicka-diplomacia
MFEA. (2024b). *Zastupiteľské úrady SR na mape*. https://www.mzv.sk/staty/zastupitelske-urady-na-mape
MFEA. (2024c). *Kontakty v oblasti ekonomickej diplomacie*. https://www.mzv.sk/sluzby/podpora-podnikania/kontakty
Ministry of Economy. (2018). *Priemyselná výroba a jej postavenie v hospodárstve SR*. https://www.economy.gov.sk/uploads/files/ezNh8gXF.pdf
Ministry of Economy. (2022). *Rada vlády SR pre konkurencieschopnosť a produktivitu*. https://www.economy.gov.sk/podnikatelske-prostredie/rada-vlady-sr-pre-konkurencieschopnost-a-produktivitu
Ministry of Economy. (2024a). *Koncepcia vonkajších ekonomických vzťahov a ekonomickej diplomacie Slovenskej republiky na obdobie 2022–2030*. https://www.economy.gov.sk/uploads/files/LMovpfgU.pdf
Ministry of Economy. (2024b). *Stratégia vonkajších ekonomických vzťahov SR na obdobie 2014–2020*. https://www.economy.gov.sk/obchod/podpora-exportu/strategia-vonkajsich-ekonomickych-vztahov-sr-na-obdobie-2014-2020
Ministry of Economy. (2024c). *About us*. Ministry of Economy of the Slovak Republic. https://www.economy.gov.sk/about-us
Ministry of Economy. (2024d). *Essential information 2024. Regional investment aid*. Ministry of Economy of the Slovak Republic. https://www.economy.gov.sk/uploads/files/ji15LmYK.pdf?csrt=13265908619619020921
Ministry of Economy. (2024e). *Podpora podnikateľov. Zoznamy*. https://www.mhsr.sk/podpora-investicii/podpora-investicii/investicna-pomoc/zoznamy
Ministry of Economy. (2024f). *Rozpočet MH SR*. https://www.mhsr.sk/ministerstvo/rozpocet-mh-sr-1?csrt=16117439304325466972
Ministry of Transport. (2024). *Od februára prechádzajú kompetencie cestovného ruchu na nové ministerstvo*. https://www.mindop.sk/media/tlacove-spravy/od-februara-prechadzaju-kompetencie-cestovneho-ruchu-na-nove-ministerstvo
NBS. (2024). *Štatistika. Priame zahraničné investície*. https://nbs.sk/statisticke-udaje/statistika-platobnej-bilancie/priame-zahranicne-investicie/
OECD. (2018). *Mapping of investment promotion agencies in OECD countries*. https://www.oecd.org/investment/Mapping-of-Investment-Promotion-Agencies-in-OECD-Countries.pdf
OECD. (2024a). *OECD data. Terms of trade*. https://data.oecd.org/trade/terms-of-trade.htm
OECD. (2024b). *Trade in value added*. OECD.Stat. https://stats.oecd.org/Index.aspx?DataSetCode=TIVA_2022_C1#
Oláhová, Z. (2023, November 4). *Slovenský export by sa mal diverzifikovať, súčasná pozícia Slovenska nie je podľa exportérov bezpečná*. SITA Webnoviny. https://sita.sk/slovensky-export-by-sa-mal-diverzifikovat-sucasna-pozicia-slovenska-nie-je-podla-exporterov-bezpecna/
Pavelka, Ľ., Ružeková, V., & Zubaľová, Ľ (2021). *Inštitucionálna podpora financovania exportu a zahraničných investícií vo vybraných krajinách EÚ*. Leges.

Ružeková, V., Zábojník, S., Hrinko, J., Parízek, L., & Hrabina, J. (2021). *Krehká realita slovenského exportu*. University of Economics in Bratislava, Council of Slovak Exporters. https://www.exporteri.sk/wp-content/uploads/2021/08/RSE_Krehká%20realita%20slovenského%20exportu.pdf

SARIO. (2024a). *Investment incentives in Slovakia*. https://www.sario.sk/sites/default/files/sario-investment-aid-eng-2024-02-16.pdf

SARIO. (2024b). *About us*. Slovak Investment and Trade Development Agency. https://www.sario.sk/en/about-us

SARIO. (2024c). *Agency profile*. Slovak Investment and Trade Development Agency. https://www.sario.sk/sites/default/files/sario-profile-2022-01-03-eng.pdf

SARIO. (2024d). *Prehľad úspešných projektov SARIO*. https://www.sario.sk/sites/default/files/sario-success-stories-sk-2023-06-21.pdf

SARIO. (2024e). *Výročná správa 2022*. SARIO. https://www.sario.sk/sites/default/files/2023-07/sario-vyrocna-sprava-2022.pdf

SARIO. (2024f). *Automotive sector in Slovakia*. https://www.sario.sk/sites/default/files/sario-automotive-sector-in-slovakia-2024-02-20.pdf

SBA. (2023). *Malé a stredné podnikanie v číslach v roku 2022*. Slovak Business Agency. https://monitoringmsp.sk/wp-content/uploads/2023/07/MSP_v_cislach_2022.pdf

SBA. (2024). *O nás*. Slovak Business Agency. https://www.sbagency.sk/o-nas

SlovakAid. (2024). *Private sector engagement program*. https://slovakaid.sk/en/programme-of-business-partnerships/

Steinhauser, D., & Boros, K. (2022). *Kam tečú slovenské exporty, pán Newton?* Inštitút hospodárskych analýz, Ministerstvo hospodárstva Slovenskej republiky. https://www.mhsr.sk/ministerstvo/centrum-pre-hospodarske-otazky/publikacie/analyzy/kam-tecu-slovenske-exporty-pan-newton

UN Comtrade. (2024). *Trade Data*. UN Comtrade Database. https://comtradeplus.un.org

UNCTADstat. (2024a). *Merchandise trade matrix, annual*. https://unctadstat.unctad.org/datacentre/dataviewer/US.TradeMatrix

UNCTADstat. (2024b). *Foreign direct investment: Inward and outward flows and stock, annual*. https://unctadstat.unctad.org/datacentre/dataviewer/US.FdiFlowsStock

UNCTADstat. (2024c). *Merchandise: Product concentration and diversification indices of exports and imports, annual*. https://unctadstat.unctad.org/datacentre/dataviewer/US.ConcentDiversIndices

U.S. Department of State. (2024). *2023 investment climate statements: Slovakia*. https://www.state.gov/reports/2023-investment-climate-statements/slovakia/

Wemer, D. A. (2013). Europe's little tiger?: Reassessing economic transition in Slovakia under the Mečiar government 1993–1998. *The Gettysburg Historical Journal*, *12*(7), 97–112. https://cupola.gettysburg.edu/ghj/vol12/iss1/7

World Bank. (2024a). *Trade (% of GDP)*. https://data.worldbank.org/indicator/NE.TRD.GNFS.ZS

World Bank. (2024b). *High-technology exports (% of manufactured exports)*. https://data.worldbank.org/indicator/TX.VAL.TECH.MF.ZS

WTO. (1995). *Slovakia: November 1995*. Trade Policy Reviews. https://www.wto.org/english/tratop_e/tpr_e/tp019_e.htm

Zaghini, A. (2003). *Trade advantages and specialisation dynamics in acceding countries*. Working Paper No. 249, European Central Bank Working Paper Series. https://www.ecb.europa.eu/pub/pdf/scpwps/ecbwp249.pdf

[illegible]

[illegible] Kingdom? [illegible]

Chapter 8

Divergence of Slovak Regions: Bumpy Road to Decentralization

Anton Marcinčin

Comenius University, Slovakia

Abstract

Large regional differences in Slovakia existed already at the beginning of the 20th century, which resulted in emigration mainly from the east of the territory. The subsequent popularity of the communist regime is explained by a successful reduction in the regional disparities and increased well-being of the inhabitants. The transformation since 1990 ignored important regional differences among the Czech and Slovak regions and this led to the disintegration of Czechoslovakia. Governance structures in Slovakia remained centralized. This harmed the welfare – weaker economic performance of the regions and worse results of the labor market. The underutilization of the economic potential of regions has consequently slowed down the catching up at the national level. Slovakia thus so far missed the opportunity to use transfers from the European Union more productively. In recent years, however, there has been some progress in changing the unsatisfactory model of public governance to a more modern one, with much greater decision-making and financial autonomy for the regions.

Keywords: Regional development; regional disparities; EU funding programs; Slovak Republic; decentralization

1. Introduction

Slovak Republic was founded only 30 years ago, on January 1, 1993. Thanks to the availability of educated and disciplined labor, the country attracted large foreign investment and quickly became an automotive powerhouse (Dębkowska et al., 2019). However, Slovakia is also known as a country of large regional disparities (OECD, 2018), which preserved a model of highly centralized

Modeling Economic Growth in Contemporary Slovakia, 145–160

doi:10.1108/978-1-83549-454-720241011

decision-making. As a result of leaving a substantial part of its territory underdeveloped, the country stopped converging with the developed economies (Hlaváč, 2023; Marcinčin, 2022) and its fiscal policy significantly deteriorated.

It seems almost obvious that the old growth model which combines cheap labor and foreign investment should be replaced by a more modern model based on educated and skilled labor, innovations, new technologies, and green energy (European Commission, 2023). However, the ongoing discussions may miss one crucial point – a need to change the quality of governance, from highly centralized and spatially-blind to decentralized and place-based. Only decentralized decision-making, which utilizes a wealth of information, can ensure the efficient allocation of scarce resources in line with the endogenous potential of regions for the economic growth of the country (Green, 2023; O'Brien et al., 2015).

In this chapter, we first briefly describe historical development from 1918 to 1992. In the third part, we compare selected indicators of regional disparities in Slovakia to other regions of the European Union (EU). In the fourth part, we briefly analyze the utilization of the major financial transfer aimed at cohesion and reduction of regional disparities. The fifth part concludes and presents public policy recommendations.

In the chapter, we use both literature available in English but especially in Slovak, and data by the Eurostat and the Slovak Statistical Office.

The main message of the chapter is that a transition from the communist regime to a free-market economy requires that the governance model be deeply restructured. Slovakia refused a centrally planned economy but retained a centralistic, spatially-blind growth model. As a result, not only do regional disparities remain considerably high but also national economic development stagnates. While recently some signs of decentralization appeared, much remains to be done.

2. Convergence by the Comrades and a Breakup of Czechoslovakia

It is widely accepted that the communist regime, especially in its first, extensive period, helped Slovakia and its regions to converge to the much more developed Czech lands.

Large regional disparities in Slovakia existed already at the beginning of the 20th century. In 1918, when democratic Czechoslovakia was established, its eastern parts were much less developed than the western Czech lands – Bohemia, Moravia, and Silesia. Slovakia – especially its eastern part – suffered from insufficient infrastructure, obsolete agriculture, and slow industrialization (Lubyová & Marcinčin, 2002).

Slovak transport network was built from the North to the South, where the capital city of Budapest was located, to serve the Hungarian and Austrian markets. Czechoslovakia with the capital city Prague on its Western part made transport from the east by up to 50% more expensive. In 1914, rail network density was only 0.062 km/km^2 in Slovakia and Carpathian Ruthenia, while 0.130

km/km^2 in Bohemia, 0.098 km/km^2 in Moravia, and 0.136 km/km^2 in Silesia (Karvaš, 1933, p. 21; quoted in Marcinčin, 2023, p. 125).

In 1910, 64% of the active population worked in agriculture in Slovakia, while only 37% in Bohemia, 46% in Moravia, and 35% in Silesia. However, agricultural productivity in Slovakia was about 40% lower than in the Czech lands, and even in 1936, Slovakia contributed to the Czechoslovak agricultural production only by 22% (Karvaš, 1933; quoted in Marcinčin, 2023, p. 126).

In the same period, only 18% of the active population worked in industry in Slovakia, but 37% in Bohemia, 30% in Moravia, and 41% in Silesia. While the number of workers in industry between 1910 and 1926 increased in western Slovakia by 34% to still low 40 thousand people, it fell by 10% in central Slovakia to 33 thousand and by 27% in eastern Slovakia to 8 thousand people (Karvaš, 1933; author's calculations).

As a result, in 1928, Slovaks were on average much poorer than Czechs: 40% of the Slovak taxpayers reported income lower than 12 thousand Koruna and 37% reported more than 18 thousand Koruna. The respective averages for the Czech lands were 34% and 45% (Karvaš, 1933, pp. 72–74; author's calculations). Even in 1937, with 25% of the Czechoslovakian population, Slovakia's share in GNP was only 15%, in industrial production only 8%, and in agricultural production 22% (Federální statistický úřad, 1985, pp. 822–824). Illiteracy in 1930 was 1.8 times higher in Slovakia than in the Czech lands (Begg, 1991, p. 245).

Emigration abroad was therefore often perceived as the only real solution to the unfavorable economic situation, especially in eastern Slovakia. Between 1900 and 1914, an estimated one-third of the population from eastern Slovakia emigrated (Hanzlík, 1967). Between 1918 and 1939, about 500 thousand people emigrated (Federální statistický úřad, 1985, pp. 822–824).

The Czechoslovak economic policy did not pay much attention to the fact that the potential and capacities of the Czech and Slovak economies were rather different. Imrich Karvaš (1903–1981), an economist and a regionalist, called for an industrial policy that would take into account those regional differences and increase the competitiveness of the Slovak economy on the domestic and foreign markets. The change came, however, only after the war and with a communist regime. And during a war, as a German ally, the Slovak economy in 1937–1943 saw a 52% increase in industrial employment and a 54% increase in industrial production, fueled by the German war demand.

In 1948–1953, the communist regime introduced its institutions by shock therapy. To secure central control over the Czechoslovak economy, a strict hierarchical structure of planning and control was established, and production was monopolized and horizontally cartelized (Mlčoch, 1997). Attempts to reform inefficient central planning started in 1957 but ended with a military occupation in 1968 under the leadership of the Soviet army (Rusek, 1996).

During the communist period, however, thanks to rapid economic growth, Slovakia and its regions experienced convergence and higher standards of living. From 1948 to 1983, Slovakia's share of the social product of Czechoslovakia increased from 19% to 30%, the gross industrial production from 13% to 29%, the monetary income from 22% to 31%, on the number of university students from

22% to 37%, and the number of physicians from 20% to 33% (Federální statistický úřad, 1985; author's calculations).

This was a result of both the after-war extensive growth and certain decentralization. However, after its initial success, the inefficient communist model (Kornai, 1996) started generating negative growth in the 80s (Begg, 1991) and Czechoslovakia in 1989 returned to a democracy and market economy.

Slovakia's catching up to more developed Czech lands could also be a reason, why an opinion poll in 1994 showed that 45% of Slovakia's respondents claimed that "the post-November regime has more shortcomings compared to the pre-November regime," while the same claimed only 20% of the Czech respondents (Černušáková, 2004). Even in 2018, the opinion poll showed that 43% of Slovaks thought that "life was better before 1989 than today," while only 21% thought the opposite (TASR, 2018).

The transition from a centrally planned to a market economy in Czechoslovakia is often described as a shock therapy – it happened in the institutional vacuum. The rapid pace of reforms, however, hurt Slovak much more than the Czech economy (OECD, 1994). Slovakia's gross domestic product (GDP) growth recovered only in 1994, reaching its peak at −15% in 1991. The unemployment rate increased to 12% in 1991 and continued to rise till 2001 when it reached 19%. Inflation reached 61% in 1991 and remained in double digits until 1995. Net exports fell to a negative 9% of GDP in 1990 and recovered in 1994 (Morvay, 2000, p. 58; Statistical Office SR). The fiscal deficit in 1990 was estimated at 12% of GDP (Tóth, 2000, p. 92).

A lack of consideration for a regional policy and different consequences of the shock therapy then led to a breakup of Czechoslovakia (Pavlínek, 1995).

3. Disparities Between Slovak Regions

Slovakia is often referred to as a country with one of the largest regional disparities. However, this evaluation differs based on the level of territorial units considered: the Slovak regional disparities grow with the more detailed area classification. So, while the European Commission takes into account NUTS 2 or NUTS 3 regions and considers Slovakia one of the countries with deep regional disparities, the OECD (2018) takes a more detailed NUTS 4 level which makes Slovakia rank among countries with the deepest regional disparities (Table 8.1). This is because 79 NUTS 4 regions do not form functional areas and often separate more productive and wealthier centers from more rural surroundings. Their definition was driven more by the political consideration and their size differed from 10,900 (Medzilaborce) to 173,200 citizens (Ministerstvo vnútra, 2007; Statistical Office SR, 2024).

In this chapter, we aim to answer two questions – what are the disparities among the Slovak regions and how did they develop over time? And are these disparities significant compared to other countries of Europe? For that, we examine the development of demography, GDP per capita, investment per capita, employment rate, and the risk of poverty and social exclusion. Disparities are

Table 8.1. Number of Population of Slovak Regions by NUTS Classification.

NUTS 2		NUTS 3		NUTS 4	
	Population		**Population**	**Number of Districts**	**Average Population**
Bratislava	726,220	Bratislava	726,220	8	90,778
West Slovakia	1,809,393	Trnava	565,333	7	80,762
		Trenčín	572,117	9	63,569
		Nitra	671,943	7	95,992
Central Slovakia	1,308,177	Žilina	688,749	11	62,614
		Banská Bystrica	619,428	13	47,648
East Slovakia	1,587,236	Prešov	807,595	13	62,123
		Košice	779,641	11	70,876
Total	5,431,026	Total	5,431,026	79	68,747

Source: Author's own calculations based on Statistical Office SR, Number of the Population by Sex – SR-Area-Reg-District, U-R (yearly) [om7102rr], Mid-year (Mean) population (Person).

calculated weighted by the total population of the regions. Furthermore, we also look at the geographical distribution of the marginalized Roma population, which could help explain some of the disparities.

The literature on the Slovak regional disparities is well summarized by Korec et al. (2016). While several studies used the static perspective, many fewer analyze the development of disparities – convergence.

3.1 Demography

Regional demographic developments indicate the availability of jobs, standards of living, and prospects. We use the latest projections by Eurostat (Population on 1st January by age, sex, type of projection, and NUTS 3 region [proj_19rp3]) from 2019 for about 1,200 NUT3 regions of member states of the European Union. First, we look at the age composition of the population in 2050 for three age groups: 0–14 years, 15–64 years (working age population), and 65+ (seniors). Second, we calculate the pace of change. Third, we calculate a percentile rank for each region and indicator. We consider the value of the regional indicator significantly different if it ranks below the 10th or above the 90th percentile. Finally, we also calculate regional disparity by each EU country in 2025 and 2050 weighted by the total size of the population.

Age composition in 2050: The ratio of 0–14 years old in 2050 will be significantly high in the Bratislava region, at 94 percentile level. On the other hand, the ratio in Trenčín and Nitra regions will be small, ranking at the 14 and 15 percentiles (Fig. 8.1). The ratio of 15–65 years old will not differ much from the

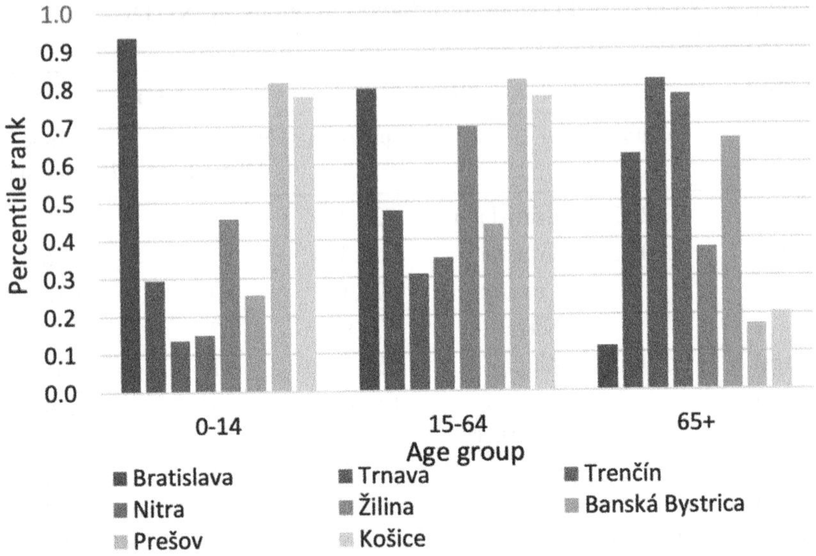

Fig. 8.1. Ranking by the Age Groups in 2050. *Source:* Author's own calculations based on Eurostat, Population on 1st January by age, sex, type of projection and NUTS 3 region [proj_19rp3].

European values. The ratio of seniors will be small in Bratislava at the 12th percentile, but also in Prešov and Košice regions, at the 17th and 21st percentile levels.

The pace of change: While the composition of the population will not be so different from the European peers, the speed of change seems considerably high. Trenčín, Nitra, and Banská Bystrica will lose some 14% of their total population and 27% of both 0–14 and 15–64 years old and gain 36% of 65+ over 25 years.

The speed of growth of the total population will be significantly high in Bratislava, which ranks at the top 6 percentile. In contrast, the speed of a decline in Trenčín, Nitra, and Banská Bystrica is also rather high at 15th to 17th percentiles. This is because Trenčín and Nitra are quickly losing child populations aged 0 to 14, raking at the seventh and ninth percentile, and Banská Bystrica at the 11th percentile. Furthermore, they are also losing the working-age population – and Nitra significantly fast. The population is significantly fast becoming senior in five regions: Bratislava, Prešov, Trnava, Košice, and Žilina. The other three regions ranked in the 80th and 81st percentiles.

Another finding is that Bratislava differs from all other regions, followed by Prešov and Košice and then Trenčín, Nitra, and Banská Bystrica. The remaining Trnava and Žilina are between the second and third groups.

The disparity between Slovak regions is rather high for the ratio of children, with only France and Portugal higher in 2025 and also with Romania and Spain higher in 2050. The disparity in the share of working age and seniors is relative to other countries low.

3.2 GDP per Capita

We used Eurostat data GDP at current market prices by NUTS 3 regions [nama_10r_3gdp] and Population on 1 January by age group, sex, and NUTS 3 region [demo_r_pjangrp3]. We do not use data in purchasing parity as they contain certain methodological problems, which, however, may not be too significant (Hlaváč, 2023).

The performance of regions in Slovakia differs tremendously. In 2021, Bratislava produced 39,000 euros per capita, while Prešov only 11,000 euros, and the average of the seven regions other than Bratislava was only 15,000 euros.

In the 2000 to 2021 period, Bratislava progressed from the 22nd to the 80th percentile in 2010 and remained there (Fig. 8.2). All other regions progressed, too, some of them – Prešov, Žilina, Banská Bystrica, and Nitra from significantly low levels in 2000. However, they achieved only the 19th percentile in 2021, with two exceptions: Trnava, 29th, and Prešov, 10th percentile. For more than 10 years, the ranking did not change.

From a weighted regional dispersion perspective, Slovak regions, however, do not differ too much – there were other 12 countries in 2020 with higher disparities in 2020.

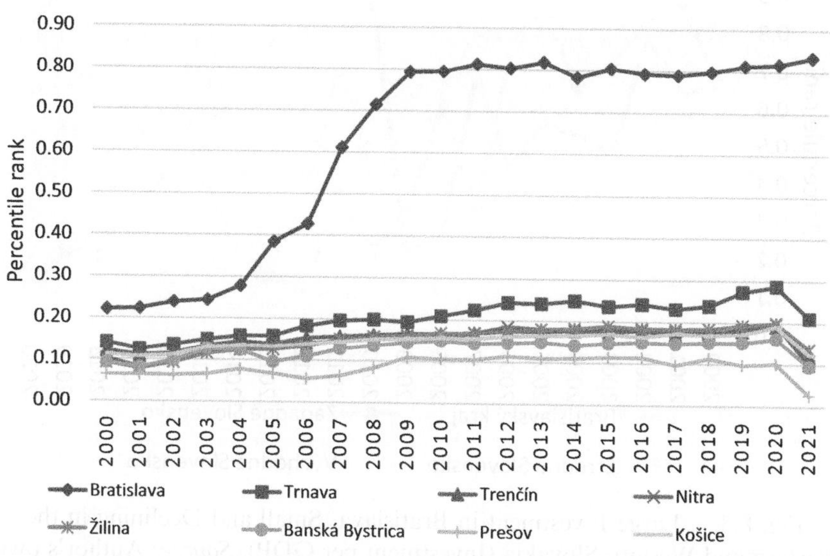

Fig. 8.2. GDP per Capita: Bratislava Among the Best and Prešov Among the Worst Performers. *Source:* Author's own calculations based on Eurostat, Gross domestic product (GDP) at current market prices by NUTS 3 regions [nama_10r_3gdp].

3.3 Investment per Capita

We calculate investment on GDP from Eurostat Gross fixed capital formation by NUTS 2 regions [nama_10r_2gfcf], GDP at current market prices by NUTS 2 regions [nama_10r_2gdp], and population weights from Population on 1 January by age, sex and NUTS 2 region [demo_r_d2jan]. We calculated investment on GDP ratio for NUTS 2 because NUTS 3 was not available.

Investment till the crisis in 2009 was similar in NUTS 2 Slovak regions, ranging on average from 24% to 28% of GDP. Interestingly, relatively the lowest investment was in the richest region of Bratislava. This has changed significantly since 2010 as Bratislava quickly increased its investment-to-GDP ratio to some 28%, while other regions, most notably Eastern and Western Slovakia, fell to much lower values, ranging from 16% to 25%.

Compared to other European regions, Bratislava remained in the top 10 percentile from 2012 to 2019 (Fig. 8.3). On the contrary, Eastern and Western fell recently from the bottom 20% to the bottom 10%, exhibiting a worrisome trend of lack of investment (including maintenance).

Regional discrepancies in 2020 are higher than in Slovakia in 5 out of 18 countries, namely in Ireland, Romania, Hungary, Germany, and the Czech Republic.

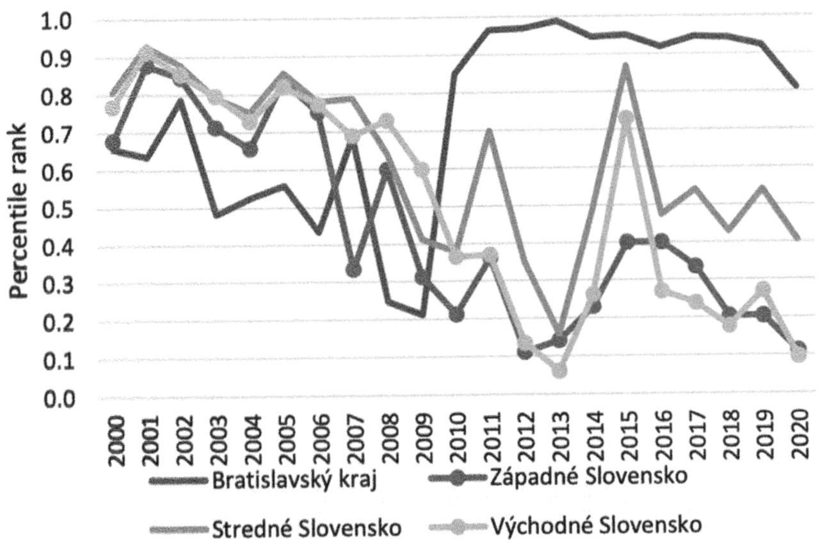

Fig. 8.3. Large Investment in Bratislava, Small and Declining in the Eastern and Western Slovakia (Investment per GDP). *Source:* Author's own calculations based on Eurostat, Gross fixed capital formation by NUTS 2 regions [nama_10r_2gfcf], Gross domestic product (GDP) at current market prices by NUTS 2 regions [nama_10r_2gdp].

3.4 Employment Rate

Two Eurostat data sets are used, Employment rates by sex, age, and NUTS 2 regions (%) [lfst_r_lfe2emprt] and Population on 1 January by age, sex, and NUTS 2 region [demo_r_d2jan].

Again, from 2000 to 2022, the employment rate in Bratislava is rather high, reaching the average of 72% and having a positive trend. The latter is true also for Western and Central Slovakia, which started from much lower values (some 55% in 2000) and reached 72% in 2022. Eastern Slovakia, however, started from a similar 52% in 2000 and reached only 66% in 2022. This was some 14 percentage points less than in Bratislava, which is almost equal to the average over the whole period of 15 percentage points.

Compared to other European regions, Bratislava reached the top 10 percentile in 2021, while Eastern Slovakia only left the bottom 20 percentile in 2022 (Fig. 8.4).

Out of 24 compared European countries at the NUTS 2 level, six have higher regional disparities than Slovakia: Italy, Belgium, Spain, Romania, Switzerland, and France.

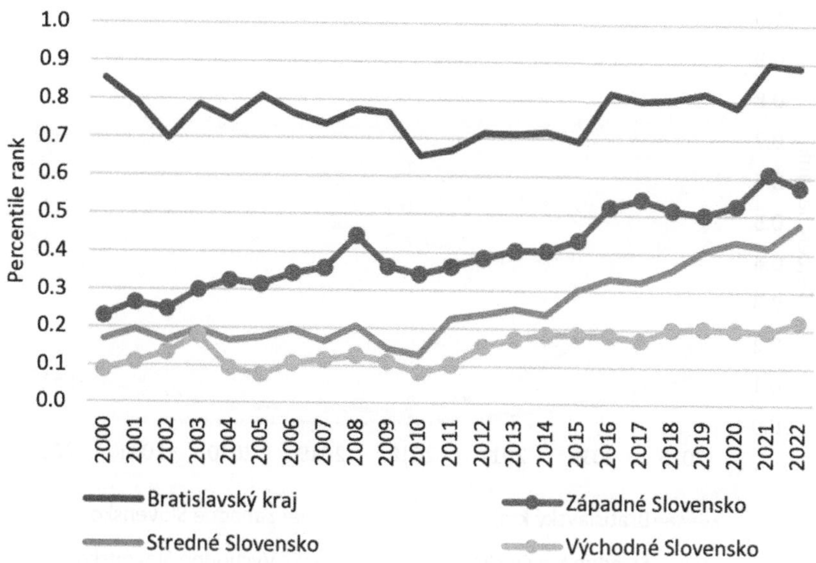

Fig. 8.4. Employment Rate: Prešov Left Alone. *Source:* Author's own calculations based on Eurostat, Employment rates by sex, age and NUTS 2 regions (%) [lfst_r_lfe2emprt] and Population on 1 January by age, sex and NUTS 2 region [demo_r_d2jan].

3.5 Poverty and Social Exclusion

By the Eurostat definition, households are facing poverty or social exclusion if they experience at least one of the three poverty and social exclusion risks: risk of poverty, severe material and social deprivation, and/or living in a household with very low work intensity (Eurostat, 2023).

Persons at risk of poverty or social exclusion by NUTS regions [ilc_peps11n] and Population on 1 January by age, sex, and NUTS 2 region [demo_r_d2jan] were used. Persons at risk of poverty or social exclusion at the regional level – NUTS 2 – are available only for 2015–2022 and the number of observations gradually increased from 108 to 248.

Before the pandemic, there were two similar groups of regions in Slovakia: Bratislava and Western Slovakia with very low values, 6% and 10%, respectively. The second group of Eastern and Central Slovakia was at 18% then. However, in 2022, the values increased, with Bratislava at 11% and Eastern Slovakia at 23%.

Compared to other European regions, Bratislava has ranked in the top 5 percentile since 2016 and Western Slovakia in the top 10 percentile since 2017 (Fig. 8.5). Eastern Slovakia rank now approaches the bottom 30%.

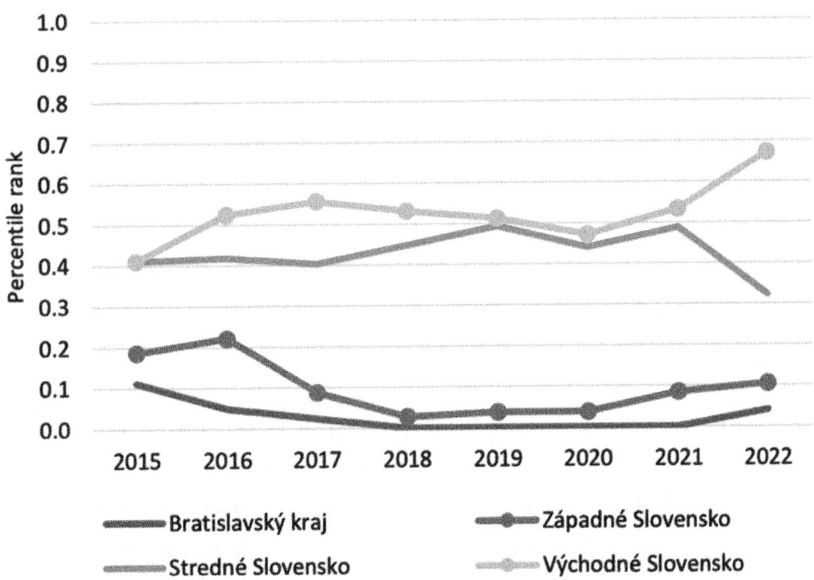

Fig. 8.5. The Risk of Poverty and Social Exclusion is Very Low in Bratislava and Western Slovakia. *Source:* Author's own calculations based on Eurostat, Persons at risk of poverty or social exclusion by NUTS regions [ilc_peps11n] and Population on 1 January by age, sex and NUTS 2 region [demo_r_d2jan].

Regional discrepancies in poverty and social exclusion increased in Slovakia, but from 24 countries, Slovakia ranked 11th, almost in the middle.

3.6 Marginalized Roma

Analysis of regional differences in Slovakia (and perhaps also in several other Central and Eastern European countries) needs to take into consideration also large minority of the Roma population which often lives in poor economic conditions, suffering from low education, low labor market participation, and employment and discrimination.

Some 60% (Grauzelová & Markovič, 2018) of the estimated 420 thousand Roma population (Ravasz et al., 2020) is estimated geographically marginalized, living in territories populated almost entirely by the Roma minority (Grauzelová & Markovič, 2018, p. 10).

Marginalized Roma communities differ from the majority significantly (Grauzelová & Markovič, 2018):

- they are much younger and their households are bigger, having 4.5 members as compared to 2.9 members in the general population;
- they are more often disabled, 8% of their members receive disability pensions as compared to only 2% in the general population;
- less than 25% of their members have higher than elementary education;
- the median annual income of a one-person household was only 31% of the median income of the general population; and
- in 2018, the probability of falling below the poverty line in the community was 12 times higher than in the general population.

These characteristics influence comparisons, especially of Eastern and Central Slovakia. An estimated 32% of Roma reside in the Košice region, 30% in the Prešov region, and 20% in Banskobystrický region. The residual 18% reside in the remaining five regions. The three largest concentrations at the district level are Košice-okolie with 28 thousand Roma residents, Rimavská Sobota with 26 thousand Roma residents, and Spišská Nová Ves with 23 thousand Roma residents (ARK, 2019).

4. Cohesion Investments

European Commission claims the regional (cohesion) policy is the EU's main investment policy which supports job creation, competitiveness of businesses, economic growth, sustainable development, and better quality of life. Therefore, it is complementary to other European policies like education, employment, energy, the environment, the single market, and research and innovation (European Commission, 2024a).

Because the regional disparities are driven by spatial productivity (OECD, 2018, p. 10), it is important to craft regional policy and industrial policy wisely, to support the development of the local economy and avoid the exclusion of people from job opportunities and generation of growth. Spatial productivity means higher specialization of the regions in the tradable sector or location in proximity to a city.

Furthermore, regional policy cannot be prepared and implemented without those most affected. But while the average participation of the self-government in public investment in 2018 was in the European Union 51%, in Slovakia, it was only 20% (OECD, 2018).

Since its entry, Slovakia received large transfers from the EU to increase economic, social, and territorial cohesion. They totaled 24 billion euros, which was 1.1% of GDP annually (Gertler et al., 2023). Slovakia however did not use all of the available EU funds: in 2014–2020, Slovakia spent 13.9 billion euros, or 79% of available funds (European Commission (2023, p. 30) mentions only 72% absorption rate), while its neighboring Czechia 95%, Poland 92%, Hungary 100%, and Austria 88% (European Commission, 2024b). However, their impact on cohesion is unclear since the country is not converging whether on the national or regional level.

In September 2023, the government admitted problems with the European funds. While in 2014–2020, European funds financed almost one-half of its public investment, Slovakia on average invested about 1.3% of GDP less than Hungary, Czechia, or Poland. At the same time, its management system was per capita twice as expensive as in comparable countries.

To increase the efficiency of EU funds, the government elaborated 10 recommendations focused on improving their predictability, procedures of public procurement, digitalization, and control. They also include a recommendation to prepare a public investment plan focused on key strategic priorities and improve communication with stakeholders – both are missing. Furthermore, the document noted that investment projects are not linked to national, regional, or local strategic planning documents (Úrad vlády SR, 2023).

The system is indeed administratively very complicated: Slovakia regularly reports by far the highest financial impact of detected fraudulent and non-fraudulent irregularities ratio within the EU, at 21% (while the second Romania and the third Spain only 3%). This is, however, a failure of the managing body to take preventive actions (OLAF, 2021).

Even more importantly, there is no coordination of public investment management: "A national strategic framework for public investment in Slovakia is largely missing. Slovakia does not have an overarching national plan setting the goals and strategies to guide investment allocations. Due to the lack of a national plan, there is no structured discussion on the prioritization of investment projects within or between sectors" (IMF, 2019). Public investment planning and financing is mostly top-down, which hinders the autonomous decision-making of self-governments (OECD, 2016). Coordination in the preparation of investment plans among self-governments and between self-governments and the central government is very low. This is despite the conclusion of the public expenditure review by the World Bank (2008) that strategic planning is limited by the priorities of EU funds and the residual space in the budget, and the medium-term budget was largely focused on the fiscal balance, excluding or obscuring the government's new priorities. Policy priorities should be separated from funding sources, a strategic plan with clearly defined investment priorities should be developed and public investment management, weak in all three phases – identification and appraisal of project proposals, implementation and monitoring of projects, and ex-post evaluation processes – should be strengthened.

The literature noted institutional problems (e.g., Marcinčin, 2021a). A lack of clear plan and strategy, monitoring and evaluation, little transparency, and emphasis on drawing funds rather than achieving results could be connected to the very centralized decision-making – contrary to the practice of the other countries. Uncertainty about EU funds prevents self-governments from carefully planning their investments and aligning them with their priorities, which then prevents businesses from planning their capacities.

Marcinčin (2021a) recommends to use of EU funds for productive investment to strengthen competitiveness by targeted interventions and utilize the existing planning and implementation capacities of cities and regions for the preparation and management of public investment projects that will support local economic development and the economic stability of local governments.

5. Conclusions

The literature on the regional disparities in Slovakia is not rich, which is surprising in light of the large influx of cohesion funds from the European Union. However, a majority of analyses conclude that there are significant disparities between the west (Bratislava) and east, although – because of underestimated population and overestimated production in Bratislava – not as high as the data suggest. History explains the rapid development of the capital region, large foreign direct investment, centralization of decision-making power and public administration, and concentration of the financial industry headquarters and qualified labor force (Korec et al., 2016, p. 273).

The World Bank (2003) noted, however, that because the national convergence is usually driven by the growth poles around capital cities and major agglomerations, the country should direct public investment to these areas, even if it initially widens the regional disparities. In that respect Bratislava region was not to be excluded from the EU funding, but quite the contrary. This approach would not necessarily contradict the OECD focus on switching from subsidizing underdeveloped regions to supporting them in maximizing returns from their specific (productive) endowments (OECD, Regional Development Policy).

Historical perspective certainly plays an important role: a chain of eastern and southern districts is called in the literature "a macro-region of poverty," "natural regions of poverty," or "chronically poor districts" (Marcinčin, 2021b).

Our analyses of disparities in the context of EU regions suggest a significantly rapid pace of demographic change in several Slovak regions and high disparities in the ratio of children in 2025 and 2050. Prešov shows a significantly low value of GDP per capita, but the disparity within Slovakia compared to other countries is not exceptionally high. Investment to GDP compared to other European regions is significantly high in Bratislava and low in eastern and western Slovakia, and disparity in Slovakia is relatively high. Employment rate is significantly high in Bratislava and disparity in Slovakia is relatively high. Similarly, poverty and social exclusion are compared to other European regions very low in Bratislava and Western Slovakia, while at the national level, the disparities in Slovakia are not high. Part of the explanation lies with the marginalized Roma community, which is concentrated in the three regions: Košice, Prešov, and Banská Bystrica. To conclude, there is not much progress in reducing measurable disparities in Slovakia and some of them are significantly different in the European comparison.

Before and especially after it entered the European Union, Slovakia received large amounts of subsidies from the European Union to reduce regional disparities and enhance cohesion. The country was expected to apply a good model of management and use the funds productively. This seems to fail and last year, the government proposed to reconsider the way the utilization of funds is planned and implemented. This is part of the first positive steps, accompanied by the assigning of 2.4 billion euros to the more autonomous competence of regions and cities. However, this approach misses the most important elements of decentralized decision-making and thus could bring disappointment.

We would recommend simply copying more successful countries and institutionalizing proper public investment management, focusing on place-based policies and allowing regions to plan and develop their local economies. A good example could be found in neighboring Poland (OECD, 2021). It would only require a transition from the centralistic to the truly central government.

References

ARK. (2019). *Atlas rómskych komunít. Databáza ARK 2019*. Inštitút Mateja Bela. https://www.institutmatejabela.sk/atlas

Begg, D. (1991). Economic reform in Czechoslovakia: Should we believe in Santa Klaus? *Economic Policy*, *6*(13), 243–286. https://doi.org/10.2307/1344628

Černušáková, B. (2004, November 8). Oľga Gyarfášová: Slovensko sa dnes už pozerá viac dopredu. *Hospodárske noviny*. https://hnonline.sk/hnporadna/civilizacia/61876-olga-gyarfasova-slovensko-sa-dnes-uz-pozera-viac-dopredu

Dębkowska, K., Ambroziak, Ł., Czernicki, Ł., Kłosiewicz-Górecka, U., Kutwa, K., Szymańska, A., & Ważniewski, P. (2019). *The automotive industry in the Visegrad Group countries*. Polish Economic Institute.

European Commission. (2023). *2023 Country Report – Slovakia*. Commission Staff Working Document. https://economy-finance.ec.europa.eu/system/files/2023-05/SK_SWD_2023_625_en.pdf

European Commission. (2024a). *Cohesion policy*. https://ec.europa.eu/regional_policy/policy/what/investment-policy_en

European Commission. (2024b). *Cohesion policy overview*. https://cohesiondata.ec.europa.eu/cohesion_overview/14-20

Eurostat. (2023). *People at risk of poverty or social exclusion in 2022*. https://ec.europa.eu/eurostat/web/products-eurostat-news/w/ddn-20230614-1

Federální statistický úřad. (1985). *Historická statistická ročenka ČSSR*. SNTL.

Gertler, P., Reiner, M., & Zeman, J. (2023). *Ekonomické prínosy členstva Slovenska v EÚ*. National Bank of Slovakia. https://nbs.sk/aktuality/ekonomicke-prinosy-clenstva-slovenska-v-eu-analyticka-studia/

Grauzelová, T., & Markovič, F. (2018). *Príjmy a životné podmienky v marginalizovaných rómskych komunitách: Vybrané ukazovatele zo zisťovania EU SILC MRK 2018*. https://www.minv.sk/swift_data/source/romovia/atlas_romskych_komunit_2019/EU%20SILC_MRK_web.pdf

Green, A. (2023). *When should place-based policies be used, and at what scale?* OECD-EC High-Level Workshop Series: Place-Based Policies for the Future. https://www.oecd.org/regional/When-should-place-based-policies-be-used-and-at-what-scale.pdf

Hanzlík, J. (1967). Vývoj obyvateľstva na území Slovenska v rokoch 1869–1961. *Geografický časopis*, *19*(1), 3–47.

Hlaváč, M. (2023). *Dobieha slovenské HDP na obyvateľa v parite kúpnej sily bohatšie krajiny EÚ? Diagnóza nepriaznivého vývoja oficiálnych štatistík*. Inštitút sociálnej politiky. https://www.employment.gov.sk/files/slovensky/ministerstvo/analyticke-centrum/analyticke-komentare/komentare_2023/hlavac_2023_dobieha_slovensko_eu_v_hdp_pks.pdf

IMF. (2019). *Slovak Republic. Technical assistance report – Public investment management assessment*. IMF Country Report No. 19/330. https://www.mfsr.sk/en/finance/value-money/missions-presentations/missions/2019/pima/

Karvaš, I. (1933). *Sjednocení výrobních podmínek v zemích českých a na Slovensku*. Sbor pro výzkum Slovenska a Podkarpatské Rusi.

Korec, P., Ondoš, S., & Rusnák, J. (2016). Regionálne disparity na Slovensku; niekoľko poznámok k ich bádaniu. *Acta Geographica Universitatis Comenianae*, *60*(2), 257–293.

Kornai, J. (1996).*The citizen and the state: Reform of the welfare system*. Discussion Paper No. 32. Collegium Budapest, Institute for Advanced Study.

Lubyová, M., & Marcinčin, A. (2002). Unemployment in Slovakia. In A. Marcinčin & M. Lubyová (Eds.), *EU – Monitoring 2002. Monitoring of Slovak Republic integration to European Union. Accession process of Slovakia and the unemployment problem* (pp. 85–124). SFPA, Friedrich Ebert Stiftung.

Marcinčin, A. (2021a). Európske fondy ako nástroj centralizmu. In A. Marcinčin & J. Csabay (Eds.), *Ročenka regionálneho rozvoja 2021* (pp. 63–72). SPEKTRUM STU.

Marcinčin, A. (2021b). Chudoba ako dôsledok centralizácie. In J. Košč & J. Ruman (Eds.), *K problematike chudoby a sociálnej neistoty na Slovensku v 21. storočí*. OZ Pracujúca chudoba.

Marcinčin, A. (2022). Regionálny rozvoj: boj proti ostrovom chudoby a cesta k udržateľnému a inkluzívnemu rastu. In B. Schmögnerová (Ed.), *Ako reštartovať Slovensko? Sociálnodemokratická obnova spoločnosti po pandémii a konzervatívno-liberálnej vláde* (pp. 88–102). Friedrich Ebert Stiftung.

Marcinčin, A. (2023). Od regionalizmu k regionálnej politike: odbornosť a odvaha. In F. Chudják & E. Zimková (Eds.), *Odkaz prof. Imricha Karvaša pre súčasnú hospodársku vedu a prax* (pp. 124–140). Vydavateľstvo EKONÓM.

Ministerstvo vnútra. (2007). *Stručný prehľad vývoja územného a správneho členenia Slovenska*. https://www.minv.sk/?strucny-prehlad-vyvoja-uzemneho-a-spravneho-clenenia-slovenska

Mlčoch, L. (1997). The restructuring of property rights through the institutional economist's eyes. In M. Mejstřík (Ed.), *The privatization process in East-Central Europe. Evolutionary process of Czech privatizations*. Kluwer Academic Publishers.

Morvay, K. (2000). Macroeconomic development. In A. Marcinčin & M. Beblavý (Eds.), *Economic policy in Slovakia 1990–1999* (pp. 18–59). CSMA, SFPA and INEKO.

O'Brien, P., Sykes, O., & Shaw, D. (2015). The evolving context for territorial development policy and governance in Europe – From shifting paradigms to new policy approaches. *L'Information géographique*, *79*(1), 72–97.

OECD. (1994). *OECD economic surveys. The Czech and Slovak Republics 1994*. OECD Publishing. https://doi.org/10.1787/eco_surveys-svk-1994-en

OECD. (2016). *Making the most of public investment in the Eastern Slovak Republic*. OECD Publishing. https://doi.org/10.1787/9789264253261-en

OECD. (2018). *OECD regions and cities at a glance 2018*. OECD Publishing. https://doi.org/10.1787/26173212

OECD. (2021). *Better governance, planning and services in local self-governments in Poland*. OECD Publishing. https://doi.org/10.1787/550c3ff5-en

OLAF. (2021). *The OLAF report 2020*. Publications Office of the European Union. https://anti-fraud.ec.europa.eu/system/files/2021-12/olaf_report_2020_en.pdf

Pavlínek, P. (1995). Regional development and the disintegration of Czechoslovakia. *Geoforum*, *26*(4), 351–372.

Ravasz, Á., Kovács, Ľ., & Markovič, F. (2020). *Atlas rómskych komunít 2019*. VEDA.

Rusek, A. (1996). *Visegrad countries (CEFTA)*. Susquehanna University.

Statistical Office SR. (2024). *Statistics*. https://slovak.statistics.sk/

TASR. (2018, May 11). *Medzi Slovákmi stále prevažuje nostalgia za socializmom*. SME. https://domov.sme.sk/c/20823306/medzi-slovakmi-stale-prevazuje-nostalgia-za-socializmom.html

Tóth, J. (2000). Fiscal policy. In A. Marcinčin & M. Beblavý (Eds.), *Economic policy in Slovakia 1990–1999* (pp. 60–93). CSMA, SFPA and INEKO.

Úrad vlády SR. (2023). *Návod pre úspešné Slovensko: Dobehnúť zameškané*. https://isa.gov.sk/wp-content/uploads/2023/10/white_paper-2_eurofondy_online.pdf?csrt=771515283529975119

World Bank. (2003). *Slovak Republic—Joining the EU. A development policy review*. The World Bank.

World Bank. (2008). *Slovak public expenditure review*. The World Bank.

Chapter 9

The Political-Economic Foundations of Slovakia's Dependent Growth Model

Jakub Szabó

Comenius University, Slovakia

Abstract

In observing several Central and Eastern European Union countries facing systemic challenges to their dependent growth models, most notably Hungary and Poland, the resilience of foreign-dependent and export-led growth in Slovakia remains puzzling, especially in the context of relatively high levels of socioeconomic disintegration. Failing to identify the systemic distinctions of Slovakia's GM growth model against the backdrop of the broader political economy of the Visegrad region, this chapter seeks to explain the apparent differences through the politics of growth model approach, adjusted for the purposes of advanced peripheral economies. It is argued that an important explanans to the resilience of foreign-dependent growth in Slovakia can be traced back to the unexpected constellation of neoliberal forces governing in the early 2000s and their implementation of avant-garde neoliberal policies aimed at outbidding regional competitors in foreign investment attraction. Facing growing socioeconomic discontent and anticipating that national populists would assume power, the outgoing neoliberal government tied the hands of its successors by committing to a euro adoption strategy, which the subsequent administration was unable to reverse. Consequently, the lasting resilience of Slovakia's growth model lies in the interactions between a cross-class enduring domestic growth coalition with a trans-coalitional commitment to catering to the needs of transnational manufacturing capital on the one hand, and external constraints, most notably membership in the European Monetary Union (EMU), on the other.

Keywords: Dependent export-led growth; dominant growth coalition; European Eastern periphery; FDI-led growth; growth models; politics of dependent capitalism; social blocs

Modeling Economic Growth in Contemporary Slovakia, 161–177

doi:10.1108/978-1-83549-454-720241012

1. Introduction

In recent years, engagement with the post-Keynesian "growth model" (GM) approach has become increasingly prevalent in the comparative political economy (CPE) literature, particularly due to the approach's explicit ambitions toward bringing a range of questions back to the center of political economy analysis. Such topics include growth and stagnation, inequality and distribution, the intersections between CPE and international political economy (IPE), and interrogation of the different social blocs that underpin national GMs (Baccaro et al., 2022). In a nutshell, the GM approach argues that the relative importance of different components of aggregate demand determine long-term cross-national diversity of capitalism. From its inception, however, a relatively broad range of CPE scholarship has pointed out that simple categorizations of the peripheral Central and Eastern European (CEE) countries along the lines of dominant drivers of economic growth will prove to be flawed by failing to acknowledge the position of countries in lower orbits of global value chains, thereby affirming the importance of intertwining CPE and IPE (Ban & Adăscăliței, 2022). The Visegrad countries (Czechia, Hungary, Poland, and Slovakia; hereafter "V4"), in particular, are an exemplary demonstration of how the immense inflow of foreign direct investment (FDI), in anticipation of the countries' entry into the European Union (EU) single market, enshrined their dependent roles as suppliers of lower value-added manufactured goods (Bohle, 2018; Nölke & Vliegenthart, 2009; Vukov, 2023). Furthermore, in addition to the systemic constraints created by FDI-led growth and the ensuing industrial interconnectivity with Western economies, further limitations on the economic decisions of these peripheral European countries are increasingly imposed by EU integration (Medve-Bálint & Szabó, 2024), making the V4 countries a *sui generis* case of export-led GMs.

In the 2010s, the V4 countries were increasingly scrutinized by the CPE and IPE scholarship as national populists ventured into development upgrading processes and attempted to regain control over their dependent market economies via unorthodox economic policies, especially in Poland (Naczyk, 2022) and Hungary (Scheiring, 2020). As opposed to their regional counterparts, however, Czechia and Slovakia experienced only contained attempts at politicizing their economic dependencies, with the former country making partial progress in transforming its economy toward higher value-added production within the parameters of liberal democracy. Slovakia, on the other hand, "is on its way to becoming as economically disintegrated as Hungary" (Scheiring, 2021, p. 1584), which makes the lack of politicization of dependent growth particularly puzzling. Indeed, even following the return of national populists to power in October 2023, Slovakia does not appear to be on the path toward becoming another "national-neoliberal" regime in Visegrad (Ban et al., 2023). While the divergent trajectory is often associated with different recoveries and responses to the global financial crisis (GFC) of 2008 (e.g., Naczyk, 2022; Sebők & Simons, 2022), I argue that the country-specific growth coalition and external constraints play a more vital role in explaining the resilience of Slovakia's GM.

Employing the politics of the GM framework, this article aims to single out the Slovak case from the broader political economy of the V4 region, which has already been analyzed by numerous authors (Bohle, 2018; Vukov, 2023), and pinpoint the political foundations and constraints of its FDI-led growth in order to shed some light on the lack of politicization of Slovakia's FDI-dependent growth. In this context, this chapter seeks to outline the contours of the growth coalition underpinning Slovakia's dependent export-led growth, including its origins and evolution against a changing political landscape. While domestic interest groups are undoubtedly instrumental in shaping the backbone of Slovakia's GM, they do not operate in a vacuum and face several constraints. Arguably, the most institutionally constraining arrangement Slovakia has faced since 2009 pertains to its membership in the European Monetary Union (EMU). This chapter argues that Slovakia's membership in the EMU represents an important explanans of the puzzle of the resilience of Slovakia's FDI-dependent GM. Backed by a specific constellation of neoliberal forces that emerged as a result of an unexpected political window of opportunity arising in the early 2000s, attempts to outbid regional competitors in attracting transnational capital became the driving impetus behind the "neoliberal turn" in Slovakia in 2003–2004 (Fisher et al., 2007). Anticipating that national populists would assume power as neoliberal reforms fueled growing socioeconomic discontent, the outgoing government unexpectedly locked the Slovak crown to the EMU's exchange rate mechanism (ERM II) at the end of 2005, effectively tying the hands of its successors from pursuing potential unorthodox developmental strategies. Given the ensuing pressure from the National Bank of Slovakia (NBS) and international financial markets to commit to the euro adoption strategy, the incoming national populist government was unable to reverse this decision and was instead compelled to bring Slovakia into the EMU in 2009, inevitably limiting the maneuvering space for domestic policymaking. Policy discretion was additionally constrained by reforms of EMU economic governance and banking supervision after the euro crisis (Johnston & Matthijs, 2022).

This chapter is structured as follows. The first section outlines the basic features of Slovakia's FDI-dependent GM against the backdrop of the broader GM of the V4 countries and its evolution before and after the GFC. At the end of the section, I zoom in on the recovery and response of the V4 countries to the GFC. The second section fleshes out the theoretical framework of the politics of GM with a particular focus on advanced peripheral countries. Based on the politics of GM framework, the third section examines the growth coalition responsible for creating, shaping, and sustaining Slovakia's current FDI-dependent GM since the late 1990s. The fourth section outlines external constraints imposed on Slovakia's GM, particularly by European monetary integration. The final section reasserts the key conclusions of this paper.

2. FDI-Led Dependent Growth in Visegrad Before and After the GFC

Following the fall of the Soviet Union-dominated economic bloc, the V4 countries underwent abrupt transformations toward capitalism with distinctive transnational features, often associated with disruptive socioeconomic disintegration. Apart from Hungary, the remaining V4 countries first experimented with varieties of national capitalism before opening up to foreign investors (Myant & Drahokoupil, 2011). The eventual stabilization of the "embedded neoliberal" regimes in the late 1990s and early 2000s can be subsequently attributed to reindustrialization, spurred by FDI that capitalized on low labor costs, welcoming regulatory environments and industrial capacities inherited from the socialist era (Bohle & Greskovits, 2012). As a result of the dominance of FDI in capital-intensive complex manufacturing sectors, the V4 countries experienced hefty export-led growth (Ban & Adăscăliței, 2022).

Despite undisputable growth benefits, the FDI-generated boom also led to the dualization of the countries' economies with profound socioeconomic consequences. On the one hand, the export-competitive and foreign-owned sector started to thrive, propelled by low wages, a deregulated market environment and access to the EU market. Furthermore, the import of new technologies kick-started productivity growth that contributed to wage increases. In this context, the automotive industry came to assume an exceptional role in the economies. In 2018, average wages in the car industry exceeded the national average by 40% (Kahancová & Staroňová, 2024, p. 106). On the other hand, inward-oriented and domestically owned firms engaged in labor-intensive production eventually began to lag on productivity, engendering declines in the share of domestically owned companies in countries' total exports (Győrffy, 2022b). Consequently, in Slovakia, foreign-owned companies and their affiliates now account for about 80% of exports (OECD, 2024d), with the share of domestic value added in total exports on a continuously declining trajectory (OECD, 2024c).

Table 9.1 provides stylized data concerning Slovakia's GM as well as the GM of the V4 region. It can be empirically demonstrated that a majority of the growth in the region can indeed be attributed to foreign demand, with a growing tendency in this direction after the GFC. The share of exports in GDP, and particularly exports of manufactured goods, has experienced a significant rise since the arrival of FDI into manufacturing sectors. With a large portion of the countries' value-added stemming from manufacturing linked to German-led value chains, the V4 region established itself as part of a robust Central European manufacturing hub (Bohle & Greskovits, 2012). The sectoral balances often used in post-Keynesian analysis (e.g., Hein et al., 2021), however, reveal that a simple decomposition of growth drivers might be misleading as it artificially puts the V4 countries at the same level as Germany, the poster boy of the European export-led mercantilist regime. None of the V4 countries, however, mimicked Germany's evolution prior to the GFC as they all experienced a "foreign-financed boom" (Holzner, 2017, p. 60), with domestic sectors constituting net borrowers in the aggregate. This explicitly concerns the inability of the V4 countries' foreign-owned private sectors to generate surpluses in the 2000s, almost exclusively in nonfinancial corporations, which helps to explain the recurring current account deficits. It can, therefore, be shown that even though the growth in the V4 region was overwhelmingly export-led throughout the period preceding the GFC, current account and trade deficits resulting from FDI inflows and imports required for manufacturing supply chains accentuated the dependent nature of the Visegrad GM.

Table 9.1. Stylized Data on the Dependent Growth Model in Slovakia and the V4 Region Before and After the GFC.

		Slovakia		V4 Average	
		pre-GFC	post-GFC	pre-GFC	post-GFC
Import-adjusted relative growth contributions	*Annual growth*	5.23%	3.00%	4.12%	2.55%
	Consumption	21.91%	10.05%	20.81%	5.73%
	Investment	16.28%	11.38%	13.34%	11.16%
	Government spending	7.33%	8.79%	11.44%	10.68%
	Exports	54.48%	69.77%	54.42%	70.51%
Sectoral balances, % GDP	Private sector	−1.42%	2.76%	−1.60%	1.75%
	Public sector	−3.04%	−3.58%	−3.33%	−3.02%
	Household sector	0.97%	0.88%	1.50%	1.29%
	External sector	3.49%	−0.06%	3.43%	−0.02%
Value added, % Total	Manufacturing	40.88%	21.85%	29.17%	21.42%
	Construction	4.89%	8.19%	6.05%	6.76%
	Finance, insurance and real estate	11.26%	12.78%	10.28%	12.24%
Merchandise trade, % GDP	Exports	35.93%	91.72%	31.58%	77.14%
	Exports of manufactured goods	30.09%	79.66%	26.62%	65.64%
	Imports	39.40%	90.03%	34.96%	74.11%
Domestic value added, share of gross exports	Domestic value in exports	68.9%	60.6%	68.9%	60.6%
FDI flows, % GDP	*Inward FDI*	8.46%	1.75%	5.95%	2.20%
Productivity and labor cost, annual growth	*Productivity*	5.17	2.2	4.65	1.79
	ULC	5.26	2.15	6.12	2.19

Source: Annual growth and import-adjusted growth contributions from Baccaro and Hadziabdic (2023), sectoral balances from Eurostat national accounts (Eurostat, 2024), value added by sectors from OECD STAN database (OECD, 2024b), merchandise trade and FDI data from UNCTAD (UNCTAD, 2024a, 2024b, 2024c), domestic value added as share of gross exports from OECD Trade in Value Added database (OECD, 2024c) and ULC and productivity growth data from OECD productivity database (OECD, 2024a).

Note: Values at constant prices. The pre-GFC period average values are for years between 1995 and 2007 whereas the post-GFC between 2008 and 2018. The V4 average denotes a simple, unweighted average of all V4 countries.

In the aftermath of the GFC, however, two recalibrations can be discerned. Firstly, the already established foreign-owned manufacturing capacities spurred an export bonanza, reinforcing the already dominant role of exports as the primary driver of growth in the V4 countries (cf. Baccaro & Hadziabdic, 2023). With relatively balanced current accounts, dependent growth in the V4 region became openly mercantilist (Hein et al., 2021), which contributed to a loosening up of balance of payment constraints (Vukov, 2023). Secondly, a distinctive recalibration can be seen even in the FDI nature of dependent growth itself. With long-term capital inflows drying up in the 2010s, other sources of external financing took the place of FDI, most notably EU structural and cohesion funds and remittances (Bohle & Greskovits, 2019). Nonetheless, the changing weights of the different types of systematically important external sources of financing have not yet exerted pressure toward recalibrating the export-led GM itself. By seeking to prod countries to comply with rule of law requirements via the withholding of EU funds, the EU unwittingly is pushing countries (such as Hungary) to turn back to FDI (Medve-Bálint & Szabó, 2024).

To summarize, the GMs of all four Visegrad countries have been markedly shaped by manufacturing FDI, cementing export-led growth, despite foreign investment inflows slowing down in recent years. It has been empirically demonstrated that the export component was further accentuated after the GFC. Therefore, from a structural point of view, Slovakia's GM does not exhibit exceptional features against the backdrop of the broader capitalism of V4 countries. However, despite sharing similar fundamentals in their GMs, the V4 countries had different experience with the GFC, especially in terms of their recoveries and responses. In general, three types of responses can be distinguished. Falling foreign demand, notably, triggered only a mild economic slowdown in Slovakia and the Czech Republic, enabling these two countries to enjoy a relatively quick recovery fueled by a resurgence of German industrial production and global trade. Given that the countries bided the crisis relatively well, the neoliberal features of the countries' GMs were not explicitly politicized and illiberal forces remained contained (Saxonberg et al., 2024). The situation unfolded slightly differently in Poland and Hungary. With a more diversified economy and exchange rate realignment absorbing part of the exogenous shock caused by the GFC, Poland managed to avoid recession (the only EU member state to do so). Yet, the attempts of foreign parent companies to seize excess liquidity from their Polish subsidiaries, managing to thrive even amid the global economic downturn, triggered discontent of "comprador bankers" who subsequently transferred this backlash onto the Polish political arena (Naczyk, 2022). Hungary was the only V4 country that suffered a more consequential economic slump. Compelled to turn to the International Monetary Fund (IMF) and the EU for financial support to overcome problems caused by extreme exposure to loans denominated in foreign currencies and high public debt, the incoming national-populist government capitalized on "disenchantment" with FDI-dependent growth (Sebők & Simons, 2022).

As the Slovak and Hungarian political economies are not that distinct as far as socioeconomic disintegration is concerned (Scheiring, 2021), it would be tempting to infer the lack of an illiberal countermovement in Slovakia as a consequence of the country's rapid recovery after the GFC, which in turn is owed to the resilient

German economy and a sufficient fiscal buffer. Instead, as I argue in subsequent sections, the origins and evolution of the domestic growth coalition as well as external constraints limiting domestic policy discretion represent crucial contributing factors to the containment of any illiberal countermovement in Slovakia. Before I delve into the molding of the basic contours of the growth coalition sustaining the current GM in Slovakia, I will first clarify the politics of the GM framework, placed into the context of the advanced periphery.

3. Politics of FDI-Dependent Growth

In the preceding section, it was established that the postsocialist model of growth in Slovakia is export-led, that is, driven by foreign demand for the country's lower valued-added manufactured goods. Yet, it goes without saying that "calculating growth contributions from national account statistics and finding perfect evidence for a growth model are not enough" (May et al., 2024, p. 6) and it is equally important to identify whether the underlying politics and social blocs are geared toward preserving the existing GM. By employing the notion of a dominant growth coalition (DGC) (Baccaro & Pontusson, 2022), adjusted for the purposes of advanced peripheral economies that are "beyond the Lockean heartland" (May et al., 2024, p. 9), this section provides theoretical background for explaining the politics of peripheral GMs.

Capitalizing on their privileged access to government circles, the DGC represents a quasihegemonic, cross-class, and enduring socioeconomic power bloc consisting of organized business interests that seek to mold public policies according to their preferences and systematically uphold the GM from which they benefit. Reflecting sectoral interests, the DGC encompasses owners and managers of firms, major business associations and even banks, depending on the key sectors underpinning the GM, that is, the sectoral interests of banks and financial institutions are more likely to be reflected in debt-led GM than in export-led GM (e.g., Ban & Bohle, 2021). Furthermore, even though the post-Fordist DGCs are not "coalitions of equals" (Hopkin & Voss, 2022, p. 383), it is not excluded that the DGC may also succeed in co-opting a fraction of labor if the "labor aristocracy" remains in a subordinate position (Baccaro & Pontusson, 2022).

In spite of the frequent over-emphasis on electoral politics in the CPE literature (e.g., Beramendi et al., 2015), the politics of GM stresses that mass politics plays a rather limited role in shaping the GM, with its part mostly resting on gaining "passive consent" of society. In general, the fundaments of GM are shielded from electoral competition as the policies sustaining the GM (e.g., firm subsidies and market regulations) belong to the "quiet politics" realm of technocrats and business-elite interactions (Culpepper, 2010) where capital tends to enjoy the upper hand. Not only are the economic policies that are essential for sustaining the GM of lower political salience and institutionally depoliticized (e.g., through EU economic governance), but the system of "cartel parties" tends to converge on their inevitability, ideationally and discursively. This is further reinforced by the existence of "revolving doors" between capital, be it manufacturing or financial, and state and EU elites, blurring the distinction between the interests of capital and society. With the backing of the media and "organic intellectuals," these policies come to be portrayed as "common sense," earning the DGC an intellectual hegemony (e.g., Nölke, 2020). This often results in political conflict revolving around identity issues and mostly ornamental changes in the welfare system (Hopkin & Voss, 2022). Only once the coalition of growth beneficiaries becomes too narrow (e.g., during a period of long-term stagnation) can the GM become electorally contested via the emergence of antisystem parties. Even then, however, the obstinance of existing GM structures often tends to prevail.

Before delving into the DGC features constituting and sustaining the FDI-led GM in Slovakia, two issues must be raised. Firstly, as opposed to the politics of GM envisaged by Baccaro and Pontusson (2022) primarily focusing on advanced capitalist countries in Western Europe and North America, the advanced peripheral countries in the CEE region generally suffer from so-called "gelatinous" civil societies. As a result, compliance is often enforced by various forms of cooptation, be it clientelism or patronage, weakening the need for intellectual hegemony (May et al., 2024) and further curtailing the importance of mass politics. Secondly, the dependent FDI-led GMs, as the name suggests, differ significantly in terms of the structure of their capital ownership. With large inflows of FDI, the rise of dualization of the CEE economies prompted the creation of two distinct capitalist blocs – transnational and domestic – with unequal bargaining positions between the two. Though often reliant on foreign-owned supply chains in the GM, the interests of domestic capitalists can at times clash with those of transnational capital, forcing the DGC to readjust (Scheiring, 2020). It is, therefore, necessary to stratify between domestic and transnational sectoral interests in an FDI-led GM, especially as the structural power of MNCs over domestic politics tends to be the primary explanans of the underlying industrial-enterprise policy regime in the advanced periphery (Bohle & Regan, 2021).

4. Mapping Dominant Growth Coalition in Slovakia

In the aftermath of the Czechoslovak split in 1993, Slovakia under the national-populist leadership of Vladimír Mečiar embarked on a path of nation-building associated with support for welfare paternalism, aspirations toward building a strong domestic capitalist class, and explicitly negative sentiment toward foreign investors. Replacing the second wave of voucher privatization with direct sales of industrial state-owned companies to political loyalists, the governing political elite sought to solidify a long-lasting social bloc encompassing the national-populist political class and pro-Mečiar state enterprise managers (Fisher et al., 2007). The resistance against the "insider-dominated series of management buyouts" (Gould, 2003, p. 295) from civil society sparked increasingly confrontational and authoritarian conduct on the part of Mečiar, further triggering a cascade of unintended consequences, such as financial capital shortages and a halt on Euro-integration ambitions. Lacking capital for the restructuring of firms, state-controlled banks struggled to keep domestic private firms afloat, often granting loans based on political criteria. With price controls and contractionary monetary policy in place, the ensuing high interest rates caused a slowdown in investment activities of nonfinancial corporations, prompting a fraction of formerly pro-Mečiar economic elites to even question their allegiance to the regime (Gould & Szomolányi, 2000). Along with the mismanagement of systematically important Slovak companies (e.g., VSZ steelworks in Košice), expansionary fiscal policy and rampant corruption, Mečiar's inward-oriented growth started to crumble under the rising twin deficits.

As trade unions turn away from the national-populist government due to the imposition of wage controls and the suspension of tripartite consultations (Bohle & Greskovits, 2012, p. 148), a broad anti-Mečiar coalition ultimately prevailed in the 1998 election, putting a definitive end to Slovakia's experimentation with domestically oriented capitalism. As a first major reform, the broad left-right coalition led by Mikuláš Dzurinda was forced to recapitalize, restructure, and then privatize the insolvent state-owned banking sector, with the cost of this reform reaching about 12% of the country's GDP (Mikloš, 2014, p. 117). Consequently, this necessarily opened up the Slovak financial sector to the dominance of foreign-owned banks, with the share of foreign-owned bank assets on overall commercial bank assets rising from 24.10% in 1996 to 95.56% in 2002, putting Slovakia in first place in the region in terms of the banking sector with the highest level of foreign ownership (cf. Mérő & Valentinyi, 2003, p. 38). A similar turnabout is discernible with respect to the metamorphosis of the industrial structure. With the aim of putting an end to Mečiar's favoritism toward national champions in heavy industries and energy sectors, the new government launched an aggressive horizontal FDI-led reindustrialization via privatization, aggressive investment schemes, the establishment of the SARIO investment agency, and the creation of industrial parks, aiming to make up for FDI that had been lacking (Duman & Kureková, 2012).

Although Dzurinda's first government succeeded in consolidating the Slovak economy and securing the country's place in the European integration process, it was nonetheless too heterogenous in implementing radical neoliberal reforms. It was not until 2002 that an unhampered right-wing majority, capitalizing on a divided opposition, launched a "neoliberal turn," a set of radical reforms envisaged by a "neoliberal epistemic community" concentrated around Minister of Finance Mikloš (Fisher et al., 2007, pp. 990–991). By coopting think tanks and journalists, the implemented reforms were portrayed as inevitable and without "meaningful or acceptable alternatives" (Mikloš, 2014, p. 132) in spite of being perceived as radical even by the IMF (Appel & Orenstein, 2018). In addition to the privatization of a large portion of the energy sector, the avant-garde neoliberal reforms included substantial changes to the tax system, such as unifying the rate of VAT at 19% (stripping exemptions on food and medicine), devising a flat tax set at 19% for personal and corporate income tax and repealing taxes on dividend, real estate transfers, gifts, and inheritances. In addition, the Labor Code was significantly deregulated with an explicit pro-employer bias, collective bargaining weakened, the availability of full unemployment benefits restricted, and a three-pillar pensions system put into operation, complementing the traditional pay-as-you-go system with a capitalization pillar as well as a voluntary, supplementary pension savings pillar (Fisher et al., 2007). Alongside changes to industrial policies already under Dzurinda's first term in office, the neoliberal reforms after 2002 helped Slovakia gain an edge in the regional bidding war over FDI in the early 2000s and enabled western Slovakia to integrate into a broader regional manufacturing cluster specialized in the automobile industry and electronics (Bohle & Greskovits, 2012, pp. 168–172). The arrival of two major automobile producers, Peugeot-Citroën (2003) in Trnava and Kia in Žilina (2004), as well as Samsung electronics in Galanta (2002) during Dzurinda's governments solidified the manufacturing FDI-led growth in Slovakia.

With Dzurinda's government coming to an end in 2006 and left-wing nationalists led by Róbert Fico's Smer assuming office, a major countermovement to the implemented neoliberal measures was expected. Capitalizing on the general fatigue from ongoing structural reforms, Smer established itself as a dominant anti-austerity force, aligning itself with the main trade union organization, the Confederation of Trade Unions (KOZ). However, in spite of pre-election politicization of the neoliberal reforms, the most radical measures were left largely intact. For instance, it was not until 2013 that Smer revoked the 19% flat tax rate on personal and corporate income and set the top marginal tax rates, respectively, at 25% and 23%, with the brackets still lower than prior to the 2004 tax reform (Appel & Orenstein, 2018, p. 157). Similarly, the Smer-led governments did not fully abolish the second pension pillar but allowed two opt-out windows in 2008 and 2009, made nonenrollment in private accounts a default option for new entrants and lowered the required contribution from 9% to 4% of gross wages. No attempts to nationalize the capitalization pillar were either communicated or attempted (Naczyk & Domonkos, 2016). And even when the national populist government attempted to nationalize the profits of private health insurance companies in one episode, it was quickly halted by Slovakia's Constitutional Court. Although certain recalibrations were made regarding the most avant-garde neoliberal reforms, mostly in terms of removing the greatest excesses, the fundamental features of the manufacturing FDI-led GM were consequently not challenged.

Perhaps compensating for its inactivity in repealing neoliberal reforms, the economic policies of governing Smer (2006–2010; 2012–2020) concentrated primarily in the noisy arena of the country's welfare system and labor regulation, with ad hoc redistributive policies (so-called "social packages") aimed at its core constituents, pensioners, and lower income workers. This strategy helped to strengthen the already cozy relations between Fico's government and representatives of the KOZ. Apart from these measures, no major changes were implemented, with the quiet politics of state-business interactions not jeopardized. For instance, many important domestic industrialists were coopted by the national populist government (e.g., owner of the Ironworks Podbrezová Vladimír Soták) with minor concessions, which contributed to the appeasement of the domestic capitalist class. The pro-government industrialists nonetheless continued to operate in a subordinate position vis-à-vis foreign investors. The interests of foreign capital forming the backbone of Slovakia's GM remained an explicit priority even of Fico's government, which proved eager to provide substantial concessions to attract even more FDI. In 2015, for example, the government of Róbert Fico announced another major investment by automobile company Jaguar Land Rover in the volume of 1.4 billion euros, with the government providing 125 million euros in investment stimulus and an additional 500 million euros for construction of the industrial park (Trend, 2018), further cementing the FDI-dependent GM.

In this regard, whether it was neoliberals in the early 2000s, governments dominated by Róbert Fico for the majority of the 2006–2020 period or an ideologically ambiguous and incoherent coalition that took the reins of government after the 2020 election, they all understood that good working relations with foreign industrialists are pivotal in retaining political power, which ultimately forced them to act as a mere extended arm of the interests of foreign industrialists. For instance, in scrutinizing an important industrial policy tool – regional investment aid – it is apparent that the instrument was predominantly used to reinforce the FDI-dependent economy, with around 95% of aid granted to companies with foreign owners, mostly of within-EU origin, regardless of the nominal ideological underpinnings of the governing coalition (Medve-Bálint & Éltető, 2024). This clearly demonstrates that support for FDI remains a trans-governmental commitment in Slovak electoral politics, free from any political contestation. To illustrate the inner workings of FDI politics in Slovakia, in July 2022, Heger's government announced the arrival of yet another 1.2-billion-euro investment from the Volvo automaker for the production of electric vehicles. To appease investors amid coalitional upheavals, the liberal Minister of Economy Sulík saw two main opposition challengers, Fico and Pellegrini, sign a political memorandum guaranteeing support for the investment regardless of a change in government. Arguing that foreign investments do not belong among issues of political competition, the opposition leaders happily complied, arguably convincing the Swedish-Chinese investors to eventually choose the Slovak offer (Pravda, 2022).

5. Euro Constraint of Slovakia's FDI-Led Dependent GM

In the section prior, it was shown that Slovakia's FDI-dependent GM is based upon a cross-class enduring social bloc, in general reflecting the interests of transnational manufacturing capital, though parts of labor and domestic industries are incorporated as well, reinforcing the export element of Slovak growth. Yet, small and open CEE economies are necessarily exposed to multiple external constraints, further limiting the space for domestic discretion even though none reach the intensity of EU integration. While undoubtedly contributing to an institutional upgrading in its "new" member states (Bruszt & Vukov, 2017), the EU was simultaneously used as a tool to exercise "remarkable control over economic transformation" and development strategies in the CEE region by the "old" member states (Jacoby, 2010, p. 418). For instance, relying on membership conditionality and soft power, the EU was crucial for attracting FDI into the region (Medve-Bálint, 2014). As a country initially excluded from the first round of EU accession negotiations due to creeping authoritarianism, this effect became particularly present in Slovakia with the post-1998 Dzurinda governments becoming markedly compliant in adopting the required acquis communautaire. In resonance with domestic neoliberal reforms, the EU conditionality, therefore, continuously reinforced FDI-led growth in Slovakia.

Recognizing the general public discontent with the socioeconomic disintegration process and the growing likelihood of an antiausterity coalition winning the 2006 parliamentary elections, the outgoing coalition proceeded to introduce an additional constraint, with unprecedented importance, only a couple of months before the general election. In a relatively unexpected move with the aim of tying the hands of its successor, the Dzurinda government approved pegging the Slovak crown to the ERM II in 2005 (Hospodárske noviny, 2005), committing Slovakia to a euro-entry strategy (Epstein & Johnson, 2010, p. 1255). Although generally supported by business, this move was never consulted with other social partners (Bohle & Greskovits, 2010) and from the perspective of external observers, it became "remarkable what a high cost Slovakia was prepared to pay for Eurozone entry" (Pechova, 2012, p. 791) where once in the ERM II, the cost of deviating from the euro-path rose disproportionately. Even though new prime minister Fico contemplated "postponing" euro adoption shortly after the election, the pressure from financial markets and the central bank forced him to reconsider this position and unwillingly bring Slovakia into the EMU in 2009 (Pechova, 2012).

By putting potential populists on the "leash" (Medve-Bálint & Szabó, 2024), a narrow circle of neoliberal policymakers in the Ministry of Finance and the NBS succeeded on two fronts. Firstly, this move allowed the government to preserve its neoliberal legacy. With neoliberal reforms aimed at fulfilling the Maastricht criteria, the quasi-fixed nominal exchange rates served as an additional constraint preventing Smer from running unsustainable deficits. This became evident in February 2008 when the government signed a stability pact with employer and employee associations, committing to public deficit reduction and wage moderation (Bohle & Greskovits, 2010). Secondly, though it is questionable to what extent this strategy was foreseen at the time, euro membership prevented an unveiling of illiberal policy diversion similar to those witnessed in post-2010 Hungary or Poland between 2015 and 2023. Not only are EMU member states under greater fiscal scrutiny than the countries retaining their monetary autonomy – especially following the reinforcement of austerity rules after the euro crisis (Johnston & Matthijs, 2022) – but the institutionalization of monetary policy and later banking supervision and regulation at the EU level has made certain heterodox policies impossible under the current system of economic governance. For instance, the NBS, even if politically controlled, can no longer serve as an executive arm of national populists aiming to increase domestic influence in the financial sector (Mérő & Piroska, 2016), backstop sovereign debt (Ban & Bohle, 2021), or conduct other forms of financial nationalism (Johnson & Barnes, 2015), which severely curtails the toolkit of potential challenges to the current GM.

The experience with illiberal challengers in the advanced periphery has shown that institutionalization of the conduct of monetary policy at the EU level, which indirectly influences the fiscal maneuvering space, represents one of the greatest obstacles that illiberal challengers to the status quo may face. Or as formulated by Győrffy (2022a, p. 13), "being outside of the eurozone is a necessary condition for entrenching authoritarianism, while being a member is a sufficient condition for keeping liberal democracy." The different experiences with the Greek and Hungarian countermovements have clearly demonstrated that while the EU was rather oblivious regarding creeping authoritarianism and rule of law noncompliance in Hungary and Poland, at times even complicit, the reaction toward economic noncompliance in Greece was swift and resolute.

6. Conclusion

Even though national populists led by Róbert Fico managed to return to power in October 2023, the FDI-led GM in Slovakia remains resilient and unlikely to be challenged in the short to medium term, in spite of the high levels of socioeconomic disintegration that the country is enduring (Scheiring, 2021). This chapter aimed to shed some light on this puzzling resilience through the lens of the GM literature. Through systemic categorization of Slovakia's GM against the backdrop of the broader political economy of V4 capitalism, it was demonstrated that the Slovak dependent market economy does not exhibit exceptional features compared to its regional counterparts, at least not before the illiberal turn in the early and mid-2010s. Instead, I argue, the explanans for the resilience of Slovakia's GM lies in the interactions between the domestic growth coalition with a trans-coalitional commitment toward catering to the needs of transnational manufacturing capital on the one hand, and external constraints, most notably membership in the EMU, on the other.

The origins to this obstinate constellation can be sourced back to the early 2000s, when a group of neoliberals occupying key socioeconomic ministries and facing the need to outbid regional competitors in foreign investment attraction embarked Slovakia on a path of avant-garde neoliberal reforms. In combination with EU conditionality, this put Slovakia on track for unconstrained and arguably unsustainable FDI-led growth. In anticipation of relinquishing power due to rising socioeconomic discontent, the outgoing neoliberal government unexpectedly brought Slovakia into the ERM II waiting room, with the aim of preventing potential national-populist successors from implementing unorthodox development strategies. Under pressure from the NBS and international financial markets, the incoming left-wing nationalist government had no alternative but to commit to the euro adoption strategy. With their hands tied, the national-populist governments dominated by Róbert Fico between 2006 and 2010 and between 2012 and 2020 were conferred limited domestic discretion in terms of implementing heterodox economic policies, such as financial repression aimed at promoting the domestic bourgeoisie, shedding some light on the puzzling absence of an illiberal countermovement in Slovakia after the GFC.

Acknowledgment

This work was supported by the Slovak Research and Development Agency under Contract no. APVV-21-0237.

References

Appel, H., & Orenstein, M. A. (2018). *From triumph to crisis*. Cambridge University Press. https://doi.org/10.1017/9781108381413

Baccaro, L., Blyth, M., & Pontusson, J. (2022). Introduction: Rethinking comparative capitalism. In L. Baccaro, M. Blyth, & J. Pontusson (Eds.), *Diminishing returns: The new politics of growth and stagnation* (pp. 1–50). Oxford University Press.

Baccaro, L., & Hadziabdic, S. (2023). Operationalizing growth models. *Quality and Quantity*. https://doi.org/10.1007/s11135-023-01685-w

Baccaro, L., & Pontusson, J. (2022). The politics of growth models. *Review of Keynesian Economics*, *10*(2), 204–221. https://doi.org/10.4337/roke.2022.02.04

Ban, C., & Adăscăliței, D. (2022). The FDI-led growth models of the East-Central and South-Eastern European periphery. In L. Baccaro, M. Blyth, & J. Pontusson (Eds.), *Diminishing returns: The new politics of growth and stagnation* (pp. 189–209). Oxford University Press.

Ban, C., & Bohle, D. (2021). Definancialization, financial repression and policy continuity in East-Central Europe. *Review of International Political Economy*, *28*(4), 874–897. https://doi.org/10.1080/09692290.2020.1799841

Ban, C., Scheiring, G., & Vasile, M. (2023). The political economy of national-neoliberalism. *European Politics and Society*, *24*(1), 96–114. https://doi.org/10.1080/23745118.2021.1956241

Beramendi, P., Häusermann, S., Kitschelt, H., & Kriesi, H. (2015). Introduction: The politics of advanced capitalism. In *The politics of advanced capitalism* (pp. 1–64). Cambridge University Press. https://doi.org/10.1017/CBO9781316163245.002

Bohle, D. (2018). European integration, capitalist diversity and crises trajectories on Europe's Eastern periphery. *New Political Economy*, *23*(2), 239–253. https://doi.org/10.1080/13563467.2017.1370448

Bohle, D., & Greskovits, B. (2010). Slovakia and Hungary: Successful and failed euro entry without social pacts. In P. Pochet, M. Keune, & D. Natali (Eds.), *After the euro and enlargement: Social pacts in the EU* (pp. 345–369). European Trade Union Institute.

Bohle, D., & Greskovits, B. (2012). *Capitalist diversity on Europe's periphery* (1st ed.). Cornell University Press. http://www.jstor.org/stable/10.7591/j.cttq439z

Bohle, D., & Greskovits, B. (2019). Politicising embedded neoliberalism: Continuity and change in Hungary's development model. *West European Politics*, *42*(5), 1069–1093. https://doi.org/10.1080/01402382.2018.1511958

Bohle, D., & Regan, A. (2021). The comparative political economy of growth models: Explaining the continuity of FDI-led growth in Ireland and Hungary. *Politics & Society*, *49*(1), 75–106. https://doi.org/10.1177/0032329220985723

Bruszt, L., & Vukov, V. (2017). Making states for the single market: European integration and the reshaping of economic states in the Southern and Eastern peripheries of Europe. *West European Politics*, *40*(4), 663–687. https://doi.org/10.1080/01402382.2017.1281624

Culpepper, P. D. (2010). *Quiet politics and business power*. Cambridge University Press. https://doi.org/10.1017/CBO9780511760716

Duman, A., & Kureková, L. (2012). The role of state in development of socio-economic models in Hungary and Slovakia: The case of industrial policy. *Journal of European Public Policy*, *19*(8), 1207–1228. https://doi.org/10.1080/13501763.2012.709018

Epstein, R. A., & Johnson, J. (2010). Uneven integration: Economic and monetary union in Central and Eastern Europe. *JCMS: Journal of Common Market Studies*, *48*(5), 1237–1260. https://doi.org/10.1111/j.1468-5965.2010.02111.x

Eurostat. (2024). *Non-financial transactions – Annual data*. https://ec.europa.eu/eurostat/databrowser/view/NASA_10_NF_TR/default/table?lang=en

Fisher, S., Gould, J., & Haughton, T. (2007). Slovakia's neoliberal turn. *Europe-Asia Studies*, *59*(6), 977–998. https://doi.org/10.1080/09668130701489170

Gould, J. A. (2003). Out of the blue? Democracy and privatization in postcommunist Europe. *Comparative European Politics*, *1*(3), 277–311. https://doi.org/10.1057/palgrave.cep.6110019

Gould, J. A., & Szomolányi, S. (2000). Slovakia: Elite disunity and convergence. In J. Higley & G. Lengyel (Eds.), *Elites after state socialism: Theories and analysis* (pp. 47–69). Rowman & Littlefield.

Győrffy, D. (2022a). Populism and authoritarianism in the EU: What is the role of the euro? *European Politics and Society*, 1–21. https://doi.org/10.1080/23745118.2022.2148916

Győrffy, D. (2022b). The middle-income trap in Central and Eastern Europe in the 2010s: Institutions and divergent growth models. *Comparative European Politics*, *20*(1), 90–113. https://doi.org/10.1057/s41295-021-00264-3

Hein, E., Meloni, W. P., & Tridico, P. (2021). Welfare models and demand-led growth regimes before and after the financial and economic crisis. *Review of International Political Economy*, *28*(5), 1196–1223. https://doi.org/10.1080/09692290.2020.1744178

Holzner, M. (2017). The financial effects of the crisis in European emerging markets. In P. Havlik & I. Iwasaki (Eds.), *Economics of European crises and emerging markets* (pp. 39–62). Palgrave Macmillan.

Hopkin, J., & Voss, D. (2022). Political parties and growth models. In *Diminishing returns* (pp. 375–400). Oxford University Press. https://doi.org/10.1093/oso/9780197607855.003.0015

Hospodárske noviny. (2005, November 27). *Koruna sa ocitla v čakárni na euro*. https://hnonline.sk/dennik/170597-koruna-sa-ocitla-v-cakarni-na-euro

Jacoby, W. (2010). Managing globalization by managing Central and Eastern Europe: The EU's backyard as threat and opportunity. *Journal of European Public Policy*, *17*(3), 416–432. https://doi.org/10.1080/13501761003661935

Johnson, J., & Barnes, A. (2015). Financial nationalism and its international enablers: The Hungarian experience. *Review of International Political Economy*, *22*(3), 535–569. https://doi.org/10.1080/09692290.2014.919336

Johnston, A., & Matthijs, M. (2022). The political economy of the Eurozone's post-crisis growth model. In L. Baccaro, M. Blyth, & J. Pontusson (Eds.), *Diminishing returns: The new politics of growth and stagnation* (1st ed., pp. 117–142). Oxford University Press.

Kahancová, M., & Staroňová, K. (2024). Arms-length influence: Public sector wage setting and export-led economic growth in Czechia and Slovakia. *European Journal of Industrial Relations*, *30*(1), 97–119. https://doi.org/10.1177/09596801231215901

May, C., Nölke, A., & Schedelik, M. (2024). Growth models and social blocs: Taking Gramsci seriously. *Competition & Change*. https://doi.org/10.1177/10245294241231992

Medve-Bálint, G. (2014). The role of the EU in shaping FDI flows to East Central Europe. *JCMS: Journal of Common Market Studies*, *52*(1), 35–51. https://doi.org/10.1111/jcms.12077

Medve-Bálint, G., & Éltető, A. (2024). Economic nationalists, regional investment aid, and the stability of FDI-led growth in East Central Europe. *Journal of European Public Policy*, *31*(3), 874–899. https://doi.org/10.1080/13501763.2024.2305834

Medve-Bálint, G., & Szabó, J. (2024). The "EU-Leash": Growth model resilience and change in the EU's Eastern periphery. *Politics and Governance*, *12*. https://doi.org/10.17645/pag.7449

Mérő, K., & Piroska, D. (2016). Banking Union and banking nationalism—Explaining opt-out choices of Hungary, Poland and the Czech Republic. *Policy and Society*, *35*(3), 215–226. https://doi.org/10.1016/j.polsoc.2016.10.001

Mérő, K., & Valentinyi, M. E. (2003). *The role of foreign banks in five Central and Eastern European countries*. https://www.mnb.hu/en/publications/studies-publications-statistics/working-papers-1-1/wp-2003-10-katalin-mero-marianna-endresz-valentinyi-the-role-of-foreign-banks-in-five-central-and-eastern-european-countries

Mikloš, I. (2014). Slovakia: The latecomer that caught up. In A. Åslund & S. Djankov (Eds.), *The great rebirth: Lessons from the victory of capitalism over communism* (pp. 113–134). Peterson Institute for International Economics.

Myant, M., & Drahokoupil, J. (2011). *Transition economies: Political economy in Russia, Eastern Europe, and Central Asia*. Wiley.

Naczyk, M. (2022). Taking back control: Comprador bankers and managerial developmentalism in Poland. *Review of International Political Economy*, *29*(5), 1650–1674. https://doi.org/10.1080/09692290.2021.1924831

Naczyk, M., & Domonkos, S. (2016). The financial crisis and varieties of pension privatization reversals in Eastern Europe. *Governance*, *29*(2), 167–184. https://doi.org/10.1111/gove.12159

Nölke, A. (2020). *Exportism as an ideology in world politics* (pp. 125–142). https://doi.org/10.1007/978-3-658-30512-3_8

Nölke, A., & Vliegenthart, A. (2009). Enlarging the varieties of capitalism: The emergence of dependent market economies in East Central Europe. *World Politics*, *61*(4), 670–702. https://doi.org/10.1017/S0043887109990098

OECD. (2024a). *Productivity and ULC by main economic activity (ISIC Rev.4)*. https://stats.oecd.org/Index.aspx?DataSetCode=PDBI_I4#

OECD. (2024b). *STAN structural indicators (iSTAN) 2022 ed.* https://stats.oecd.org/Index.aspx?DataSetCode=STANI4_2020#

OECD. (2024c). *TiVA 2023 ed. Principal indicators*. https://stats.oecd.org/Index.aspx?DataSetCode=TIVA_2022_C1

OECD. (2024d). *Trade by enterprise characteristics (ISIC rev4): TEC by ownership*. https://stats.oecd.org/Index.aspx?DataSetCode=TEC2_REV4

Pechova, A. (2012). Legitimising discourses in the framework of European integration: The politics of Euro adoption in the Czech Republic and Slovakia. *Review of International Political Economy, 19*(5), 779–807. https://doi.org/10.1080/09692290.2011.633477

Pravda. (2022, July 1). *Volvo bude mať podporu aj v prípade zmeny vlády, tvrdí Fico.* https://spravy.pravda.sk/domace/clanok/632407-volvo-bude-mat-podporu-aj-v-pripade-zmeny-vlady-tvrdi-fico/

Saxonberg, S., Sirovátka, T., & Csudai, E. (2024). Crisis? What crisis? Social policy when crises are and are not crises in Czechia, Hungary and Slovakia. *Social Policy and Administration, 58*(2), 228–247. https://doi.org/10.1111/spol.13004

Scheiring, G. (2020). *The retreat of liberal democracy: Authoritarian capitalism and the accumulative state in Hungary.* Palgrave Macmillan.

Scheiring, G. (2021). Varieties of dependency, varieties of populism: Neoliberalism and the populist countermovements in the Visegrád four. *Europe-Asia Studies, 73*(9), 1569–1595. https://doi.org/10.1080/09668136.2021.1973376

Sebők, M., & Simons, J. (2022). How Orbán won? Neoliberal disenchantment and the grand strategy of financial nationalism to reconstruct capitalism and regain autonomy. *Socio-Economic Review, 20*(4), 1625–1651. https://doi.org/10.1093/ser/mwab052

Trend. (2018, November 7). Investorom roka je Jaguar Land Rover. https://www.trend.sk/trend-archiv/investorom-roka-je-jaguar-land-rover

UNCTAD. (2024a). *Foreign direct investment: Inward and outward flows and stock, annual.* https://unctadstat.unctad.org/datacentre/dataviewer/US.FdiFlowsStock

UNCTAD. (2024b). *Merchandise: Intra-trade and extra-trade of country groups by product, annual.* https://unctadstat.unctad.org/datacentre/dataviewer/US.IntraTrade

UNCTAD. (2024c). *Merchandise: Total trade and share, annual.* https://unctadstat.unctad.org/datacentre/dataviewer/US.TradeMerchTotal

Vukov, V. (2023). Growth models in Europe's Eastern and Southern peripheries: Between national and EU politics. *New Political Economy*, 1–17. https://doi.org/10.1080/13563467.2023.2189695

III

Characteristics and Performance of Selected Industries

III

Chapter 10

Slovakia as an Automobile Superpower or Factory Economy?

Monika Martišková[a] *and Katarína Lukáčová*[b]

[a]Central European Labour Studies Institute (CELSI), Slovakia and Charles University, Czechia
[b]Scuola Normale Superiore in Pisa, Italy and European Training Foundation, Italy

Abstract

The automotive industry in Slovakia underwent a steep development pathway during the last 20 years, mostly thanks to the inflow of foreign direct investments, resulting in increasing production outputs, exports, and employment. In this chapter, we highlight the limits of this growth, pointing out on production function of the industry heavily based on foreign capital. Under the current challenges of production digitalization, automatization, and car electrification, the position of the country seems uncertain. As a response, the government of Slovakia, but also others in the region, embarked on supporting new wave of foreign direct investments mostly in battery production and in the case of Slovakia also attracting a fifth car manufacturer. We conclude that this strategy fixes the current dependency on foreign capital and know-how rather than allows for upgrading.

Keywords: Automotive; Slovakia; global production networks; transformation; foreign direct investments; industrial policies; integrated periphery; electromobility

1. Introduction

The automotive industry in Slovakia has experienced significant growth over the last 20 years, positioning the country as the world leader in per capita car production. With a population of five million, the country produces millions of cars per year, industry contributes to 12% of the GDP and one-third of the overall

Modeling Economic Growth in Contemporary Slovakia, 181–200

doi:10.1108/978-1-83549-454-720241015

exports of the country. While some view this as a success story of postsocialism upgrading and effective industrial policies that have integrated the country into Western European and global markets (Cagáňová et al., 2019; SARIO, 2024; Saxunova et al., 2018; Šipikal & Buček, 2013), others see it as a situation of extensive dependence on the global industry, over which local government and other actors have limited control and emphasize the risks associated with relocation to other countries, potentially leading to job losses (Gažo et al., 2022; Guzik et al., 2020; Kureková, 2018; Martišková, 2019; Pavlínek, 2016, 2022).

The automotive industry is a highly competitive, and globally interconnected sector, with a relatively closed set of companies figuring in the value chain. It is an example of a producer-driven chain, marked by integrated production with highly specialized, segment-specific, and vertically organized transnational firms (Fernandez-Stark & Gereffi, 2019). Vertical integration causes also a high local concentration of some suppliers around plants of final car producers as many components are supplied in just-in-time and just-in-sequence mode (Dicken, 2007). This industry is also distinguished by its high dependence on technology, capital, and skilled labor, coupled with a strong emphasis on lean manufacturing practices (Sturgeon et al., 2008).

Global Production Networks (GPNs) showcase fragmented production chains and diverse value-added activities, dispersing high and low-value tasks geographically. This dispersion leads to varied automotive production locations classified as core, periphery, and semiperiphery, emphasizing prevalent functions within the production cycle. Despite the industry being vertically integrated, core regions and home countries of multinational corporations (MNCs) retain strategic functions related to production and investments, while peripheral locations maintain production functions. Integration of Slovakia into the automotive value chains was driven by geographic expansion of foreign companies leading to the establishment of production capacities, which are labor-intensive and low-value-added, leaving Slovakia in dependent position of assembly of cars and its components with limited high value-added functions (Pavlínek, 2016, 2022).

As we show in this chapter, the Slovak automotive industry was developed with the enormous support of foreign direct investments (FDIs) where the state played a crucial role in attracting global investors. This was possible not only by conscious government policies in attracting automotive production but also contextual factors such as low labor costs and membership in the European Union (EU) which facilitated an access to its single market and proximity to wealthy West European markets. All these factors made the locations of Central and Eastern Europe (CEE) attractive for investors in the automotive industry. As a result, the Slovak economy grew with the automotive industry, creating hundreds of thousands of jobs directly and indirectly. The dominant function of the companies residing in the region is production function, with limited outreach to higher value-added activities, like R&D.

In this chapter, we aim to introduce the development and reasons for attracting foreign investors in the automotive industry to Slovakia, examine its impact on the local economy, and shed light on the prospects of the industry amid decarbonization, automation, and digitalization, which are simultaneous trends shaping the industry. Throughout the chapter, we combine statistical evidence with available research studies about the automotive industry and our work in mapping industrial developments and their prospects through interviews and action research with local stakeholders. Where possible, we emphasize the local and European context of the automotive industry in Slovakia.

We first describe the process of the development of the automotive industry in Slovakia and discuss the consequences for the economy and labor, and then look at the prospects of the sector to transform along with the requirements of increasing digitalization and automatization of the production and to deliver the zero-emission vehicles in full scale by 2035.

2. Development of the Automotive Industry in Slovakia

The Slovak automotive industry was built on foreign investments and the inflow of global companies, both final producers and a dense network of suppliers. After the split from Czechoslovakia and the establishment of the independent state in 1993, Slovakia had in its territory only Volkswagen, which privatized formerly state-owned company BAZ near the capital city Bratislava in 1991. During the 1990s, because of a political decision to support domestic capital in privatization processes and a lack of subsidies offered to foreign investors, Volkswagen remained the only car producer in the country. Nevertheless, investments and production in VW were gradually increasing, reaching 125 thousand cars in 1998, compared to 3,000 in 1993 (Jacobs, 2017).

In 1998, when the pro-European government was formed, new economic incentives were introduced to attract FDIs in the automotive sector (Jacobs, 2017). In 2000, Slovakia also reopened the accession talks to the European Union which increased the political reliability of the country for foreign investors, who were already investing in neighboring countries of Czechia, Hungary, and Poland. Slovakia entered bidding competition later and with aggressive offers which along with subsidies for the companies, included also indirect costs for building infrastructure such as roads, but also schools or flats for managers. The costs per one created workplace reached 75,000 EUR for investment in KIA near Žilina and 44,000 EUR for PSA in Trnava (now Stellantis) (Martišková, 2019). Both investments were announced in 2004 and started operating in 2006. Jaguar Land Rover was opened in 2018 as the fourth car manufacturer in Slovakia and it was supported by 44,600 EUR per working place created. The last investment in the automotive industry was announced by Volvo in 2022 in the Košice region, where only electric cars are planned to be produced since 2026. The state subsidy for attracting Volvo as the fifth car producer was again high, reaching 72,000 EUR per workplace created. As a result, Slovakia has the third largest stock of FDIs in the region, amounting to 53,2% of GDP, after Czechia and Hungary (Eurostat, 2022).

The car production in Slovakia witnessed a continuous increase, reaching one million cars annually since 2015. The output has been fluctuating around this level since 2010. This trend is reflected in both the volumes and values of exported products, given that car production in Slovakia is mainly export oriented. As a result of FDIs and increasing production volumes, Slovakia, as well as other countries in the region, became a net exporter. The volume of exports of motor vehicles has quintupled since the 2000s in both Slovakia and Czechia and significantly increased also in Poland and Hungary (Fig. 10.1).

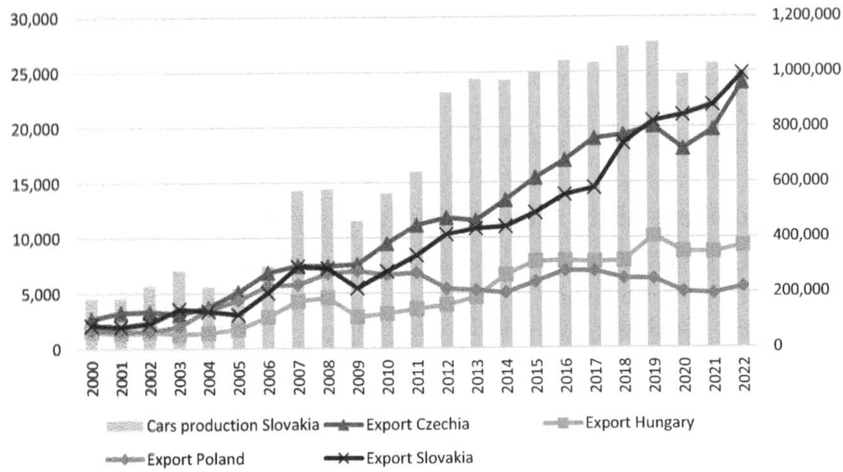

Fig. 10.1. Car Production in Slovakia and Exports of Motor Vehicles in V4 Countries 2000–2022. *Source:* Cars production OICA, the value of exports of motor vehicles Eurostat [ds-045409], in million EUR, own compilation.

2.1 Labor Costs and Position of Labor

Along with generous subsidies, low wages in the region were the main reason for investors to come (Guzik et al., 2020; Pavlínek, 2018). Labor costs in the region in 2000 ranged between 3 and 4 EUR per hour, compared to 27 EUR per hour in Germany, 24 EUR in France, and 22 EUR in Italy (Fig. 10.2). The relocation of jobs from Western to Eastern countries was the intentional strategy of the companies to maintain or increase profitability via labor costs reductions. As a result, jobs in manufacturing in the automotive industry were vanishing in Western Europe and created in Eastern Europe as a part of the profit-seeking investments of foreign companies (Pavlínek, 2020).

Between 2000 and 2022, wages in Eastern European countries increased three to five times, in Slovakia, which meant an increase from 3 to 15 EUR per hour. Despite the convergence rate between Eastern and Western European countries being positive, this was still not sufficient to catch up with old EU member states, resulting in a persistent "wage curtain" between new and old member states. The difference with German wages thus remains significant, and the region remains attractive for labor-intensive investments.

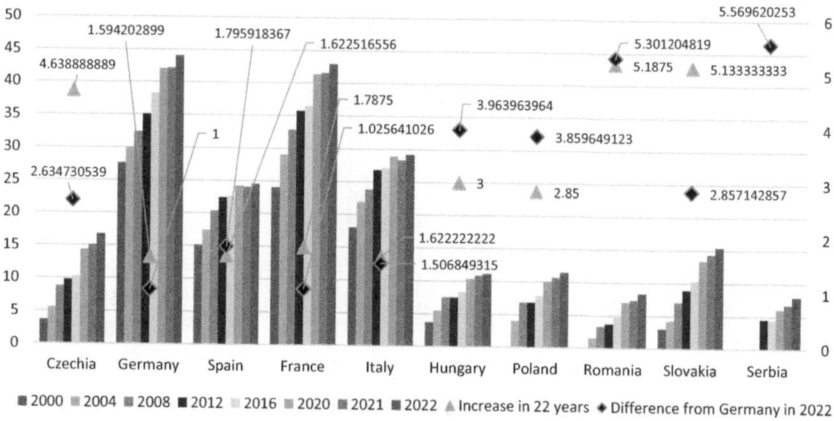

Fig. 10.2. Labor Costs in Manufacturing. *Source:* Eurostat [lc_lci_lev], own computation.

The average wage in the automotive industry is almost at the level of the national average (in 2022, it was 1,518 EUR per month), but for blue-collar workers, the average was lower (1,300 EUR in 2022) (SSO, 2024). There is a high share of variable pay in blue-collar workers' wages estimated at 40% (SSO, 2024). To get decent payment, workers undertake night shifts, weekend shifts, and overtime work. In Slovakia, 11% of employees work at night, which is by far the largest number in the EU-27, where the average is 4.3% (Eurostat, 2024).

The position of labor in the automotive industry is weak. CEE region, including Slovakia, represents the countries with low trade union density rates as well as low collective bargaining coverage (Kahancová & Uhlerová, 2023). Collective bargaining within the automotive industry predominantly occurs at the company level. The estimated density of employers' organizations in the metal sector is approximately 18%–20%, and the density of trade unions is even lower (Kahancová, 2016). Collective bargaining coverage is estimated to be 22%–25% which is at a similar level as the national average (Benedeková et al., 2019).

Over time, employment within the industry experienced consistent growth, with nearly 140,000 individuals directly employed in automotive roles (NACE 29) by 2022. This accounted for 5.3% of total employment, a significant rise from the 3.9% recorded in 2013. Likewise, the workforce engaged in automotive production constituted one-fifth of all industrial employment by 2022, up from 16.6% in 2013. Interestingly, employment was increasing also during the COVID-19 pandemic, the reason being the launch of the production in Jaguar Land Rover during 2019 and 2020.

The predominantly manufacturing function of the companies in Slovakia is manifested in a significantly higher share of middle-skilled occupations compared to Germany (see Fig. 10.3). Within the last 10 years between 2013 and 2022, there

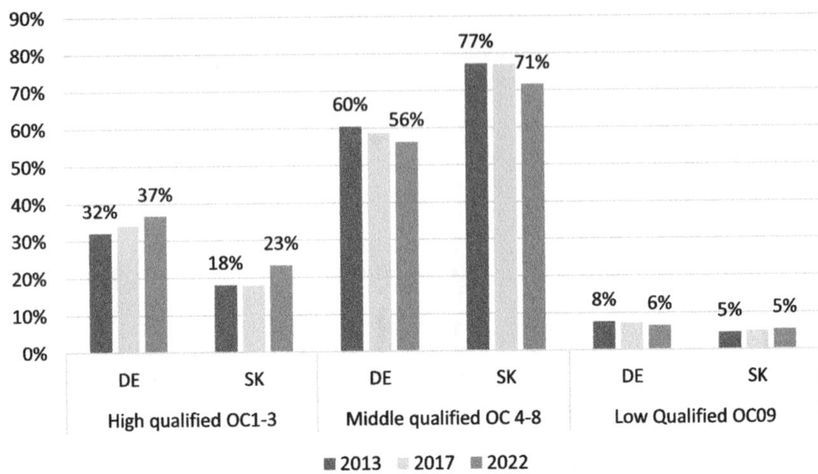

Fig. 10.3. Qualification Levels in Manufacturing, SK and DE. *Source:* Own computation based on Eurostat data [lfsq_egan22d].

has been a systemic change in the composition of the workforce, when we can observe an increasing number of highly qualified workers and decreasing the middle-skilled occupations. This reflects digitalization and automatization processes, which require more and more highly qualified workers, while diminishing job opportunities for middle-skilled workers (Acemoglu & Autor, 2011). In Slovakia, the share of middle-qualified occupations remains high, around 70%, but dropped by seven percentage points since 2013, while the number of high-qualified increased from 18% to 23%. This trend was identical to Germany (see Fig. 10.3).

2.2 Position of Slovak Automotive in the Global Value Chains

High production of cars and their increasing volumes throughout the years suggested that the country, as well as the region of CEE in general, undertake mostly production functions (Pavlínek, 2018, 2020; Pavlínek & Ženka, 2011; Szalavetz & Sass, 2023). For Slovak automotive companies, it means that the activities with high value-added are less often relocated in the subsidiaries.

A good proxy of the limited presence of high value-added activities is the extent of expenditures and employment levels in R&D. Thanks to persistent cost differences, R&D activities have been relocated to the CEE countries to some extent in the last years, but this was not the case for Slovakia. In terms of R&D business expenditures, Slovakia spends only 0.33% of the total value of production on R&D in the automotive industry compared to 7.06% in Germany. Consequently, only a small portion of R&D personnel and researchers are employed in the industry. In 2021, R&D personnel represented only 0.8% of total

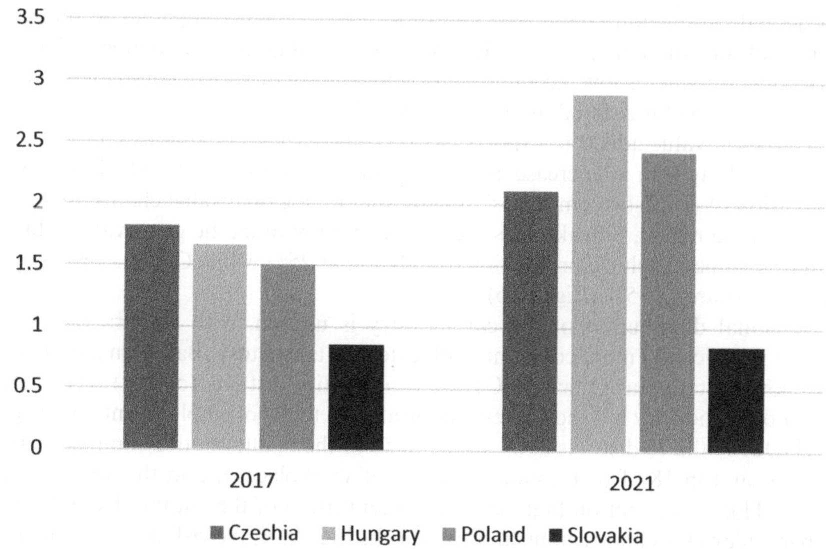

Fig. 10.4. Share of R&D Personnel and Researchers on Total Employment in Automotive Manufacturing (NACE 29), in %. *Source:* Own computation based on Eurostat data [rd_p_bempoccr2h].

employment in automotive compared to 16% in Germany or 2.1% in Czechia (Fig. 10.4). Slovakia thus only partially upgraded its production function and keep lacking behind other CEE countries.

2.3 Dominance of MNCs and Local Economy

The presence of foreign companies, especially multinational corporations, was considered important for economic restructuring and upgrading the economy, which would be facilitated through the spill-over effects based on cooperation and know-how exchange between foreign and domestic companies. The linkages between domestic and foreign companies were supposed contribute to regional development and upgrading, but as Pavlínek (2018) showed, the Slovak automotive industry has developed only weak tights between domestic and foreign companies leading to limited benefits for the regions and local economies. An important factor behind loose linkages between foreign and domestic companies is the fact that the majority of Slovak-owned firms operating in the automotive industry are small companies with up to 10 employees and their performance is low with an estimated gap of 65% from foreign-owned companies (OECD, 2022). Nevertheless, medium-sized Slovak-owned businesses are better integrated into the global production chains and cooperate with foreign companies in innovations and information exchange. The problem remains that the number of these types of companies is low, accounting for a maximum of 10% of companies in the sector out of 350 registered as suppliers (SARIO, 2023).

Domestic value added in exports has been increasing continuously in the last 20 years, along with an increase in gross output and gross exports, which suggests stagnation of domestic companies' integration in the global value chains (OECD, 2019). In the region, Slovakia has the lowest share of domestic gross value added on gross value in vehicle production, oscillating at 25%, while Czechia or Poland have this share at 35% (Fig. 10.5).

Regional distribution of the car industry is uneven, with western Slovakia having significantly more companies allocated in its territory. Based on data from the Slovak Statistical Office (SSO), we can identify districts (okresy) where the automotive industry has the highest importance in terms of employment and wage level. Out of the 78 districts in Slovakia, in 58 of them, automotive companies are present, and in 18 of them, more than 5% of workplaces are in the automotive sector. This points out on high level of concentration of the automotive industry in particular cities and regions in Slovakia. In Fig. 10.6, the risk index of Slovak regions is depicted providing an aggregate view on the four indicators:

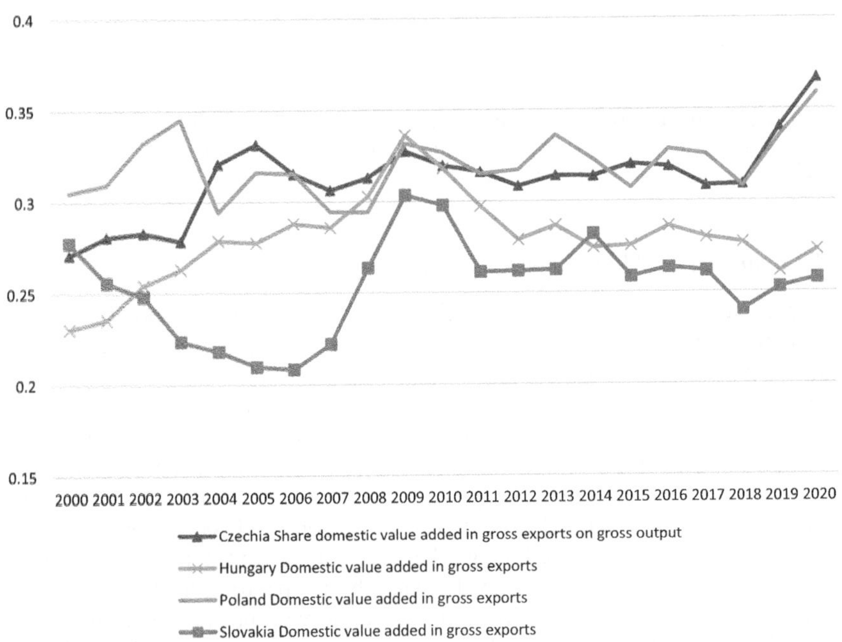

Fig. 10.5. Share of Domestic Value Added in Gross Output in Vehicle Production. *Source:* TiVA database OECD, own compilation.

(1) the share of automotive employment on overall employment in the given district;
(2) the share of automotive employment on industrial employment in the given district;
(3) the share of average wage on the overall average wage in the given region; and
(4) the share of the average wage in automotive on the overall average wage in the industry in the given region.

Based on this methodology, we can distribute regions into four clusters, ranging from the cluster where the automotive industry is very important (reaching a score of 4), to the region where the industry is moderately important (score of 3), to the regions where the industry is partially important (score 2), to the regions where automotive is present but not that important (score 1 and 0). Based on this methodology, automotive industry is having an important or very important impact on employment and wage levels in 15 regions and this number is expected to increase with new investment of Volvo near Košice (for details see Fig. 10.6).

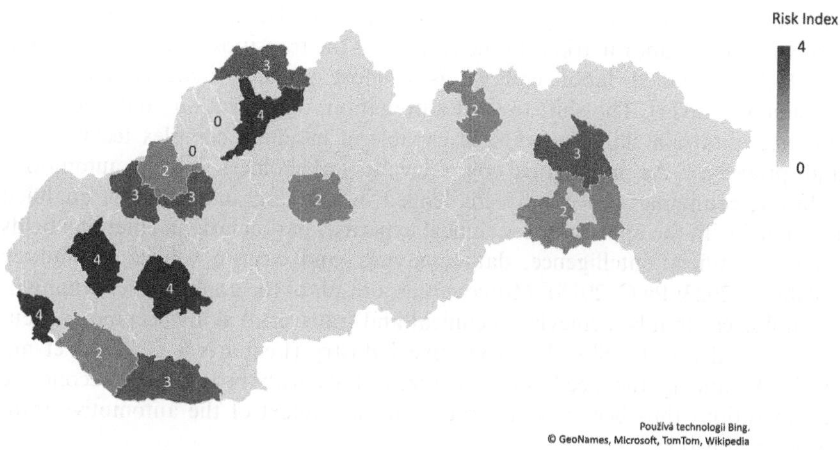

Fig. 10.6. Risk Index in Slovak Regions. *Source:* Own computation based on the data of the Slovak Statistical Office (2019).

3. Current Challenges for the Automotive Industry

As we have shown in the previous chapter, automotive manufacturing has emerged as a cornerstone of Slovak's economic model over the past 20 years. Such a model has brought prosperity for socioeconomic development, but also several vulnerabilities stemming from a strong economic integration into foreign markets (Bohle & Greskovits, 2012; Pavlínek, 2022). The industry is currently undergoing a transformation characterized by a shift to a digital and green economy which includes multifaceted challenges, originating from a combination of factors such as technological advancements, economic dynamics, regulatory frameworks, and societal influences. For the Slovak economy, transition-related challenges are particularly mentioned and can be presented as twofold.

Firstly, the challenges align with broader global industrial trends. Rapid technological advancements, resulting in intensifying automation, digitalization, and electrification necessitate continuous adaptation of manufacturing production and organization. Amid the shift to electromobility, automotive companies are investing even more in the implementation of new technologies. While Slovakia and its Visegrad counterparts have experienced a slower kick-off in both the production and consumption of electric cars compared to the rest of the Europe (Hillebrand, 2023; Slovak Electric Vehicle Association, 2023; Studená et al., 2023), implementing automation and digitalization throughout the restructuring process intensifies the associated risks, such as skill obsolescence and job destruction (Abdul-Hamid & Ambasz, 2023; Arntz et al., 2016; Majzlíková & Vitáloš, 2022; Nedelkoska & Quintini, 2018; Studená et al., 2023).

The second set of challenges in Slovakia's automotive industry is linked to the structure of the labor market. In the context of the transition, the utilization and the lack of skilled labor emerge as a most pressing issue (Lukáčová & Kahancová, 2024). The shift toward automation, digitalization, and electrification necessitates a skilled workforce capable of handling complex technologies and processes. As highlighted by relevant stakeholders in the automotive industry, companies are greatly challenged in sourcing and retaining qualified personnel with the appropriate technical expertise, particularly in emerging fields such as artificial intelligence, data analytics, and electric vehicle technology (Oláhová, 2023; PwC, 2018). Moreover, as a result of the gradual intertwining of technological trends, achieving technical and transversal skills become particularly critical for the Slovak automotive industry (Lednárová Dítětová et al., 2022). Balancing the need for specialized skills with broader socioeconomic considerations thus becomes imperative in the context of the automotive transition in Slovakia.

The current challenges in the Slovak labor market however extend beyond a lack of technical skills. From the employment perspective, the Slovak automotive sector is characterized by various disparities. There is a persistent pattern of gender gap and regional disparities in employment levels as well as in wages. In addition to that, there are divergences in working conditions forming alongside the automotive hierarchy, that is, the position of the company in production chains, the so-called tier gap. Navigating these challenges by relevant stakeholders requires a holistic approach that considers the technological demands of the industry, the situation in the labor market, and the overall structure and the position of the sector in the economy.

4. Digitalization and Decarbonization of the Industry and Employment and Reskilling Challenge

Similar to other European countries, the shift toward electromobility is expected to bring about gradual restructuring within Slovakia's automotive industry affecting overall structure as well as employment in the sector. In this regard, the production of electric cars will likely impact automotive suppliers producing parts and components as well as final producers of cars, particularly those which manufacture combustion engines. Manufacturing of electric engines is less labor-intensive than the production of combustion engines; therefore, there are expected implications for labor as well (Bauer et al., 2020; CLEPA, 2021; Pavlínek, 2023).

The cars manufactured in Slovakia are destined in majority for export, thus as in the case of other Visegrad countries, the transition to electrified vehicles' production will largely be influenced by foreign demand. Moreover, given that the automotive industry in Slovakia is dominated by foreign capital (97.9% of auto companies are almost solely of foreign ownership compared to 14.9% in Germany, and 23.6% in Italy), the process and pace of the transition in Slovakia will heavily rely on the strategic decisions made by foreign-owned assembly firms and component suppliers (Eurostat, 2020; Pavlínek, 2023).

Several academic works emphasize that the production factories in Slovakia predominantly exhibit the characteristics of assembly halls of foreign-owned companies, with strategic developmental activities such as R&D centralized in the home countries of foreign companies (Baldwin & Lopez-Gonzalez, 2013; Bohle & Greskovits, 2012; Kureková, 2018; Šćepanović, 2015). Throughout long-term operations in Slovakia, foreign-owned manufacturing companies had both direct and indirect effects on productivity. The source of productivity growth was based on the ability to foreign technology absorption, rather than domestic technological capabilities (Alguacil et al., 2015; Radosevic, 2017). While the increase in productivity led to impressive socioeconomic growth, however, the growth has not been accompanied by systemic investments into R&D, skill formation systems, and other areas that would help build resilience and domestic technological potential (Pavlínek, 2022). As a result, the lack of a highly qualified workforce is emerging as a potential barrier to digital transformation for automakers (PwC, 2018).

Exploring the decarbonization challenge in the automotive industry in Slovakia means looking at companies' readiness for the transformation from combustion engine production to zero-emission vehicles. The second topic relevant to decarbonization would be discussing the transportation sector and the reduction of emissions from mobility, but since car production and consumption are poorly connected in the case of Slovakia, in the following section, we focus on the cars and their components production and changes related to decarbonization.

While the effects of green and digital transition bring inarguably transformative implications for the labor market, various researchers point out that it is quite difficult to estimate exact trends, when it comes to effects on employment due to the complexity of changes related to the transformation of the automotive sector (Bauer et al., 2020; Lukáčová & Kahancová, 2024; Pavlínek, 2023). The shift to electromobility not only leads to the restructuring of production, but some aspects of electric vehicle manufacturing also boost the closely intertwined processes of digitalization and automation of production. For instance, the production of electric vehicles involves a high degree of automation, as manufacturers utilize advanced robotics and automated systems to assemble batteries, electric drivetrains, and other components. Digitalization on the other hand plays a crucial role in managing supply chains, coordinating production processes, and ensuring quality control in EV manufacturing facilities. In this regard, there will not necessarily be an overarching trend but a complex mixture of new job creation, job reduction as well as job upgrading (Bauer et al., 2020).

According to predictions, the production of electric cars will reach 20%–30% share by 2025 (Elektromobilita, 2020). Each of the four companies in the Slovak automotive industry has already started production of fully electric vehicles along with ICE and hybrid versions of their models. This increases production costs and may pose a challenge to remain competitive when compared to newly built fully electric plants mushrooming in Europe and the US and already operating in China (Pavlínek, 2023). As a result, wage pressures may even intensify along with further digitalization and automatization of production.

The presence of battery gigafactories operating is considered an indicator of a positive future for the automotive industry in the country (Schade et al., 2022). Notably, Slovakia boasts two battery producers who have announced their operations in the country, one of which is the gigafactory InoBat. This Slovak-owned startup specializes in providing customized solutions for various transportation sectors, including cars, buses, and airplanes. In 2023, InoBat signed a memorandum of understanding with the Chinese company Gotion High-Tech and the Slovak government to establish a gigafactory with an initial capacity of 20 GWh, with potential expansion to 40 GWh. The Slovak government has committed to supporting this investment by preparing the necessary infrastructure for the factory, which is slated to commence production in 2026. Furthermore, Volvo is considering integrating battery production into its forthcoming manufacturing facility situated in eastern Slovakia.

Slovakia thus joined the renewed race for investments in the region, competing with Hungarian, Czech, and Polish governments to secure growth and employment in the region (Hillebrand, 2023). The estimated impact of the successful automotive transformation is a 4% employment increase compared to the baseline scenario, while an unsuccessful transformation could mean a 10% decrease in GDP and a 4% in employment (Pirie et al., 2022). Despite in the short-term, the support for investments in batteries production seems to be a vital precondition of automotive industry transformation, in longer run, several other aspects are highlighted, such as low quality of jobs in batteries assembly and limited employment growth stemming from these investments (Czirfusz, 2023; Schade et al., 2022). As a potential growth based on the value-added activities, R&D associated with the battery circular economy and smart vertical integration of the value chains is recommended along with continuous exploration of raw materials availability and development of recycling value chains (Javid & Nejat, 2017; Schade et al., 2022).

Given its high share of manufacturing jobs, Slovakia ranks among the European countries most susceptible to automation and digitalization. According to the report by Georgieff and Milanez (2021), nearly 34.6% of jobs in Slovakia are at high risk of automation by 2030. Another analysis by the Slovak National Bank (NBS, 2021) predicts that 62% of existing jobs face potential risks of robotization, with about 10% of positions anticipated to be replaced by robots. Moreover, by 2030, significant population aging is expected, transitioning from an almost five-to-one ratio of the working-age population to the elderly population to a three-to-one ratio. Approximately 20%–30% of job roles are confronting the simultaneous challenges of digital and green transformations, with particular vulnerability observed in car manufacturing positions.

The transition carries significant implications for labor demand and overall skill structure in the labor market as well. As report by NBS (2021) further suggests, due to anticipated shifts, 30% of jobs will necessitate higher skill levels, leading to reduced demand for middle-skilled workers, while approximately 40% of forthcoming job roles remain yet to be defined in the transforming and emerging sectors such as renewable energy etc. The report also highlights the disadvantaged position of young people, noting that current schoolchildren are anticipated to enter the labor market with below-average proficiency in reading literacy, mathematics, and science, likely due to widespread school closures during the COVID-19 pandemic. Concerning young graduates, there is a potential risk of heightened brain drain among highly skilled workers (NBS, 2021). The current lack of labor in the industry is substituted by employing workers from foreign, mostly third-world non-EU countries. Indeed, employment of foreigners increased from less than 14,000 in 2016 to 54,000 in 2023 (UPSVaR, 2023).

4.1 Reskilling Infrastructure and Policy Dialog

Automation, as well as digitalization amid automotive transition and electrification, has one of the greatest potentials in terms of the automotive industry and engineering; however, they have a direct impact on human capital and work and encompass a large social dimension. At the same time, the specifics of the education system are decisive about the trends in the automotive industry (Grenčíková et al., 2021), which makes employers increasingly engaged in the public discourse about VET (vocational education training) programs and possible learning provisions.

Slovakia's low rankings in various international education assessments highlight the underperformance of its education system. This underperformance is emphasized by the rising mismatch between the skills acquired through educational programs and the requirements of the automotive industry, which concentrates on some of the largest employers in the country. Automakers thus often rely on their in-house training. According to Eurostat data, in 2020, almost 63%

of industrial companies provided training for workers, which is above the national average. Similarly, in 2020, 65% of industrial workers participated in retraining in companies that provided courses, which is above the European average (Eurostat, 2023).

Skill development tools such as VET or adult learning become particularly important for Slovakia in the context of digital and green transition and labor market challenges (OECD, 2020). Slovakia belongs to the countries with a traditionally strong school-based VET system which is predominantly youth-centered (Duman & Kureková, 2012; Fazekas & Kureková, 2016). Despite the decline in VET participation since the 90s, the reintroduction of a dual system of VET became an often-used tool in the auto industry to mitigate labor shortages and to better align skill provisions with the employer's needs. In contrast to other EU countries, vocational education and training in Slovakia predominantly takes place at the secondary school level, but there are pilot programs of dual higher education at some universities. For example, Volkswagen in collaboration with the Slovak Technical University in Bratislava initiated the professional bachelor's degree with an internship directly at the VW Bratislava factory (STU BA, 2017). Moreover, in 2023, Kia initiated study programs and pilot projects in collaboration with three technical universities. The OEM management has implemented a financial aid program, sponsoring preselected employees to enhance their technical qualifications in the university VET program.

In terms of adult learning, a report by Studená et al. (2023) suggests that the overall participation and culture of adult learning is underdeveloped and weak in Slovakia. Slovakia has been positioned among the weak-performing countries within the EU in terms of the participation of adults in learning. According to Labor Force Survey data which measures participation of adults in a learning activity in the past 4 weeks, the participation rates of adults in the age group between 25 and 64 years old remained constantly low with minor changes; the rate would vary slightly around 3%–4%, in 2020 only at 2.8%. The 2021 brought more significant rise to 4.8%, but it remains to be one of the lowest participation rates in the EU.

While various policy frameworks and strategies touch upon the reform of the education system and reskilling, the available statistics do not yet reflect the effects, for instance, in the participation rate (for more, see: Marcinčin et al., 2023). Employers from the Slovak automotive industry have been very influential in bringing up and navigating the debates at the national and cross-sectoral level about reforming the education system to mitigate skill mismatch with market needs, workers training, reskilling, up-skilling, and investing in enhancing digital competencies (Studená et al., 2023). A recent report by Lukáčová & Kahancová (2024) found that despite being active in policy debates about skill development, car makers are reluctant to unions' attempts to adopt training-related clauses in the collective agreements as they prefer to have full discretion over on-job training. In the newly institutionalized Alliance of Sectoral Councils, the representatives of auto companies, however, cooperate with other social partners on tripartite and sectoral principles to create a new qualification framework for future occupations.

5. Conclusion: Searching Ways to Decrease Dependency on the Automotive Industry

Slovakia, despite being able to attract such a high volume of foreign capital in the automotive industry in last 20 years, was not able to fully benefit from its presence. This is manifested in remarkably high level of output, exports, and employment levels in the foreign companies, but with in very low level of R&D and share of domestic capital. The dependency on foreign capital is manifested in the weak linkages between domestic and foreign companies and the low level of embeddedness of foreign companies in local economies.

Transformation of the industry driven by the simultaneous occurrence of digitalization, automatization, and decarbonization efforts may represent a challenge to the industry with increasing uncertainties about its future worldwide and in integrated peripheries particularly. Despite the ongoing upgrade in production methods, and increasing use of automatization and digitalization, this is not geared toward upgrading of the position subsidiaries of MNCs residing in Slovakia, nor toward increasing R&D or wage. Moreover, the switch to electric vehicles seems to reproduce the old model of industrial policies building on incentives for foreign investments to establish production plants, as in the case of giga factories.

Slovakia is thus expected to remain in a specialization trap, which is difficult to break (Grieveson et al., 2021). That is why it is not easy to abandon the policies of attracting investments in the automotive industry and support different pathway. Nevertheless, partial steps toward functional upgrading should be taken. These include changes in the focus of the direct support of foreign investments and changes in the education system and R&D support and building linkages with domestic capital. New battery value chains and mobility shift may represent opportunity to diversify production and aim at higher value-added production activities (e.g., in the clean public transport vehicles, last-mile vehicles and digital tools of mobility sharing, or in recycling) (Gažo et al., 2022; Schade et al., 2022).

Acknowledgment

This work is based on the research conducted between 2022 and 2024 within BAR-METAL project supported by the European Commission & European Social Fund Plus (no. 101052331). This work was also supported by the Czech Science Foundation [Grant Number 23-07819S].

References

Abdul-Hamid, H., & Ambasz, D. (2023). *Steering the human development strategy for a sustainable green economy in the Slovak Republic*. World Bank.

Acemoglu, D., & Autor, D. (2011). Skills, tasks and technologies: Implications for employment and earnings. In D. Card & O. Ashenfelter (Eds.), *Handbook of labor economics* (Vol. 4, pp. 1043–1171). Elsevier. https://doi.org/10.1016/S0169-7218(11)02410-5

Alguacil, M., Éltető, A., & Martínez–San Román, V. (2015). *International R&D spillovers in Central and Eastern Europe. The role of capital imports and local conditions*. Working Papers 2015/12, Economics Department, Universitat Jaume I.

Arntz, M., Gregory, T., & Zierahn, U. (2016). *The risk of automation for jobs in OECD countries: A comparative analysis*. OECD Social, Employment and Migration Working Papers, No. 189. OECD Publishing. https://doi.org/10.1787/5jlz9h56dvq7-en

Baldwin, R., & Lopez-Gonzalez, J. (2013). *Supply-chain trade: A portrait of global patterns and several testable hypotheses*. NBER Working Papers 18957. National Bureau of Economic Research, Inc. http://www.nber.org/papers/w18957

Bauer, W., Riedel, O., & Herrmann, F. (2020). *Employment 2030: Effects of electric mobility and digitalisation on the quality and quantity of employment at Volkswagen*. Fraunhofer Institute for Industrial Engineering IAO.

Benedeková, M., Drobný, M., Bartovicová, M., Kasanová, M., Stolárová, I., & Krabáč, J. (2019). *Extenzia kolektívnych zmlúv vyššieho stupňa – princíp, realizácia, dopady*. Konfederácia odborových zväzov SR. https://www.kozsr.sk/wp-content/uploads/2020/06/Extenzia-kolekt%C3%ADvnych-zmlúv-vyššieho-stupňa.pdf

Bohle, D., & Greskovits, B. (2012). *Capitalist diversity on Europe's periphery*. Cornell University Press.

Cagáňová, D., Hlásniková, P. R., Vraňaková, N., & Chlpeková, A. (2019). Intellectual capital as a key factor in the automotive industry. *Mobile Networks and Applications*, *24*(6), 2024–2031. https://doi.org/10.1007/s11036-018-01206-2

CLEPA. (2021). *Electric vehicle transition impact assessment report 2020–2040: A quantitative forecast of employment trends at automotive suppliers in Europe*. European Association of Automotive Suppliers. https://clepa.eu/wp-content/uploads/2021/12/Electric-Vehicle-Transition-Impact-Report-2020-2040.pdf

Czirfusz, M. (2023). *The battery boom in Hungary*. Friedrich Ebert Stiftung. https://library.fes.de/pdf-files/bueros/budapest/20101.pdf

Dicken, P. (2007). *Global shift: Mapping the changing contours of the world economy*. SAGE Publications Ltd.

Duman, A., & Kureková, L. (2012). The role of the state in the development of socio-economic models in Hungary and Slovakia: The case of industrial policy. *Journal of European Public Policy*, *19*(8), 1207–1228. https://doi.org/10.1080/13501763.2012.709018

Elektromobilita. (2020). Ročenka 2020 Všetko, čo potrebujete vedieť o elektormobilite v SR. (Annual Journal 2020. All you need to know about electromobility in Slovakia). ISBN 978-80-973581-0-5. https://www.pcrevue.sk/library/PDF%20ARCHIV/Elektromobilita%202020+inz.pdf

Eurostat. (2020). *Foreign control of enterprises by economic activity and a selection of controlling countries (from 2008 onwards)*. [fats_g1a_08] [dataset]. https://doi.org/10.2908/FATS_G1A_08

Eurostat. (2022). *Inward FDI stocks in % of GDP*. [tec00105] [dataset]. https://doi.org/10.2908/TEC00105

Eurostat. (2023). *Participants in CVT courses by sex and NACE Rev. 2 activity – % of persons employed in enterprises providing CVT courses*. [trng_cvt_13n2] [dataset]. https://doi.org/10.2908/TRNG_CVT_13N2

Eurostat. (2024). *Employed persons working at night as a percentage of the total employment, by sex, age, and professional status (%)*. [lfsa_ewpnig] [dataset]. https://doi.org/10.2908/LFSA_EWPNIG

Fazekas, M., & Kureková, L. M. (2016). *OECD reviews of vocational education and training. A skills beyond school review of the Slovak Republic*. OECD Publishing. https://www.oecd.org/publications/a-skills-beyond-school-review-of-the-slovak-republic-9789264233348-en.htm

Fernandez-Stark, K., & Gereffi, G. (2019). Global value chain analysis: A primer. In S. Ponte, G. Gereffi, & G. Raj-Reichert (Eds.), *Handbook on global value chains* (2nd ed., pp. 54–76). Edward Elgar Publishing. https://doi.org/10.4337/9781788113779.00008

Gažo, P., Martišková, M., & Smith, T. S. J. (2022). The transformation of the Slovak and Czech automotive industries: Stakeholders' perspectives and barriers towards an ecological mobility industry. *International Journal of Automotive Technology and Management*, *22*(2), 202–221. https://doi.org/10.1504/IJATM.2022.124360

Georgieff, A., & Milanez, A. (2021). *What happened to jobs at high risk of automation?* OECD Social, Employment and Migration Working Papers, No. 255. OECD Publishing. https://doi.org/10.1787/10bc97f4-en

Grenčíková, A., Kordoš, M., Bartek, J., & Berkovič, V. (2021). The impact of the industry 4.0 concept on Slovak business sustainability within the issue of the pandemic outbreak. *Sustainability*, *13*(9), 4975. https://doi.org/10.3390/su13094975

Grieveson, R., Bykova, A., Hanzl-Weiss, D., Hunya, G., Korpar, N., Podkaminer, L., Steher, R., & Stoellinger, R. (2021). *A new growth model in EU-CEE. Avoiding the specialisation trap and embracing megatrends*. Friedrich Ebert Stiftung. https://library.fes.de/pdf-files/id-moe/17843.pdf

Guzik, R., Domański, B., & Gwosdz, K. (2020). Automotive industry dynamics in Central Europe. In A. Covarrubias V. & S. M. Ramírez Perez (Eds.), *New frontiers of the automobile industry: Exploring geographies, technology, and institutional challenges* (pp. 377–397). Springer International Publishing. https://doi.org/10.1007/978-3-030-18881-8_15

Hillebrand, E. (2023). *The transition to electric vehicles in CEE*. Friedrich Ebert Stiftung. https://eastern-europegrowth.fes.de/e/the-transition-to-electric-vehicles-in-cee

Jacobs, A. J. (2017). *Automotive FDI in emerging Europe: Shifting locales in the motor vehicle industry*. Palgrave Macmillan.

Javid, R. J., & Nejat, A. (2017). A comprehensive model of regional electric vehicle adoption and penetration. *Transport Policy*, *54*, 30–42. https://doi.org/10.1016/j.tranpol.2016.11.003

Kahancová, M. (2016). *The rise of the dual labour market: Fighting precarious employment in the new member states through industrial relations (PRECARIR)*. CELSI. https://celsi.sk/media/research_reports/RR19.pdf

Kahancová, M., & Uhlerová, M. (2023). Trade unions in Slovakia: From politics to bread-and-butter unionism. In T. Müller, K. Vandaele, & J. Waddington (Eds.), *Trade unions in Europe* (pp. 945–978). Peter Lang. https://www.etui.org/sites/default/files/2023-06/Chapter25_Slovakia_From%20politics%20to%20bread-and-butter%20unionism_2023.pdf

Kureková, L. M. (2018). *The automotive industry in Central Europe: A success?* IZA World of Labour. https://doi.org/10.15185/izawol.448

Lednárová Dítětová, L., Hrnčiar, M., Cibíková, N., Čierna, Z., Pálová, V., Škodová, M., Varačka, M., & Vittek, J. (2022). *Zručnosti pre budúcnosť konkurencieschopného trhu práce na Slovensku*. Republiková únia zamestnávateľov. https://www.ruzsr.sk/media/e5cec396-eadc-477a-8129-ea880222621l.pdf

Lukáčová, K., & Kahancová, M. (2024). *Digitalization, automatization and decarbonization: Opportunity for strengthening collective bargaining in the metal sector*. Slovak Policy Report. BARMETAL project. https://celsi.sk/media/datasource/BARMETAL_country_report_Slovakia_vXKTt8Q.pdf

Majzlíková, E., & Vitáloš, M. (2022). Potential risk of automation for jobs in Slovakia: A district-and industry-level analysis. *Eastern European Economics*, *60*(5), 452–478. https://doi.org/10.1080/00128775.2022.2099421

Marcinčin, A., Benedeková, M., Dubecová, A., Gažo, P., Hužiková, A., Košč, J., Lacko, M., & Lukáčová, K. (2023). *Spravodlivá transformácia*. https://www.kozsr.sk/wp-content/uploads/2023/10/AV22_Spravodliva-transformacia.pdf

Martišková, M. (2019). *The future of employment in the car sector. Four country perspectives from Central and Eastern Europe*. Friedrich Ebert Stiftung. https://prag.fes.de/e/the-future-of-employment-in-the-car-sector-four-country-perspectives-from-central-and-eastern-europe

NBS. (2021). *Structural challenges*. National Bank of Slovakia. https://nbs.sk/_img/documents/_publikacie/sktrukturalne_vyzvy/2021/strukturalne_vyzvy_2021_en.pdf

Nedelkoska, L., & Quintini, G. (2018). *Automation, skills use and training*. OECD Social, Employment and Migration Working Papers, No. 202. OECD Publishing. http://dx.doi.org/10.1787/2e2f4eea-en

OECD. (2019). *OECD economic surveys: Slovak Republic 2019*. OECD Publishing. https://doi.org/10.1787/eco_surveys-svk-2019-en

OECD. (2020). *OECD skills strategy Slovak Republic: Assessment and recommendations*. OECD Skills Studies. OECD Publishing. https://doi.org/10.1787/bb688e68-en

OECD. (2022). *Strengthening FDI and SME linkages in the Slovak Republic*. OECD Publishing. https://doi.org/10.1787/972046f5-en

Oláhová, Z. (2023, November 18). *Slovenský automobilový priemysel má problém, pomôcť by mohla zahraničná pracovná sila*. SITA. https://sita.sk/vpriemysle/slovensky-automobilovy-priemysel-ma-problem-bori-sa-s-nedostatkom-kvalifikovanej-pracovnej-sily/

Pavlínek, P. (2016). Whose success? The state–foreign capital nexus and the development of the automotive industry in Slovakia. *European Urban and Regional Studies*, *23*(4), 571–593. https://doi.org/10.1177/0969776414557965

Pavlínek, P. (2018). Global production networks, foreign direct investment, and supplier linkages in the integrated peripheries of the automotive industry. *Economic Geography*, *94*(2), 141–165. https://doi.org/10.1080/00130095.2017.1393313

Pavlínek, P. (2020). Restructuring and internationalization of the European automotive industry. *Journal of Economic Geography*, *20*(2), 509–541. https://doi.org/10.1093/jeg/lby070

Pavlínek, P. (2022). Relative positions of countries in the core-periphery structure of the European automotive industry. *European Urban and Regional Studies*, *29*(1), 59–84. https://doi.org/10.1177/09697764211021882

Pavlínek, P. (2023). The transition of the automotive industry towards electric vehicle production in the East European integrated periphery. *Empirica*, *50*(1), 35–73. https://doi.org/10.1007/s10663-022-09554-9

Pavlínek, P., & Ženka, J. (2011). Upgrading in the automotive industry: Firm-level evidence from Central Europe. *Journal of Economic Geography*, *11*(3), 559–586. https://doi.org/10.1093/jeg/lbq023

Pirie, J., Suta, C.-M., Hidi, J., Barbieri, L., & Kőműves, Z. (2022). *Electromobility in the Visegrad region – Slovakia*. Cambridge Econometrics. https://www.camecon.com/what/our-work/electromobility-in-the-visegrad-region-slovakia/

PwC. (2018). *Automotive supplier survey 2018*. PwC. https://www.pwc.com/sk/en/odvetvia/automobilovy-priemysel/automotive-supplier-survey-2018.html

Radosevic, S. (2017). *Upgrading technology in Central and Eastern European economies*. IZA World of Labour. https://doi.org/10.15185/izawol.338

SARIO. (2023). *Automotive sector in Slovakia*. Slovak Investment and Trade Development Agency. https://www.sario.sk/sites/default/files/2023-10/sario-automotive-sector-in-slovakia-2023-10-26.pdf

SARIO. (2024). *Automotive industry*. SARIO, Slovak Investment and Trade Development Agency. https://www.sario.sk/en/invest-slovakia/industries-regions-overviews/automotive-industry

Saxunova, D., Novackova, D., & Bajzikova, L. (2018). Focus on the automotive industry in the context of a globalization process in Slovakia. *Journal of Eastern Europe Research in Business & Economics*. https://doi.org/10.5171/2018.435685

Šćepanović, V. (2015). Have your competitiveness and eat it, too: The pull and limits of cost competition in Hungary and Slovakia. In M. Bernaciak (Ed.), *Market expansion and social dumping in Europe* (pp. 190–209). Routledge.

Schade, W., Haug, I., & Berthold, D. (2022). *The future of the automotive sector: Emerging battery value chains in Europe*. ETUI Research Paper – Report 2022.02. http://dx.doi.org/10.2139/ssrn.4220540

Šipikal, M., & Buček, M. (2013). The role of FDIs in regional innovation: Evidence from the automotive industry in Western Slovakia. *Regional Science Policy & Practice*, *5*(4), 475–491. https://doi.org/10.1111/rsp3.12022

Slovak Electric Vehicle Association. (2023). *Slovensko a elektromobilita 2023. Trh, infraštruktúra a opatrenia pre rozvoj sektora*. https://www.seva.sk/wp-content/uploads/2023/06/SEVS_VS_23.pdf

SSO. (2024). *Composition of the average nominal monthly wage of employee based on occupations [Štruktúra priemernej nominálnej mesačnej mzdy zamestnanca podľa klasifikácie zamestnaní (SK ISCO – 08)]*. [np2004rs]—DATAcube. [dataset]. Slovak Statistical Office. https://datacube.statistics.sk/#!/view/sk/VBD_SLOVSTAT/np2004rs/v_np2004rs_00_00_00_sk

STU BA. (2017). Volkswagen a STU otvárajú nový odbor [HN]. https://www.stuba.sk/sk/diani-na-stu/volkswagen-a-stu-otvaraju-novy-odbor-hn.html?page_id=11185

Studená, I., Kováčová, L., & Kureková, L. M. (2023). *I SKILL National Report – Slovakia*. Working Paper. I SKILL Project - Industrial Relations and Social Dialogue to Kick-in Inclusive Adult Learning – Deliverable 3.1. https://cdn.ceps.eu/wp-content/uploads/2023/12/D-3.1-I-SKILL_National-Report_-Slovakia_final.pdf

Sturgeon, T., Van Biesebroeck, J., & Gereffi, G. (2008). Value chains, networks and clusters: Reframing the global automotive industry. *Journal of Economic Geography*, *8*(3), 297–321. https://doi.org/10.1093/jeg/lbn007

Szalavetz, A., & Sass, M. (2023). Disentangling the semi-periphery: Evolutionary trajectories and perspectives of the Austrian and Hungarian automotive industries. *Post-Communist Economies*, *35*(3), 211–235. https://doi.org/10.1080/14631377.2023.2171179

UPSVaR. (2023). *Zamestnávanie cudzincov na území Slovenskej republiky*. Office of Labour, Social Affairs and Family. https://www.upsvr.gov.sk/statistiky/zamestnavanie-cudzincov-statistiky/zamestnavanie-cudzincov-na-uzemi-slovenskej-republiky-za-rok-2022.html?page_id=1156941

Chapter 11

Slovak Innovation Ecosystem: Information Technology and Digital Innovations

Jaroslav Vokoun

Slovak Academy of Sciences, Slovakia

Abstract

Innovation is a pillar of competitiveness and a tool for transforming society toward sustainable development. Investment in research, development, and innovation comes from both private and public sources. However, corporate investment is lower than the European Union (EU) average, partly due to the structure of Slovakian companies within value chains. A significant portion of innovation comes from imports, reflecting a low focus on pre-production and postproduction phases of production within Slovakia. The government provides varied institutional support for research and development, including tax incentives for innovation. Additionally, digitalization is underway through the Industry 4.0 concept. Retaining and attracting skilled information technology (IT) professionals from abroad is crucial, as the IT sector offers an attractive environment for talented individuals. Enhancing the knowledge society requires collaboration from all stakeholders to employ more creative people within Slovakia. Imported innovations dominated the scene, but in recent years, companies have been increasingly investing in the domestic R&D and innovation. The necessity of digital transformation is a theme in discussions of Slovak society. It's a prerequisite for successful adaptation to the ongoing changes the country is facing.

Keywords: Innovation; digitalization; research and development; education system; strategy

1. Introduction

Innovation covers broad spectrum, extending to products, services, technologies, processes, and even the built environment. Success in research and development

Modeling Economic Growth in Contemporary Slovakia, 201–217

doi:10.1108/978-1-83549-454-720241016

(R&D) activities relies on the collaboration of several actors. The quality of an innovation system hinges on the degree of integration between these actors. Main actors in the innovation system include firms (this encompasses employees of all levels, owners, management, corporate research centers, and industry clusters), research institutions (this includes researchers and their institutions), schools (this refers to students and teachers within the educational system), and support institutions (these institutions provide strategies and support measures for innovation). Innovation is a key driver of both sustainable development and efficiency. It strengthens a nation's competitiveness and is fostered by strong connections within the innovation system. The knowledge triangle, a symbolic representation of the interactions between research, education, and innovation, highlights the importance of these connections.

Slovakia's historical context significantly influenced its approach to R&D and innovation. Between 1948 and 1989, as part of Czechoslovakia, Slovakia operated under a centrally planned economy. State ownership of companies, limited domestic competition, a state monopoly on foreign trade, and restricted imports due to currency limitations played a role. In this environment, a strong focus was placed on R&D and innovation to develop domestic technologies and materials in place of unavailable imports. Additionally, restrictions on exporting new technologies from economically advanced countries, often due to potential military applications, further fueled domestic innovation efforts. Following the split from Czechoslovakia in 1993, Slovakia began transitioning to a market economy. Privatization of state-owned companies, the emergence of new businesses, and the arrival of foreign investors transformed the landscape. This shift fostered the development of globally competitive firms, reflected in Slovakia's position as a major export-oriented nation with a high export-to-gross domestic product (GDP) ratio (93.4% in 2022).

While Slovakia has a well-defined innovation ecosystem with standard actors, its efficiency remains a challenge. Despite having an innovation strategy in place, implementation issues hinder its effectiveness. Numerous support programs exist to assist companies with domestic innovation, yet participation remains low. Currently, imported innovations hold a dominant position in enhancing product competitiveness. To address these issues, fostering a talent pool of creative and motivated researchers is crucial. Their education and development play a vital role in driving domestic innovation. Furthermore, with digital transformation permeating all aspects of life, upskilling the entire workforce in digital competencies is essential.

2. Innovation Ecosystem

The innovation system reflects a country's level of economic development. Key actors within this system, such as companies, universities, and research institutions – shape the "knowledge triangle" of innovation, education, and research. Weaknesses within these actors can hinder the overall development of the innovation system.

Several factors contribute to Slovakia's lower innovation performance, including shortcomings in the education system, the national R&D system, and the business sector's limited focus on domestic innovation. Additionally, the structure of the economy and the institutional environment may not be conducive to fostering innovation. Slovakia lags behind in various areas such as R&D spending, technology transfer, and research collaboration with industry. Slovakia's lower innovation performance stems from weaknesses in the education system, the national R&D system, and a business sector with a limited focus on domestic innovation. The economic structure and institutional environment may also play a role. Strong interconnectedness between these actors is crucial for a well-functioning national innovation ecosystem (Šikulová et al., 2014).

According to the EC, 2023a; European Innovation Scoreboard, 2023, Slovakia falls into the category of "emerging innovators," indicating the lowest innovation performance within the European Union (EU).[1] This group significantly lags behind the "moderate innovators" in terms of development dynamics. With an innovation performance of only 65.6% of the EU average, Slovakia needs to accelerate its progress to achieve successful convergence (Table 11.1). While Slovakia surpasses the EU average in exports of medium and high-tech goods (+19.9%), sales of innovative products (+14.5%), lifelong learning (+8.8%), and air emissions with fine particles (+7.6%) (EC, 2023b), these areas often rely heavily on imported innovations. Non-R&D innovation expenditures, which can foster domestic innovation, are at par with the EU average. A relative strength lies in the level of human resources available in Slovakia.[2]

Joining the EU in 2004, Slovakia faced a significant innovation gap. The knowledge-intensive sector and the share of innovative companies lagged behind the EU average by 20%–30% and 50%, respectively, and patent activity remained low (Klas et al., 2005). While there have been improvements in recent years, the overall situation remains similar. Domestic R&D is underutilized, with innovative companies favoring purchased technologies over in-house R&D.

A significant gap exists between Slovakia's domestic spending on R&D and that of economically developed countries, which typically allocate around 3% of GDP to R&D. In 2000, Slovakia's R&D spending was just 0.64% of GDP (compared to the EU average of 1.81%) (Eurostat, 2023c). This share even dipped to 0.45% by 2007, while the EU average remained steady. Fortunately, there has been a gradual increase since 2015, reaching 0.98% in 2022. However, Slovakia still falls short of the EU average (2.23%). The structure of the Slovakian economy, with lower R&D expenditures by both companies and the government, contributes to this gap. While government and academic sectors rely on state budget funds for R&D, corporate spending remains low. Furthermore, Slovakia's

[1]The European Innovation Scoreboard classifies Romania, Bulgaria, Latvia, Poland, Slovakia, and Croatia as "emerging innovators," with all scoring lower than 70% of the EU average.

[2]The significant increase observed in 2023 compared to 2022 is due to a change in methodology.

Table 11.1. European Innovation Scoreboard Country Profile (Slovakia, 2023).

	Performance Relative to EU in 2023 (%)	Performance Change 2016–2023 (%)	Performance Change 2022–2023 (%)
Summary innovation index	65.6	6.4	4.2
Human resources	91.6	1.7	21.3
Attractive research systems	51.7	18.2	2.8
Digitalization	67.1	12.0	5.2
Finance and support	38.1	3.7	1.7
Firm investments	56.0	16.5	0.3
Use of information technologies	74.7	−9.7	−2.5
Innovators	42.3	15.6	14.2
Linkages	49.8	10.7	−3.6
Intellectual assets	49.4	7.0	−1.7
Employment impacts	55.9	11.7	9.6
Sales impacts	101.8	0.4	11.5
Environmental sustainability	95.5	−2.8	−5.7

Source: EC (2023b).

competitiveness in production currently relies more heavily on imported innovations than on domestic R&D efforts.

Historically, company spending on R&D has lagged behind in Slovakia, hovering between 0.2% and 0.3% of GDP from 2003 to 2012 (Eurostat, 2023c). While there's been a gradual increase in recent years, reaching 0.56% in 2022, this still falls short of the 2% typical in developed economies. Government R&D spending has also remained relatively flat, averaging around 0.18% of GDP after 2000, with some fluctuations. The EU average for government spending sits at 0.25% of GDP. The academic sector shows a more positive trend. While its share of R&D funding started low at 0.06% after 2000 (compared to the EU's 0.38%), it has steadily climbed to 0.25% in 2022, approaching the EU average of 0.48%. However, this overall low level of R&D expenditure in Slovakia limits research opportunities and restricts job creation in the R&D sector. This, in turn, contributes to the outflow of skilled and creative minds from the country.

Slovakia's R&D workforce has historically lagged behind the EU average. For a long time, the share of R&D workers hovered around 0.6% of the total workforce (compared to the EU's 1.2%) (Eurostat, 2023d). However, there have been positive developments in recent years. By 2022, this share had increased to 0.86%, and it remains the sixth lowest among EU countries. The most significant growth has occurred within the corporate sector, where the R&D workforce was below 0.2% until 2016. This share has risen to 0.34% in 2022, but it's still the fourth lowest in the EU (only Latvia, Cyprus, and Romania have a lower percentage). Traditionally, the academic sector employed the largest share of R&D workers, with a current level of 0.36%, which is close to the EU average (0.42% in 2022). However, due to stagnant growth in the academic sector, the increase in corporate R&D workers is narrowing the gap. The government sector maintains a share similar to the EU average (around 0.16%–0.17%).

Integration into the global economy significantly impacted Slovakia's innovation landscape. An influx of foreign direct investments brought a surge in labor productivity and a massive transfer of technology. These factors helped compensate for existing technological deficiencies through the import of modern technologies, products, and services. Furthermore, widespread privatization transformed ownership structures, with many large firms becoming foreign-owned and export-oriented. These foreign-owned companies often integrate Slovakia into their global value chains, with subsidiaries typically focusing on the production phase (assembly) and having a limited presence in preproduction (R&D) and postproduction (support services). This focus on production has historically resulted in lower demand for highly skilled R&D workers. However, this trend is gradually shifting. We are now seeing a positive development in activities like R&D, programming, and information technology (IT) support within companies, suggesting a growing role for higher-skilled workers in Slovakia's innovation ecosystem.

Venture capital plays a limited role in financing innovative startups in Slovakia, despite its potential to mitigate risk through shared resources and expertise. However, several active funds are present, including the National Holding Fund, the Slovak Development Fund, the Innovation and Technology Fund, and Eterus Capital. Private equity capital also plays a part, with funds entering innovative companies for a defined period. The Innovation and Technology Fund specifically targets young companies with developed products or services ready for market introduction. This fund prioritizes sectors like environmental technologies, renewable energy, industrial innovation, e-commerce, IT, telecommunications, life-improving technologies, and software solutions.

Industry 4.0 hinges on expertise in IT and fosters automation and robotization. In Slovakia, this is most evident in the automotive industry, where car manufacturers' high-quality standards drive robot adoption throughout the supply chain. Around 78% of robots deployed in Slovakia in 2019 were used in automotive production (Nacero, 2023). This focus is reflected in the national robot density: 4.3 robots per 1,000 employees in 2021, compared to the European average of 11.1 robots per 1,000 employees. One successful example of automation and robotization is PPS Group, a Detva-based engineering company specializing in steel frames and structures. PPS Group even operates its own Welding School, annually training roughly 50 new skilled workers to support their advanced manufacturing processes. Green innovation is also gaining traction. PPS Group is exploring methods to reduce their environmental impact, such as producing steel with a zero-carbon footprint (Trend, 2024).

Slovakia faces challenges in fostering corporate partnerships for innovation. Limited production in technologically advanced sectors restricts the pool of potential collaborators. A smaller economy often lacks the "critical mass" of companies needed to drive robust partnerships (Brzica et al., 2011). Furthermore, lower levels of trust in Slovak society compared to many European countries can make collaboration more difficult (Bunčák et al., 2009). Small and startup companies often demonstrate a greater willingness to collaborate. Example of successful collaboration is the Smart Cluster – StartUP HUB, which exemplifies this trend, acting as a partner institution that fosters partnerships specifically in technology-oriented ventures. Initiatives like FinTech Hub Slovakia create valuable ecosystems for collaboration. This organization provides support platforms for both large corporations and startups in the financial sector. Their services encompass technological guidance, legal assistance, and consulting. These hubs play a crucial role by helping innovators verify and refine their ideas (product, concept, or prototype). Ultimately, their goal is to support financial sector innovation and digitization in Slovakia. Additionally, they create a safe environment for companies to test the validity of their solutions. The ambition behind these initiatives is to cultivate a more interconnected innovation ecosystem in Slovakia, facilitating collaboration between domestic and international innovators.

3. R&D and Innovation Support

Slovakia's R&D activities are largely concentrated in academic institutions. A significant portion of scientists work at the Slovak Academy of Sciences (SAV) and universities. As of 2022, the country boasted 23,344 full-time equivalent (FTE) R&D workers, reflecting a 28.8% increase compared to 2012.[3] Notably, the public and university sectors employ roughly 60% of the total R&D workforce. This translates to 18,394 researchers (FTE) excluding technical and support staff, as many researchers combine research work with university teaching.

While research remains concentrated in academia, the business sector is demonstrating increasing dynamism. The number of researchers in industry has grown significantly, with car manufacturing employing the most researchers (1,149 FTE in 2022), followed by machine manufacturing (986 FTE) and electrical equipment manufacturing (490 FTE).[4] This growth reflects a 40% increase

[3]Data from the Statistical Office of the Slovak Republic: https://datacube.statistics.sk/.

[4]In 2008, the number of researchers employed (FTE) in these sectors was significantly lower: only 43 in car manufacturing, 278 in machine manufacturing, and 133 in electrical equipment manufacturing.

in researchers within the business sector since 2012. Furthermore, R&D expenditure in this sector has skyrocketed by 154% during the same period.[5] Fueled by this surge in funding and personnel, the corporate sector is emerging as a key player in Slovakia's R&D and innovation landscape.

For a long time, inadequate technical infrastructure hampered research efforts in Slovakia. However, a significant investment push supported by the EU helped bridge this gap. Between 2013 and 2020, 14 strategic R&D infrastructure projects were established, along with 7 science parks and 7 research centers. Despite this progress, the long-term sustainability of these projects remains a challenge. The initial phase of any science park typically requires financial support to foster its activities. Unfortunately, due to a lack of continued funding, these Slovakian parks and research centers struggle to fully utilize their potential. Attracting corporate partners also presents a hurdle. As a result, the most successful parks/centers tend to attract startups with high innovation potential.

Participation in the European research area offers significant advantages. Research institutions and companies benefit by concentrating large-scale human and financial resources, crucial for conducting top-tier research. However, current conditions in Slovakia limit its ability to compete with the well-established national innovation systems of more economically advanced EU countries. A prime example of Slovakian scientific contribution is their involvement with the European Organization for Nuclear Research (CERN) in Geneva. Slovakian scientists play a vital role in research at the Large Hadron Collider, contributing to both basic and applied research of global significance. Beyond research, Slovakian companies have successfully supplied CERN with cutting-edge equipment, including magnets and highly sophisticated robots. The Slovak Experiment IS521 focuses on studying the deformation of atomic nuclei. Additionally, the TATRA spectrometer, an invention by scientists from the Slovak Academy of Sciences, examines the deformation of the atomic nucleus at its birth. The transfer of cutting-edge technologies from CERN empowers Slovakian specialists to leverage their expertise in diverse fields like electronics, metal physics, cryogenics, medical detector development, superconducting magnets, computer networks, and artificial intelligence applications (Veda na dosah, 2023).

Globally, several industries are recognized for their high level of innovation, including information and communication technology (ICT), electronics production, pharmaceuticals, and car manufacturing. In Slovakia, electronics and car production are significant contributors to industrial output. However, these sectors currently focus on assembly with a high reliance on imported innovations, resulting in low added value. This dependence on external R&D limits domestic R&D activities. Similarly, the pharmaceutical industry has a limited presence in Slovakia, primarily concentrated on the production of generic drugs, which

---

[5]Historically, expenditure on buildings and technological equipment dominated R&D spending, accounting for roughly 80% of the total up to 2010. However, this trend has shifted. By 2022, the share of these expenditures has decreased to 47%, while the allocation for personnel costs in in-house R&D activities is on the rise.

require less investment in R&D. While some small research firms participate in global drug trials, overall domestic R&D efforts remain low.

Climate change risks are driving a carbon transformation, incentivizing R&D efforts focused on eco-innovations. These innovations aim to reduce the environmental impact of production and product use across various sectors like energy, industry, transportation, and construction.[6] The European Eco-Innovation Scoreboard helps us evaluate progress in environmental innovation. Slovakia currently falls within the group with the lowest eco-innovation performance, reaching only 77.7% of the EU average (Varga, 2023). Despite this, several recent strategic documents highlight the government's commitment to tackling environmental and climate challenges. "Greener Slovakia," the environmental policy strategy for the Slovak Republic until 2030 outlines key goals (MŽP SR, 2020).[7] One such goal is to encourage green public procurement, aiming for at least 70% of public sector purchases to be environmentally friendly. Looking ahead, innovations will be crucial in areas like water management in urban environments, preventing landscape desertification, and fostering sustainability across industry, buildings, and households.

The government hesitated to introduce R&D tax credits for companies, fearing potential misuse. However, a transparent system was finally established in 2015, allowing companies to deduct R&D expenses from their income tax. The rules are subject to change. The number of companies utilizing this program has been inconsistent. In 2015, there were 83 participants, rising to a peak of 415 in 2020. Only 16 companies used the R&D tax deduction in 2023 (Financial administration of Slovak Republic, 2024). Uptake of this support tool remains low.

Public institutions play a leading role in supporting R&D and innovation in Slovakia. The Slovak Innovation and Energy Agency (SIEA) identifies various challenges in this area and offers solutions for businesses. SIEA offers an "innovation voucher" program that finances collaboration between small and medium enterprises (SMEs) and research institutions, universities, companies, and municipalities. In partnership with the European digital innovation hub EXPANDI 4.0, SIEA helps SMEs initiate their digitalization journeys (Expandi, 2023). They also assist SMEs in finding funding for digital projects. Supported projects exemplify this focus, including digitalization of buildings and spaces, 3D geodetic mapping, innovative applications of alternative energy sources, and advancements in robotics and mechatronics (SIEA, 2023). SIEA announces calls and finances projects targeting both public and private entities. In the public sector, the focus is on reducing energy consumption and promoting renewable

[6]Innovations for the company's functioning and product life cycle.

[7]Other important strategic documents are the Low Carbon Development Strategy of the Slovak Republic until 2030 with a view to 2050, the Integrated National Energy and Climate Plan for the years 2021–2030, the Waste Prevention Program of the Slovak Republic for the years 2019–2025, and the Action Plan for the Development of Electromobility in the Slovak Republic.

energy use in public buildings. For households, SIEA supports projects that encourage the adoption of renewable energy sources and improve air quality.

Several agencies play a key role in financing R&D projects in Slovakia:

- Scientific Grant Agency of the Ministry of Education (VEGA): This internal grant system primarily supports basic research projects conducted at universities and institutes within the Slovak Academy of Sciences (SAV).
- Research and Development Support Agency (APVV): APVV funds both basic research and, to a greater extent, applied R&D projects. However, companies currently underutilize these programs.
- Research Agency: This agency facilitates applications for the European Horizon Europe program, offering grants for early-stage researchers, support for established researchers, and projects focused on decarbonization and economic digitization.
- Research and Innovation Authority (VAIA): VAIA aims to attract talent through initiatives like the Innovation Fellowship for returning Slovaks and provides other R&D and innovation support schemes. Recognizing the fragmented nature of current support systems, VAIA is working to unify the process of preparing, publishing, evaluating, submitting, and monitoring research projects. These efforts aim to increase transparency, fairness, and overall program effectiveness.

4. Educational System

A well-educated and well-trained workforce is key to a country reaching its full potential. Demographic trend significantly influences the development of the educational system. Primary school enrollment is declining. Fewer students enrolling in vocational schools leads to a critical gap in skilled professionals available for the labor market. University enrollment is rising, but the structure of graduates presents a challenge. Slovakia has a low share of university graduates in science, technology, engineering, and math (STEM) fields, with only 1.3% of its population aged 20–29 holding a STEM degree compared to the EU average of 2.2% (Eurostat, 2023a). One of the factors in the deterioration of the quality of the educational process at universities is the irrational increase in the number of universities. Student mobility offers another perspective. Slovakia boasts a high rate of students studying abroad, with 20% seeking education elsewhere, the highest in the OECD after Luxembourg (OECD, 2023a). The Czech Republic, with its welcoming approach to Slovakian students, is a popular destination. Estimates suggest that approximately half of these students might return to Slovakia, bringing back valuable experiences and international knowledge.

The Program for International Student Assessment (PISA) gauges the quality of educational outcomes for 15-year-old students. Slovak students' performance on PISA tests is below the OECD average in mathematics, reading, and scientific literacy (OECD, 2023b). In recognition of these skill gaps, Slovakia's education system is undergoing curriculum reform to better equip graduates for the demands of the labor market.

A study by Bunčák et al. (2009) found that investing in personal development is a relatively neglected strategy among Slovak citizens. This trend is particularly prevalent among older, less educated, and economically inactive individuals. Additionally, the study revealed a low prevalence of life strategies focused on creativity, innovation, and entrepreneurship within the Slovak population.

Slovakia is taking steps to ensure its workforce has the skills needed to thrive in a changing world. As part of a comprehensive curricular reform, the new State Educational Program aims to equip students with the skills and knowledge necessary for success in the 21st century. The government's Lifelong Learning Strategy (MŠVVŠ SR, 2021) aims to create a more flexible educational system that can better adapt to the evolving demands of the labor market. Additionally, the Digital Skills Strategy focuses on providing adult learning opportunities to equip individuals with the skills necessary to participate effectively in an increasingly digital society.

5. The Talent Challenge

Talented individuals are the lifeblood of a knowledge-based economy. They drive innovation, generate new ideas, and possess the skills critical for competitiveness. However, in globalized world, retaining talent in less innovative countries presents a significant challenge. Favorable conditions for labor mobility can lead to a brain drain, where talented individuals migrate to more economically developed regions and countries seeking better opportunities for growth and career development. This creates a paradoxical situation: as the importance of talent rises, so does the difficulty of attracting, retaining, or developing a skilled workforce. To address this challenge, countries need to create an environment that fosters talent development and offers attractive opportunities for talented individuals to contribute and thrive.

The Slovak Republic faces a challenge in retaining its highly skilled workforce. Unlike countries with favorable conditions for talent, Slovakia experiences a net loss of skilled professionals due to emigration. The country's current mobility policy prioritizes filling immediate labor shortages, particularly in sectors like the automotive industry.

The government introduced a support scheme to incentivize Slovak experts working abroad to return in 2015. This 4-year program offered financial assistance to offset barriers and ease the transition back to Slovakia. Despite its goal, the scheme attracted only a small number of participants (26), primarily young professionals and senior experts. Additionally, the majority (18) found employment in Slovak Academy of Sciences.

The government continues its efforts with a renewed support scheme for the return of experts (2020–2024 with a view to 2027). Additionally, the SASPRO 2 project aims to foster international research collaboration by attracting 40 foreign researchers to scientific clusters within the Slovak Academy of Sciences, Comenius University, and the Slovak Technical University. Recognizing the value of foreign talent, the program also aims to attract back Slovak scientists currently working abroad (UK, 2020).

Emigration waves in the 20th century significantly depleted Slovakia's pool of skilled workers, creating a challenge that persists today. Historically, Slovak society wasn't as open to immigration. A 2018 survey (Table 11.2) showed a significant gap between Slovaks and the EU average in perceiving immigration benefits. However, recent years have witnessed a shift. The lack of skilled workers in key industries necessitated an influx of immigrants. This trend accelerated due to the war in Ukraine, with over 100,000 Ukrainians finding refuge in Slovakia and more than 35,000 filling vacant positions. These developments are gradually changing Slovak society, fostering greater acceptance of immigrants compared to the past.

A 2019 survey of creative people with international work experience revealed key differences between domestic and foreign work environments (Brzica et al., 2020).[8] The survey found that creative workers perceive several advantages to working abroad compared to Slovakia:

- More opportunities for professional development (74.2%).
- Better-equipped workplaces (67.6%).
- Valuable networking opportunities (62.2%).
- Experience gained abroad is beneficial upon returning home (56.0%).[9]

Slovakia also experiences significant internal migration, with a net migration flow from the eastern to western regions. Bratislava, as the capital and center of education and research, attracts creative professionals. This leads to the growth of the Bratislava region and the weakening of other parts of the country.

Table 11.2. Degree of Agreement With the Statement: Immigrants Contribute a Lot to Our Country (%).

Country	Totally Agree	Tend to Agree	Tend to Disagree	Totally Disagree	Don't Know
EÚ	13	37	26	17	7
Slovakia	2	14	39	37	8

Source: EC (2018).

[8]The online survey was conducted by researchers from the Economic Institute of the Slovak Academy of Sciences in November and December 2019. The sample consisted of 225 respondents.

[9]The percentages in parentheses represent the share of respondents who gave a positive answer for each factor.

6. Digital Transformation

The development of digitalization is dependent on the development of ICT. The availability of technology and applications enables the provision of solutions for a wide range of activities. Digitalization saves resources, facilitates work, and increases interaction between actors. It changes the labor market because, on the one hand, it creates jobs, and on the other hand, changes in process technology create pressure for new skills or reduce the need for some professions. The path to the digital decade is a political program of the EU. Ensuring better access to digital goods and services is a pillar of the Digital Single Market in the EU.

Citizens use the internet for various activities. In 2022, 65% of the Slovak population used online banking services. 97% of young people aged 16 to 24 made online purchases. Only 4.4% of the Slovak population uses smart home elements, compared to the EU average of 11% (Eurostat, 2023b). The EU aims to have at least 80% of all adults with basic digital skills by 2030. Half of the adult population in Slovakia has basic digital skills, which is slightly lower than the EU average (51.3% for Slovakia and 55.5% for the EU). High shares above 80% are in the Netherlands, Finland, and Norway.

Approximately 15% of companies in Slovakia train their employees in ICT. In the EU, this is approximately 22% of companies. The level of digital intensity in companies in Slovakia is lower than the EU average. 38% of companies have a very low intensity. In contrast, 22% of companies achieve a higher intensity. Only 3% of companies have a very high level of digital intensity. Digitalization is more common in large companies (Eurostat, 2023b).

The state, through laws, creates many obligations for various types of entities and offers a variety of services. This requires an efficient public administration. Electronic public administration solutions bring benefits for government, citizens, and businesses. It is a key tool for improving the efficiency, transparency, and accountability of government. According to the EU Digital Decade goals, all key public services for businesses and citizens should be online by 2030.

The level and progress of digitalization is assessed using the Digital Economy and Society Index (DESI) (EC, 2022; EC, 2023b). In terms of digitalization, Slovakia is below the EU average (Table 11.3). In 2022, it ranked 23rd out of EU member states in the DESI assessment. The area of human capital is better evaluated (19th place), where Slovakia reaches 96% of the EU average. Slovakia

Table 11.3. Digital Economy and Society Index (Score, 2022).

	DESI 2022	**Human Capital**	**Connectivity**	**Integration of Digital Technology**	**Digital Public Services**
Slovakia	43.4	44.1	49.8	27.8	52.0
EU	52.3	45.7	59.9	36.1	67.3

Source: EC (2022).

is close to the EU average in the indicators of basic digital skills of the population (55% SK, 54% EU), the share of ICT specialists in total employment (4.3% SK, 4.5% EU). Slovakia has an above-average rating in terms of the share of ICT graduates in total graduates (4.4% SK, 3.9% EU). Several initiatives are aimed at strengthening the digital competencies of all population groups.

Slovakia's internet connectivity is good in some areas, but we fall behind in infrastructure requiring larger investments. Specifically, Slovakia performs well in terms of basic broadband internet access. However, we lag behind in providing high-speed connections (exceeding 1 Gbps). The coverage of 5G networks is less extensive compared to other countries.

In terms of digital technology integration, Slovak companies lag behind in almost all areas. The extent of this lag in digitalization compared to the EU average is 23%. A more significant area of lag is the use of electronic invoices, which is used by 50% fewer companies than the EU average.

Slovakia lags behind the EU average by 23% in terms of public digital services. The Digital Public Services Index shows a score of 52.0 for Slovakia compared to 67.3 for the EU. While the proportion of e-government users is similar to the EU average (62% in Slovakia vs. 64% in the EU), there is a lag in the range of digital public services provided to citizens and businesses.

A 2023 survey by EXPANDI 4.0, Industry4UM cluster, and Go4insight research agency investigated the adoption of Industry 4.0 by Slovak companies (Industry4UM, 2023).[10] The number of companies initiating digitalization efforts jumped from 32% in 2021 to 50% in 2023. Conversely, the proportion of non-engaged companies decreased significantly, from 42% to 23% in 2023. Paradoxically, the percentage of businesses viewing digital transformation as very important has dipped from 58% in 2022 to 48% in 2023 (46% in 2021). The share of companies considering Industry 4.0 "necessary, but not essential" has grown from 27% in 2022 to 38% in 2023. The complexity of the business environment, with challenges in supply chains, energy markets, and high inflation, may be limiting the pace of digitalization efforts.

Digital transformation faces numerous internal hurdles within companies. The most significant obstacles hindering digitalization efforts are high investment costs of solutions (59%), insufficient employee skills (44%), lack of prioritization of Industry 4.0 by top management (31%), resistance to change within the company (28%), absence of a dedicated digitalization leader (27%), and ineffectiveness of offered solutions (15%). A long-standing challenge is the scarcity of qualified workers. The most significant skill gaps are in programming and software application management (41%), data analytics (36%), and industrial engineering (35%). There is a significant difference in digitalization efforts between domestic and foreign-owned companies. Among the companies surveyed, only 20% of domestic companies are actively digitalizing, compared to 41% of companies with

[10]An online survey was conducted from October 5, 2023 to November 13, 2023 with a sample of 113 respondents.

foreign ownership. A potential disadvantage for foreign-owned companies may be the lower autonomy of subsidiaries in decision-making.

The availability of skilled IT workers has attracted foreign companies, which have become major employers in Slovakia. Top Employers in IT & Telecommunication Service in 2021 were Slovak Telekom (2,717 employees), Deutsche Telekom IT & Telecommunications Slovakia (1,703), DXC Technology Slovakia (1,264), Orange Slovensko (1,163), Accenture Technology Solutions (1,046), Eset (1,004), IBM Slovensko (798), Scheidt & Bachmann (719), UNIQA Group Service Center Slovakia (670), Siemens Mobility (558). Notably, only one of the top 10 employers, Eset is a domestic company (SARIO, 2022).[11]

Several key platforms exist in Slovakia that foster collaboration and diverse activities within the IT industry:

- ITAS: This association brings together over 100 ICT firms, representing roughly 80% of the Slovak IT market. Their projects encompass both the private and public sector's digital transformation through collaborative efforts on the Digital Coalition project. Additionally, ITAS supports educational initiatives and conducts IT skill verification.
- KOŠICE IT VALLEY: This cluster boasts 55 members, including entities from the private, public, and academic sectors. Their focus areas include educational activities, fostering innovation, research and development, and promoting collaboration within the industry.
- ZAICT: This association unites 14 members from the private, public, and academic sectors. Their activities involve supporting lectures by ICT companies at secondary schools, offering educational programs, and organizing school camps aimed at raising IT skills among students.

Digital applications are undergoing significant development in the educational system. Their availability was crucial in mitigating the disruptions caused by the COVID-19 pandemic. Additionally, several cities are actively developing the Smart City concept.

While digitalization offers numerous advantages, it also introduces certain risks: cyberattacks, misuse of personal data, prejudices in algorithms, inequality in access to technology, threats of job loss, unhealthy dependencies on technology, etc. Given the aforementioned risks, it is crucial to incorporate ethical considerations into the digitalization process. Digitization itself also becomes a problem for the environment as it expands, because some ICT-related solutions are energy-intensive. Digitalization itself can pose environmental challenges, as some ICT solutions are energy and raw material intensive.

Several strategic government documents address the issue of Slovakia's digitalization lag. The 2030 Strategy for Digital Transformation of Slovakia aims to achieve convergence in the field of digitalization. The strategy focuses on innovative technologies such as artificial intelligence, the Internet of Things, 5G

[11] Eset is a global company specializing in digital security.

technology, big data and analytics, blockchain, and high-performance computing, which will strengthen competitiveness. The National Concept for Informatization of Public Administration for 2021–2026 focuses on developing strategic priorities within the government's competence. The National Coalition for Digital Skills and Jobs (Digital Coalition) operates in the country, bringing together ministries, universities, associations, technology companies, and key initiatives aimed at improving people's digital skills.

Digital transformation and green transformation are closely intertwined. The EU's recognition of this connection as a political agenda will benefit Slovakia's own solutions. Digital technologies are becoming essential tools in the transition to a climate-neutral and circular economy.

7. Conclusion

Slovakia's innovation ecosystem is improving, but significant gaps remain compared to the EU. While investments in domestic R&D are rising, a significant portion of innovations still come from abroad. Furthermore, government support for R&D and innovation falls short of the EU average. The key to unlocking a knowledge-based economy lies in government prioritization. Educational reforms are essential to adapt to demographic shifts, evolving labor market needs, technological advancements, and environmental challenges. To thrive in this changing landscape, Slovakia needs to cultivate an environment that fosters talent development and attracts skilled individuals by offering opportunities for contribution and growth. Low level of R&D expenditure limits research opportunities and restricts job creation in the R&D sector.

Digital transformation is another societal imperative impacting all aspects of life. While Slovakia is actively developing and utilizing digital applications, international comparisons reveal a persistent gap compared to the EU average. Continued efforts are needed to bridge this digital divide. Recognizing these challenges, the Slovak government has recently approved several strategies aimed at propelling the country toward success in R&D, innovation, education, and digitalization. By prioritizing R&D, investing in education and skills training, and accelerating digital transformation initiatives, Slovakia can unlock its potential and thrive in a rapidly changing global environment.

References

Brzica, D., Gabrielová, H., Jeck, T., Kačírková, M., Klas, A., Lábaj, M., & Vokoun, J. (2011). *Spolupráca aktérov v technologickom a inovačnom rozvoji*. Institute of Economic Research SAS.

Brzica, D., Kačírková, M., Ostrihoň, F., & Vokoun, J. (2020). *Atraktivita územia a mobilita talentov: veľké mestá priťahujú talenty*. Institute of Economic Research SAS.

Bunčák, J., Džambazovič, R., Hrabovský, M., & Sopóci, J. (2009). *Názory občanov na budúcnosť Slovenska*. Institute of Economic Research SAS.

EC. (2018). *Standard Eurobarometer 90. Public opinion in the European Union. National report an annex.* https://ec.europa.eu/commfrontoffice/publicopinion/index.cfm/Survey/getSurveyDetail/instruments/STANDARD/surveyKy/2215

EC. (2022). *Digital economy and society index (DESI) 2022, Slovakia.* European Commission. https://digital-strategy.ec.europa.eu/sk/policies/desi-slovakia

EC. (2023a). *European innovation scoreboard 2023.* European Commission. https://op.europa.eu/en/web/eu-law-and-publications/publication-detail/-/publication/04797497-25de-11ee-a2d3-01aa75ed71a1

EC. (2023b). *European innovation scoreboard 2023 – Country profile Slovakia.* European Commission. https://research-and-innovation.ec.europa.eu/statistics/performance-indicators/european-innovation-scoreboard_en#country-profiles-eu

Eurostat. (2023a). *Number of tertiary education students by sex and level of education, 2021.* https://ec.europa.eu/eurostat/statistics-explained/index.php?title=Tertiary_education_statistics

Eurostat. (2023b). *Digitalisation in Europe – 2023 edition.* Interactive publications. https://ec.europa.eu/eurostat/web/interactive-publications/digitalisation-2023

Eurostat. (2023c). *Gross domestic expenditure on R&D by secto.* [dataset] [rd_e_gerdtot]. https://doi.org/10.2908/RD_E_GERDTOT

Eurostat. (2023d). *Share of R&D personnel and researchers in total active population.* [dataset] [rd_p_perslf]. https://ec.europa.eu/eurostat/databrowser/view/RD_P_PERSLF/default/table?lang=en

Expandi. (2023). O nás. EDIH EXPANDI 4.0, Bratislava. https://www.expandi40.sk/o-nas/

Financial administration of Slovak Republic. (2024). *Zoznam daňových subjektov s odpočtom výdavkov (nákladov) na výskum a vývoj podľa §30c ods. 8.* https://www.financnasprava.sk/sk/elektronicke-sluzby/verejne-sluzby/zoznamy/exporty-z-online-informacnych

Industry4UM. (2023, December 6). *Prieskum: Industry 4.0 sa v priemyselných podnikoch presadzuje pomaly.* Association of intelligent industry – Industry4UM. https://industry4um.sk/industry-4-0-sa-v-priemyselnych-podnikoch-presadzuje-pomaly/

Klas, A., Brzica, D., Frank, K., Gabrielová, H., Chovan, I., Juríčková, V., Kačírková, M., Košta, J., Morvay, K., Petrík, B., Staněk, P., & Vokoun, J. (2005). *Technologický a inovačný rozvoj v Slovenskej republike.* Institute of Economic Research SAS.

MŠVVŠ SR. (2021). *Stratégia celoživotného vzdelávania a poradenstva na roky 2021–2030.* The Ministry of Education, Science, Research and Sport of the Slovak Republic. https://rokovania.gov.sk/RVL/Material/26635/1

MŽP SR. (2020). *Zelenšie Slovensko – Stratégia environmentálnej politiky Slovenskej republiky do roku 2030.* Ministry of Environment of the Slovak Republic. http://www.minzp.sk/iep/strategicke-materialy/envirostrategia-2030/

Nacero. (2023). *Slovakia is starting to fall behind in robotics.* National Centre of Robotics. https://nacero.sk/slovakia-is-starting-to-fall-behind-in-robotics/

OECD. (2023a). *Education at a glance 2023. OECD indicators.* OECD Publishing. https://doi.org/10.1787/e13bef63-en

OECD. (2023b). *PISA 2022 results (Volume I): The state of learning and equity in education, PISA.* OECD Publishing. https://doi.org/10.1787/53f23881-en

SARIO. (2022). *Information & communications technology sector in Slovakia*. Slovak Investment and Trade Development Agency. https://www.sario.sk/sites/default/files/sario-ict-sector-in-slovakia-2022-09-23.pdf

SIEA. (2023). *Výzva na podporu inovácií v podnikoch je otvorená aj v roku 2024*. Slovak Innovation and Energy Agency. https://www.siea.sk/vyzva-na-podporu-inovacii-v-podnikoch-je-otvorena-aj-v-roku-2024/

Šikulová, I., Dujava, D., Frank, K., Gabrielová, H., Habrman, M., Hudcovský, M., Hvozdíková, V., Jeck, T., Lábaj, M., Morvay, K., Nežinský, E., & Vokoun, J. (2014). *Slovenská ekonomika: desať rokov členstva v Európskej únii. Vybrané témy a problémy*. Institute of Economic Research SAS. https://ekonom.sav.sk/sk/publikacie/slovenska-ekonomika-desat-rokov-clenstva-v-europskej-unii-vybrane-temy-a-problemy-p257

Trend. (2024, February 15). *PPS Group patrí medzi firmy, ktoré proces transformácie úspešne zvládli. Okrem investícií do automatizácie si vychováva aj vlastných zamestnancov*. TREND. https://www.trend.sk/biznis/cielime-pridanu-hodnotu-tvrdi-sef-pps-group-daniel-futej

UK. (2020, June 24). *Prioritami klastra sú internacionalizácia vo vede a podpora slovenských vedcov*. Comenius University. https://uniba.sk/detail-aktuality/browse/11/back_to_page/tlacove-spravy-3/article/prioritami-klastra-su-internacionalizacia-vo-vede-a-podpora-slovenskych-vedcov/

Varga, H. (2023). *Eco-innovation country profile 2022: Slovakia*. European Commission. https://circabc.europa.eu/ui/group/96ccdecd-11b4-4a35-a046-30e01459ea9e/library/72da759a-5d35-4756-9db4-0fd6c9b1e8ca?p=1&n=10&sort=modified_DESC

Veda na dosah. (2023, June 20). *Oslavujeme 30. výročie členstva Slovenskej republiky v CERN-e*. Veda na dosah, Slovak Centre of Scientific and Technical Information. https://vedanadosah.cvtisr.sk/priroda/fyzika/oslavujeme-30-vyrocie-clenstva-slovenskej-republiky-v-cern-e/

Chapter 12

Business Service Centers: A New Growth Impulse for the Slovak Economy

Tomáš Dudáš

Pan-European University, Slovakia

Abstract

Business service centers (BSCs) are a crucial part of Slovakia's economy, employing around 40,000 highly skilled workers and playing a significant role in the growth of service exports. The industry is mainly concentrated in Bratislava, the capital city of Slovakia. However, Košice, located in Eastern Slovakia, is playing an increasingly important role in information technology (IT) outsourcing. The employees of BSCs create higher value compared to other industries, which allows BSC operators to offer higher wages. Despite experiencing layoffs in the past, BSC operators in Slovakia currently have stable positions. However, to ensure the long-term sustainability of the industry, the government needs to provide more focused support. This support should aim to secure the highly skilled workforce required for the industry, whether from Slovakia or abroad. Although the industry is not immediately threatened by the ongoing artificial intelligence (AI) revolution, most BSC operators are preparing their units for the further automation of their processes.

Keywords: Business service centers; shared service centers; business processing outsourcing; Slovakia; government support; artificial intelligence

1. Introduction

The emergence of global value chains in the world economy has also led to a change in the organization of business activities. Multinationals have sought to take advantage of lower labor costs in less developed countries by setting up business service centers (BSCs) in those countries, units that provide in-house services to their parent and sister companies or third parties in areas such as

Modeling Economic Growth in Contemporary Slovakia, 219–233

Published under exclusive licence by Emerald Publishing Limited
doi:10.1108/978-1-83549-454-720241017

finance, information technology (IT) services, customer services, human resources, purchasing, or sales (Klimek, 2021). As well as reducing costs, the establishment of a BSC is driven by the need to standardize business processes, and modern technology is key to enabling people to collaborate on tasks in real-time.

BSCs can be divided into two basic groups – shared services centers (SSCs) and business process outsourcing (BPO). SSCs are typically responsible for performing specific corporate functions (e.g. finance and accounting, IT support, HR) that support the core business of the company. BPO involves contracting out the operation and responsibility for specific business processes to a third-party service provider.

In Slovakia, the first significant foreign direct investment (FDI) in BSCs could be observed at the end of the 1990s, but their real boom occurred only in the 21st century. As of March 2024, 56 companies were included in the list of BSCs maintained by the Ministry of Economy of the Slovak Republic, but based on other sources (AmCham Slovakia, SARIO), it can be assumed that more companies are active in this field in Slovakia. According to data from a survey conducted annually since 2015 by the American Chamber of Commerce, BSCs employed almost 40,000 people in 2023. It can be concluded that BSCs, together with the automotive and electrotechnical industries, are one of the main pillars of the Slovak economy today.

2. Business Service Centers in Central Europe

While the center of the BSC industry could be found in Asia (India, China, Philippines, Malaysia), Central Europe certainly plays an important role in the operations of multinationals. According to Deloitte's 2023 Global Shared Services and Outsourcing Survey, Poland is the second most popular location for SSCs globally (Deloitte, 2023). The size of the available skilled workforce and favorable wage conditions make Poland a clear choice for BSCs, and it is not surprising that by the end of 2022, half of the Central European BSC units were located in the country.

According to the ABSL publication Business Services Sector in Poland in 2023, at the end of the first quarter of 2023, there were 1,800 business centers (BPO, SSC, IT, and R&D units) operated by 1,106 companies in Poland. The sector employed 435,300 people in 2023 and was completely dominated by foreign companies. This represents 6.7% of total employment in the Polish business sector, and BSCs generated about $30 billion in knowledge-intensive business services exports in 2022. BSCs in Poland were created in two main waves. The first coincided with Poland's accession to the European Union (EU) and the second started after the global financial and economic crisis of 2008/2009 (ABSL, 2023). Most of the centers are concentrated in large cities, there are seven Polish cities with at least 100 of them (Warsaw, Kraków, Wroclaw, Tricity, Poznaň, Katowice, and Łódź). Most of the centers are owned by American companies, but the UK, France, and Germany are also major investors in the industry (Ślusarczyk, 2017).

The Czech Republic is another important hub for the business services sector in Central Europe, with 380 centers employing 175,000 people. The Association of Business Service Leaders in the Czech Republic estimates that the number of employees in the sector will reach 200,000 by 2025. As in Poland, most centers in the Czech Republic are located in large cities, with Prague being the most important host city (52% of all centers). The industry composition of the centers is standard, with manufacturing, telecommunications, and business and professional services playing the most important role. Most centers in the Czech Republic operate as in-house centers, with the majority of employees working in finance, accounting, and IT services (ABSL, 2024).

Hungary may not be as popular as the similarly sized Czech Republic for setting up BSCs, but it still had 201 active companies in the industry employing around 100,000 people in 2023. Budapest is the dominant city in the industry with around 75,000 jobs, while Székesfehérvár, Debrecen, Miskolc, and Szeged also play a minor but growing role. The majority of BSCs in Hungary deal with finance, accounting, and controlling activities (81%), but human resources (73%), IT (64%), and procurement (60%) also play an important role in the services provided. It's not surprising that most BSCs in Hungary are foreign-owned, with American and European companies being the main players (HIPA, 2023).

Always looking for lower operating costs, global companies expanded their presence to countries like Romania, Bulgaria, and Serbia. Most companies are active in Romania, with 280 units and 131,000 employees in 2020. The country offers a large talent pool of highly skilled employees willing to work for wages lower than those in the Visegrád Four (V4 – Czech Republic, Hungary, Poland, and Slovakia) countries (InvestRomania, 2023). Bulgaria's attractiveness as a location for BSC units is also steadily increasing, with approximately 79,000 employees in 2022 (InvestBulgaria, 2024). Although Serbia is not a member of the EU, the attention of foreign investors in the BSC industry has increased in recent years. The skilled and multilingual workforce gives Serbia a great perspective to soon become a top country for the shared services and BPO industry (Deloitte, 2022).

3. Business Service Centers in Slovakia

Slovakia is known worldwide as a stronghold of the automotive industry. Car manufacturers in Slovakia produce about 1 million cars per year, and the industry directly or indirectly employs more than 261,000 people. The share of the automotive industry in the total industrial production is about 50% and it generates 11% of the Slovak gross domestic product (GDP). Not surprisingly, the automotive sector also plays a dominant role in Slovak exports, as it consists of export-oriented, foreign-owned units of global automotive companies (SARIO, 2024a).

Despite the dominance of the automotive industry, since the beginning of the 21st century, there has been an increase in FDI in the service sector. As global companies discovered Central Europe as an attractive location for BSCs, Slovakia also became a viable destination. Initially, call centers for German-speaking countries were established, but the services provided by local units soon branched out into finance, accounting, and IT services. American technology company Dell was the first global company to establish a BSC in Slovakia, and dozens of others followed in the following years (Trend, 2003).

When it comes to the current state of the industry in Slovakia, the most comprehensive data source is the annual survey conducted by the Business Service Center Forum, an organization that aims to bring together operators of SSCs and BPOs in Slovakia. This survey started in 2015, and in its latest edition, 39 business centers were surveyed, representing 95% of the total employment in the industry. According to the 2023 edition of the survey, the number of employees in the participating companies reached 37,843 as of August 2023, bringing the total number of employees in the industry to approximately 40,000 (BSCF, 2023). For comparison, the number of employees in the BSC sector is equal to the employment in the electrotechnical industry, which is the second largest exporting industry in Slovakia. This is shown in Fig. 12.1 below:

As in all Central Europe, BSCs in Slovakia are almost exclusively the product of FDI, with investors mostly being globally known multinational corporations. These include companies from the IT (IBM, Dell, Lenovo, Alcatel/Lucent), financial (SwissRe, Allianz, Zurich Insurance), telecommunications (O2 Slovakia,

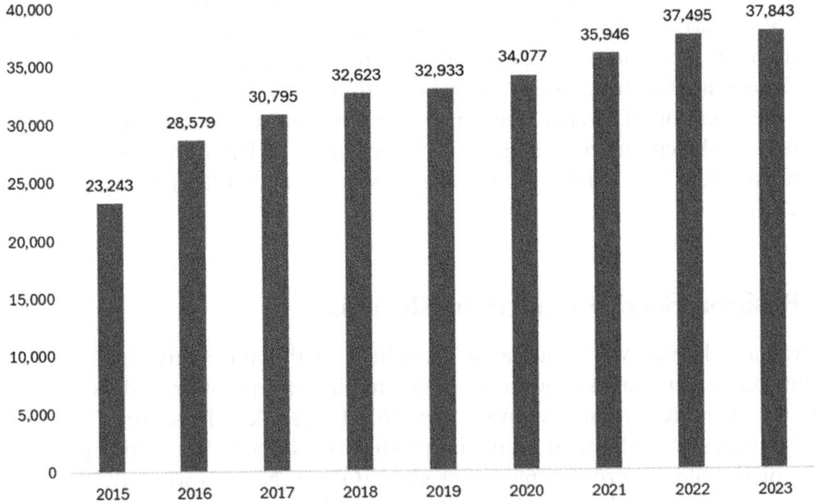

Fig. 12.1. The Number of Employees in the Slovak BSC Sector (2015–2023). *Source:* BSCF Surveys 2015–2023.

Deutsche Telecom, AT&T, Orange), and industrial (Mondelez, Embraco, Henkel) sectors. The companies operating BSCs in Slovakia are mainly from the USA and Western Europe. A quick look at the list of BSCs registered with the Slovak Ministry of Economy reveals 20 companies from the USA (including companies based in Ireland), followed by a strong group of German (8) and Swiss (8) companies. The dominance of foreign-owned subsidiaries is underscored by the fact that there is only one domestic company among the 56 companies registered with the Ministry of Economy (Ministry of Economy of the Slovak Republic, 2024).

As for the regional distribution of BSCs, they are located mainly in large cities, with Bratislava being the dominant city, where 44 centers were in 2023, according to the list of companies registered with the Ministry of Economy. Košice also has an important position in the sector, with another five centers in 2023. However, BSCs can also be found in other regional cities and several smaller towns. The dominance of the largest cities is due to the requirements for the functioning of BSCs, which include an educated workforce and quality office space. In this respect, Bratislava and Košice have a clear advantage, as they are the largest university cities in Slovakia and at the same time have the largest supply of quality office space. Other regional cities do not have these advantages but on the other hand offer lower wage demands for potential employees and the possibility of regional investment aid at the maximum level allowed by the EU. In the case of BSCs outside large cities, these are usually centers with fewer employees, typically located near the production facilities of foreign companies.

BSCs in Slovakia can be divided into three basic groups according to their focus – IT, finance, and other business activities. BSCs in Slovakia perform a wide range of activities, including financial services and accounting, IT services, customer services, human resources support, sales, and order processing or purchasing. However, it is possible to define three service areas that dominate BSCs in Slovakia (Fig. 12.2). These are IT services (including software development), customer services (including sales and technical support), and financial services, with these three areas accounting for 77% of the centers according to the BSCF 2023 survey. Meanwhile, the structure of the activities provided has been stable over the long term, and the share of the three key activities has already been roughly the same since the first BSCF survey in 2015 (BSCF, 2015).

According to a report by BSCF in 2016, the Corporate Service Centers in Slovakia cater to all regions of the world. The primary region served is Europe, which is supported by all the BSCs. North America is the second most common region served, with 54% of the centers catering to it. Africa follows closely at 50%, the Middle East at 46%, South America at 38%, and Asia Pacific at 35%.

Regarding the size of BSCs, it is more common to find centers with a larger number of employees. According to the BSCF 2023 survey, there were 15 centers in Slovakia with over 1,000 employees and 22 centers with at least 100 employees. The biggest employer in this sector in Slovakia is IBM International Services Center, which currently employs around 3,000 people.

Measuring the contribution of the BSC industry to the local economy can be difficult because GDP and industry statistics typically do not have a separate

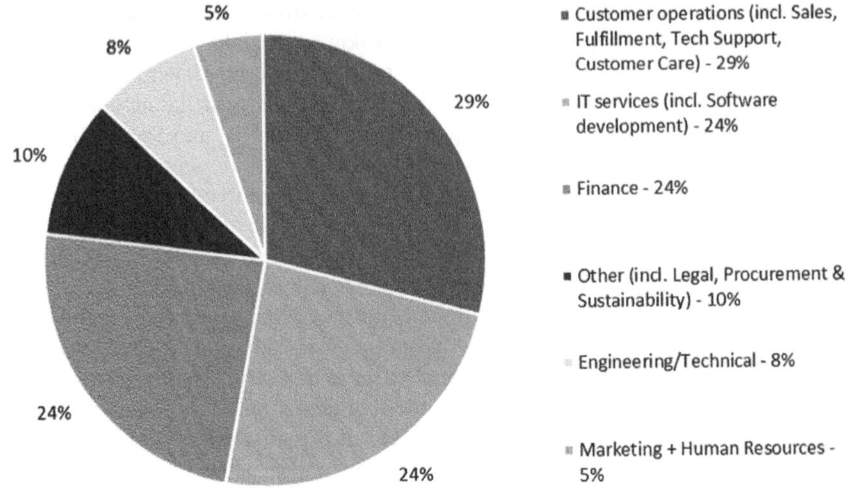

Fig. 12.2. Business Services Provided by the Slovak BSCs in 2023. *Source:* BSCF Survey 2023.

entry for BSCs. However, there are data available that highlight the industry's contribution in three key areas: employment, export of services, and public finances. The BSC industry employs approximately 40,000 individuals, making it a significant employer, on par with sectors such as the manufacture of electronic equipment or the manufacture of food products (Statistical Office of the Slovak Republic, 2024). Additionally, the BSC industry contributes to the export of services, with the most important part being the export of Information and Communications Technology (ICT) and financial services. Together, these two areas had a total value of 6.25 billion euros in 2021, and most of this export likely originated from the BSC industry. Regarding the contribution of public finances, BSC operators participating in the BSCF 2023 survey paid 27.4 million euros in corporate income taxes and 400 million euros in social contributions for their employees. The employees contributed an additional 180.2 million euros in income taxes and 146.7 million euros in social contributions.

4. Employees of Business Service Centers in Slovakia

The growth of the BSC industry in Slovakia is visible in the available employment data, as the number of employees will increase by about 62% between 2015 and 2023. This makes the average annual growth rate of employment 5.8%, which is above the average of the Slovak services industry. The growth seems to slow down considerably in 2023 (1%), but 85% of the companies participating in the survey expect to increase their number of employees in the next 12 months. The great advantage of the BSC sector is that it employs a high percentage of university-educated employees, who can create a higher added value compared to industry or other service sectors. While it is true that the share of university-educated employees in the BSC sector decreased significantly between 2015 and 2023 (82% vs. 66%), it is still significantly higher than the average of most sectors in the Slovak economy. This leads to higher wages, as the BSC sector is one of Slovakia's sectors with the highest nominal monthly wages (Fig. 12.3). Companies participating in the BSCF 2023 survey reported an average monthly salary of 2,417 euros, which is 69% higher than the average monthly salary in the Slovak economy (BSCF, 2023).

BSCs in Slovakia have a predominantly young and educated workforce. The average age of BSC employees is 36.2 years, though it has increased notably from 31 years since 2015. The industry primarily employs domestic workers, who make up 89% of the workforce in 2023. The gender balance of employees in BSCs is remarkable, with women making up approximately half of the workforce in 2023 (50.5%). Moreover, the proportion of women in managerial positions is relatively high, accounting for 41% in both 2018 and 2019 (BSCF, 2019). BSCs are efficiently managed organizations, with management comprising only 9% of the workforce in the long term (BSCF, 2023).

BSCs in Slovakia offer their services globally, which makes language skills of their employees a crucial factor in their operations. While English is a must-have, employers prefer their workers to be fluent in at least one other foreign language.

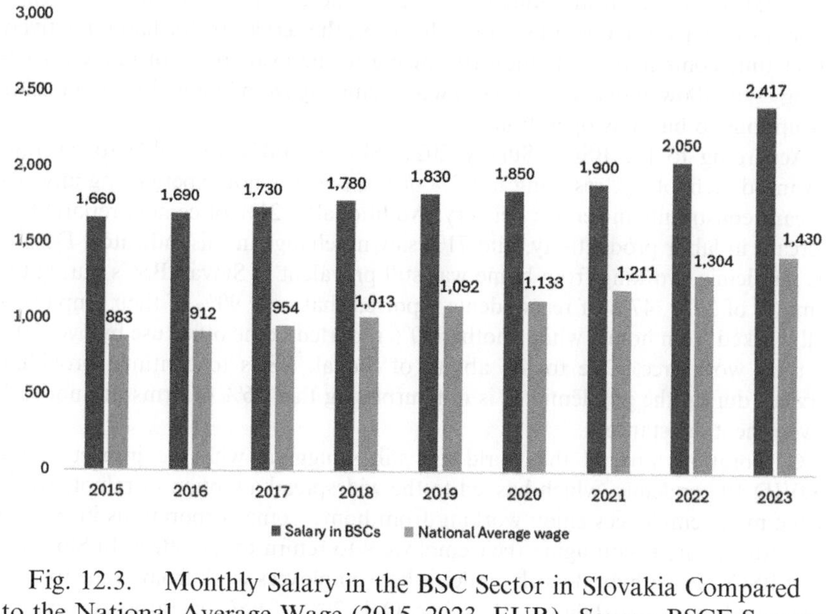

Fig. 12.3. Monthly Salary in the BSC Sector in Slovakia Compared to the National Average Wage (2015–2023, EUR). *Source:* BSCF Surveys 2015–2023.

According to the BSCF Survey 2023, all BSC employees speak English at an advanced level, and other essential languages include German (87%), French (56%), and Spanish (54%). Regional languages such as Polish or Hungarian, as well as other major world languages like Russian and Chinese, are also highly valued.

The educational qualifications of BSC employees are closely related to the services they offer. Since a significant portion of the activities of Slovak BSCs involves finance and accounting, it is not surprising that most corporate service centers hired graduates of the University of Economics in Bratislava (68%) according to data from 2017 (BSCF, 2017). Graduates of Comenius University in Bratislava (64%) are also well represented, and graduates of technical study programs are supplied by the Slovak University of Technology in Bratislava (57%), University of Žilina (57%), and Technical University in Košice (46%). As the employment of recent graduates has become increasingly important in Slovak BSCs over time, the operators of these centers have established closer cooperation with the most important universities in Slovakia. Consequently, the number of students already working with one of the BSCs during their studies is increasing.

5. Shared Service Centers and the Global Pandemic COVID-19

The COVID-19 pandemic of 2020 has had a significant impact on the global economy. To contain the spread of the virus, various measures such as quarantines and movement restrictions were put in place, which posed a serious challenge for managers across all sectors. However, the service sector had a relatively easier time compared to the industry, owing to the availability of modern technology that allowed many workers to work remotely from home, thus minimizing disruptions to business operations.

According to the BSCF Survey 2021, Slovak BSCs were able to leverage advanced technology, resulting in 97% of respondents not experiencing any significant constraints in service delivery. Additionally, 21% of centers reported an increase in labor productivity, and 71% saw no change in this indicator. Despite the pandemic, working from home was still prevalent in Slovak BSCs during the summer of 2021. 47% of respondents reported that over 90% of their employees still worked from home, while another 30% reported home office use by over 70% of their workforce. Due to the ability of Slovak BSCs to continue providing services during the pandemic, it is not surprising that 76% of firms did not seek government assistance.

Corporations around the world are still struggling with the impact of the COVID-19 pandemic, which has led to the widespread adoption of remote work. While many employees enjoy working from home, some corporations in the service industry are encouraging their employees to return to the office. In Slovakia, most BSCs have a hybrid work model, where employees work from home for 3 to 4 days and spend 1 to 2 days at the office. Only 20% of BSC operators surveyed in 2023 said they wanted their employees to work mostly from the office. While most Slovak BSC operators are satisfied with the hybrid work model, they use various methods to encourage employees to return to the office, such as improving the physical workspace, setting positive examples by team leaders, offering complimentary food and beverages, and providing on-site programs that support employees' mental and physical health. However, even with these incentives, the hybrid work model seems to be a permanent feature in Slovak BSCs.

6. Current Challenges of Slovak Business Service Centers

In early 2021, there were reports in the media about job cuts in several BSCs. It was rumored that these jobs were being outsourced to India and other developing countries with lower labor costs. The first wave of layoffs was announced by AT&T Global Network Services Slovakia, which planned to terminate the contracts of 300 employees. At around the same time, Johnson Controls also disclosed that it was relocating some of its services to India and letting go of over 500 employees. This news came as a surprise to many, as BSCs have been one of the success stories of the Slovak economy over the previous decade (Aktuality, 2021).

The recent layoffs in Slovak BSCs have sparked discussions about their competitiveness and future, especially in comparison to their counterparts in India and other Asian countries. Cost-cutting remains a significant factor when deciding where to locate BSCs. According to the 2021 Global Shared Services and Outsourcing Survey conducted by Deloitte, 84% of the participating companies cited cost reduction as their primary goal for investing in enterprise service centers. The second most important factor was to standardize and improve the efficiency of business processes, identified by 88% of the businesses (Deloitte, 2021). This is shown in Fig. 12.4 below:

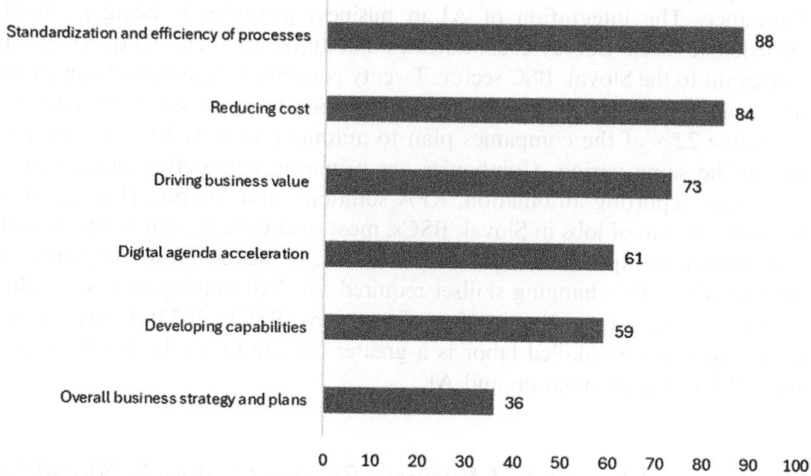

Fig. 12.4. The Objectives of Investing in GBS and SSC Capabilities in 2021 (%). *Source:* Deloitte 2021 Global Shared Services and Outsourcing Survey Report.

The increase in labor costs in Slovakia has become a concern for firms operating BSCs, as Slovak wages are no longer competitive compared to wage costs in countries like India, the Philippines, or Malaysia. This is especially a problem for routine and repetitive work tasks, which may gradually move out of Slovakia. However, BSCs are replacing these tasks with higher value-added activities. Even though some Slovak BSCs had to let go of workers, this did not cause significant problems as the redundant workers were able to find employment elsewhere in the sector. Furthermore, Slovakia still has certain advantages that Asian competitors cannot offer. For instance, knowledge of European languages is limited in India and similar countries. Additionally, Slovakia's location provides a different time zone than Asian countries, and cultural proximity is appreciated by some customers.

A major challenge to the development of BSCs in Slovakia is the shortage of qualified workforce. According to the BSCF Survey 2023, BSC operators in Slovakia are struggling to recruit new employees due to the limited availability of suitable candidates. As a result, 48% of firms are facing critical labor shortages, leading to a continuous increase in labor costs. With the growing complexity of roles, finding candidates with relevant experience and skills has become increasingly difficult, especially in the IT sector (BSCF, 2023). This issue is particularly acute in the Bratislava, Košice, and Banská Bystrica regions, where most BSCs are located. Furthermore, the acute shortage of IT specialists, which has been highlighted by the IT Association of Slovakia for several years, is also impacting Slovak BSCs since IT is one of their primary activities.

The use of artificial intelligence (AI) and automation presents a major challenge for BSCs. Shared service centers are increasingly implementing AI and automation to enhance efficiency in transactional activities. Companies are identifying repetitive tasks and automating them to improve cost and quality performance. The integration of AI in business processes is being gradually extended. The BSCF Survey 2023 indicates that automation and AI questions are also relevant to the Slovak BSC sector. Twenty percent of the surveyed companies plan to automate over 20% of the relevant corporate processes in the next 2–3 years, while 22% of the companies plan to automate at least 10% of their processes in the same period. Companies are primarily considering process automation, data reporting automation, RPA solutions, and chatbots (Fig. 12.5). In terms of the future of jobs in Slovak BSCs, most operators are optimistic, as only 5% of companies expect major job displacement. However, most companies are concerned about the changing skillset required for their employees (56%), while 31% of companies expect the creation of new jobs (BSCF, 2023). Currently, the limited availability of skilled labor is a greater constraint on the functioning of Slovak BSCs than automation and AI.

7. Government Support of Business Service Centers in Slovakia

To maintain its appeal to BSCs, Slovakia must address the main challenges currently faced by its BSC operators. While companies must accept the rising cost

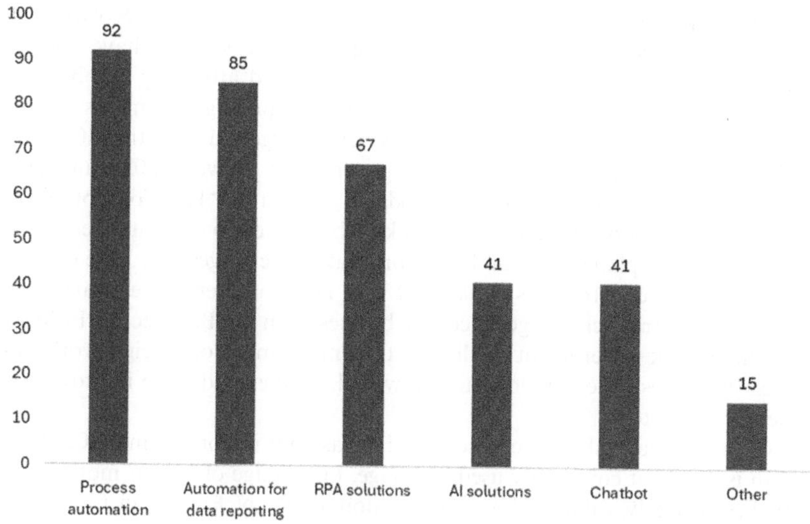

Fig. 12.5. Automatization/Robotization Processes Implemented in Slovak BSCs (%). *Source:* BSCF Survey 2023.

of labor in Slovakia, they require assistance in securing a skilled workforce. This is also reflected in the annual BSCF Survey, where companies operating BSCs in Slovakia have expressed the need to simplify the process of hiring foreigners from third countries. Nearly half of the companies suggest state support for firms that provide work experience to students and recent graduates. Additionally, one-third of companies would appreciate increased support for the relocation of employees to other regions of Slovakia.

The Slovak government recognized the significance of BSCs for the national economy quite early, and thus, adopted a document named "The Concept of Support for Business Service Centers in Slovakia" back in 2016. This document highlights the current state of the industry and its growth potential, and it outlines a three-pronged strategy to support BSCs in Slovakia. The first objective of the government is to ensure an adequate workforce for BSCs by providing education and training opportunities, as well as facilitating the arrival of highly skilled professionals from abroad. The second objective is to create a conducive environment for the development and expansion of BSCs. In this regard, the government aimed to establish an official definition of BSC and to raise awareness about their importance, as they are often perceived as call centers where specialized skills are not required. The third objective was to actively promote new investments in BSCs. The government aimed to create 20,000 new job opportunities in the BSC industry by 2020, through the implementation of a specialized investment promotion program conducted by the Slovak Investment and Trade Development Agency (SARIO).

Based on feedback received from companies operating BSCs in Slovakia, it is evident that the goals outlined in the 2016 government strategy have not been fully achieved. A skilled labor force is still scarce, and attracting highly skilled professionals from abroad remains challenging. The prior governments failed to assess whether the 2016 goals were met, which is largely due to the COVID-19 pandemic and the frequent changes in government between 2020 and 2023. Therefore, it is recommended that an updated version of "The Concept of Support for Business Service Centers in Slovakia" be created to evaluate the progress toward the action plan's goals and to incorporate the changes that have occurred in the sector since 2016. This could lead to a new comprehensive strategy that addresses the current challenges faced by businesses in the BSC sector. In March 2024, the Slovak government facilitated the employment of foreign workers in selected industries. The next logical step would be to extend these improvements to the service sector.

Foreign language skills are becoming increasingly important in BSCs. While English is the most commonly used language, knowledge of two or more foreign languages is highly valued. However, the dominance of English in foreign language teaching has led to a decline in the teaching of other major European languages like German, French, Spanish, and Italian. Although the choice of the first foreign language has been liberalized, English remains the dominant language. Therefore, it is essential to strengthen the teaching of other European languages to meet the demand and fill the gaps in the market. The shortage of qualified teachers in these languages may be a challenge. It is also highly recommended that university students learn a second foreign language to increase their job opportunities in the BSC sector.

To provide more targeted government support to BSCs, it is important to gather more data on their activities. Currently, the only consistent source of data on the state of BSCs is the annual survey conducted by AmCham Slovakia in partnership with the Business Service Center Forum since 2015. State agencies can collaborate with these organizations to expand the survey data set to gain a better understanding of the operations and needs of firms that run BSCs.

BSCs in Slovakia can receive investment incentives based on the number of new jobs and wages paid to employees. Under this aid scheme, businesses providing services in priority areas are offered more favorable conditions. In these areas, companies can qualify for investment support by creating as few as 20 new jobs, given that the wages of employees are at least 1.8 times the average wage in the district. In areas that are not considered a priority, investors must create a minimum of 50 jobs if they want to be eligible for government support. Additionally, they must pay their employees wages that are at least 1.5 times the average wage in the district. There is no limit on the size of the investment, which means that even smaller investments can qualify for the government aid scheme (SARIO, 2024b).

It is helpful to compare state support available for BSC projects in Slovakia with other Visegrád Four countries, as they often compete for such projects. In the Czech Republic, BSCs are also given special conditions based on the size of the investment. However, the only investment aid offered is in the form of corporate tax relief and has a maximum duration of 10 years. Only strategic investments with a minimum value of 200 million CZK can receive additional government support in the form of financial support for the acquisition of assets up to 20% of eligible costs (CzechInvest, 2024). The maximum intensity of investment aid granted is comparable to the maximum values for investment aid in Slovakia.

Hungary offers BSCs a wide range of investment assistance tools, including corporate tax relief, financial support for job creation, employee training, and research and development activities. Job creation support is only available for projects located outside the capital, and there are regional regulations governing the benefits provided. The VIP cash subsidy is available based on the Hungarian government's individual decision and can be combined with the development tax allowance (CIT allowance) up to the regional maximum aid intensity threshold in locations that are eligible for regional aid under European regulations (HIPA, 2023).

Poland has a separate investment aid scheme for BSCs based on a program document aimed at supporting key investments for the Polish economy between 2011 and 2030. This scheme is designed to assist BSCs with advanced activities and includes financial grants for job creation and employee training. However, to qualify for this support, companies must meet both qualitative and quantitative criteria, and are required to establish cooperation with a Polish higher education institution. It is important to note that this support goes beyond the standard investment aid available to all foreign investors (Polish Investment and Trade Agency, 2024).

Upon comparing the investment aid schemes for BSCs in the V4 countries, we can conclude that the Slovak aid scheme is similar to other countries in the region. The criteria for obtaining investment aid are clear-cut and, unlike the Polish criteria, are only quantifiable. This means that it is possible to receive income tax relief, a contribution toward newly created jobs, real estate at a preferential price, and, for priority areas, a financial subsidy. However, the disadvantage for potential applicants is that investment aid is not available in Bratislava, just like in other V4 capitals. Nevertheless, the total possible intensity of investment aid is comparable in the V4 countries as it adheres to the EU regulations.

8. Conclusion

Over the past 20 years, BSCs have emerged as a significant component of the Slovak economy. Although they cannot compete with the automotive industry in terms of long-term economic impact, BSCs still offer tens of thousands of well-paying jobs. Employees in these centers generate greater value-added compared to their counterparts in the industry and contribute to the much-needed export of services.

Despite experiencing layoffs in previous years, the BSC operators in Slovakia currently have a stable position. However, to ensure the long-term sustainability of the industry, the government needs to provide more focused support. This support should focus on securing the skilled labor force required for the industry, whether from Slovakia or abroad. The industry does not face an imminent threat from the ongoing AI revolution. However, many Slovak BSC operators plan to automate their processes to increase operational effectiveness.

References

ABSL. (2023). *Business service sector in Poland 2023*. Association of Business Service Leaders (ABSL). https://shop-absl.pl/Business-Services-Sector-in-Poland-2023-p122

ABSL. (2024). *Business service sector in the Czech Republic 2024*. Association of Business Services Leaders in the Czech Republic (ABSL). https://absl.cz/wp-content/uploads/2024/03/ABSL_Report_2024_everze-1.pdf

Aktuality. (2021). Jeden z najdôležitejších sektorov sa otriasa pod vlnou prepúšťania. Je to jeho definitívny koniec? *Aktuality.sk*. https://www.aktuality.sk/clanok/858612/jeden-z-najdolezitejsich-sektorov-sa-otriasa-pod-vlnou-prepustania-je-to-jeho-koniec/

BSCF. (2015). *Business Service Center Forum Survey 2015*. file:///C:/Users/dudas/Downloads/bscf-conference-brochure-1.pdf

BSCF. (2017). *Business Service Center Forum Survey 2017*. http://www.amcham.sk/download.pl?hash=Llqh8RkXLxRN8T09IcdWhlg8pWoC1kRp&ID=4819

BSCF. (2019). *Business Service Center Forum Survey 2019*. https://amcham.sk/download.pl?hash=437RsBogyvIJupOyVdGNLhNtyZcVGR0a&ID=5393

BSCF. (2021). *Business Service Center Forum Survey 2021*. https://amcham.sk/download.pl?hash=UIPCpf54Quajo13QJmkjcNFbk9oAcv2G&ID=5957

BSCF. (2023). *Business Service Center Forum Survey 2023*. https://amcham.sk/download.pl?hash=Vt0DU521GtFnAAMD13itUrS1pj5V2ooc&ID=6486

CzechInvest. (2024). *Centra strategických služeb*. Czechinvest.org. https://www.czechinvest.org/cz/Sluzby-pro-investory/Investicni-pobidky-a-dotace/Centra-strategickych-sluzeb

Deloitte. (2021). *2021 global shared services and outsourcing report*. https://www.deloitte.com/content/dam/assets-zone1/au/en/docs/services/consulting/2023/deloitte-au-con-2021-global-shared-services-report-190821.pdf

Deloitte. (2022). *Investing in Serbia – At your glance 2022*. https://www2.deloitte.com/content/dam/Deloitte/rs/Documents/tax/Investing%20in%20Serbia%202022.pdf

Deloitte. (2023). *2023 global shared services and outsourcing survey*. Deloitte US | Audit, Consulting, Advisory, and Tax Services. https://www2.deloitte.com/content/dam/Deloitte/us/Documents/process-and-operations/us-2023-global-shared-services-and-outsourcing-survey-executive-summary.pdf

HIPA. (2023). *Business services Hungary 2023*. HIPA – Hungarian Investment Promotion Agency. https://hipa.hu/uploads/insight/6/5/6/9/6569c5d07780f7005066461.pdf

InvestBulgaria. (2024). *IT & BPO industry*. https://investbg.government.bg/it-bpo-industry/

InvestRomania. (2023). *Romania's business service sector*. https://investromania.gov.ro/web/wp-content/uploads/2023/08/InvestRomania.ITC_BPO_SSC.pdf

Klimek, A. (2021). Offshoring of white-collar jobs: Theory and evidence. *International Journal of Management and Economics*, *57*(1), 69–84. https://doi.org/10.2478/ijme-2021-0003

Ministry of Economy of the Slovak Republic. (2024). *Zoznam centier podnikových služieb pri MH SR*. https://www.mhsr.sk/uploads/files/yYSfzk1d.pdf?csrt=13799980959778607526

Polish Investment and Trade Agency. (2024). *Investment incentives*. Paih.gov.pl. https://www.paih.gov.pl/en/why_poland/investment_incentives/

SARIO. (2024a). *Regional investment incentives*. https://www.sario.sk/en/invest-slovakia/support-investors/regional-investment-aid

SARIO. (2024b). *Shared service & business process outsourcing centers in Slovakia*. https://www.sario.sk/sites/default/files/sario-ssc-2024-02-21.pdf

Ślusarczyk, B. (2017). Shared services centres in Central and Eastern Europe: The examples of Poland and Slovakia. *Economics & Sociology*, *10*(3), 45–58. https://doi.org/10.14254/2071-789x.2017/10-3/3

Statistical Office of the Slovak Republic. (2024). *DATAcube*. https://datacube.statistics.sk/

Trend. (2003). Nemeckým klientom americkej firmy zdvihnú telefón Slováci. *Trend.sk*. https://www.trend.sk/financie/nemeckym-klientom-americkej-firmy-zdvihnu-telefon-slovaci

Chapter 13

Culture and Tourism: Hidden Potential for Slovak Economy

Kristína Baculáková

University of Economics in Bratislava, Slovakia

Abstract

The aim of the chapter is to clarify the importance of culture and tourism in the economy of Slovakia in the context of social and economic changes in recent years. Culture as a part of every society, an element that defines, unites, and at the same time divides, today undoubtedly belongs to the economic activity of the country with its material outputs. In the last two decades, the share of culture and creative industry in gross domestic product (GDP) has been growing both in the entire Union and in Slovakia. Despite the fact that Slovakia has a huge cultural capital that can be transformed into cultural output, this area is often outside the interest of policymakers. However, culture is a catalyst for economic growth, a tool for regional development, a source of employment, and a contributor to social inclusion. Together with tourism, they represent a significant potential for regional development in Slovakia.

Keywords: Culture; cultural capital; creative industries; tourism; regional development; sustainable development

1. Introduction

Culture, which represents a summation of values, norms, beliefs, symbols, and rituals is the basis of every society. Individual communities create their own culture, which is specific. Moreover, culture is alive, that is, it is constantly changing. It is necessary to cultivate it, that is, improve it. Currently, the question of the importance of culture for society and culture as a source of creativity and a catalyst of knowledge is coming to the fore. The basis of the current, so-called knowledge economy is the quality of information, knowledge, ideas.

Modeling Economic Growth in Contemporary Slovakia, 235–251

doi:10.1108/978-1-83549-454-720241019

According to Castells and Cardoso (2005), knowledge is also the basis of culture. Nowadays, we think about the economization of culture. This means that certain economic benefits are attributed to culture. Compared to other economic sectors, culture shows a number of fundamental differences and is economically presented as a tool for the development of regions, a catalyst for economic growth, an important source of employment, and a positive factor for social integration and cohesion. The basis of cultural diversity is also the strengthening of cultural identity, both at the national and regional level. Today, diversity is understood as one of the basic prerequisites for sustainable growth and prosperity on a global scale.

John Hawkes offers the definition that culture is The Fourth Pillar of Sustainability. According to Hawkes (2001), culture allows people to express themselves, creates a sense of connection and cooperation. Traditional cultural production (such as crafts) allows people who are for various reasons not employed to participate in the economic process. This effect is mostly present in developing countries where there is hardly any job opportunity. It enables women to be better involved (not only on maternity leave) in social life and fosters community feeling and belonging, which ultimately leads to strengthening of cultural identity.

Cultural activities bring together people with different opinions, habits, and beliefs from different conditions and thus contribute to increasing intercultural competences and mutual understanding. Recognizing and understanding each other's differences contributes to the prevention of unwanted attitudes such as bullying, racism, and improves the involvement of disadvantaged groups. The role of culture in every society is therefore undeniable. Together with tourism, which is often connected to creative industries, it represents the hidden potential for future Slovak economy.

2. Culture in the Slovak Economy

Slovak culture was born on the background of European culture; hence, it is based on the European cultural context with the strong Christian tradition. Starting from the historical context, Slovak culture built its nationality under the influence of political, economic, and social changes. After 1989, it began to fully open up to the influence of world culture (Mistrík, 2006). Today, the economization of culture as a trend manifests itself throughout the European Union (EU) through the concept of the creative industry. The concept of creative industry is developing relatively slowly in Slovakia. Compared to the countries of Western Europe, this development was also influenced by the country's socialist past. The rebirth of the post-Soviet society also means rediscovering its cultural values.

In Slovakia, the creative industry was not included in any policy until recently, and therefore its contribution to economic development was not even mapped. However, the Government of the Slovak Republic adopted in 2011 the Basic concepts for the support of the cultural and creative industries in the Slovak

Republic, which should have served for the inevitable updating of Slovakia's national economic policy in relation to the creative industries (Ministerstvo kultúry SR, 2011). The understanding and definition of the creative industry in Slovakia is based on the EU's methodology for determining the creative industry. It divides the creative industry into the cultural sector and the creative sector. According to the materials of the Government of the Slovak Republic, the creative industry "is a summary of industries that are built on the use of the results of mental creative activity in the field of art, culture and other industries; creates an entire exploitation chain, ranging from the creation of conditions for creative activity, through production to the restoration (redesign) of its results" (Ministerstvo kultúry SR & Ministerstvo hospodárstva SR, 2014). The creative industry falls under the purview of the Ministry of Culture, which, in addition to the initial material, also prepared the Initial Strategies for the Development of the Creative Industry in the Slovak Republic. From the point of view of conceptualization, the year 2015, when the government adopted the Action Plan, is particularly significant. The plan promised to apply the ESS-net Culture methodology in practice (Ministerstvo kultúry SR & Ministerstvo hospodárstva SR, 2015). The result is now finally a functional satellite account of the creative industry in Slovakia, which allows statistical mapping of individual industries and thus monitoring their development. The satellite account of the cultural and creative industry in Slovakia is methodologically and content-wise based on the final documents of the ESSnet-Culture project, which was created by Eurostat in 2009–2012 and which became the starting point for building international harmonized statistics on culture and formed the basis for the development of European statistics on culture and creative industry. The account was created as a subsystem of the national accounts of the Slovak Republic, which is based on the methodology and concepts of the system of national accounts of the Slovak Republic. The branches of cultural and creative industries make up nine areas in the satellite account, namely Cultural Heritage, Periodical and Non-Periodical Press, Visual Arts and Crafts, Architecture, Performing (Scenic) Arts, Audiovisual Media, Advertising, Art Education, and Support Services for CCIs Areas (Ministerstvo kultúry SR, 2022).

Before the existence of the satellite account of the creative industries, it was rather problematic to accurately identify the units that can be included. The first attempt at comprehensive mapping of individual cultural and creative sectors came in 2013, when a study by Neulogy was published. The study chose a composite work methodology, mapping macroeconomic indicators but also regional characteristics (Neulogy, 2013). In March 2020, the renowned KEA agency in cooperation with the European Commission completed the annual project of strategic evaluation of measures to support the development of the cultural industry in Slovakia, while also issuing a package of recommendations. According to the study, the Slovak government has recognized the importance of the cultural industry for the economic and social development of the country. It also considers it remarkable that Slovakia allocated 270 million EUR from the Integrated Regional Operational Program (IROP) 2014–2020 to support the development of the cultural and creative industry in the regions (KEA, 2020).

Overall, the perception of the creative industry has become more holistic, but the biggest shortcomings can be identified as the low competitiveness of the industries and the very short standardized statistical survey.

In the pre-COVID period, the cultural and creative industries were developing very dynamically. The EY's study on the creative industry in the EU has already revealed that during the global economic crisis, when almost all other industries recorded a decline in production and income, it was the regional industries that grew. They thus became a source of employment, especially for young people (EY, 2014).

The period before the pandemic was positive for the cultural and creative industry in Slovakia. The sector as a whole grew year-on-year. The added value in 2020 amounted to 1,498.28 million EUR, which was a decrease of 44.758 million EUR compared to 2019 (Horecká & Némethová, 2022). One of the most analyzed economic indicators of the economy is, of course, the gross domestic product (GDP). The GDP of cultural and creative industries in 2020 was 1,550.505 million EUR, which represented a decrease of 47.474 million EUR compared to 2019. According to statistics, three sectors have the largest share on the GDP of the entire sector, namely the sector outside the direct activity of the creative industry (but producing creative production) with a share of about 24%, followed by the advertising sector with a share of 15% and audiovisual production with a share of 11%. In 2020, the share of the cultural and creative industry in the entire economy of Slovakia was up to 1.68%, which is more than tourism with only 1.45% (Horecká & Némethová, 2022).

In Slovakia, the total revenues of the cultural and creative sector in 2017 amounted to 963.7 million EUR. The most prosperous and most potential subsector was gaming industry with the significant growth of +267% (revenues) and +1568% (employment) during the period 2013–2017 (KEA, 2020). Overall, the audiovisual sector of the creative industries recorded growth of +46,6% (KEA, 2020). Music industry itself generated +30% revenue. Majority of the Slovak creative industries are composed of micro and small enterprises (less than 10 employees). Self-employment represented 61% of the total employment in the sector. In the period 2013–2017, employment in the audio-visual sector grew most (16%). However, the largest percentage of people employed in the creative industries work in the book sector (KEA, 2020). Some aspects of the culture and creative industries in Slovakia are illustrated in Fig. 13.1.

3. The COVID Times

According to the EY (2021) study, creative industries is one of the sectors most affected by the pandemic. In total, the cultural and creative economy in Europe lost up to 31% of its turnover, which is more than, for example, tourism (27%) or the automotive industry (25%). The only sector that matched creative industries in this unpleasant comparison was air transport (31%). The total turnover of cultural and creative enterprises thus fell by 199 billion EUR. The impact of the pandemic on culture and the creative industry are the worst in the area of Central and

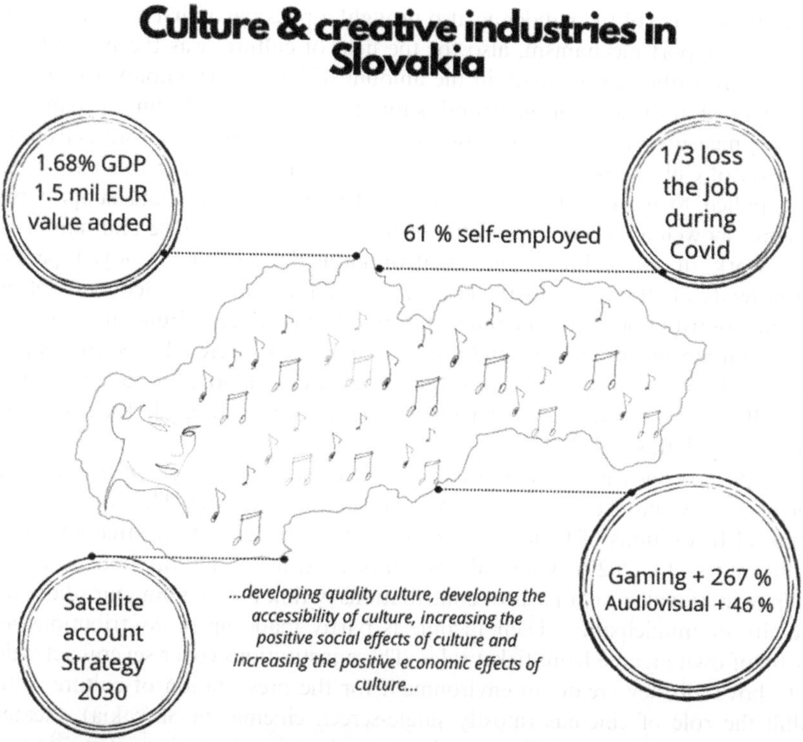

Fig. 13.1. Culture and Creative Industries in Slovakia. *Source:* Author's own processing.

Eastern Europe, and the shocks are felt in all cultural and creative industries. The most affected are performing arts (−90%) and music (−76%). The only area of creative industries that managed to maintain its income in 2020 was the gaming sector (+9%).

When the world was hit by the COVID pandemic, 220,000 people worked in the cultural and creative industry in Slovakia (9% of the workforce). About one third of them have been facing the decline in the performance by more than 80%, in some industries up to 90% (Collective of authors, 2020). According to SOZA (2020) data, only around 2,000 events were reported throughout Slovakia in 2020. For comparison, in 2019, there were more than 11,000 of them. In April 2020, the survey of the platform "We stand by culture" collected the data to identify the basic impacts of pandemics on the creative industries. The Institute of Cultural Policy also provided a basic analysis. The results showed that people working in the sector of cultural events are at existential risk of income loss (Inštitút kultúrnej politiky, 2020).

The first wave of the pandemic also brought a package of first measures. Basic financial support mechanism, also for the field of culture, was the possibility to obtain a contribution to wages in the amount of 80% if the employer maintains employment at the level of the period before the pandemics. Within the pandemic support measures, particular attention was paid to the Law on Subsidies from the Ministry of Culture, which was approved by the parliament in October 2020. The law applied to workers in culture, arts and crafts, technical and support professions, as well as professions in the field of audiovisual culture and film artists who work in the cultural and creative industries as self-employed persons (Ministerstvo kultúry SR, 2020). The law allowed the voluntary deduction of two percent contribution to artistic funds (Literary Fund, Musical Fund and Fine Arts Fund). Organizers of festivals and other cultural events were allowed to postpone the validity of purchased tickets for events that were supposed to take place until June 30, 2021, but due to the pandemic, they were canceled. Extension was possible until June 30, 2022.

Despite the measures taken, it can be stated that not a single scheme affected one of the key actors of culture in Slovakia – cultural facilities. The Association of Cultural Institutions of Cities and Towns of Slovakia also drew attention to this problem (AKIS, 2020). Cultural institutions, such as cultural houses, mostly operate in Slovakia on a basis of contributions within the founding jurisdiction of the city or municipality. Their income is partly made up of contributions and partly of own income from ticket sales. These institutions cover several activities, but above all they create an environment for the presentation of culture – they fulfill the role of cinemas (mostly single-screen cinemas in Slovakia), theaters, concert halls, exhibition halls, participate in educational activities. Thus, in most municipalities and towns in Slovakia, they have multifunctional cultural houses that have the necessary equipment material and technical equipment and especially a dignified space that is directly created and maintained to fulfill the role of a cinema hall and a theater hall. Cultural centers have their permanent staff employees who, as a result of the pandemic, found themselves in the same unfavorable situation as the artists themselves. If adequate help is not provided to these cultural institutions, there is a risk the disappearance of spaces for the presentation of culture at the local and regional level. This may lead to a narrowing of the cultural offer, which ultimately can bring serious consequences in the form of a change in values and attitude of society toward art and culture, influence on the development of society, especially youth and the threat to social inclusion of excluded groups.

4. Hidden Potential of Culture for the Slovak Economy

The financial support from the European funds represents a very good opportunity for the development of creative industries in the regions. Entrepreneurship in creative industries in Slovakia is very volatile, the financial incentive can therefore be motivating. Development of creative industries at the regional level is the key for stable functioning of the whole sector. Regional development of cultural and creative industry will help to bring the culture and creativity closer to the general public. Support for the regional development of creative work will also enable a better understanding for the needs of creative workers. Although the action plan was designed in cooperation and discussion with the professional public, the creative workers themselves see the support so far as theory rather than practice. Only practice can show more effective solutions and support models (including non-financial ones, for example).

The introduction of the ESSnet-Culture methodology is also a considerable benefit and opportunity, that is, the allocation of creative industries according to NACE codes. Such division enables to precisely define industries and its subcategories. The biggest benefit of the methodology is the possibility to measure creative industries. Cultural and creative industries have recently become interesting for economists, because several studies have indicated that they behave differently from other industries. One example was demonstrated during the Global Financial Crisis back in 2008/2009. Despite the crisis, creative sector was growing and providing employment opportunities mostly for young people.

Development of creative thinking is also associated with innovative potential. Creativity as a creative process can be the first step which later may (but not necessarily) lead to innovation. So, it is impossible to identify creativity as innovation, but we understand creativity as an important part of innovation process. Creativity represents the process of creating new ideas and thoughts, while invention denotes a new idea or thought. For an even better understanding of the mutual relation between the concepts of creativity and innovation we should return to Schumpeter and his creative destruction (Schumpeter, 1976). That represents an innovative subversion of old systems. It is an ongoing process of changes – innovations of products and processes when new ones replace obsolete ones. At the same time up to 50% of productivity growth is precisely the process of creative destruction. Innovation means a shift, always for the better. Creativity is a constant change, unrest. However, this change may not automatically lead to the better, on the contrary, creativity (as a change) leads to the destruction of old systems. While creativity represents a process of absolute change, innovation is a strategic and long-term preparation to this change. Creativity and innovation are therefore closely related from an economic point of view. Creativity can be the basis of innovation, but unlike innovation, it does not always bring a positive shift.

Anderson et al. (2014) see creativity and innovation as inseparable parts of the same process. He therefore proposes one common definition of both creativity and innovation: "Creativity and innovation at work is the process, attempts and results of attempts to develop and introduce new and improved ways of doing things. Creativity is the phase of this process, in which new ideas are generated and innovation represents the next stage of implementation thoughts and ideas to improve work procedures, practices or products. Creativity and innovation can occur at the individual, team, organization or combined at more than one of these levels." In simple terms, it could be said that creativity represents the beginning of something new, but we can only innovate what already exists. Creativity is, according to several authors (Amabile, 1996; Anderson et al., 2014), the first step to innovation. On the other hand, creativity alone does not necessarily lead to innovation.

Culture has its central place in the knowledge economy. The communication of culture plays a dynamic role in the world of ideas, as it provides direct creative input through its ability to inspire and implement new ideas and new approaches. It helps to structure creative endeavors and promote quality through the application of traditional disciplines, the involvement of specialized skills, and the respect for authenticity that marks a truly cultural endeavor.

The problem for the future development of the sector and the release of its full potential is the underestimation of the influence and importance of the cultural and creative sector. While before the pandemic the economic value of the cultural and creative industry came to the fore, in recent years, we have been witnessing a return to the so-called public value. Culture and creative industries have a number of indirect effects in addition to their direct impact on the economy. Cultural wealth can be considered an important capital, for example, for the country's tourism. In addition, culture creates the morale of society and contributes to social inclusion. In very simple terms, culture distinguishes man from other creatures on this planet. At the same time, we learn culture, and during life, it is necessary to constantly improve it, that is, to cultivate it.

Slovak legislation and European structural funds help to develop the potential of the cultural and creative industry in Slovakia. The aim of the last support was to build creative centers in individual regions. Some creative centers (such as in Trnava or Trenčín) have already been built. Creative centers as institutions help the development of the cultural and creative industry in individual regions, that is, through activities that generate employment growth in the sector. These activities represent the development of creative talent, entrepreneurial skills, and the support of nontechnological innovations. The creative center helps support entrepreneurship in the creative industry, facilitates market access, helps build networks and clusters, and increases the demand for creative production. Creative centers cooperate with public administration, educational institutions. At the same time, their infrastructure is very complex, they provide workspaces, so-called co-working space, administrative spaces, laboratories, workshops, studios, and sales premises.

In 2023, the Culture Strategy 2030 was adopted by the Ministry of Culture. The extensive and complex document, which determines the future direction of culture and the creative industry in Slovakia, was created in extensive collaboration with experts, external collaborators, members of the Platform for Cultural and Creative Industry, as well as with the public. The document is based on the principles of participation, nonpartisanship, long-term perspective of development, and social impact. The new strategy proceeded with the definition of the main goal and subgoals of the cultural policy in Slovakia so that the cultural policy was assessed according to measurable parameters and the results were comparable to other public policies (Ministerstvo kultúry SR, 2023).

These goals include developing quality culture, developing the accessibility of culture, increasing the positive social effects of culture, and increasing the positive economic effects of culture. Individual subgoals are connected to each other and influence each other. Cultural diversity can be a suitable way to protect society from dangerous phenomena that threaten democracy, such as extremism or xenophobia. Culture has, as well, potential in addressing climate change.

For a long time, a major obstacle to the development of the full potential of culture and the creative industry in Slovakia is its underestimation and under-dimensioning of its financing. This underestimation was supposed to be eliminated precisely by the introduction of the satellite account, with which it is possible to map the economic benefits of the industry. However, the individual activities included in the Slovak satellite account are not completely identical to foreign statistics. This does not allow a comparative analysis of the creative industry in Slovakia and abroad. Moreover, as far as international trade is concerned, the Slovak creative industry is largely closed to the outside world (Ministerstvo kultúry SR, 2023). Even though the share of public spending on culture in GDP in Slovakia is comparable to the EU average, the country has long been lagging behind other European countries in terms of the volume of private resources in culture. These detected shortcomings and threats are solved by the vision of the development of culture until 2030. The vision is based on seven strategic goals, it is a well-managed, high-quality, responsible, dignified, inclusive, respected, and effectively financed culture.

For the gradual improvement of the quality of services in culture, it is necessary to improve management processes systematically and continuously in cultural institutions. The national and regional self-government established cultural institutions are currently functioning in the legal forms of budget or contribution organization, while voices are heard seeking a legal form with greater flexibility and independence in financing and management. For the need to link the department of culture and key actors in the sector on various levels, the ministry responded already in 2020 by creating a platform for the cultural and creative industry as a potential tool for the development of culture and creativity, small and medium-sized businesses, innovations, employment, permanently sustainable urban and regional development, economic and social development, artistic education, tourism, and establishing international cooperation. This should be further transformed as a communication tool for the actors in the culture and creative industries (Ministerstvo kultúry SR, 2021).

The new strategy for the development of culture and the creative industry in Slovakia is based on global megatrends in the field of culture. Due to its rich cultural heritage, traditions, and crafts, Slovakia has a huge cultural potential. The inspiration for its development is also the overall development of the creative industry on the territory of the EU, of which Slovakia is a part. The dynamics of creative industry development in the EU before the pandemic represented a potential economic miracle. The industry grew by an incredible 17% between 2013 and 2019. In 2019, the creative industry employed around 4.4% of the workforce, which is 8.4 times more than, for example, the telecommunications sector (EY, 2021). In comparison with other countries, Slovakia belongs to the medium group of European countries with a share of CCI's GDP between 1.5% and 2% (EY, 2021). Only four countries with a highly developed cultural policy have a higher share of the creative industry in GDP. In addition, the Central

European market is one of the fastest growing, especially in the segment of video games and audiovisuals. Creative jobs tend to be held by younger and higher-educated people than the average.

The COVID pandemic has caused a huge external shock to the creative industry. Along with air transport, these were the sectors that paid the most for the crisis. In addition to financial aid for the creative sector, other priorities for its support are emerging as new, postpandemic challenges. An example is leveraging broader cross-sectoral links, especially with tourism, research and innovation, energy, transport and active mobility, and construction. Creative industry promotes and strengthens the European model of a social economy, where key players can help shape the EU's economy and welfare through sustainable, inclusive, democratic, and cooperative programs.

5. Tourism in the Slovak Economy

Tourism as such began to develop more significantly in the 18th century. Today, the term tourism is understood much more broadly. We are talking not just about leisure travel but about any movement of person with various goals. Tourism generally has a distinct economic and social impact. Tourism can be defined from the perspective of demand and from the perspective of supply. The demand perspective is largely based on leisure and related recreation. The supply perspective is broader and includes many other reasons for travel. For a standardized measurement of tourism performance, it is important, as with culture, to start from a satellite account that precisely defines individual areas. The satellite account of tourism in Slovakia began to be compiled in 2001, while the first data were published in 2007 (Matlovičová et al., 2015).

Tourist interest is derived from several key determinants. These determinants include the degree of economic growth, the population factor, the political factor, and today we can also include individual preferences and trends (Matlovičová et al., 2015). The higher the degree of economic growth, the greater the assumption of growth in interest in tourism. However, this premise does not apply completely across the board. A typical example is still developing countries in the region of Latin America or Southeast Asia. Countries such as Brazil or Thailand began to attract tourists while still in the process of industrialization. The population factor is closely linked precisely with the degree of economic development. The political factor is also important. These determinants include the degree of economic growth, the population factor, the political factor, and today we can also include individual preferences and trends.

The variety of forms of tourism is huge today. The most common forms include recreational tourism, water tourism, agritourism, cultural tourism (which also has several branches), or specialized tourism, which mainly attracts sports fans. Among the forms mentioned, in Slovakia, we find mainly cultural tourism, and within the specific forms mainly hiking tourism, cycle tourism, ski tourism, and among the recreational forms are water tourism and spa and wellness tourism.

Until the COVID pandemic, tourism in Slovakia had been recording an average growth of 5% year-on-year for about a decade (Özoğlu, 2020). Participation in domestic trips (together with foreign trips) exceeded participation in foreign trips alone. Preference was given to short-term trips. The most common reasons for not participating in any trip were health reasons, insufficient funds, or motivation to travel. It was mainly about the category of elderly. Since 2013, the number of employees in the tourism industry in Slovakia has been continuously growing. At the beginning of 2020, 162 thousand jobs were recorded in the tourism industry. In 2019, tourism share in GDP was up to 2.86% (Štatistický úrad, 2021a). In 2019, tourism produced a total value of 10.2 billion EUR. It is a summary of the production of characteristic tourism industries that are internationally comparable, as well as industries specific to tourism in Slovakia. The gross value added of all these industries amounted to 4.6 billion EUR (Štatistický úrad, 2021b). Participants in the tourism industry spent a total of almost 6.8 billion EUR (expenses of locals and foreigners on the territory of the Slovak Republic as well as expenses of citizens of the Slovak Republic on trips abroad). Total expenses increased by 15.8% year-on-year. Domestic tourism was particularly successful. Among the sectors, the largest volume was made up of domestic tourism expenditures (3.0 billion EUR). These expenses achieved year-on-year growth of almost 24%. However, the striking fact is that up to two thirds of visitors from abroad spent only one night in Slovakia. Slovakia is therefore becoming a destination especially for visiting the capital as part of traveling around Central Europe (especially the Prague-Vienna-Budapest triangle). At the same time, Slovak citizens spent almost 2.1 billion EUR on goods and services on trips abroad and foreigners who came to Slovakia 1.6 billion EUR (Štatistický úrad, 2021b). Some aspects of tourism in Slovakia are illustrated in Fig. 13.2.

6. The COVID Times

After the outbreak of the COVID pandemic, tourism in Slovakia recorded a year-on-year decrease of 54% in 2020, while the number of tourists from abroad decreased by more than 70% (Tajtáková, 2021). During the favorable year 2019, average year-on-year increase in domestic trips represented 23.7% while for foreign trips even 10.1% (Štatistický úrad, 2020). In 2020, however, there was a strong decrease of 45.6% for the domestic trips and 81.1% for foreign trips (Štatistický úrad, 2022). The pandemic has caused the loss of about one-tenth of jobs in tourism. In 2021, the share of tourism in Slovakia's GDP decreased to 1.4%, which is less than half the value compared to the best result in 2019. The average expenses for domestic trips decreased in 2020 compared to 2019 by 3.2 EUR and for foreign trips by 114 EUR (Štatistický úrad, 2022). In 2020, residents took domestic trips with staying overnight for personal purposes in particular in order to get to know new cities. Other reasons for domestic trips were a visit of rural and mountainous areas.

Due to ongoing pandemic, in 2021, 496 gastro and tourism enterprises were deleted from the commercial register (FinStat, 2021). The data for the year 2022,

Fig. 13.2. Tourism in Slovakia. *Source:* Author's own processing.

when further impacts of the pandemic were shown, have, unfortunately, not yet been evaluated by the statistical office. Entrepreneurs in the tourism industry used state aid to mitigate the consequences of the pandemic. In addition, after the adoption of the amendment proposal, tourism organizations in the regions could temporarily use the provided subsidy from the state budget in the amount of up to 15% for operating costs in 2022 and 2023. Without aid schemes from the Ministry of Transport, 72% of tourism entrepreneurs would have to close their businesses. This follows from a survey conducted by the Department of Transport among 1,101 recipients of pandemic aid in the field of tourism (Trend, 2023). Despite the fact that, according to their own words, three-quarters of entrepreneurs would not have survived the pandemic without state aid, 62% of respondents described the amount of aid for tourism as insufficient or completely insufficient.

7. Hidden Potential of Tourism for the Slovak Economy

Considering global socioeconomic trends, tourism is one of the most promising economic sectors in the world economy. Increasing the standard of living of the population in the rapidly developing countries of Eastern Europe and Asia or the tendency to shorten the length of working hours in Western Europe create conditions for the growth of demand for services in the field of travel and tourism. Global trends in tourism are also changing dynamically. Crowded world monuments are changing the interest of travelers. This causes a shift away from mass tourism and a return to regional and local tourism. According to the World Economic Forum's index, which measures the competitiveness of tourism in individual countries, Slovakia was ranked 60th. It is thus at the bottom of the EU member states. Slovakia has a huge tourist potential. The rich cultural heritage and diverse geomorphology create conditions for summer and winter tourism, sports and recreation, as well as educational tourism and spa industry. However, this potential is not fully exploited.

Tourism is developed on two levels – central and regional. The central level primarily provides support to regions and promotes Slovakia abroad. However, the greatest weight on the development of tourism lies with the regions themselves. Tourism is the so-called cross-cutting sector of the national economy, which means that it affects many other economic sectors (e.g. transport, construction, food industry, agriculture). Tourism contributes to the growth of tax and foreign exchange revenues and thus the growth of the GDP of the state and the region. It directly and indirectly creates jobs. It contributes to value creation and has a multiplier effect. The development of tourism stimulates structural changes in the regional economy in connection with the decline of traditional economic activity. At the same time, tourism participates in international cooperation. In addition, the development of tourism and the income obtained from it help preserve and enhance cultural heritage.

In Slovakia, the tourism development policy is governed by regionalization. The first regionalization was adopted in the 1960s. The last, most recent one, divides Slovakia into 21 regions (Gregorová et al., 2015). The division was based on the most general common characteristics of the territories, although it is not universal (Ministerstvo dopravy SR, 2005). In 2021, the first mapping study of tourism potential in Slovakia took place. When comparing the actual and potential market share, the study found that Slovakia is not in line with the market, which is a situation where the actual market share corresponds to the potential market share. Slovakia with a potential market share of 17% and an actual market share of 11% lags behind by 6% (HAM, 2021). According to the study, the technological environment represents a major threat to Slovak tourism. Slovakia lags behind significantly in science and research, and even in the field of tourism there has been no technological change. As a result, competitiveness against other countries deteriorates, despite favorable entry conditions. Other threats include still insufficiently developed infrastructure, weak electronification of public administration, strong bureaucracy, and public policy. Recently, in addition to the progressing climate change, more and more emphasis is being placed on the greening of tourism. The tourists themselves are interested in seeing intact nature, on the other hand, he demands perfect infrastructure, which often disturbs the protected area. This is a long-standing problem in locations such as the Tatras, where the interests of investors, tourists, and conservationists collide, and it is very difficult to reconcile these different interests.

Other economic threats are rising inflation and a drop in disposable income of the population. In addition, the pandemic has paradoxically increased the demands on the quality of the services provided (especially with regard to safety and accessibility). For the successful development of tourism potential, it is necessary to pay attention to the determinants that decide the choice of a tourist destination, such as the quality of the location, the quality of the services provided, the available facilities and products, and marketing. In 2016, Slovakia introduced a new marketing brand, Good Idea Slovakia (Čiefová & Goda, 2019). According to the Ministry of Foreign and European Affairs (2016), the aim of this national branding was to create and introduce into the presentation practice of the Slovak Republic a set of attractive, trustworthy communication messages and their graphic renderings, which relevant domestic actors identify with, and which will help in creating a positive image of Slovakia abroad. The Good Idea Slovakia brand covers not only tourism but creates the already mentioned national branding for Slovakia as such. Moreover, such a national strategy significantly helps tourism, as it represents a unifying element in communication abroad.

A positive assumption for tourism is that the target group of tourists traveling for recreation should return to the level of the 2019 by 2025. The scenario suggests that the volume (of overnight stays) is, however, recovering faster than revenues, which means that tourism revenues will not return to the 2019 level until 2030.

8. Conclusion

Culture and creativity are the basis of human being. In today's understanding, creativity is transformed into an economic result – it produces profit. The creative industry contributes to economic growth, sustainable development, promotes social inclusion, and preserves cultural heritage. When thinking about the benefits of the creative industry, in addition to economic values, its key role in global value chains should be emphasized. The creative industry stimulates innovation, brings added value as an element of social cohesion, and serves as an effective tool in the fight against the current recession. It helps preserve cultural heritage and helps promote social inclusion.

Slovakia has a huge cultural potential. Historical crafts together with modern art and dynamic sectors, such as video games, represent a promising potential for the Slovak economy. However, the cultural sectors in Slovakia have long been underfunded, marginalized, and on the sidelines of government priorities. Since culture also determines morality, these negative tendencies are also reflected in society. Despite this, it was the cultural community in Slovakia that mobilized and, together with other stakeholders as well as the wider professional public, prepared an extensive strategy for the development of culture and the creative industry until 2030. The strategically set goals, as long as they are fulfilled, will enable the full release of the potential of this sector for economic growth and development of society.

Hand in hand with the development of the potential of culture, we also monitor the growing potential of tourism in Slovakia. Culture and tourism are very close to each other. It is the cultural heritage in any form that motivates the development of tourism in the region. At the same time, together with recreational tourism, cultural tourism also prevails in Slovakia. However, tourism, like the cultural industry, was affected by the COVID pandemic. Travel restrictions radically cut incomes, and even attendance itself. Without the necessary financial assistance from the state or the Union, many entrepreneurs working in culture and tourism would not survive. Both industries showed their most dynamic growth just before the pandemic, in 2018–2019. Slovakia is trying to support its tourism potential with national branding, but also with the identification of weaknesses, which was brought about by the first mapping study. The dynamics of traveling is increasing, and it seems that after the pandemic, people are returning not only to travel but also to cultural experiences. It remains to be believed that the full recovery and growth will be at least as sharp as the entire world was hit by COVID.

References

AKIS. (2020). *List Vláde Slovenskej republiky*. Asociácia kultúrnych inštitúcii Slovenska. https://www.1akis.sk/index.php

Amabile, T. (1996). *Creativity and innovation in organizations*. Harvard Business Schools. 9-396-239. https://edisciplinas.usp.br/pluginfile.php/4927750/mod_resource/content/0/Creativity%20and%20Innovation%20in%20Organizations.pdf

Anderson, N., Potočnik, K., & Zhou, J. (2014). Innovation and creativity in organizations: A state-of-the-science review, prospective commentary, and guiding framework. *Journal of Management*, *40*(5), 1297–1333. https://doi.org/10.1177/0149206314527128

Castells, M., & Cardoso, G. (2005). *The network society. Form knowledge to policy*. Johns Hopkins Center for Transatlantic Relations.

Čiefová, M., & Goda, N. (2019). Význam nation brandingu pre Slovensko: súčasné trendy a výzvy. *Ekonomické, politické a právne otázky medzinárodných vzt'ahov 2019: zborník vedeckých prác. Vydavatel'stvo EKONÓM*, *2019*, 91–98.

Collective of authors. (2020). *Otvorený list premiérovi: Začnite okamžite riešiť túto neúnosnú situáciu!*. https://www.omediach.com/tv/18979-otvoreny-list-premierovi-zacnite-okamzite-riesit-tuto-neunosnu-situaciu

EY. (2014). *Creating growth: Measuring cultural and creative markets in the EU*. EY Building a better working world. http://www.creatingeurope.eu/en/wp-content/uploads/2014/11/study-full-en.pdf

EY. (2021). *Rebuilding Europe. The cultural and creative economy before and after the COVID-19 crisis*. EY. https://www.rebuilding-europe.eu

FinStat. (2021). *Výmazy z Obchodného registra v roku 2021*. FinStat. https://news.finstat.sk/clanky/vymazy-z-obchodneho-registra-v-roku-2021/

Gregorová, B., Neradný, M., Klaučo, M., Masný, M., & Balková, N. (2015). *Cestovný ruch a regionálny rozvoj*. Belianum, Banská Bystrica.

HAM. (2021). *Mapovacia štúdia CR Slovenska*. Koncepčný dokument Ministerstva dopravy SR. https://www.mindop.sk/ministerstvo-1/cestovny-ruch-7/legislativa-a-koncepcne-dokumenty/koncepcne-dokumenty/regionalizacia-cestovneho-ruchu-v-sr

Hawkes, J. (2001). *The fourth pillar of sustainability. Culture's essential role in public planning*. Common Ground Publishing Pty Ltd in association with the Cultural Development Network (Vic).

Horecká, J., & Némethová, R. (2022). *Zhrnutie výsledkov satelitného účtu kultúry a kreatívneho priemyslu SR (2015-2020)*. INFOSTAT – Inštitút informatiky a štatistiky. https://www.culture.gov.sk/posobnost-ministerstva/umenie-a-kreativita/kulturny-a-kreativny-priemysel/satelitny-ucet-kultury-a-kreativneho-priemyslu-sr/

Inštitút kultúrnej politiky. (2020). Odhadujeme dopady pandémie na kultúru a kreatívny priemysel Facebook. https://www.facebook.com/notes/inštitút-kultúrnej-politiky/odhadujeme-dopady-pandémie-na-kultúru-a-kreatívny-priemysel/1401112776765644/?_rdr. Accessed on March 25, 2020.

KEA. (2020). *Cultural industries in Slovakia. Report on the AS-IS situation*. Analysis and recommendations to boost growth in Cultural Industries in Slovakia N° SRSS/SC2018/097. https://www.culture.gov.sk/wp-content/uploads/2020/11/AS-IS_sprava.pdf

Matlovičová, K., Klamár, R., & Mika, M. (2015). *Turistika a jej formy*. Grafotlač, Prešov.

Ministerstvo dopravy SR. (2005). *Regionalizácia cestovného ruchu v Slovenskej republike*. https://www.mindop.sk/ministerstvo-1/cestovny-ruch-7/legislativa-a-koncepcne-dokumenty/koncepcne-dokumenty/regionalizacia-cestovneho-ruchu-v-sr

Ministerstvo kultúry SR and Ministerstvo hospodárstva SR. (2014). *Stratégia rozvoja kreatívneho priemyslu v Slovenskej republike*. https://www.culture.gov.sk/wp-content/uploads/2019/12/strategia.pdf

Ministerstvo kultúry SR and Ministerstvo hospodárstva SR. (2015). *Akčný plán realizácie Stratégie rozvoja kreatívneho priemyslu v Slovenskej republike*. https://www.culture.gov.sk/wp-content/uploads/2019/12/akcny_plan.pdf

Ministerstvo kultúry SR. (2020). *Národná rada schválila kľúčový zákon ministerstva kultúry o dotáciách*. https://www.culture.gov.sk/ministerstvo/medialny-servis/aktuality-ministerstva-kultury/narodna-rada-schvalila-klucovy-zakon-ministerstva-kultury-o-dotaciach/

Ministerstvo kultúry SR. (2021). *Platforma pre kultúrny a kreatívny priemysel*. https://www.culture.gov.sk/posobnost-ministerstva/umenie-a-kreativita/kulturny-a-kreativny-priemysel/platforma-pre-kulturny-a-kreativny-priemysel/

Ministerstvo kultúry SR. (2022). *Satelitný účet kultúry a kreatívneho priemyslu*. https://www.culture.gov.sk/posobnost-ministerstva/umenie-a-kreativita/kulturny-a-kreativny-priemysel/satelitny-ucet-kultury-a-kreativneho-priemyslu-sr/

Ministerstvo kultúry SR. (2023). *Stratégia kultúry a kreatívneho priemyslu Slovenskej republiky 2030*. https://www.culture.gov.sk/ministerstvo/strategia-kultury-a-kreativneho-priemyslu-2030/

Ministerstvo kultúry SR. (2011). *Východiská koncepcie na podporu kultúrneho a kreatívneho priemyslu v Slovenskej republike*. https://www.culture.gov.sk/wp-content/uploads/2019/12/Vychodiska-strategie-rozvoja-kreativneho-priemyslu-v-SR.pdf

Ministry of Foreign and European Affairs. (2016). *Branding krajiny – Značka Slovensko*. https://www.mzv.sk/ministerstvo/prezentacia-slovenska-v-zahranici/znacka-slovensko

Mistrík, E. (2006). *Slovenská kultúra v multikulturalizme*. Univerzita Konštantína Filozofa, Filozofická fakulta, Nitra.

Neulogy. (2013). *Správa o stave a potenciáli kreatívneho priemyslu na Slovensku*. Neulogy, a.s. https://www.tvba.sk/imageuploads/1207/sprava-kreativny-priemysel-mksr-neulogy.pdf

Özoğlu, M. (2020). *Základné ukazovatele za dovolenkové a služobné cesty za rok 2019*. Štatistický úrad Slovenskej republiky. https://slovak.statistics.sk/wps/portal/

Schumpeter, J. A. (1976). *Capitalism, socialism & democracy*. Taylor & Francis e-Library edition, 2003. https://periferiaactiva.files.wordpress.com/2015/08/joseph-schumpeter-capitalism-socialism-and-democracy-2006.pdf

SOZA. (2020). *Koronakríza a hudobný priemysel na Slovensku*. SOZA. https://moja.soza.sk/aktuality/315/koronakriza-a-hudobny-priemysel-na-slovensku

Štatistický úrad. (2020). *Ubytovacie zariadenia SR v auguste mali takmer 800 tisíc hostí a 2,5 milióna prenocovaní*. https://slovak.statistics.sk/wps/portal/ext/products/informationmessages/inf_sprava_detail/

Štatistický úrad. (2021a). *Cestovný ruch v roku 2019 vytvoril 2,86 % z výkonu slovenskej ekonomiky*. https://slovak.statistics.sk/wps/portal/ext/products/informationmessages/inf_sprava_detail/

Štatistický úrad. (2021b). *Satelitný účet cestovného ruchu v Slovenskej republike za rok 2019*. https://slovak.statistics.sk/wps/wcm/connect/f33cb77a-5029-4323-ad5b-42f0d7da3606/Prilohy_satelitny+ucet_CR_2019_SK.zip?MOD=AJPERES&CVID=nTo42ya

Štatistický úrad. (2022). *Satelitný účet cestovného ruchu v Slovenskej republike za rok 2020*. https://slovak.statistics.sk/wps/portal/ext/products/informationmessages/inf_sprava_detail/

Tajtáková, M. (2021). Dopady pandémie COVID-19 na domáci cestovný ruch na Slovensku. *Ekonomika cestovného ruchu a podnikanie*, *13*(1), 10–80. https://of.euba.sk/www_write/files/veda-vyskum/ecrp/ecrp-2021-01.pdf

Trend. (2023). *Cestovný ruch by sa bez pandemickej pomoci dlho zviechal. Podnikatelia podporu očakávali skôr*. Trend. https://www.trend.sk/spravy/cestovny-ruch-bez-pandemickej-pomoci-dlho-zviechal-podnikatelia-podporu-ocakavali-skor

Chapter 14

Economic Trajectories of Slovakia and Czechia: Twins or Unique Cases?

Lubor Lacina and Dunja Spasojević

Mendel University in Brno, Czech Republic

Abstract

Chapter concentrates on similarities and dissimilarities of both Czech and Slovak economy since start of the economic transformation at the begin of 90s. Authors closer look on economic development before both countries joining the European Union (EU) May 1st, 2004 and before Slovakia joining Eurozone by January 1st, 2009. Both impact of membership in EU and Slovak membership in Eurozone provides ground for identification of economic trajectories of both economies during economic transformation and after joining EU and in case of Slovakia Eurozone. Authors try to solve the puzzle if both economies behave rather as a twins or unique cases.

Keywords: Czech economy; Slovak economy; economic transformation; economic trajectories; EU membership; structural breaks

1. Introduction

The historical development of former Czechoslovakia and Slovak Economy is covered in Chapter 1 by Juraj Sipko. This chapter will concentrate on similarities and dissimilarities of both Czech and Slovak economy since start of the economic transformation at the begin of 90s. Authors closer look on economic development before both countries joining the European Union (EU) May 1st, 2004 and in case of Slovakia after joining Eurozone by January 1st, 2009. Both impact of membership in EU and Slovak membership in Eurozone provides ground for identification of economic trajectories of both economies during economic transformation and after joining EU and in case of Slovakia Eurozone.

Following the peaceful dissolution of Czechoslovakia, the Slovak Republic and Czech Republic emerged as independent countries and embarked on a

Modeling Economic Growth in Contemporary Slovakia, 253–264

Published under exclusive licence by Emerald Publishing Limited
doi:10.1108/978-1-83549-454-720241021

journey of economic transition and reform. During the 30 early years of independence, both Slovakia and Czechia faced many challenges, including establishing new economic policies, institutions, and legal frameworks (Myant & Drahokoupil, 2013).

The beginning of the 1990s marked the start of economic transformations in both economies, which were very inefficient after 40 years of central planned economy. That was a result of combination of central planning system and general nationalization of economy (almost nonexistence of private sector). Central planned organization of economy led to lots of distortions (e.g., fixed prices, multiple exchange rates, trade orientation to other central planned economies, redistribution of profits from more successful to less successful state-owned companies). The fiscal federal system of Czechoslovakia generated permanent transfers from the Czech Republic to Slovakia. This led to strong industrialization of Slovak economy and a shift away from agriculture. The Czech economy was slowly depleting its capacity from interwar period, and the growth of efficiency of the production were slowing down (Žídek, 2017).

Due to permanent lagging behind the West (e.g., Austria, West Germany), both economies strongly negatively diverge in terms of gross domestic product (GDP) per capita. The fact that citizens of former Czechoslovakia wanted to follow the path of development of Austria and West German economy was definitely one of the reasons for the so-called velvet revolution in autumn 1989 (Žídek, 2006).

From January 1991, federal Czechoslovak government started radical reform – price liberalization, opening of the domestic market to foreign competition, simultaneous monetary and fiscal restrictions; and a small privatization too. Subsequently, mass privatization – two waves with the unique so-called voucher method. In addition, government realized the direct sales of so called "silver gold companies" to foreign direct investors – for example, Skoda car VW.

As a result of inflation (almost 60% in the first year of economic transformation) and a drop in GDP led to increased unemployment. But unemployment increase was much intensive in Slovakia than in the Czech Republic (roughly 13% vs 3%) partly due to the different impact of transformation on both economies and higher impact of change strategy toward arms industry which was traditionally more concentrated at Slovak part of federation (Žídek, 2017).

1992 elections in Slovakia combined with the worsening of economic situation led at Slovakia to the victory of populism – Vladimir Mečiar government. Prime minister of the Czech Republic Vaclav Klaus continued in relatively radical reform and the inability to agree on common policy for both part of federation the compromise led to disintegration of the state from January 1st· 1993, so-called "velvet divorce."

In the Czech Republic, year 1993 was characteristic by continuation of reforms – including the second wave of mass privatization. In Slovakia, the process of privatization was stopped and direct sales primary to "politician's friends" and foreign direct investors were prioritized.

In first half of 90s, the Czech Republic was kind of economic transformation star – rapid growth and low unemployment and inflation. However, in the end, currency crisis occurs – May 1997, which contributed to banks problems. In the end, cleaning up the banking sector was very expensive.

Slovak government led by Vladimír Mečiar halted reforms and increased indebtedness of Slovak economy. Subsequently, Dzurinda and Mikloš reforms helped Slovak economy recover and fulfill Maastricht criteria as requirement for membership in Eurozone.

Following part of the chapter is devoted to comparison of time series of main economic indicators of Slovak and Czech economy.

2. GDP Growth

The trajectory of GDP per capita in Fig. 14.1 is clear. Slovak economy started convergence process from lower level compared with Czech economy. Slovak economy is still lagging behind the Czech one but at significantly higher levels of GDP per capita in both economies than begin of 90s. Both economies started after quite painful transformation in 90s strong economic convergence process at the beginning of the new millennium. The impact of process of preparation for EU membership and then May 1st, 2004 entrance to EU played important role in dynamics of convergence process. In last decade, we can observe kind of convergence trap problem in both countries. The convergence process slowdown and in case of Czech economy even reverse. This slowdown is partly connected with the impact of Covid pandemic and consequent energy crisis. Both economies follow the development of Spain and Portugal, countries which were also partly

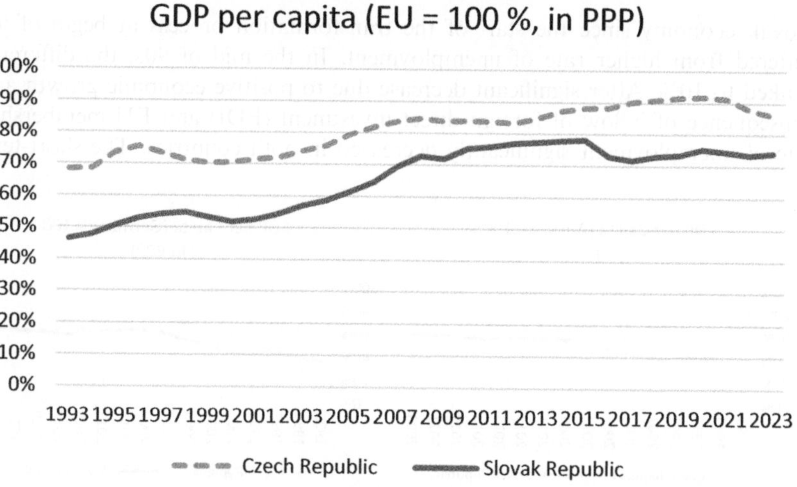

Fig. 14.1. Economic Convergence Process of Czech and Slovak Economy to EU Average. *Source:* Own processing using IMF (2024a,d) data (estimate for year 2023).

caught at convergence trap (middle income trap) around/close to 80% of EU GDP per capita average. Both Slovak and Czech economy were not able to follow the trajectory of Irish economic tiger; even the factors of Irish economic success are country specific (Fig. 14.3).

The question here is whether we can celebrate the convergence process toward the EU average as a success or view it as an unused opportunity? Partly the public opinion is influenced by prevailing comparison with nearest neighboring countries – Austria and Germany. Both countries are those which significantly benefit from EU membership/enlargement of EU by CEE countries. The GDP per capita of both countries is above EU average and Germany itself is globally one of the most developed economies. If we compare Czech and Slovak GDP per capita with our neighboring, above reach economies in EU, the picture of convergence process is little bit more skeptical. For more details, see Figs. 14.2 and 14.3. Both Czech and Slovak economy lagging behind German and Austria level which for most citizens of both countries is quite frustrating, especially if they compare the status quo with their expectations about speed of the process of convergence at the start of transformation process in begin of 90s. If we compare the process of convergence with other catching up EU countries like Spain, Italy, or Portugal, the citizens will be much more optimistic about the success of their countries. At certain years, Czech economy even skip economic level of Portugal and Spain and catch up to the economic level of Italy. Slovak economy made comparable progress in the process of economic convergence toward Mediterranean countries as Czech economy.

3. Rate of Unemployment and Inflation

Slovak economy since the start of the transformation process at begin of 90s suffered from higher rate of unemployment. In the mid of 90s, the difference peaked to 10%. After significant decrease due to positive economic growth as a consequence of inflow of foreign direct investment (FDI) and EU membership, rate of unemployment significantly decreased in both countries. The short-term

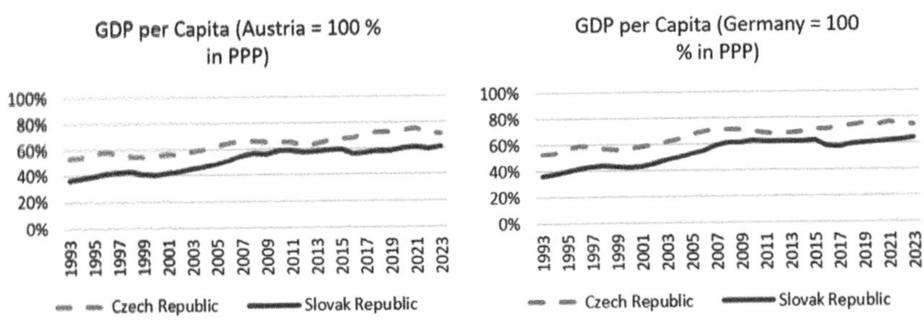

Fig. 14.2. Economic Convergence Process of the Czech and Slovak Economies to the Level of Germany and Austria. *Source:* Own processing using IMF (2024d) data (estimate for year 2023).

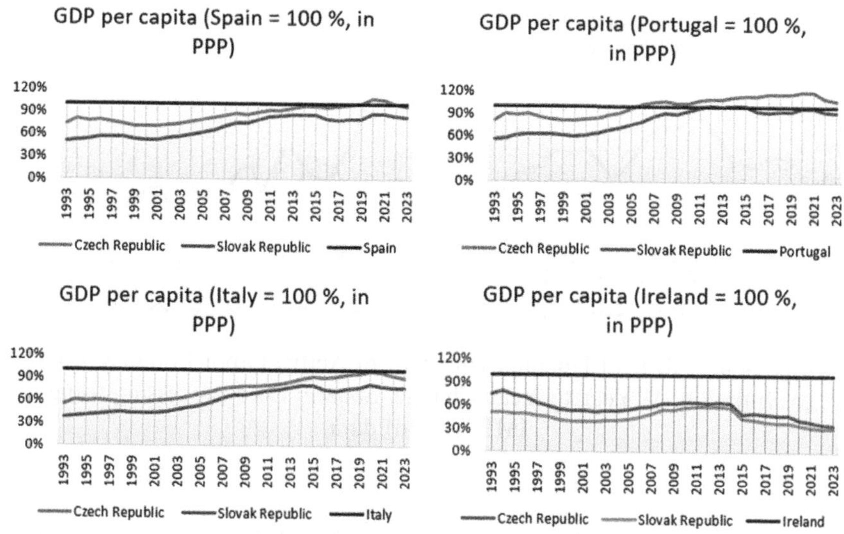

Fig. 14.3. Economic Convergence Process of the Czech and Slovak Economies to the Level of Spain, Portugal, Italy, and Ireland. *Source:* Own processing using IMF (2024d) data (estimate for year 2023).

worsening was observed as the consequence of financial and Eurozone crises following the year 2008.

Due to huge fiscal interventions via national and EU budget (Next Generation EU budget), both Covid crisis and energy crisis had almost no effect on unemployment rate in both countries and especially Czech labor market did stay rigid and slightly overheated. The unemployment rate gap was persistent during the whole observed period, but Slovak trend was significantly downward sloping toward levels of unemployment close to 5%.

Both economies were able to stabilize inflation at low levels after transformation shocks. Then since year 1999 Slovakia had positive inflation differential compared with Czech Republic until the process of fulfilling Maastricht criteria which started in year 2007. Since the introduction of euro at Slovakia January 2009, both economies follow pretty same path in terms of inflation with intensive inflation period during the years 2021–2024. It became clear that for small economies, it is difficult to control inflation, does not matter if country use own currency and have full control over monetary policy or if the country is part of Eurozone and has very limited influence on common monetary policy. An indictor of this is shown below in Fig. 14.4:

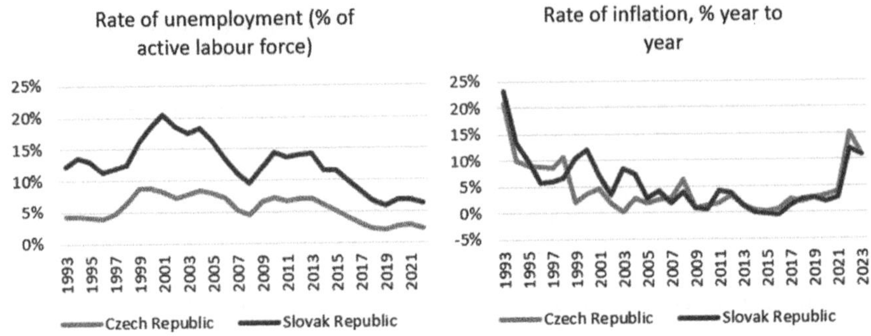

Fig. 14.4. Rate of Unemployment (% of Active Labor Force) & Rate of Inflation, % Year to Year Change. *Source:* Own processing using IMF (2024d) data.

4. Openness of the Economy – Sectoral and Territorial Structure of Exports

Fig. 14.5 firstly shows the evolution of openness of Czech and Slovak economy (export in terms of GDP) during the period 1993–2022. Both economies used the opportunity to use its comparative advantages and the size of EU internal market with free movement of goods. The openness of both countries increased to highest levels among all EU 27 countries. In case of Slovakia, the rate of openness more than doubled.

Sectoral structure of export of three countries (Czech, Slovak, and German) for the reference year 2022 is shown on the right side of the figure. All three countries' most important export sector is machinery and transport equipment, where both Czech and Slovak republic share is even higher than German one and exceeds 50% on total exports. The second most important sector for all three

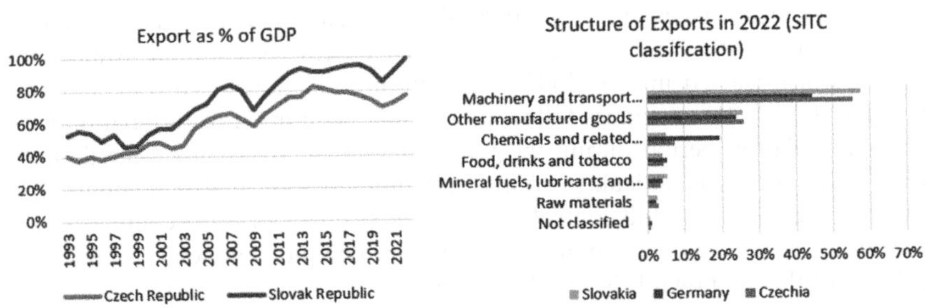

Fig. 14.5. Economic Openness and Structure of Exports. *Source:* Own processing using WB (2024a) and Eurostat (2024b) data.

countries is other manufactured goods with proportion around 25%. The third position is held by chemicals and related products with strongest sector share on total exports in Germany.

The dependence on both small open economies on EU trading partners is visible in Fig. 14.6. Years 1999, 2004, and 2023 were taken in consideration. In all observed years, Germany is the most important trading partner, even in the case of the Czech economy, the share of Germany is slowly decreasing. Other important trading partners are other neighboring countries in the region, Austria, Poland, and Hungary. There is quite strong and persistent historical interdependence between Czech and Slovak economy via its common trade.

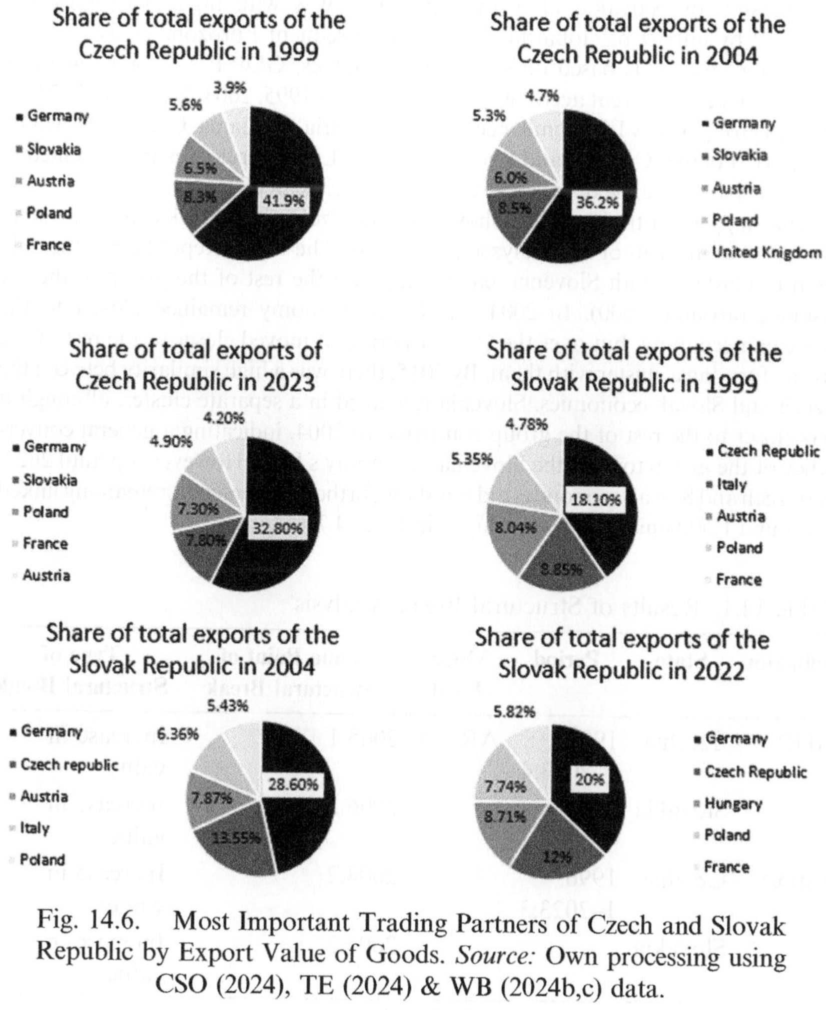

Fig. 14.6. Most Important Trading Partners of Czech and Slovak Republic by Export Value of Goods. *Source:* Own processing using CSO (2024), TE (2024) & WB (2024b,c) data.

5. Are Slovakia and Czechia Twins or Unique Cases?

To add further dimension to comparative analysis of main economic indicators of Czech and Slovak economy, the analysis of structural breaks in GDP growth time series and cluster analysis were employed.

Structural breaks analysis identified that both economies positively reacted with some delay to membership in EU in May 2004. The structural analysis identified the positive impact on both export and GDP. For details, see Table 14.1. The impact of EU membership was identified as the most statistically significant structural break during the whole observed period. Other factors like inflow of money from EU budget or FDI inflow had also potential to positively influence the economic development. The potential positive impact of Eurozone membership on Slovakia after the year 2009 was with high probability out weighted by impact of global financial and consequent Eurozone crisis.

Cluster analysis is based on set of four variables: GDP Per Capita, Inflation, Unemployment, Current account Balance for years 1995, 2004, 2015, and 2022 for selected group of new EU member countries (Bulgaria, Romania, Czechia, Slovakia, Hungary, Poland, Croatia, and Slovenia). Single Linkage rule was implemented in each analysis, while the distance measure was Euclidean distances.

The analysis for the year 1995 shows that the Czech and Slovak economies were quite diverse in terms of the analyzed parameters. The Czech Republic was the only country clustered with Slovenia, employing with the rest of the group in the far distance (around 3,500). In 2004, the Czech economy remained closest to the Slovenian economy, but over the 10-year period, it moved closer to the rest of the group, forming a cluster with them. By 2015, there was a high similarity between the Czech and Slovak economies. Slovenia remained in a separate cluster, although it was closer to the rest of the group compared to 2004, indicating a general convergence of the group toward the Slovenian economy's level. However, up until 2022, the Czech and Slovak economies did not show further convergence, remaining linked at around 1,500 units. This is displayed in Fig. 14.7.

Table 14.1. Results of Structural Break Analysis.

Indicator	State	Period	Model Used	Time Point of Structural Break	Type of Structural Break
GDP	Czechia	1995: 1–2023:4	AR (1)	2005:1	Increase in value[a]
	Slovakia			2006:2	Increase in value
Export	Czechia	1996: 1–2023:3		2004:2	Increase in value
	Slovakia			2005:3	Increase in value

Source: Own processing using Eurostat (2024a,c) data.

[a]This structural break was not statistically significant in AR model, only OLS.

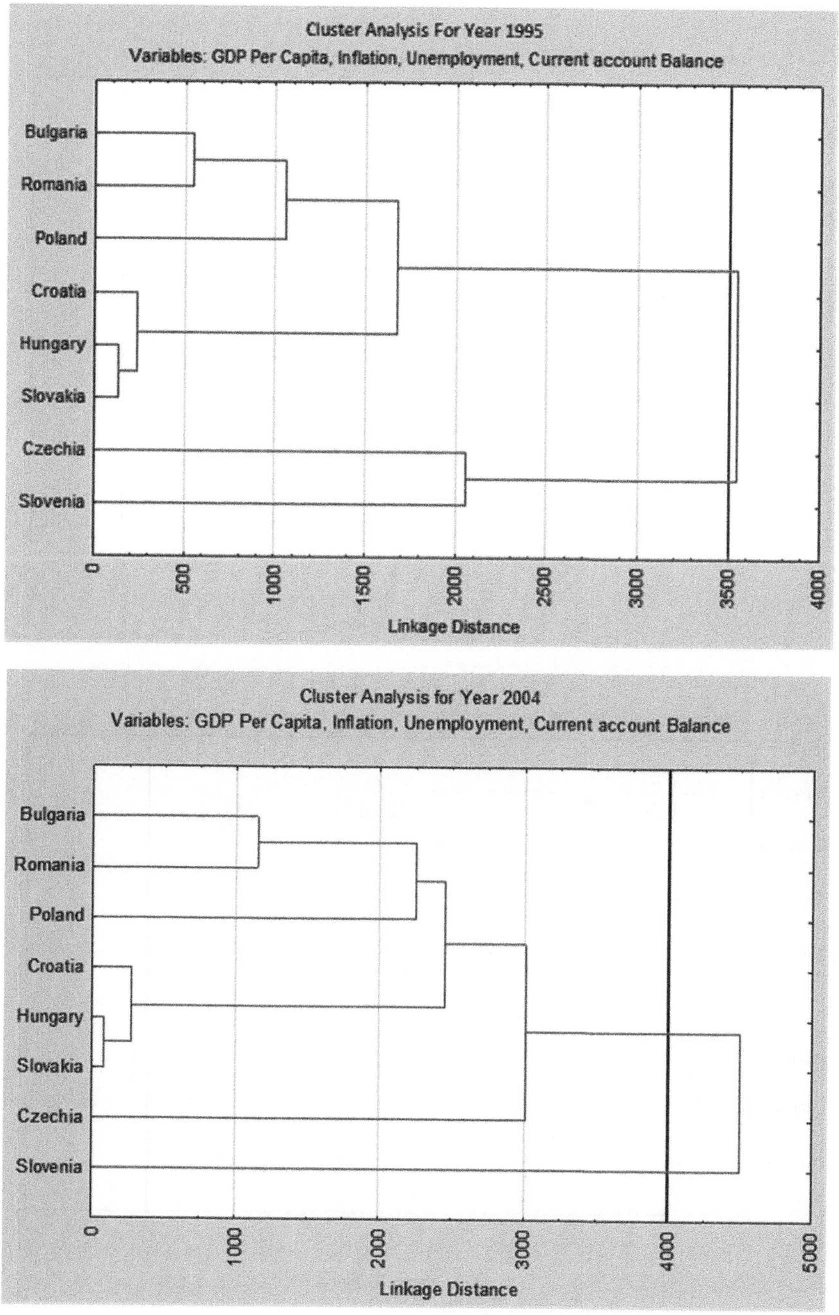

Fig. 14.7. Results of Cluster Analysis.
Source: Own processing using IMF (2024b,c) data.

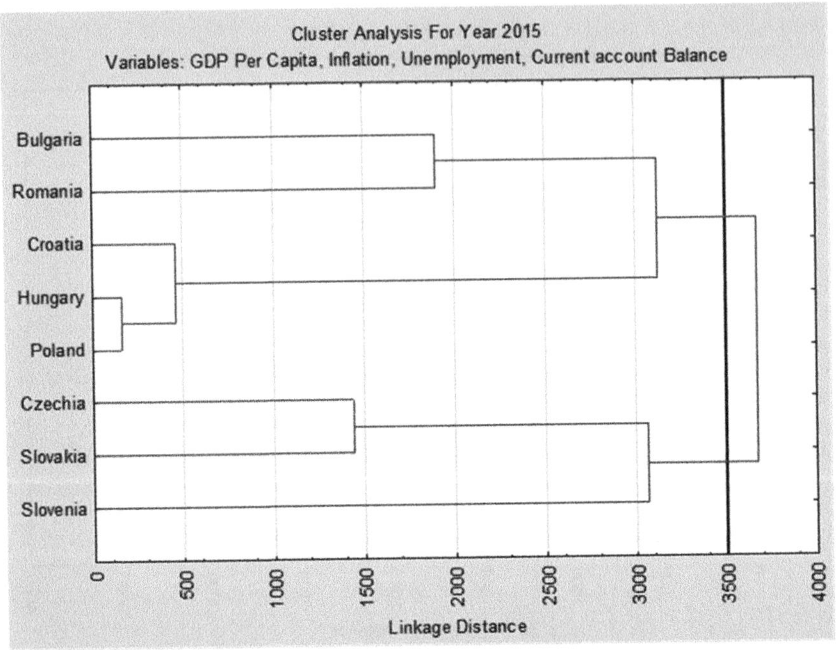

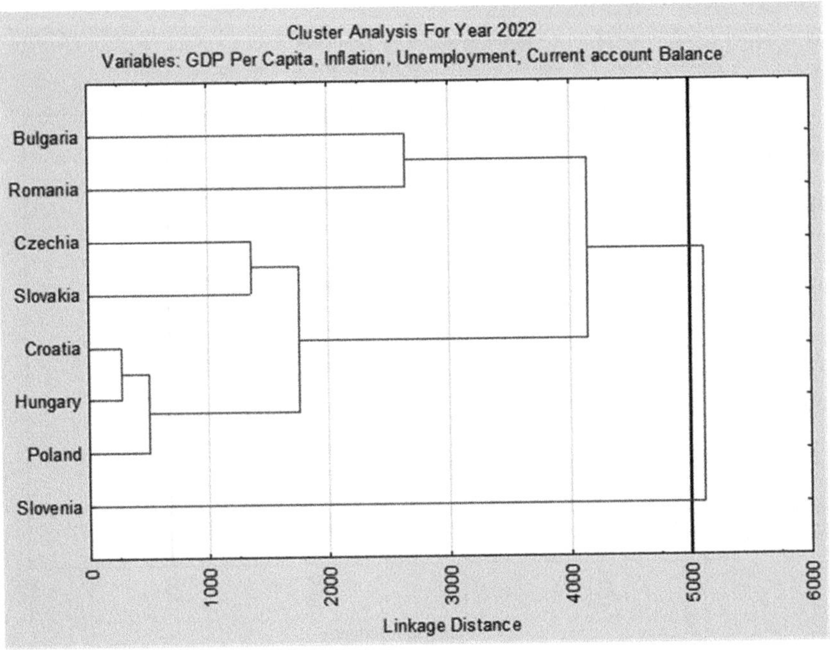

Fig. 14.7. *(Continued).*

6. Conclusion

After the politically and economically turbulent 1990s, both Czech and Slovak Republic made significant economic progress. The EU membership opened up new opportunities for trade and investment, contributing to further economic growth. Over the years, the country's strong export orientation and integration into EU internal market have played a crucial role in its economic growth. While challenges persist, the country's journey since 1993 reflects a remarkable transformation into a dynamic competitive market economy in Europe. Main challenges for the near future are adjustment of both economies to process of automatization and danger of narrowing the car industry due to upcoming trend of electromobility. Both countries are strongly dependent and devote significant part of national resources to automotive industry. Both countries have globally highest numbers of car production per 1,000 inhabitants. The dependence on automotive a transport sector is strengthening by huge inflow of FDI to companies producing semiparts for automotive industry since star of economic transformation until the end of observed period. To be more specific, from 2003 to 2022, the number of cars produced per 1,000 persons increased by 171% in the Czech Republic and by 253% in the Slovak Republic (International Organisation for Motor Vehicle Manufacturers, 2024).

The ability to break up convergence ceiling will decide if both economies will cope with higher levels of unemployment or if they will be able to follow the path of Irish economy based on economies of scale and higher added value production.

Above mentioned arguments allow us to conclude that Slovak and Czech economy follow more or less the same economic path, strong convergence in first decade of 20th century, and kind of convergence trap in last decade. Both economies significantly benefit as typically small open economies from membership in EU which allows approach to EU internal market with almost 450 million quite reach consumers. Both economies will have to cope with the risk of overdependence on automotive industry and on economic development of German economy. Higher diversification in terms of structure of production toward higher added value products and services is necessary. Also higher diversification of territorial structure of trade toward countries outside of EU could help diversify a lot of risk connected to future economic development of EU integration project and individual economic condition of member countries' economies with which both economies are strongly interconnected via foreign trade and FDI investments.

References

CSO. (2024). *Cross-border movements of goods (CBmG)*. Czech Statistical Office. https://apl.czso.cz/pll/stazo/STAZO.STAZO?jazyk=EN&prvni=N

Eurostat. (2024a). *GDP and main components (output, expenditure and income)*. https://ec.europa.eu/eurostat/databrowser/view/namq_10_gdp__custom_10542386/default/table?lang=en

Eurostat. (2024b). *International trade of EU, the euro area and the member states by SITC product group*. https://ec.europa.eu/eurostat/databrowser/view/EXT_LT_INTERTRD/default/table?lang=en&fbclid=IwAR1ruE3i_KeHGZVTkjTWCHFQsq55r6GBEq_Zo7_J3yb9ayUi8mXCc4BijSM

Eurostat. (2024c). *Exports and imports by member states of the EU/third countries*. https://ec.europa.eu/eurostat/databrowser/view/namq_10_exi__custom_10542336/default/table?lang=en

IMF. (2024a). *European Union data – Gross domestic product per capita & inflation*. International Monetary Fund. https://www.imf.org/en/Publications/WEO/weo-database/2023/October/weo-report?a=1&c=998,&s=PPPPC,PCPIPCH,&sy=1993&ey=2023&ssm=0&scsm=1&scc=0&ssd=1&ssc=0&sic=0&sort=country&ds=&br=1

IMF. (2024b). *Advanced economies – Gross domestic product per capita, unemployment, current account balance & inflation*. International Monetary Fund. https://www.imf.org/en/Publications/WEO/weo-database/2023/October/weo-report?c=122,935,134,178,136,182,936,184,&s=NGDPRPPPPC,PCPIPCH,LUR,BCA,&sy=1993&ey=2028&ssm=0&scsm=1&scc=0&ssd=1&ssc=0&sic=0&sort=country&ds=.&br=1

IMF. (2024c). *Emerging and developing Europe – Gross domestic product per capita, unemployment, current account balance & inflation*. International Monetary Fund. https://www.imf.org/en/Publications/WEO/weo-database/2023/October/weo-report?c=918,944,964,968,&s=PPPGDP,PCPIPCH,LUR,BCA_NGDPD,&sy=1995&ey=2028&ssm=0&scsm=1&scc=0&ssd=1&ssc=0&sic=0&sort=country&ds=.&br=1

IMF. (2024d). *Particular countries data – Gross domestic product per capita, unemployment & inflation*. International Monetary Fund. https://www.imf.org/en/Publications/WEO/weo-database/2023/October/weo-report?c=122,935,134,174,178,136,182,936,184,&s=PPPGDP,PCPIPCH,LUR,&sy=1993&ey=2023&ssm=0&scsm=1&scc=0&ssd=1&ssc=0&sic=0&sort=country&ds=.&br=1

International Organisation for Motor Vehicle Manufacturers. (2024). *World motor vehicle production by country/region and type*. https://www.oica.net/category/production-statistics/2022-statistics/

Myant, M., & Drahokoupil, J. (2013). *Tranzitivní ekonomiky: Politická ekomie Ruska, východní Evropy a střední Asie*. Academia.

Trend Economy. (2024). *Slovak republic – Imports and exports (2022)*. https://trendeconomy.com/data/h2/SlovakRepublic/TOTAL

WB. (2024a). *Exports of goods and services (% of GDP) – Czechia, Slovak republic*. World Bank. https://data.worldbank.org/indicator/NE.EXP.GNFS.ZS?locations=CZ-SK

WB. (2024b). *Slovak republic trade balance, exports, imports by country (2004)*. World Integrated Trade Solution. https://wits.worldbank.org/CountryProfile/en/Country/SVK/Year/2004/TradeFlow/EXPIMP/Partner/by-country?fbclid=IwAR1B3z6LERdiG-r6bh9OTInEMoZ8aWRZO6bL36wR_p0mjAFiWlKJNc3_HcM

WB. (2024c). *Slovak republic trade balance, exports, imports by country (1999)*. World Integrated Trade Solution. https://wits.worldbank.org/CountryProfile/en/Country/SVK/Year/1999/TradeFlow/Export/Partner/by-country?fbclid=IwAR3Vyq7HE0hcwBaGnGNyqn3JWKsIH3Lz3dfI3Nt1XpieWORfrCpnp8Vd5MI

Žídek, L. (2006). *Transformace české ekonomiky. 1989–2004* (1st ed.). C.H.Beck.

Žídek, L. (2017). *From central planning to the market*. CEU Press.

Printed and bound by CPI Group (UK) Ltd, Croydon, CR0 4YY
18/09/2026
14965017-0002